Out of Paper

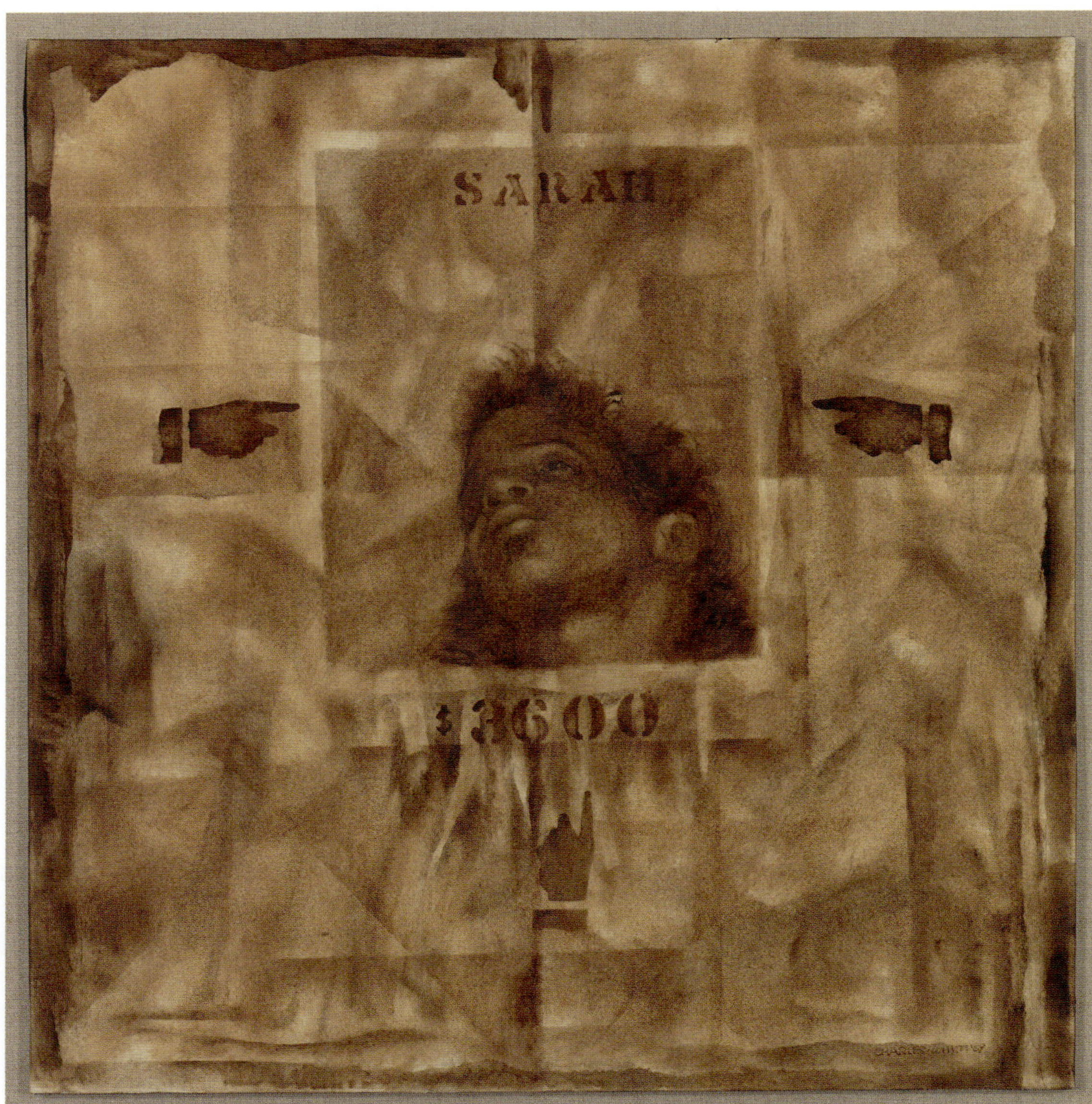

SARAH
$3600

Out of Paper

Drawing, Environment, and the Body
in 1960s America

Katie Anania

Yale University Press
New Haven and London

yalebooks.com/art

Designed by Jeff Wincapaw; with additional design by Tina Henderson, Miko McGinty Inc.
Jacket designed by Rita Jules and Tina Henderson, Miko McGinty Inc.
Set in Adobe Text Pro and Akagi Pro type by Tina Henderson, Miko McGinty Inc.
Printed in China by 1010 Printing International Limited

Library of Congress Control Number: 2023947544
ISBN 978-0-300-27223-9

A catalogue record for this book is available from the British Library.

This paper meets the requirements of ANSI/NISO Z39.48–1992 (Permanence of Paper).

10 9 8 7 6 5 4 3 2 1

Jacket illustrations: (front) fig. 11; (back) fig. 90.
Frontispiece: fig. 94; page v: fig. 54; page vi: fig. 19; page viii: fig. 73; page xii: fig. 14; page xiv: fig. 2 (detail).

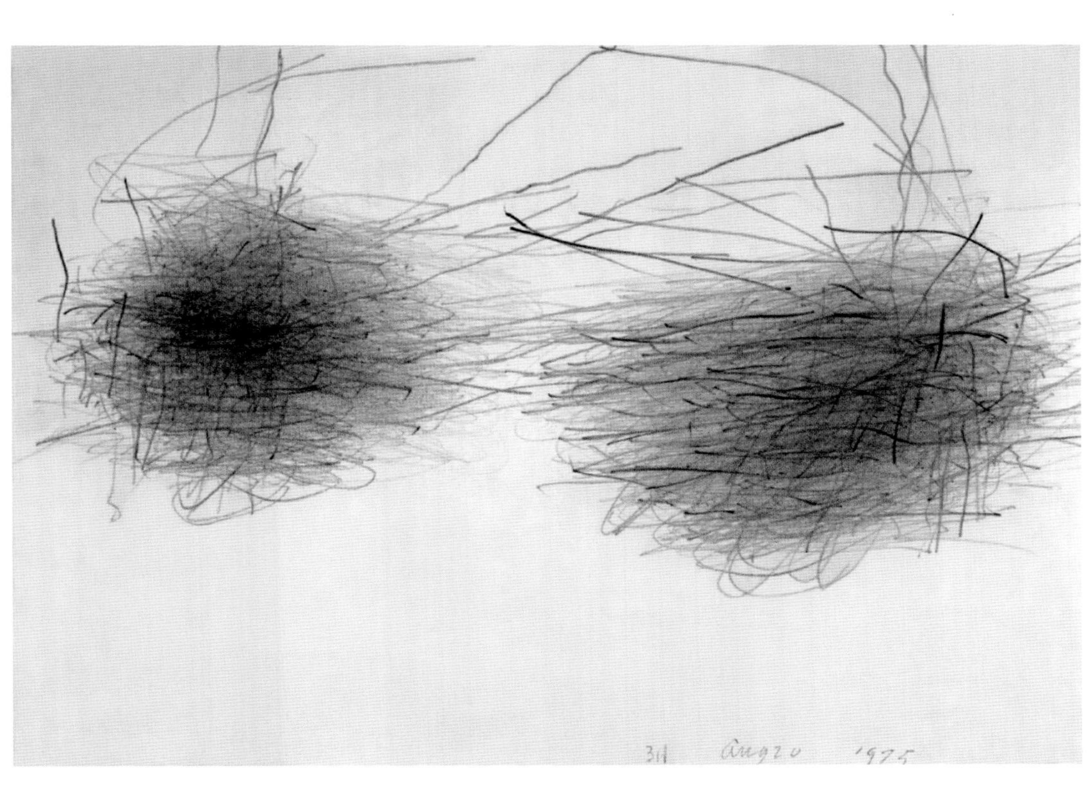

31 Aug 20 1975

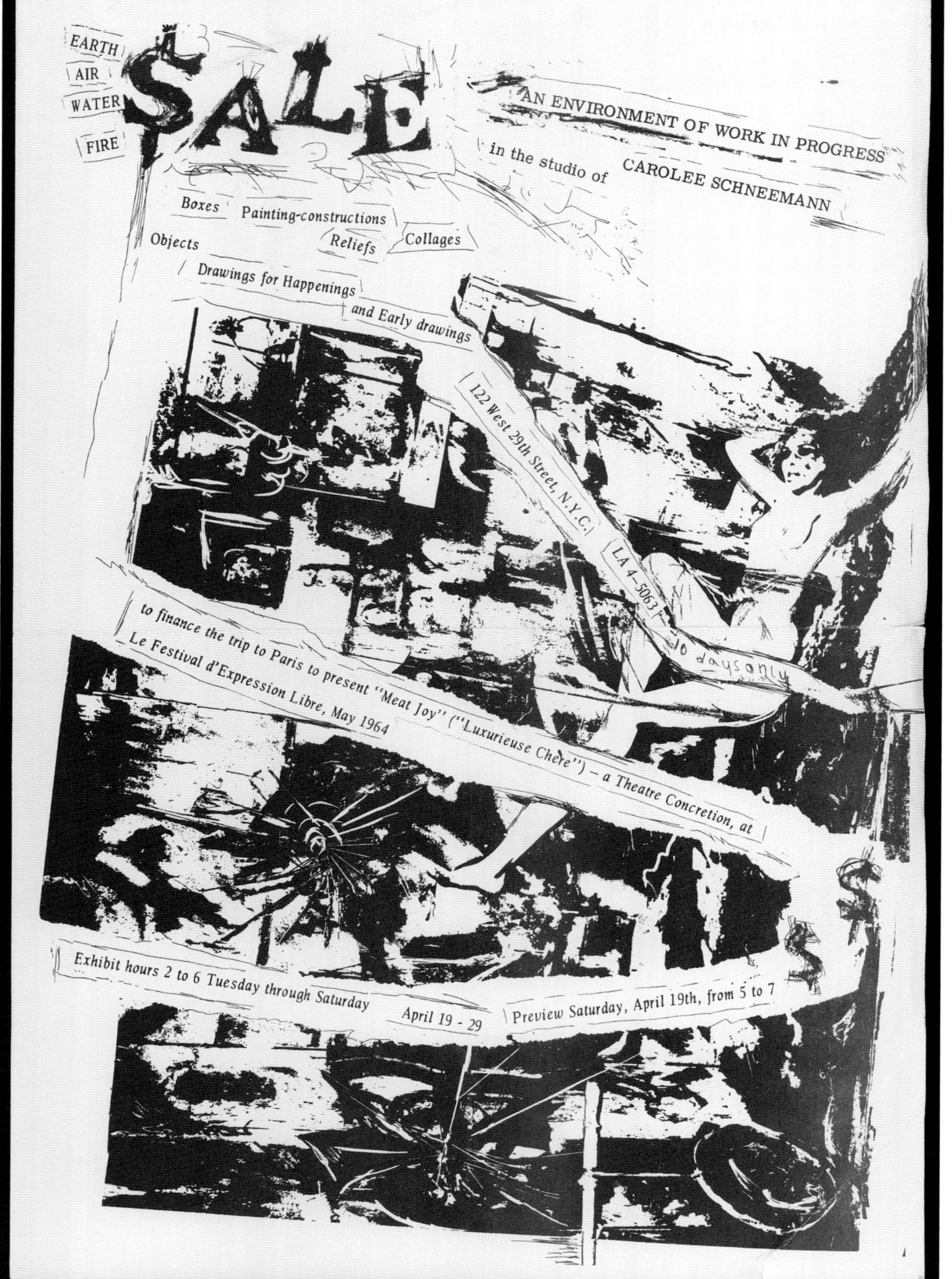

EARTH
AIR
WATER
FIRE
SALE
AN ENVIRONMENT OF WORK IN PROGRESS
in the studio of   CAROLEE SCHNEEMANN
Boxes   Painting-constructions
Objects   Reliefs   Collages
Drawings for Happenings
and Early drawings
122 West 29th Street, N.Y.C.
LA 4-5063
10 days only
to finance the trip to Paris to present "Meat Joy" ("Luxurieuse Chère") – a Theatre Concretion, at
Le Festival d'Expression Libre, May 1964
Exhibit hours 2 to 6 Tuesday through Saturday
April 19 - 29   Preview Saturday, April 19th, from 5 to 7

Contents

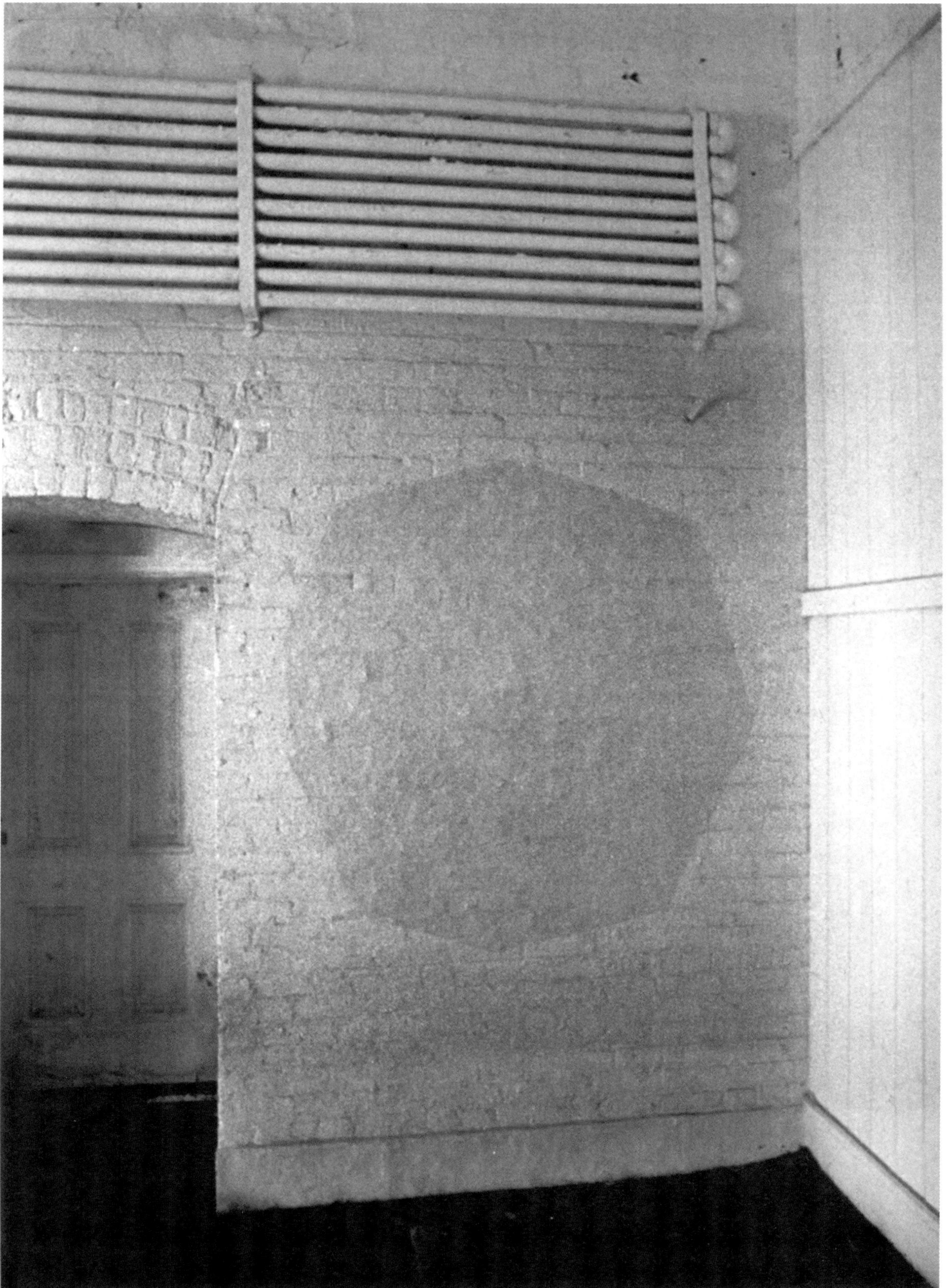

Acknowledgments

The late, great David Graeber wrote, "We don't really know how to think about debt." This is so very applicable to the task of writing academic books. I feel profoundly moved when I remember the friends who have supported *Out of Paper* in the thirteen years that it took to write, and to try and narrate these dues as fully as possible feels paramount here. First on the list are my editors at Yale University Press, including Amy Canonico, Laura Dooley, Alison Hagge, and Elizabeth Searcy, production manager Sarah Henry, proofreader Bob Land, indexer Enid Zafran, interior designer Tina Henderson, and cover designer Rita Jules. They made this text cogent and readable, and presented it beautifully as well. William Anastasi, Dove Bradshaw, Carolee Schneemann, Richard Tuttle, Lynda Benglis, Lucile Morris of the Robert Morris Estate, Paulina Alvarez of the Charles White Archive, Janet Passehl of the Sol LeWitt Collection, and the staff at the Archives of American Art, including Lindsey Bright, went deep into storage to answer my questions. Richard Tuttle was an especially generous collaborator; his poem "Is the Line Fulmination?" for my symposium in 2017 at the Morgan Library and Museum, *Minding the Time,* changed the course of the book. Adrian Piper, Dorothy Vogel, Joan Semmel, Dorothea Rockburne, Robert Barry, David Platzker, Lauren O'Neill-Butler, Vincent Wilcke at Pace Gallery, Rachel Churner at the Carolee Schneemann Foundation, Pablo Delano, Amanda Hunter Johnson, Jody Hauptman, Steven Nelson, Anthony Meier, and Stephen Urice all supplied crucial background information and support. So did Rafael Ferrer, in his own way—in his refusal to participate, he made this book better.

At the University of Texas at Austin, Richard Shiff contributed incomparable intellectual ballast to my graduate research. Early in the project, my colleagues at Fluent~Collaborative provided access to rare artists' books and conceptual ephemera from the 1960s. The work of John Clarke, Ann Reynolds, Judy Coffin, Linda Henderson, Jonathan Bober, Eddie Chambers, Cherise Smith, Stephennie Mulder, Roberto Tejada, and Ann Johns helped to fortify many bad first drafts. Prophetically, Ann Reynolds wondered, "What if this is really a book about paper?" And that is exactly what it became. A University Continuing Fellowship and a research assistantship at the Center for the Study of Modernism kept me fed, while the Austin Valkyries Division I women's rugby team and, later, Kathy Matta Ballet disciplined my body. Alexis Salas, Andy Campbell, Melissa Warak, Ariel Evans, Lauren Hamer, Lauren Hanson, Kim Gant, Katie Geha, Rebecca Giordano, Jason Goldstein, Caitlin Haskell, Rose Salseda-Gomez, Tatiana Reinoza, Allison Myers, Robin Williams, Roja Najafi, Alexis Harasemovitch-Truax,

Mary Walling-Blackburn, Caitlyn Murray, Laurence Miller, Mary Katherine Matalon, Claire Ruud, julia elizabeth neal, Claudia Zapata, Jeanne Stern, Kyle Nicola, Erica Nix, Libby Lumpkin, and George Pasterk were some of the best interlocutors one could ask for. During a research fellowship at the Georgia O'Keeffe Museum Research Center, Eumie Stroukoff, Barbara Buehler Lynes, and Carolyn Kastner provided feedback and archival assistance, and my cohort of fellows, Kate Lemay, and Maggie Cao encouraged me to widen the foundations of the project. A summer residency at the Getty Research Institute gave me time in Carolee Schneemann's and Allan Kaprow's archives, and Aliya Kalla helped me gather high-quality images from the GRI when the book reached the publication stage ten years later. A grant-in-aid to the University of Wisconsin–Madison's archives clarified the many links between drawing and Happenings, while Veronica Roberts, who supervised my Andrew W. Mellon Foundation Curatorial Fellowship at the Blanton Museum, drew out this book's nascent connections to performance studies. At the Menil Collection in Houston, Rebecca Ahrens, Geraldine Aramanda, David Breslin, Jan Burandt, Paul Davis, Toby Kamp, Karl Killian, Frances Lazare, Joseph Newland, and Michelle White helped me see this project through to its first full draft, including their support of the TRESPASS symposium, where Peggy Phelan, Connie Butler, Judith Rodenbeck, Anna Lovatt, Sandra Zalman, and Natilee Harren and I tried out drawings together and fomented one another's ideas in the best of ways. The Houston community is legendary for its support of scholars and makers, and my work was no exception; Dean Daderko, Sara Marcus, Patricia Restrepo, Nicole Burisch, Danielle Dean, Ryan Dennis, Taraneh Fazeli, Pete Gershon, Sondra Perry, Josh Pazda, and Sarah Luna also influenced this book with their brilliant projects and conversation.

The Morgan Library and Museum's Drawing Institute hosted me for a postdoctoral fellowship, while William Galperin and Henry S. Turner at the Center for Cultural Analysis at Rutgers University graciously invited me into the CCA's circle for their "Arts and Aesthetics" theme year. Alexander Nagel proved an imaginative collaborator during this time, as did Jennifer Tonkovich, John Marciari, Michael Reid, Rachel Federman, Isabelle Dervaux, Sheelagh Bevan, Steffani Jemison, Lorenzo Clayton, Timothy Corbett, Brett Littman, and Nova Benway. Villa I Tatti, Harvard's Research Center for Italian Renaissance Studies, also hosted me for a term, where Ingrid Greenfield, Martin Schwarz, Andrew Leach, Niall Atkinson, Bobby Brennan, Stephanie Leone, David Nee, Jesse Rodin, Thomas Wisniewski, Emily Wilbourne, and Amelia Saul sat with me at various editing stages and located a few original, unalloyed ideas in the pile of writing I'd assembled. Alina Payne and Robin Kelsey also gave wise counsel at critical moments.

A faculty research grant at Georgia College & State University, plus the steady support of Elissa Auerbach, Ernesto Gomez, Emily Gomez, Sandra Trujillo, Bill Fisher, Brantley Nicholson, and Stephanie Opperman, got this book to the proposal stage. Autumn Knight helped push everything over the edge, in more ways than one. Raasha Gutierrez and Cheyenne Balliew provided research assistance during this time, and their labor was the tip of a very large iceberg; many students at Georgia College contributed to this book's formation through their diligent commitment to thinking through joy.

While completing this book I received generous invitations to try out its arguments in front of an audience. For these experiences I have Alexis Salas, Mandy Malloy, Jessamine Batario, Ann Johns, Natilee Harren, Brett Littman, Tyler Coburn, Emmanuel Ortega, and Zachary Tate Porter to thank. The University of Nebraska–Lincoln provided me with much-needed time off from teaching to finish the manuscript; this time off took place in the serene, snowy biome of northwest Arkansas at the Crystal Bridges Museum of American Art, where Robert Gordon-Fogelson, Julia Silverman, Erika Doss, and Xuxa Rodriguez helped me sharpen and specify the final version. To support publication costs, UNL provided me with a Research Council Grant-in-Aid, a Hixson-Lied Faculty Research and Creative Activity Grant, and a share of an EPSCoR grant from the National Science Foundation. At UNL I also found close colleagues, specifically Andrea Bolland, Wendy Katz, Michael Hoff, Dana Fritz, Jesse Fleming, Ash Eliza Smith, Robert Twomey, Anna Henson, Sandra Williams, Francisco Souto, and Chris Marks, who contributed to this book's organization and its orientation (or not) toward rapid prototyping, inscription, and other design concepts. My atlouisplace writing group, especially Laura August, Erica Edwards, Ladi'Sasha Jones, Katie Lennard, and Saaret Yousef, were points of light in the long, dark pandemic.

Since most of this writing sprung up in a peripatetic way, often when I was living between cities, a core set of voices provided fundamental ground throughout the life of the project. These voices included Nicole Archer, Eric Talbert, Elizabeth Travelslight, Jamie Vasta, Michele Senitzer, Margaret MacNamidhe, Lauren Payne, Yasmin Golan, William Ma, Chelsea Knight, Leah Dyjak, Leah and Macauley DeVun, Aisling Hamrogue, Ariel Schrag, Anne Reeve, David X. Levine, Lydia Daniller, and my editor Abigail Rosenthal. My time as an adjunct faculty member at the San Francisco Art Institute, the California College of the Arts, and Hunter College was also nourishing—the students in all my classes, particularly my "Art of the Early Renaissance" course, bore special witness to *Out of Paper*'s turn toward the usable past. Most important, my family—my grandparents, parents, brother, aunts, uncles and cousins, and exacting editor Mel Plaut—never wavered in their confidence that I would one day draw the past into the present through writing. I owe them book after book, always.

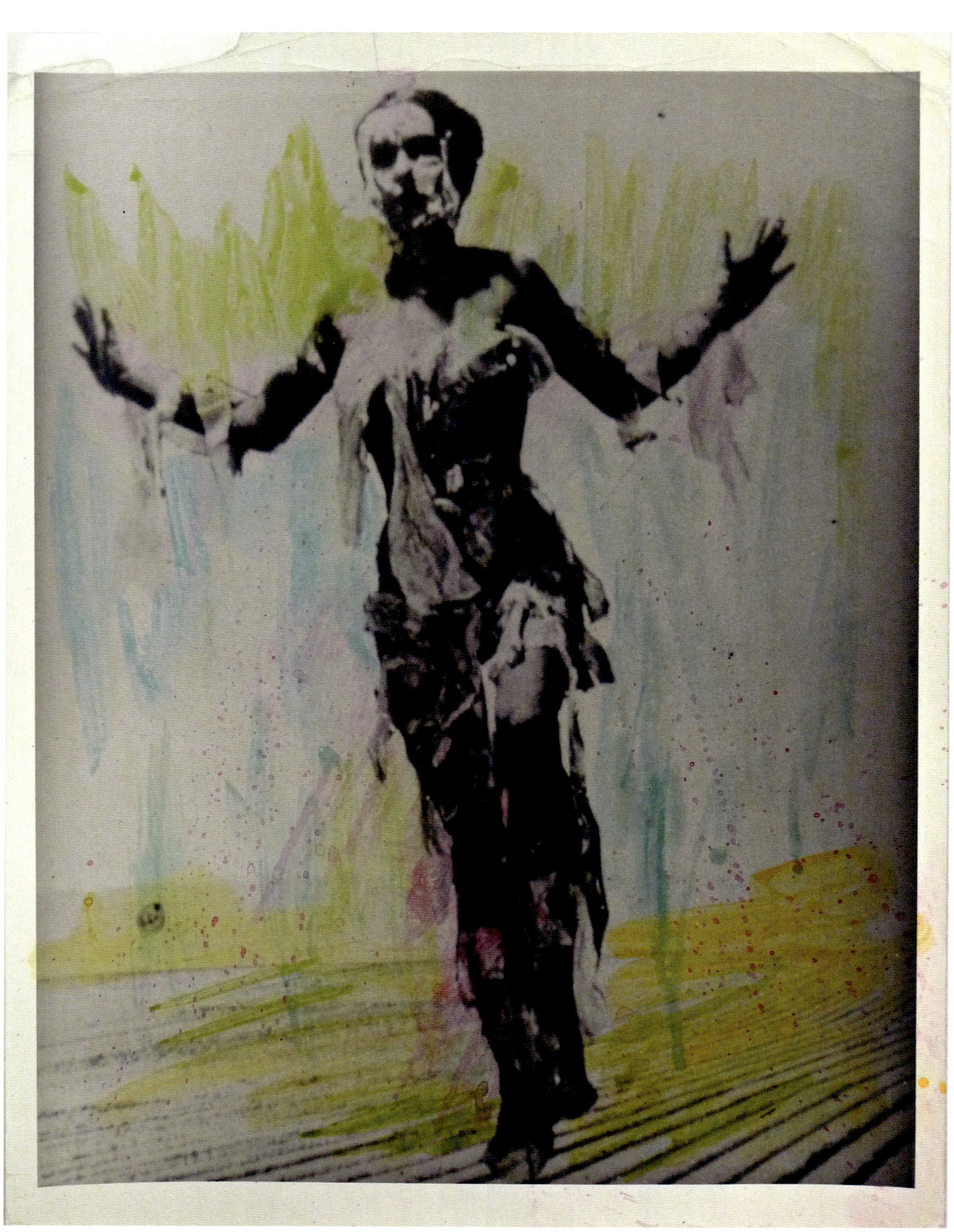

Extension is an attribute of God, or God is an extended thing.
—*Spinoza,* Ethics, *Proposition 2*

Ecologies of the Page

Crumpled in piles, scattered in the streets, stapled to telephone poles, bound into notebooks, and tacked to studio walls, paper was everywhere in US media culture and thrummed quietly through its urban avant-gardes in the 1960s. Performances invariably began with a diagram or event score, and discarded newspapers and cardboard provided costumes or signage for new projects. For artists, paper was also the ground and surface for preparatory drawings, which had long been a mythologized part of art making and whose attendant clichés were the subject of increased discussion.[1] In studios, exhibitions, and performance spaces in New York and Los Angeles, these techniques and materials all fused with one another as artists' drawings used architectural interiors, bodily gestures, social conventions, and even the city itself as both their driving force and support. This book chronicles how makers in the 1960s traversed these different material pathways in complicated ways—by taking up paper as a "borderline area," as the artist Robert Morris put it at the time, where it could model other materials' specific qualities as well as those materials' participation in ecological destruction and state violence.[2] Paper thus became vital for testing new parameters for the term *environment* and for orienting it toward embodied, lived life through drawing, cutting, shredding, and other processes.

The apparent paradox of Robert Morris's phrase—not a border but a borderline *area,* a region of space between one thing and another—is implicit in paper's very makeup. Paper is a mobile surface with uniquely flexible properties. While both canvas and paper are the principal supports for modern picture-making, paper alone mobilizes information as infinitely translatable and transmissible, detachable from the realities of its current ground, space, or environment.[3] And in a decade in which paper media lay at the center of public life and revolutionary politics, it is no accident that artists' drawings both colluded with and separated from paper to make such borders, and others, more porous. Drawings could happen on a wall or within a performance, providing physical structure even as they availed themselves of the iterative, bounded qualities of a plan drawing or sketch. Since drawing's material poverty lacked the expressionist baggage of painting, drawings could also become a theater for staging value, including the value of paper currency. They could harness the idea of surface as a technologically charged substrate or act as a deeply social medium in a moment when communication and information exchange were frontal concerns. This book charts its points of intervention, then, not across paper as a passive surface, but through new methods for manipulating one of the most widely produced industrial products on the planet.

This reappraisal of paper's capabilities contributed to a broad shift in the perception of drawings and their role in art history and artistic display. Was a drawing an escape from an object, or was it a reification of art's objecthood? If one drew on a wall rather than on the surface of the page, how might this shift viewers' perceptions of their surroundings? And how could paper act as an accessible tool for making new worlds or forestalling the old ones? In looking beyond drawing's history as a private working document used for formal clarification, this story shows how artists instead used paper's multiple states and afterlives to create material entanglements and confusion. Drawings in this period could thus became public learning tools, merging feminist and antiracist perspectives with existing scientific arguments to broaden emerging discourses on ecology. They frequently engaged with the dynamic capabilities of paper—as the main conduit for daily news, its doubling as both an object and a surface, as a precious fragment and a cheap substrate, and frequently a metonym for the body's vulnerability to poisons and violence—to turn seemingly simple material possibilities into urgent commentary on the ethics and politics of artistic practice. Like painting's canvas and sculpture's pedestal, drawing's paper provides an invitation to examine the material realities that subtend creative life, literally and figuratively.

Throughout this book, I use the word *drawing* not only to signal both the physical act of dragging an implement across a surface but also to include the acts that artists themselves named as drawings or referred to as being *like drawing:* tracing templates for sculpture, for instance, as Richard Tuttle did, or posing one's body for the camera "like a drawing class," as Carolee Schneemann did.[4] These expansive acts, done with (and sometimes referencing the absence of) the paper surface, demonstrate what performance studies scholar Diana Taylor has called the "back and forth" relationship between embodiment and its documentation.[5] Such projects also call us to attend to artists' numerous and varied references in the postwar period to the "total environment," the "art environment," and related concepts—which themselves were copresent with the consolidation of ecology as a scientific discipline, as James Nisbet has pointed out.[6] And although the curator Laurence Schmidlin has cogently historicized drawing in the postwar moment in terms of its "intermediality," the medium's entanglements between the artist's body and other notions of space read more as a question prompt for further sociohistorical inquiry rather than its answer.[7]

The artists in this book all address the environment from a combination of disciplines, which suggests that science studies and materiality studies have much to learn from their projects. Considering drawing as part of its larger, entangled media ecology positions the medium as both separate from its support but also wholly dependent on it, capable of staging dynamic relations among an image, its ground, its circuits of transit, and its embodied viewers. Carolee Schneemann, for instance, clothed her performers in shredded paper to revivify the dying tradition of figure drawing and to position human beings and their nonhuman counterparts as immanently vulnerable to violence. William Anastasi devised stenographic drawing methods with his own body that merged copying with listening. In the wake of artists' calls to make their work accessible to everyone, Richard Tuttle's cut, folded, and glued paper objects reimagined scalar relationships between the human body and architectural space. At the end of the decade, Robert Morris and Rafael Ferrer's performance plans probed US colonial interventions in Puerto Rico while undermining the postwar construction of the artist as a "world man" and visionary designer.[8] And Charles White's *Wanted Poster* series activated the paper surface as an analog of human flesh, mining a sophisticated Marxist humanist tradition to indict US print culture in its commodification of human bodies.

Robert Morris again put language to this problem when he wrote in his essay "Notes on the Phenomenology of Making" late in the decade that "a close look at the nature of art making remains to be undertaken." He was referring specifically to "the nature of art making of a certain kind," one that occurred before the artist completed the finished product, where different materials could heavily influence—even transform—the body's range of possibilities for behavior. Morris names many materials in the essay: rubber, stone, cloth dipped in hot wax, bronze, thread, and glass. All could lead to a variety of accidental discoveries "beyond taste or labor" that were prompted not by the artist's actions but by the behavior of the matter itself.[9] To Morris, these spontaneous interactions with material were both vital and elusive. A year earlier, he had lamented the fact that modern human beings were structuring their lives in a way that prevented them from exploring materials thoroughly. "An advanced, technological, urban environment is a totally manufactured one," he wrote. "Interaction with the environment tends more and more toward information processing in one form or another and away from interactions involving transformations of matter. The very means and visibility for material transformations become more remote and recondite. Centers for production are increasingly located outside the urban environment in what are euphemistically termed 'industrial parks.'"[10] As organic human-material interactions were perceived to be disappearing from public and private life, recycling, recording, cutting, planning, and erasing took on renewed potency for makers. It would make sense for them to envision new supply chains from their studios in New York's SoHo and West Village, close to vacant factories that typified a bygone model of product demand fulfillment. Others sourced cheap materials from hardware stores to give their drawings a new structure, body, or design interface.

Across the country in Los Angeles, Charles White's three successive series of ink wash drawings also reacted to the same traumatic distancing between urban life and human experience. But his drawings, and indeed his overall project, stood wholly apart from Morris's observations. Instead of commenting on the vanishing opportunities for material transformations, White's drawings offered a reparative proposition: one might represent Black bodies in an explicit way, singular and strong, and show them against the runaway slave posters and flyers that had historically rendered their living, breathing flesh a commodity. White described these drawings as depicting the "total environment" of the Black experience, using inks and liquid media to render the Black body as itself a transformation of matter from inhuman to human.[11] For Morris and White, environment and matter were key components in activating new relations to agency, both human and more-than-human. But what kind of relations exactly?

The cross-continental comparative study of US drawing that this book undertakes, reveals that drawings could change their surroundings. They could help along a humanist revival or reformulate the spaces in which human beings could live and work, or promulgate new collecting and marketing strategies, or propose new, antihumanist tactics to foreclose on the possibility of commodification altogether. For Morris, the starting point for this was the nexus between urban infrastructure and mass media. He executed his series now known as the *Crisis* drawings over the course of all thirteen days of the Cuban Missile Crisis in late October 1962 (fig. 1). Morris

Introduction

would call these the "Crisis drawings" despite their reliance on the preparatory materials commonly used for paintings. It was among the first works that the artist made after moving out of Yoko Ono's loft, on Chambers Street in New York's SoHo, and into a small flat under the loft of his friend the sculptor Mark di Suvero.[12] All thirteen works in *Crisis,* one for each day, used that morning's copy of the *New York Post* as their support.[13] In his part of the apartment, under a hand-built makeshift ceiling that barely accommodated his own height, Morris began covering copies of the newspaper in layers of paint and gesso.[14] The two weeks in which President John F. Kennedy battled Soviet ballistic missile launch stations in northern Cuba, just ninety miles from Florida's coastline, became one of the most acute moments of global tension in the Cold War, rendering the risk of nuclear conflict as a direct and dire possibility. Newspapers were one of the crisis's key conduits. Their headlines spoke of nothing else, and a nuclear war seemed imminent.

On their own, the printed newspaper pages narrate Kennedy's decisions leading to a naval quarantine of the Havana harbor on October 22. The president's attempt to sequester the Soviet missile stations would keep the reading public in a state of suspense for the crisis's duration. But Morris's drawings cover the printed text with a nebulous mist of color, forcing a criticism of mass media's theatrical storytelling as well as modern art's distanced, formalist viewing protocols.[15] Instead of the newspaper's standardized type and serial form, the drawings show the facticity of the paint, pale and viscous, as brushstrokes obscure key elements of the story. This is paint *performing as* drawing; Morris created the series, as he said later and as I noted earlier, to investigate "the borderline area in art where something is both looked at and read at the same time."[16] And true to form, instead of illuminating or amplifying the crisis, the works (figs. 1, 2) put the viewer into the role of archaeologist picking through a civilization's

Fig. 2 Robert Morris, *Crisis (Photograph of Kennedy, New York Daily News, Tuesday, October 23, 1962),* 1962. Newspaper page painted gray, 15 × 21 in. (38.1 × 53.3 cm).

remains. Only gradually does the printed page support become visible. A diaphanous cloud of gray paint obscures the particulars of this conflict that came to be defined by a nation obsessively mapping pinpoints of risk and making collective preparations against explosive shock. Morris's roller and handheld brushes obscure the *New York Post*'s famously feverish prose style as well as John F. Kennedy's Associated Press photograph (see fig. 2) that circulated to national and local newspapers and became one of his most iconic likenesses. The layers of paint do not just occlude; they also turn the newsprint sheets into discrete objects rather than a throwaway mass media publication for transmitting content. Even their orientation suggests misuse. Instead of folding them like a conventional newspaper, Morris has stretched them out to face upward like a landscape. Rotating the pages manipulates them at a semiotic as well as behavioral level: we cannot read the

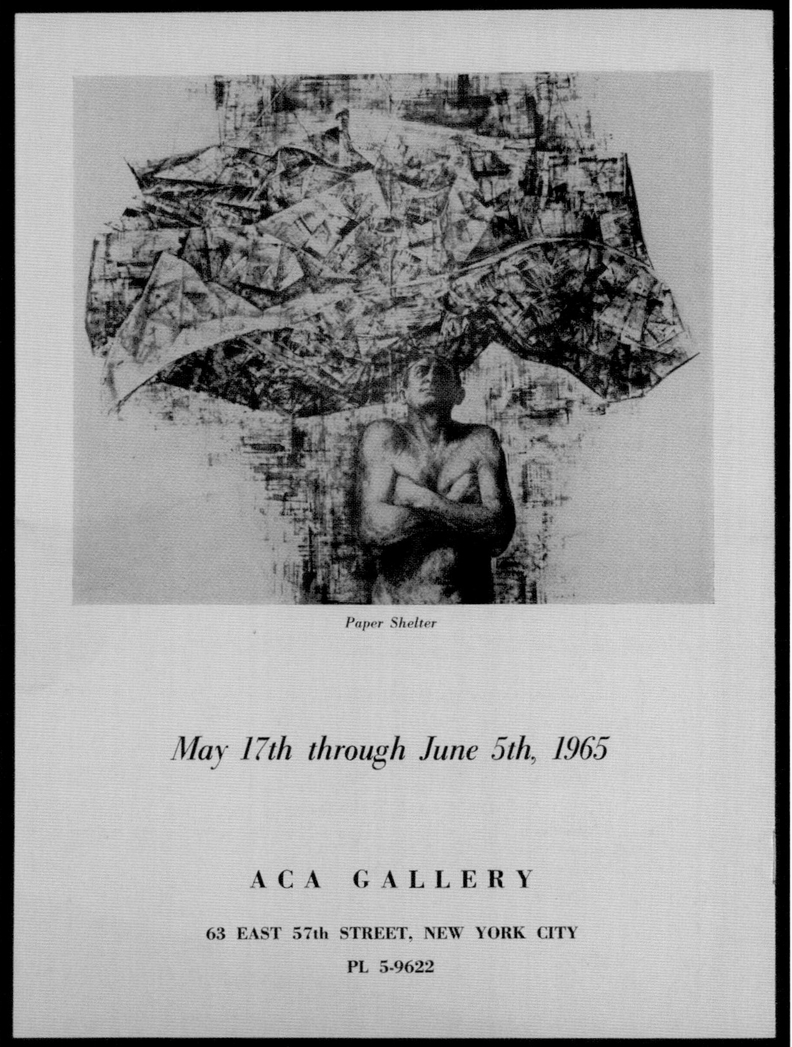

Fig. 3 Cover of Charles White's solo exhibition catalog at the ACA Gallery, New York, May 1965, with a reproduction of his drawing *Paper Shelter*. Archives of American Art, Smithsonian Institution.

Introduction

newspaper in the mode to which we are accustomed. Instead of providing the reader with up-to-the-minute information, crucial until the moment it becomes obsolete, the drawings' bleary surfaces underscore the fact that most newspapers, like much of the data recorded on them, will not survive the end of the day, much less a nuclear holocaust.[17]

Morris drew on not just paper but "the paper," as it was known in modern parlance. This taxonomic jump turned each sheet into both an object and a site for demonstration: because the news itself manipulates, the paint registers as a homeopathic gesture, matching like with like. By obscuring the paper's columns of text and pictures, Morris's paintings revealed the paper's calculated design features; one headline screams CRISIS, another shows only a flash of the charismatic Kennedy.[18] Occluding the surface of "the paper" not only distilled the anxieties of the nuclear age but showed the medium of the newspaper as instrumental to both consumer culture and idea culture—both of which Morris would later criticize for aiding "industry's ever-accelerating demand for new materials."[19] Works such as the *Crisis* drawings, made in and around New York's downtown loft neighborhoods, drew together the private acts of looking and reading. These works also extended the social action around the page to amplify the embodied experiences of writing, sitting, folding, discarding, and possibly being blown to ash, as well as cognitive processes such as sensation and perception. The *Crisis* drawings imbricate the act of making within a larger ecosystem, pitched against the anxieties about the intellectual and corporeal effects of media's omnipresence that the postwar period set in motion.

This series gives fresh context to Charles White's Chinese ink drawing *Paper Shelter* from three years later, which shows a shirtless man from the torso up standing under an umbrella-like cloud made of folded and tented paper. This work served as the cover illustration for White's solo exhibition at the ACA Gallery in 1965 and was featured in the Second Biennial Invitational Drawing Exhibition, held at Otis Art Institute of Los Angeles County College of Art the following year (fig. 3).[20] It was part of a long arc of White's pictures that employed sharp cuts of graphite, charcoal, or ink medium to create a thick atmospheric central passage. An image from his exhibition at the ACA gallery in 1965 shows two similar works in which the graphite and ink medium creates a human figure materially and energetically inseparable from its environment (fig. 4). In a slant rhyme on Morris's paint accretions, these drawings show another way of being "unforgiving . . . about layering," as the artist Toyin Ojih Odutola has put it.[21] Unlike Morris's series, however, the liquid medium insists rather than occludes. A dry brush pulled across the Chinese ink creates texture in spaces that might otherwise be aerated and thick passages of ink on the paper's surface to create weight. As a result, the looming form above the man's head feels imminent to the atmosphere while at the same time heavy and impregnable. The face tilts upward in a dreamy arc, a barometer for the allure and comfort of media narratives as well as for their precarity.

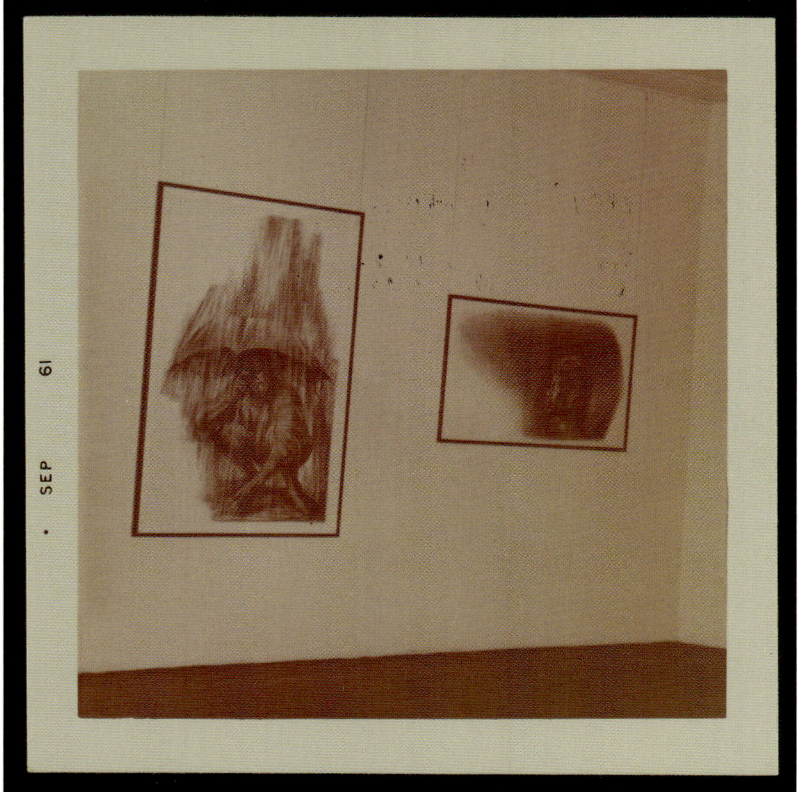

Fig. 4 Charles White, installation photograph of White's solo exhibition in 1961 at the ACA Gallery, New York. Archives of American Art, Smithsonian Institution.

Paper Shelter's tangle of references also act as a media critique of a different kind. In gardening, a paper shelter is a small, homemade structure used to keep vulnerable young shoots growing. In the US military, paper shelters were an emerging technology, developed in partnership with corporations such as Kimberly-Clark to create plastic-coated textiles—first for World War II military tents and then for suburban car campers. (Ford Motor Company's issue of *Station Wagon Living* for 1959 featured the paper tent on its cover, with images inside of happy families enjoying their paper roof shades and bedding, packing an indispensable stack of paper plates.)[22] White's drawing, however, with its paper cloud that both envelops and misleads, shows the fantasy in looking to external resources for refuge. It also highlights this man's protection by the "system"—by the very same bureaucracy that commits violence on Black bodies and resources—as it communicates white people's exclusive access to certain kinds of knowledge and spaces. "Remember a few years ago when everybody was building bomb shelters?" White said about this work in a public talk at the Los Angeles County Museum of Art the following year. "They'd go to [the luxury department store] I. Magnin, get all the furniture, clothes to sit there, you know, the dress garments. . . . They'd call the interior decorators in, they had TV down there, and a bar, and while this big holocaust was predicted to take place, they were gonna be sitting there! You know, sitting in their finery, sipping on their liquor, enjoying TV and by god, the world is going to pieces."[23] Like

     Introduction

Morris, White pictures a social matrix scrambled so profoundly by violence that the gaps between racial and class positions become pure fiction. When the bomb that this man has convinced himself to fear goes off, the "shelter" will not remain, but the yearning for protection will endure.

Despite the differences in these two artists' styles, each participated in the seismic shift in drawing's position in American art practice that was underway. Morris activated drawing's materiality in opposition to human technology and humaneness, while White used it to center the resilience of the human body and human faculties. Both artists, crucially, incorporated movement in space. Erica Moiah James has written that White's strategic deployment of form "turns theories of abjection away from the body, to the physical and symbolic spaces where these bodies live, move, and survive."[24] This remark illuminates how profoundly White reframed the work on paper: as a portable record that could make human action visible and could also show how social life accrued in all made things.

Media coverage of White's drawings, too, depicted paper as part of the general ecology of creativity. The artist's studio was an important nucleus of this ecology, a place for processing the outside world to survive. An interview spread in *Soul Illustrated* magazine from 1968 shows White sitting on a chair in front of a wall of sample pages and paste-ups, hands supporting his chin in thought, as a rounded fish-eye lens captures a curved panoramic view of the studio (fig. 5). Photographs of the artist's hands at work and another of his coffee cup appear below the caption: "A man's real

Fig. 5 Charles White, interview spread, *Soul Illustrated* 1, no. 3 (1968). Archives of American Art, Smithsonian Institution.

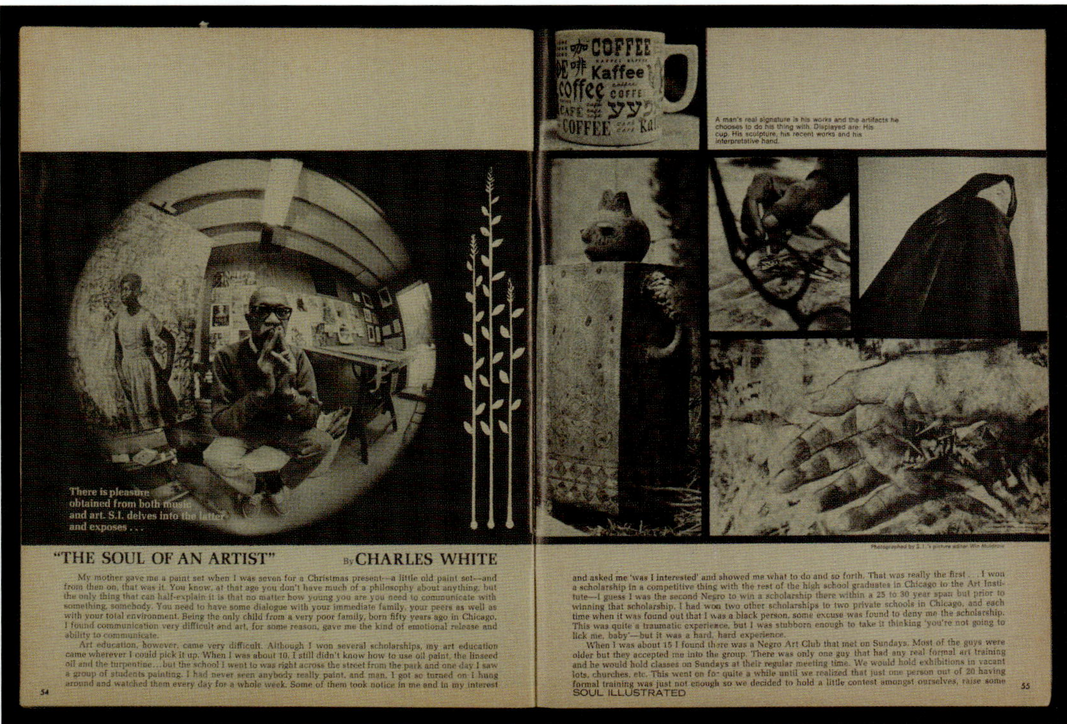

signature is his works and the artifacts he chooses to do his thing with."[25] At first, these images appear to typify what Caroline Jones has called "the auratic mechanisms of modern art"—a set of references that affirm individual creative ability and yoke the studio space to its related Latin word, *studium,* signifying private study.[26] But here, White's hands and possessions act as a metonym for relationality as well as individuality. One hand marks a collaged image of a hand, which would eventually become his charcoal drawing *I Have Seen Black Hands,* titled after Richard Wright's poem of the same name from 1934 that called for interracial activism. White's mug, too, binds to private experience but is also an artifact of social life, imbued with the chumminess of the coffee hour. Unsurprisingly, then, the article below contains multiple references to the problem of representing one's "total environment" and the social and relational aspects of lived experience. White names his own artistic milieu as inspiration: Richard Wright, Gwendolyn Brooks, Katherine Dunham, and others whose works conceded to the material reality of Black life and the intellectual value of Black cultural forms. This *Soul Illustrated* spread shows how drawings and studio objects rendered the studio environment special by activating its permeability to long histories of lived experience, and by displaying an individual intellect's debt to history, lineage, and kin.

Robert Morris was also widely promoted as an artist-thinker, as his photograph for the exhibition *Art in Process IV* in 1969 attests (fig. 6). *Art in Process* was a series of teaching exhibitions organized by the curator Elayne Varian at Finch College, an all-women's liberal arts institution on Manhattan's Upper East Side. Morris was a natural candidate for this series focusing on practical knowledge, having designed props for dance

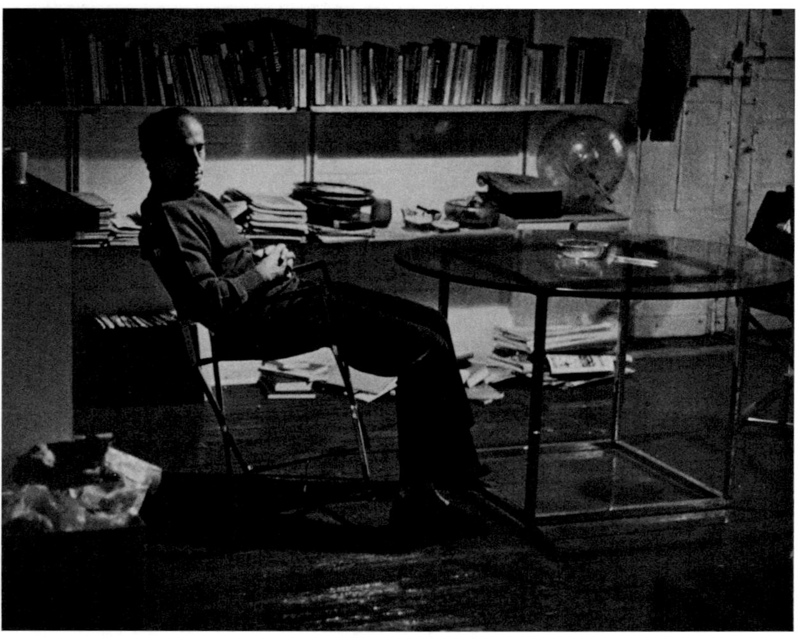

Fig. 6 Robert Morris in his studio, reproduced in *Art in Process IV,* edited by Elayne Varian, Finch College Museum of Art, October 1969. Archives of American Art, Smithsonian Institution.

Introduction

performances and by then well known as a minimalist sculptor.[27] Here, too, auratic mechanisms abound, but this time tracking to streams of materials in and beyond the studio. Morris leans back in thought, wearing soft house shoes with his hands clasped in his lap, in front of a shelf that holds a celestial star globe, film canisters, and piles of newspapers and magazines pooling on the floor to his left. These papers, as well as the overflowing trash can behind him, plot the coordinates of everyday life under capitalism: incoming and outgoing materials juxtaposed, in mutual relation with one another as two clear stages of creativity and value. Amid this metabolism of ideas and their gradual discharge as art—Morris's eventual contribution to the show *Art in Process IV* was a hand-drawn map specifying the correct installation space for his work, and he designed at least one event score for an object that was "to be deposited in the street with a toss"—he is pictured also with scientific apparatus, not unlike early modern images of artist-inventors or the astronomy-crazed Marcel Duchamp, whose work Morris admired.[28] (Duchamp, Rembrandt, Michelangelo, Leonardo, Donatello, and Pontormo all form a sort of usable past for the artists in this book. By the postwar period, these elder artists' names indexed high value and esteem for creative activity, and the historical record had revealed them to have been building on—and stumbling over—the presumed classical inheritances of Western civilization, just as the advanced conceptual and post-minimal artists of the 1960s were grappling with their own lineage.)

In emphasizing the work of the mind alongside inertia and garbage, this picture reads as a different kind of genealogical mapping, one that creates a counterpoint to White's pasteups. Knowledge comes from somewhere, but it discharges everywhere. Whatever the pause in paper's process, there's a supply chain of which you are a part. If the page was a ready-made object-form, then Morris's performances of thinking and remembering drew attention to its effects, much like his rotation of the newspaper's support. This was a way of reading and looking that challenged causality and history—the very things that these anxious newspapers purported to deliver.

The art historian and critic Leo Steinberg, who had taught Morris during his MA studies in art history at Hunter College, famously reflected on this in 1972, when he wrote about a shift in pictures he'd observed since 1950. "[Contemporary artworks] no more depend on a head-to-toe correspondence with human posture than a newspaper does," wrote Steinberg. He proposed that, in opposition to the "erect posture" that had guided visual thinking since the advent of one-point perspective in the Renaissance, artists were turning to a kind of "flatbed picture plane" that made a "symbolic allusion to hard surfaces such as tabletops, studio floors, charts, bulletin boards—any receptor surface on which objects are scattered, on which data is entered, on which information may be received, printed, impressed—whether coherently or in confusion."[29] But artists' engagements went much further than just orientation and symbolism. In Morris's and White's respective propositions, the drawing or preparatory model becomes an example of what the political philosopher Jane Bennett calls an "entanglement": a set of entities acting at different scales that involve one another and complicate each other because of each component's power and influence. Paper becomes a new pathway into practices that were equally ill-defined, in-between, and categorically nebulous. In the case studies in this book, drawings and paper hold power under limited and intermittent conditions—when a piece of media information spreads from writer to reader, for example; or when a drawing implement generates material resistance that has significance to the maker but transmits a different provocation to the viewer; or when a notation is either preserved or thrown away. I proceed here from a theoretical framework that allows us to consider these things as hybrids of thought and external action.

In taking up art history, environmental theories, and the genealogies of twentieth-century materialist philosophy, this book traces new perceptions of the body and its surroundings that drawing permitted, particularly as the term *environment* became *the environment,* a planetary sphere that was increasingly understood to be fragile and subject to violence from human-made disasters.[30] Paper was a medium for, an extension of, and a symbolic link between bodies and their surroundings, and thus a key agent in the semantics of environment. Works on paper could be in dialogue with one's environs and also with global systems. By the end of the decade, this notion of *surroundings,* circumscribed in various ways, would become a defining critical term for makers, supplanting the notion of the object altogether. "The social context and surroundings of art are more potent, more meaningful, more demanding of an artist's attention than the art itself!" wrote Allan Kaprow in a reply to Robert Morris's essay on sculpture in 1968, marking a terminus to the decade's debates on artistic form.[31]

ANTI-CARTESIANISM IN THE INFORMATION AGE

Out of Paper expands on the work of recent publications concerned with drawing practices in the 1960s and 1970s, including those by Anna Lovatt, Laurence Schmidlin, and Kelly Chorpening and Rebecca Fortnum.[32] It also builds on research on embodiment and ecology in the art of the 1960s, including works by Elise Archias, Orit Halpern, Jason A. Hoelscher, and James Nisbet.[33] The principal difference in my study is its focus on anti-Cartesian and nondualist philosophies, which emerged in the 1960s through different channels to address the seemingly incommensurable divide between subject and object; between materials and those who acted upon those materials. Most important, this manifested through new questions about mind-body relations: Must a controlling agent mandate the behaviors and habits of each body? Might physical experience be organized in different relation to the mind, allowing the two to work together instead of one commanding the other? Occurring across many branches of discourse, but especially in civil rights speeches and writings, the idea of synthesis, wholeness, and oneness became a way of facing the world.

This premise is distinct from other studies on drawing in the late twentieth century that begin with theories of language. Laurence Schmidlin discusses the 1960s' surge of interest in drawing in terms of what Roland Barthes called the "allusive field" of language—how some kinds of drawing establish gesture as "the surplus of an action." For Barthes, gesture is "the indeterminate and inexhaustible total of reasons, pulsions, indolences which surround the action with an atmosphere (in the astronomical sense of the word)."[34] This indeed prompts careful thought about the ramifications of human action in relation to artistic materials. But in this formulation, all possibilities come from human impulses, acted out upon a receiving surface. Even color appears in relation to human gesture, for "it is precisely the stroke which makes the color."[35] Similarly, Anna Lovatt asserts that drawing in the 1960s, like writing, disavowed the subject-position of the author—and thus proposed to make writing a form of labor, detached from style and content. She shows that, just as Barthes proposed that writing could operate within "the relationship between creation and society" rather than adhere to a stylistic template, New York artists' drawings emerged in antagonistic relation to cultural norms.[36] While this recuperates beautifully the commitments that some New York artists held with respect to meaning and inscription, it does not account for the complicated relations between the subject and the body that many paper-based artworks set forth in other parts of the United States, including its territories, like Puerto Rico.

In Morris's *Crisis* drawings, for instance, the above assertions about writing appear to be true at first—Morris called his drawing experiments of this period "unilluminated manuscripts," indicating a hostility to the acts of assimilation that accrue when a text is read.[37] However, several other remarks he made later reorient us toward an artwork's surface as a potentially disruptive field—specifically, as a field that both held onto and resisted Cartesian understandings of space. It was the nature of the mapping space itself—that is, the picture surface—that encouraged this separation between the thinking viewer and the actual field being looked at. Years after making the *Crisis* series, Morris observed that "all twentieth-century art seems compelled by a type of Cartesian projection that will net every visual experience by a vertical plane interposed between the viewer and the world. . . . Seeing is directed straight out, 90° to the wall or at an object never far from a wall. The pervasive spatial context is one of room space with its strongly accentuated divisions between vertical and horizontal and the subsequent emphasis on orientations of plumb and level. Within such a context for vision, the seemingly phenomenological dichotomy between flat and three-dimensional, marking and making, painting and sculpture, has been nurtured."[38] Again, we see emerging the problem of planarity and its incommensurability with the ways that most bodies, both human and more-than-human, move through the world. Jason Hoelscher, in his book *Art as Information Ecology,* attributes this to the "entropic surface quality" of Morris's works, which "have the effect of enabling a dense entanglement of the work with its larger context."[39] But drawing represents a special challenge—one worth taking up in this book—as being the site at which these entanglements are first made.

The theoretical foundations of my analysis find their futures in the vital materialist theories of Karen Barad, Jane Bennett, and Bruno Latour, but they begin with Baruch Spinoza. Spinoza was an Enlightenment philosopher whose treatise *Ethics,* posthumously published in 1677, set out to "consider human actions and appetites just as if it were an investigation into lines, planes, or bodies."[40] He spent much of his career working as an optical lens grinder, and as an avid draftsman himself, he was deeply interested in vision.[41] Spinoza's main proposal, which was well known among amateur and academic philosophers alike in the postwar period, was that both the mind and the body—or, as he framed them, thought and extension—were divine attributes, issuing from the same central impulse. In Spinoza's *Ethics,* extension was the material counterpart to thought, the material action that showed ideas and the external world to be deeply connected. Spinoza argued that "the power of Thought to think about or to comprehend things, is not greater than the power of Nature to exist and to act."[42] Any material form could be an extension of an idea, and any idea was the inevitable result of material interactions between different constituents. His term *extended substance* describes, in a beautifully inexact way, the surfeit of things that artists wanted drawings or paper-based practices to do: perform or demonstrate metaphors, stage the annihilation of the earth's atmosphere, or trace the body's changing somatic state from moment to moment.

Spinoza's claim is no less radical now than it was in the late seventeenth century when it shifted philosophy's boundaries. Matter, whether a constituent of an artistic material or an artwork's frame or support, is active no less than thought. In the long 1960s, considering the extension (and motion) of matter, whether an atom bomb or the resistance of a fountain pen, could help human beings, in their limited intellectual range, to understand that the differences between mind and matter largely reflect human categorization. Because we have privileged access to thought through language, we use thought to clarify and understand matter. Jane Bennett identifies Spinoza's proposition as central to, and a precursor for, the "ecological sensibility" that flourished from the later twentieth century onward.[43] Even as Spinoza relies on Descartes's dualism, he offers a radical departure from it. We must perceive and speak of the world dualistically, but the dualistic framework is only made available to us by examining the very things that separate mind and body from one another.

This interest in anti-Cartesianism, and in nondualism generally, had a wider-ranging reach than the scientifically oriented ecological discourses that James Nisbet deftly traces in his book *Ecologies, Environments, and Energy Systems in Art of the 1960s and 1970s.* The anti-Cartesian tradition in postwar philosophy made space for affect and embodiment as counterpoints to rote, mechanistic ideas about scientific knowledge. The French philosopher Gilles Deleuze drafted one of his first books on philosophy, a treatise on Spinoza and expressionism, in the fall of 1968. In it, he aligned Spinoza's material monism with the work of the French philosopher Henri Bergson, whose studies of time, matter, and motion felt to Deleuze like a modern effort to place matter in a frontal role in the philosophy of mind. In 1965, Louis Althusser described Spinoza's ideas as a powerful force against "the latent dogmatic empiricism of Cartesian idealism" and a precursor for Marxist thought. "Spinoza warned us that the object of knowledge or essence was in itself absolutely distinct and different from the real object," Althusser wrote. "Only an ideological world outlook could have imagined societies without ideology and accepted the utopian idea of a world in which ideology (not just one of its historical forms) would disappear without a trace, to be replaced by science." He repeated Spinoza's "favorite aphorism" as a parable for the modern age: "the two objects must not be confused: the idea of the circle, which is the object of knowledge, must not be confused with the circle, which is the real object."[44]

Many artists and thinkers were also considering thought and material, not as separate entities, but as things that could unfold in mutual relation. Nondualist thought flourished within antiracist and New Left discourses; it found lively form in the speeches and letters of Martin Luther King Jr., who had read René Descartes and Spinoza in divinity school. "Life at its best is a creative synthesis of opposites in fruitful harmony," he wrote in 1963.[45] This assertion encompassed not only the unifying power of love in the midst of racial violence, but also linked writings on "soul," in the tradition of civil rights thought, to a broader rehearsal of such theories. Nonduality also worked to amplify invisible traditions. After writing his volume on Spinoza in 1968, Deleuze would propose the idea of "minor literature" with Félix Guattari in 1975, which eventually consolidated into his affect theory. Deleuze's definition of affect rests squarely on his quotation of Spinoza: "By affect I understand affections of the body by which the body's power of acting is increased or diminished, aided or restrained."[46] From 1968 onward, the relationship between the past and the present for Deleuze was transversal, tracking back and forth between Spinoza's theories of the body and the urgent physical realities of the current moment.

In Lower Manhattan the references to nondualistic philosophies were more direct. Barnett Newman spoke and wrote about Spinoza's vision of the world as a single substance in a constant state of flux.[47] Carolee Schneemann's most beloved philosophy professor, Heinrich Blücher, was an ethics scholar, and she attended his lectures on Spinoza, pantheism, and metaphysics while a student at Bard College in the late 1950s.[48] Others made more personal citations. "Sol [LeWitt] is our Spinoza," Carl Andre declared in an essay for the artist's midcareer survey exhibition catalog in 1970.[49] Andre also kept a copy of Lewis Browne's biography of Spinoza from 1932 and made a collage out of clips of the book in an artwork to describe Sol LeWitt.[50] Matter, which was something that human beings make intelligible to one another through language, has demonstrative qualities that both exceed language and point to our eternal reliance on it as a field of reference. By considering the specificity of the material support in its many different modes, these artists moved closer to the ways that thought and imagination structure the terms for art making. Probing the intersection of thought and matter was especially relevant and urgent in a moment when matter was frequently instrumentalized at the service of the state and of capitalism. Diagramming ideas, making structures, and merging different components of lived experience created surprising usable pasts, from Schneemann's and Morris's reference to early modern "plumb line" techniques to the discussions of the way those knowledges became exclusive, extractive, or violent, as with Charles White's taking up of nineteenth-century bills of sale. And so, just as ways of knowing (or learning about) the world are a leitmotif in this book, so, too, is the seizure of knowledge and its stakes for art and picture making.

Authors such as Gwen Allen have brought avant-garde art histories to bear on media history, literature, alternative publishing, and the history of the book by observing the central role of the art magazine in disseminating ideas through media channels designed to be thrown away.[51] JoAnn Yates and Craig Robertson analyze paper through the framework of the history of management; Lisa Gitelman does so through a history of knowledge.[52] The proliferation of mail art in this period also routed paper through an intimate, yet resolutely public, system of connectivity—the national postal system—and recent transnational histories of mail art have exhumed enormous differences in artists' approaches to the mail as a public media form.[53] These media-rich and materially fungible drawings were contemporaneous with the mimeo revolution, paperback publishing, little magazines, and self-publishing, and they occasionally even foreshadow paper's role in punk and zine cultures of the 1980s. It is no coincidence that the artists in this book, including Sol LeWitt, Robert Morris, Carolee Schneemann, Adrian Piper, and Richard Tuttle, all contributed to experimental book projects; Charles White accrued a robust reputation as a graphic illustrator in an emerging wave of books on Black history. Their projects often concerned the book's specific materiality in relation to other types of information or leveraged other small-scale distributable printed materials including the calendar, the broadsheet, the auction poster, and even the centerfold.

A page from Carolee Schneemann's contribution to the experimental book *Fantastic Architecture* (1970) outlines an interior that Morris had begun to complicate in his critique of media hysteria eight years earlier: the human body. The book contained proposals and other "documentation of ideas and concepts of a new polymorphous reality" to create "a demand for new patterns of behavior—new unconsumed environments."[54] Its cover reproduces Richard Hamilton's *Guggenheim Collage* (1967), in which a cutout of Hamilton points an aerosol sprayer at Frank Lloyd Wright's iconic

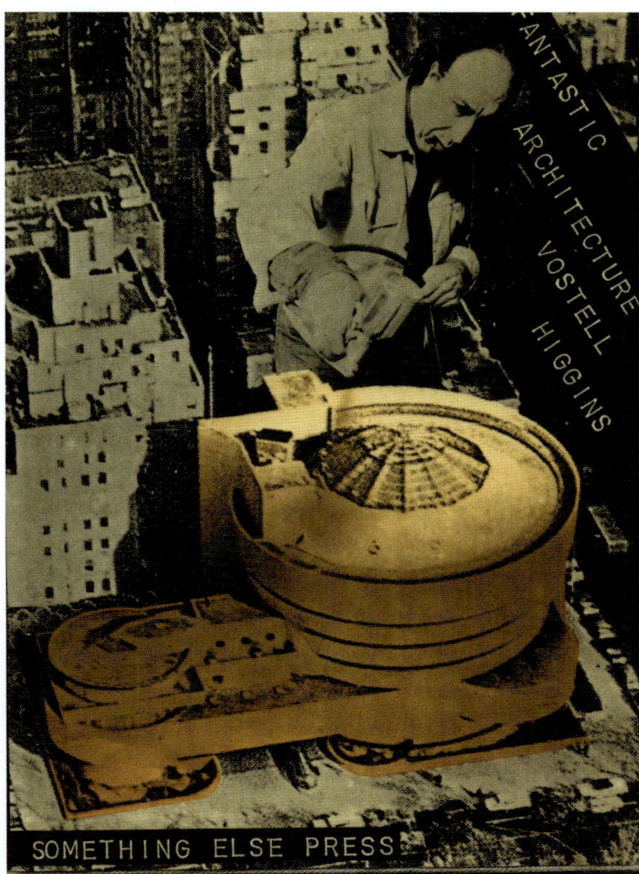

Fig. 7 Cover of *Fantastic Architecture,* edited by Wolf Vostell and Dick Higgins (New York: Something Else Press, 1970), featuring Richard Hamilton's *Guggenheim Collage* of 1967.

Guggenheim Museum building in a gesture of annihilation (fig. 7). A turn to the frontispiece revealed a photograph of Great Britain's first successful hydrogen bomb test in 1957, detonated over Christmas Island in the South Pacific. Other insets at the beginning and end of the book bespeak nuclear detonation as a spent space, a "consumed environment" that these new propositions were designed to expand. In *Fantastic Architecture* were essays and proposals by Claes Oldenburg, Douglas Huebler, Carolee Schneemann, and Richard Hamilton, as well as Buckminster Fuller's designs for Tetra City and Joseph Beuys's proposal to raise the height of the Berlin Wall by five inches. Schneemann's project departs from the aerosol's destruction and the bomb's monumentality, presenting instead an architectural complex to imitate the functions of the human body (fig. 8). Her submitted proposal included drawings, though the editors, Dick Higgins and Wolf Vostell, did not include them in the volume. In his introduction, Higgins cautioned that architects "have only just begun to escape from the drawing board mentality, the architectural equivalent of easel painting," and encouraged designers of the built environment to consider instead the "real needs for creating space, which may or may not be functional, but which is at least relevant to the sensory environment in which we live."[55] The page from Schneemann's contribution features a full-length photograph of the artist, who stands, nude, stooped over. She makes her proposition explicit a few pages earlier when she defines ecology as "a relationship, perhaps, between the body politic and the body physical?"[56] (Notably, this image was cropped from a photograph of Schneemann posing with several other artists of varying genders.) Her proposal is unique in the book in its indictment of numerous kinds of architectures that construct and encase femininity. For example, the cropped photo acts as a countermapping of the centerfold, a visual form that would have been familiar to the book's readers, for whom pornographic magazines and circulars often shared table space with art magazines. Instead of stretching out in ecstasy to make her body available to the viewer, however, Schneemann's figure stoops in the two-page spread, as though compressed by its spatial and ideological parameters. Two pages in Mylar break up the upper and lower half of her body, which share space on the page with a printed text proposing different rooms in her "Parts of a Body House."

The two facing pages exploit the artist's nude body and turn the book's own anatomy—that is, its diaphanous vellum pages—into a peep show. As with the other artists in this book, Schneemann's proposition expands the field of visionary architecture, drawing, and design to include the human corpus; specifically, here, the ecology of the human gut. In fact, this work and the ink-on-paper drawings Schneemann made to accompany it—again, never shown in the decade of its making—affirm my larger theoretical

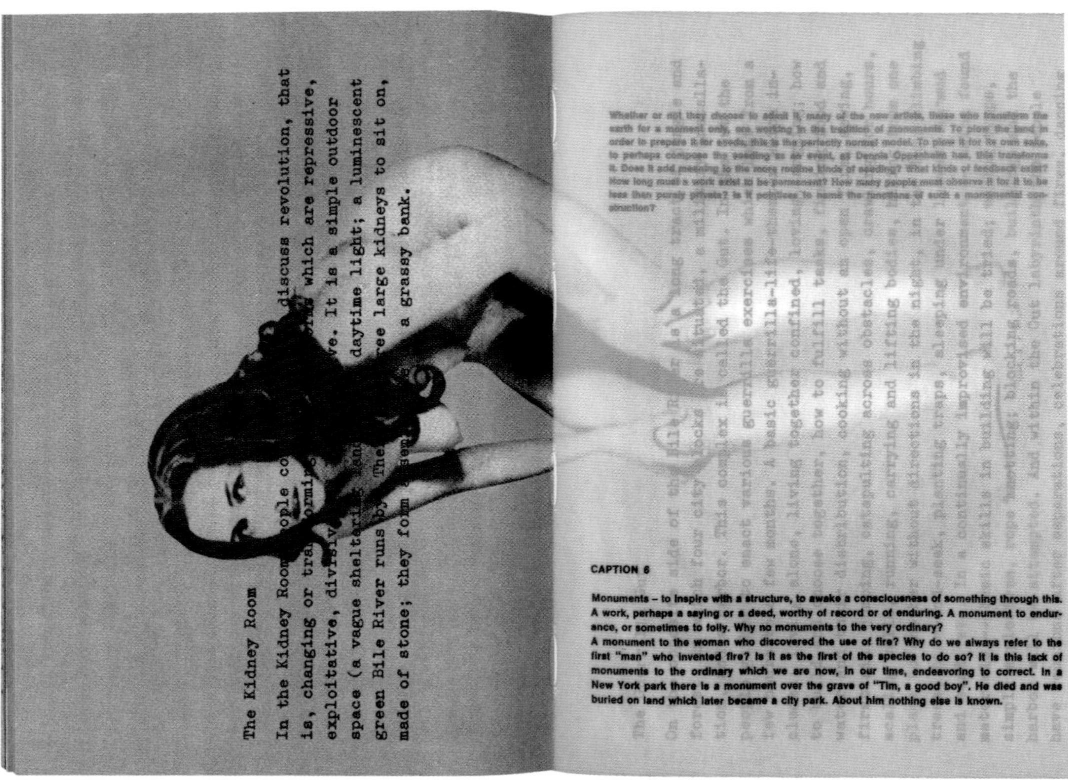

Fig. 8 Carolee Schneemann, two-page spread from "Parts of a Body House," in *Fantastic Architecture,* edited by Wolf Vostell and Dick Higgins (New York: Something Else Press, 1970).

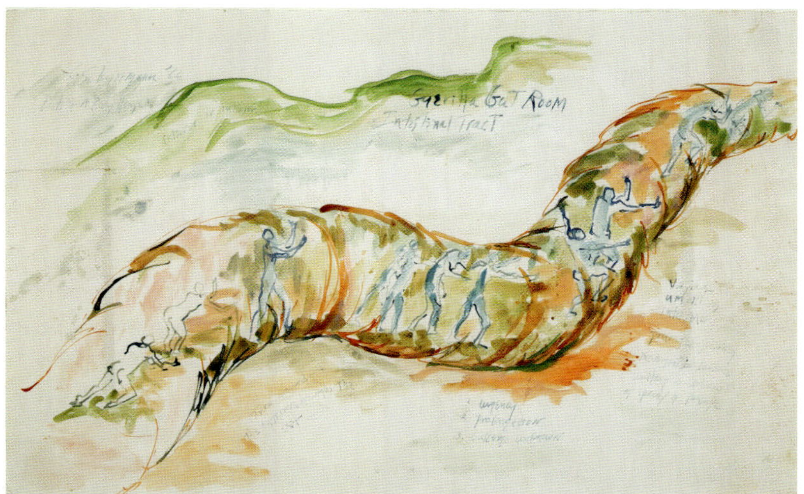

Fig. 9 Carolee Schneemann, *Parts of a Body House—Guerilla Gut Room (I)*, 1966. Watercolor and ink on paper, 22¾ × 34¼ in. (57.79 × 86 cm).

ambit: that designs for new environments lay at the center of this embattled historical moment and were attached to questions about who would imagine, design, and control the future. Such designs in this period created what Bruno Latour has called "immutable mobiles"—readouts and inscriptions that create "easily readable and presentable" versions of the complexities of lived experience.[57] For Latour as well as for my own historical work, these "immutable mobiles" are not only central to critiques of knowledge but also follow and footnote strategies like Schneemann's, which turn drawings into templates for resistance. Her *Guerilla Gut Room* drawing literalizes the intestines as a "complex," or, as she describes it in her published essay, a "long tract of jungle and forest" in which human beings might live in experimental ways (fig. 9). Its tubular tunnels extend across the paper end to end, to form "a basic guerilla-life-theater . . . in a continually improvised environment—using found materials—basic skills in building will be tried: making traps, simple explosives, rope knotting, blocking roads, buildings, and the harbor will be attempted."[58] Schneemann's plans are both a precursor and a challenge to Latour's assertion that "there is nothing you can dominate as easily as a flat surface; . . . there is nothing hidden or convoluted, no shadows, no 'double entendre.'"[59] Significantly for Schneemann, Anastasi, Tuttle, Morris, and White, this claim proves untrue.

My position relies on a feminist political ecology in the longue-durée, flowing from Heraclitus to Spinoza and through the vital materialist and posthumanist debates of the present day. Such a feminism helps us to perceive two principal points: how living matter and "inert" materials alike are often put to rigorous systems of control that mask their potentialities; and how theory resides in cursory objects just as it issues from discourses. I share Sarah Ahmed's interest in "how the word *theory* itself is distributed; how some materials are understood as theory and not others."[60] In the postwar United States, where the separations between matter and human beings seemed immanent, it became crucial to imagine that matter might be itself a theory. We can follow Karen Barad's assertion that matter is not "a support, location, referent, or source of sustainability for discourse" but rather a potent medium for reimagining who and what counts.[61] Within Morris's "borderline area," Charles White's "total environment," and Schneemann's "pantheistic excursions," there are many occasions for theories of knowledge based on human and other-than-human interactions and buttressed by the structural languages of drawing and painting.[62] Such a poststructuralist feminist ecological approach can help art history to abandon its attachment to the finished object and attend instead to what artist Steffani Jemison calls "technologies of representation and transcription as symbolic systems from which we are periodically compelled to escape."[63] I wonder also if, in considering the paper as a specific surface, we might also understand the larger question of "surface" for makers today as something requiring both tight specificity (water or garbage, for instance, are surfaces) and a much greater degree of distance and freedom. The digital document surface is, after all, also a highly surveilled surface.

Each chapter of this book examines a distinct generative process that drawing mobilized between the Cold War and the early environmentalist movement. The chapters track paper as a key agent in recycling, recording, rapid prototyping, erasing, and cutting—an account that not only shows how artists in this era changed what Donald Preziosi called art history's standard of "the tradition of individual-image interpretation" but also brings art history into dialogue with adjacent fields such as design studies and media studies.[64] Chapter 1 examines a central problem in drawing that was given renewed meaning through paper's materiality: the human figure. The chapter opens in Carolee Schneemann's loft studio in 1967, one month before her paper-based performance *Illinois Central* was rejected from the *Made with Paper* exhibition at the Museum of Contemporary Art Chicago. In the studio, she staged *Body Collage,* a nude mock-up performance for the camera that got her ejected from the exhibition. In *Body Collage,* Schneemann painted her flesh with wheat paste and jumped into a pile of wastepaper, allowing her body's spontaneous movements to choose and configure the paper scraps, rather than paper capturing her nude figure. This material reversal usurped modernist collage practice both to undercut media's tendencies to freeze and fix the female form and to use paper's fragility to implicate waste systems within state violence. This chapter clarifies the key role that Schneemann's drawing played in her engagement with Intermedia, Fluxus, and performance circles as she envisioned paper as part of a violent supply chain, as likely to *cause* death as it was to crumple, tear, or shred. In a historical moment in which miniskirts and bikinis could make women's flesh seem desirable just as melted fallout from armed conflict could inflict trauma on Vietnamese bodies, Schneemann's novel method for observation illuminated the degree to which human bodies are linked with others through distant supply chains. A microhistory of *Illinois Central* shows Schneemann's dialogue with New Left writers such as Herbert Marcuse, who called for a "new science" that treated nature as a subject in its own right, rather than one to be captured, extracted, and used.[65]

As written and printed metaphors came under fierce scrutiny due to new considerations of gender, race, and empire, other artists stripped down their commitments to language in favor of rote transcription. Recording, recordkeeping, seismographic measurements—these had long been the tools of twentieth-century modernist avant-garde movements to fuse together the active, ideating mind with the dynamic and permutational movements of machines.[66] But drawing created a link among bodies, written records, and postwar artificial intelligences that became uniquely relevant to emerging conceptual artists. Chapter 2 discusses William Anastasi's experiments with unsighted drawing methods as he entered the minimal and conceptual circles of Virginia Dwan's gallery. Anastasi's series of *Walking Drawings, Pocket Drawings,* and *Subway Drawings* were done on paper that was inserted into the artist's pocket or set on his lap. For these untitled works, Anastasi converted his body and the paper into a sightless recording device. Without their maker's sight for guidance, these works create friction against Renaissance-era mythologies of artists as guiding their bodily behaviors with divine light. Instead, in gazing at all three of these series as they traced New York's public spaces, a different set of paraprofessional behaviors comes to light in this chapter: the trained gestures of emerging secretarial and blue-collar classes, from stenography to lever-pulling. Just as paper's connections to recycling and reuse prompted artists to deconstruct their own media landscape, unsighted drawing methods facilitated a surrender to public space as they emphasized such habitual gestures as breathing, walking, and sitting.

Anastasi explored the body's embeddedness within larger systems, while other artists were deconstructing the many binaries that separated the human form from its nonhuman surroundings. Richard Tuttle approached these topics from a much broader position: through the question of scale, in the sense of both size and dimensionality. Drawing was in step with numerous thinkers' and philosophers' calls to think critically about scale and environment; even the smallest and most subtle gestures could transform space.[67] Scale was also a topic of debate in countercultural circles, as young people in the Vietnam era became acquainted with militarized barriers and boundaries that could generate inauthentic scalar relations, often mediated through paper means. Chapter 3 analyzes Tuttle's series of sculptural forms made from drawn templates, which eventually reduced in volume to the flat space of two dimensions. Tuttle cut up and sewed numerous bodies of work from these paper templates; all were light and easily portable and could be folded into a duffel bag or tacked to the wall with thumbtacks. This chapter considers cutting as a very particular line-based process, one that not only facilitated productive disruptions and augmentations in Tuttle's practice but also provided a model for thinking about scale and agency. By making new cuts into physical and social space, these works responded to scientists' and philosophers' demands to withdraw from the consumer economy. Enacted through the cut, drawing was in step with numerous thinkers' and philosophers' calls to think critically about scale and environment; even the smallest and most subtle gestures could transform space.[68]

As the utopian projects of the long 1960s gave way to violent crises late in the decade, plan drawings became a key method by which to question the possibility of structural change. Chapter 4 is an inquiry into the potentials and limitations of the prototype drawing, focusing on its relation to technology and corporate life. Prototypes and proposals on paper were a common practice for postwar artists and designers, necessary for visualizing and mobilizing a project in its early stages, but by late in the 1960s they had become marketed public objects, the subject of exhibitions and fairs. This shift prompted makers to examine planning and rapid prototyping as a reflexive method. The chapter examines sixteen extant proposal drawings for Robert Morris's live work *Frarmrroreerofibseaterlr,* which he staged with fellow artist Rafael Ferrer at the University of Puerto Rico–Mayagüez in September 1969. Each proposal drawing sketches out a different interactive scene between the artists and an unspecified set of student collaborators. Together, Morris used the prototype drawing as a way of dreaming on the page—and a way to illuminate ecological injustice and transnational state violence. A project executed in the twilight of Happenings and other performance modes, as Morris and Ferrer were contemplating their respective positions within postminimalist art movements, *Frarmrroreerofibseaterlr* shows drawings' complicated relations to plans. Even as plans and prototypes were becoming increasingly valued, they could interrogate the relations between conceptual planning and actual space.

But planning and prototyping have very clear limits besides the page's edge. The book's fifth chapter is a close study of Charles White's *Wanted Poster* series, begun in Los Angeles in 1969 after the assassination of Martin Luther King Jr. and after Black Panther Eldridge Cleaver's flight from US soil following an FBI-supported police raid. The chapter attends to White's interest in the dialectical play of accretion and removal, which came out through his oil wash drawings of the late 1960s, which had little precedent in his work up until that point. I argue that White used oil wash to simulate the archival page, thus overlaying the present with the past in order to challenge the United States' ongoing erasure of its own racist history. The *Wanted Poster* drawings galvanized support for the Black Power movements of the 1970s and made three important interventions into the art world of the late 1960s. First, they indicted US print culture as a key instrument in upholding the legal grounds of slavery, showing how slave posters and auction advertisements naturalized the body to the condition of flight. Second, they proposed a copresence of abuse and bodily integrity—that is, they suggest that it was possible for a body to appear simultaneously vulnerable to abuse and also resilient to it. Third, in melding human figures with national symbols and racist legal constructions, White demonstrated

		Introduction

the fragility of each and made them both speak to what he called the "total environment" of Black lived experience.

Several different ecologies of the page, some literalized and others figurative, created new means for twentieth-century American artists to interrogate the terms that constituted their surroundings. The unstable timelines of ecological and humanitarian disasters, the mythologized space of the studio, and the capricious critical designations of artistic knowing were all vital concerns for makers in New York and Los Angeles at the close of the Cold War and the beginning of the Information Age and the dawn of ecological thinking. These concepts also underpin my methodology. I highlight the moments when media surfaces were made to perform as objects or when the boundaries that purported to separate the interior self with public space became visible and permeable or when a work on paper could become instrumental in constructing a new and better world. Each of these artists either directly or indirectly examined the body's relation to the larger contexts in which flesh might find itself situated (such as within a social milieu or as part of an ecology) and how we might see or remake the socially inscribed categories of work, home, and street.

Especially visible here are the critical and curatorial methods that either mixed, or artificially separated, the downtown milieu of Morris, Schneemann, Ferrer, Tuttle, and Anastasi from the Midtown Manhattan and Los Angeles galleries that exhibited Charles White's work. It is important to discuss their drawings' critical fortunes together, however. When considered this way, these artists' works point to new critical positions on each city's ability to absorb and support new artists, including the institutional forces that upheld certain kinds of artworks as suitable for display and suppressed others. These works show, too, the astonishing degree of collaboration among artists that drawing and writing facilitated. Carolee Schneemann collaborated with Robert Morris but also made works as a member of the Judson Dance Theatre, Fluxus, and Intermedia. Morris and Yvonne Rainer lived downstairs from William Anastasi; Morris, Anastasi, and Rainer were all deeply influenced by John Cage and gravitated into Virginia Dwan's stable to consolidate postminimalist and early conceptualist strategies. And Richard Tuttle was the inheritor of 1960s drawing practices, primed from having visited pop art, Happenings, and avant-garde dance performances during his time as a student at Trinity College. Making work in this interdisciplinary mode—which made paper notations and drawings a necessity—generates uncanny object lessons in the ways that a seemingly private practice might absorb or reflect political struggle.

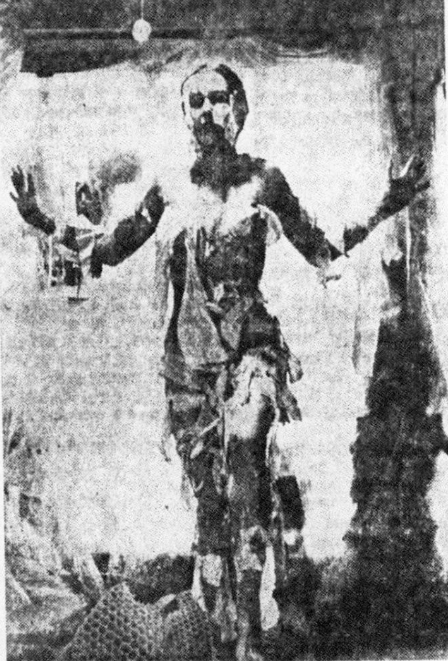

Carolee stuck with it

Gooey 'celebration' to happen at museum

By Van Gordon Sauter

What do you have when a partially nude woman douses herself with glue and thrashes around in piles of shredded paper while slides depicting pastoral scenes are bounced off the walls and a tape recorder blares forth rural noises?

You have a "Celebration of the mid-Western Landscape," of course.

The landscape will be celebrated here Jan. 26 and 27 when Carolee Schneemann stages a happening as part of the Museum of Contemporary Art's new exhibit featuring more than 400 objects made from paper and paperboard.

MISS SCHNEEMANN previewed her happening in Manhattan recently for the press. She dashed into the room, tore off her clothes and quickly whipped up a glue by mixing flour with water paste. Using a wide brush, she painted her body with the goo.

Then she nosedived into the pile of paper, rolling about to attach the paper to the glue. It didn't work. One wag commented that Betty Crocker had never intended her flour to be part of the contemporary art scene.

Undaunted, Miss Schneemann switched to a more fitting medium—wallpaper paste. Another nosedive and it worked. Emerging from the pile was an apparition that resembled a toronado barreling through a Boy Scout paper drive.

It was promptly dubbed the Abominable Schneemann.

MISS SCHNEEMANN will bring this epic to Chicago, and recruit about eight local persons to join in the festivity. So she won't end up doing a "Celebration of the Women's Tier in the County Jail," she and her troupe will be somewhat clothed.

"You can say we'll be wearing work clothes," she said.

If anyone is interested in applying for the cast, Miss Schneemann said her performers must be people "responsive to any kind of immediate environment. They must be sensitive to one another, sexually healthy, trusting.

"People who are well integrated inside are good at this. You see someone eating their soup in a wonderful way and you ask them if they would like to work with you. Painters and sculptors are very good at this."

Miss Schneemann said her happening is "basically a development of landscape sensations. The Illinois landscape. It is basically an empty landscape."

The museum will stage the event in a yet undetermined location. The audience will sit on mats around the performers, and will be able to help apply the glue. Tickets are available at the museum, and Smoky the Bear will be admitted free.

Photo © 1967 by Fred McDarrah

Carolee Schneeman in wallpaper paste and paper: Anyone who eats his soup in a wonderful way might be asked to join her.

Taking no chances

Fig. 10 Photograph by Fred McDarrah of Carolee Schneemann, *Body Collage*, 1967, published in *Chicago Daily News*, January 6, 1968.

CHAPTER 1

Wild Waste

Carolee Schneemann's Shredded Figures

Just three photographers and one filmmaker saw Carolee Schneemann's live work *Body Collage* in person, but its dissemination in print media had wide-ranging consequences. Schneemann staged the solo performance in her studio loft on West Twenty-First Street in Manhattan in early January 1968, over the course of an hour, as a preparatory exercise for a longer work, *Illinois Central.*[1] When the four visitors stepped into her space whose brick walls barely insulated them against the chilly outdoor air, Schneemann emerged from behind a screen, stripped off her clothes, and began to paint her body with a mixture of molasses and wheat paste from a plastic bucket. When her arms and legs were coated with the adhesive, she plowed through a pile of shredded paper and other studio debris. A minute later she dropped her body into the pile, then rolled. The cameras, too, advanced and rolled, and caught her sitting on a stool and posing a few times, stopping to lift both her legs off the floor; then bending at the waist, picking up handfuls of debris and loosely balling them against her body. At the work's climax, she climbed the three iron steps that led to her loft's fire escape, flapped her arms, and dove back into the pile.

Body Collage was not a drawing in any orthodox sense. However, in producing it, Schneemann referenced a wide range of quick perceptual exercises, including the sketch, the collage, and the media encounter at large. *Body Collage*'s pairing of paper and homemade adhesive paste would have been very legible in New York activist circles, where posters had to be mounted onto walls, telephone poles, and other nonporous surfaces quickly and often.[2] But in the press, this work's transposition of urban wall to human flesh—public to private, inert to alive—went unremarked upon in favor of flour's more gendered application: baking. One reviewer noted a dismissive comment from a viewer in the room: "Betty Crocker never intended for her flour to be part of the contemporary art scene." The press's displeasure with *the work* seemed to lie in Fred McDarrah's photo of the work, a photo that had spread virally among news and culture papers in New York and Chicago (fig. 10).[3] McDarrah's photo showed Schneemann facing the camera, her arms spread wide, striding with one paper-clad leg forward out of the picture plane. This pose caught the Chicago writer Van Gordon

Sauter's attention. Sauter bemusedly identified Schneemann as "an apparition that resembled a tornado barreling through a Boy Scout paper drive."[4] Rather than see her pose as a means to disrupt the authoritative framing of the camera, using paper's pliability as a lighthearted foil to power, Sauter perceived errant debris propelled by a force of nature.[5] An *apparition,* Sauter called her. To him, her flesh was unstable, imbuing clean materials like paper and flour with the foul freight of waste, disorder, and death.

Schneemann, though, positioned her body as a living, productive part of the artistic process—"not as an object," she said, but as a material like any other.[6] And in a letter the night before to her friend Michael Kustow, a British writer and theater producer, Schneemann wrote that the performance was meant to unite two other distinct phenomena: the fragmentary surfaces of collage with the lively, spontaneous gestural qualities of drawing. "[The photographers] will get what they want—like a drawing class," she told Kustow, "and from their images I will find what I need."[7] Like a drawing class, the photographs would be guided by both chance (the position of the camera, the angles of the light) and intention (Schneemann's own vision and that of the photographers). The result would be a collaboration among waste materials, image technologies, and the artist's body: a metaphorical but also deeply literal set of entanglements that amounted to a constructed ecology.

Ecology is an alluring term here, and this chapter suggests that *Body Collage* and its companion performance, *Illinois Central,* consolidated Schneemann's nascent feminist ecological position based on the human figure's embattled relationship to paper. Just a few years earlier, Schneemann stated in her notes that if something could be perceived, then it was active.[8] Looking at paper this way imbues every part of *Body Collage* with liveliness, including the "apparition" at its center. A viewer might be reminded of paper's role in helping crystallize ideas, as happens when we draw. But they are more likely to notice the paper's material flexibility and friability, which signals that every medium is also fugitive, emerging from a supply chain and always on its way to someplace else. To use a word that Bruno Latour has invoked in reference to Baruch Spinoza that is not far from Schneemann's own statement, each component becomes an actant—an entity that generates action, regardless of its human or nonhuman status.[9] Performance enhances our ability to see and notice different actants, such as the paper armor that drips off Schneemann's leg in the photograph. But many critics and contemporaries perceived only material disorder in her work. This chapter investigates *Body Collage* and the critical reaction to her other paper-based works of this moment, all of which distilled a lifetime interest in drawing for Schneemann. Taken together, the works offer a full ecology of the page, an ecology that eluded many reviewers and curators in the 1960s but was an essential part of debates about science, capitalism, and subjectivity. Drawing's viewing protocols, together with paper's material changes, brought forth a new way of observing the world.

The photographs taken during *Body Collage* were intended to generate "sketches" for Schneemann's larger performance, *Illinois Central,* which

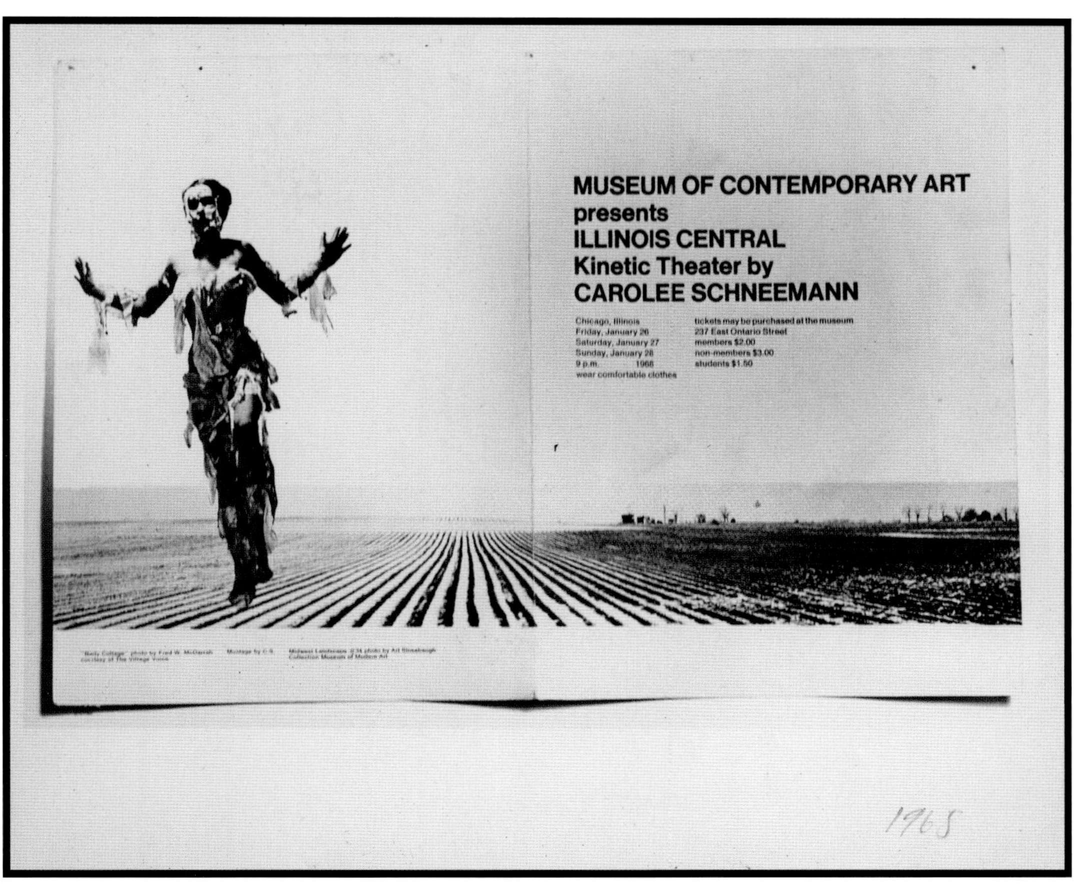

the Museum of Contemporary Art (MCA) Chicago had commissioned as part of its exhibition *Made with Paper* the following January. *Illinois Central* was planned as "a celebration of the Mid Western landscape" and would stage paper's full supply chain, complete with soil, agriculture, trees, pulp, surface, shreds, and leftover material, showing the human and nonhuman agents that were implicated within the chain.[10] In a flyer for the performance, Schneemann pasted McDarrah's photograph above a wide, flat stretch of cropland, connecting paper with the industrial agriculture necessary to produce it (fig. 11). The work's whole trajectory extended from drawing's fragmentary, momentary inscriptions, and it foregrounded drawing's components as a complex material entanglement rather than a passive surface with active agents. This all took place in a historical moment when paper (and other goods, for that matter) was imagined to be a unidirectional source of plenitude for humans to use, a central thematic to the other works in the *Made with Paper* exhibition. Instead, Schneemann staged different scenarios that alternately privileged human and nonhuman forces. In working with waste matter, she was better able to manifest an image ecology— one where materials, images, and human bodies all acted on one another (and where power imbalances and symmetries could be visible). As a result, a central quandary comes to the fore: that bodies may be vulnerable,

Fig. 11 Carolee Schneemann, collaged flyer for *Illinois Central*, 1968. Carolee Schneemann Papers, Getty Research Institute.

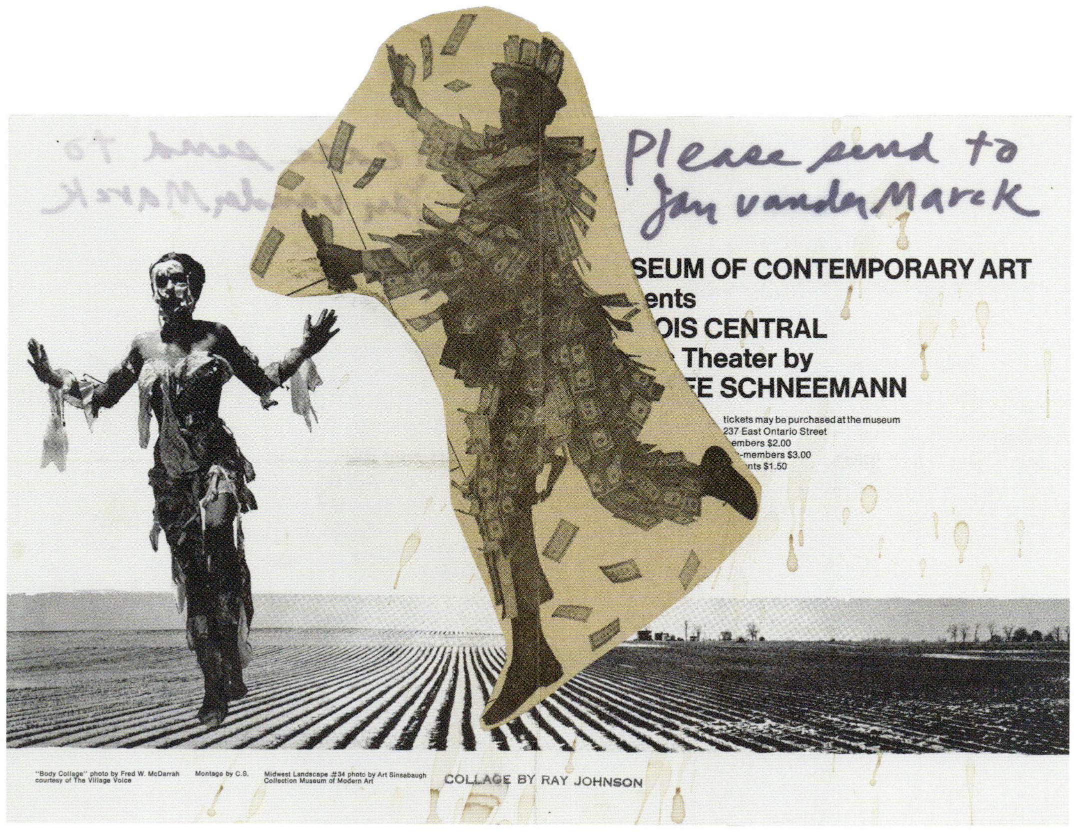

Fig. 12 Ray Johnson, undated collage for Carolee Schneemann. Carolee Schneemann Papers, Getty Research Institute.

the stuff of organic and authentic exploration, but they are also products of trade within the market economy, subject to narratives of being brand-new, virginal, or ruined. And while the political theorist Jane Bennett argues that the actant distinguishes itself from other modes such as "resource, commodity, or instrumentality," revealing the constructedness of these latter modes through its own liveliness, I maintain a different position about these remarkable paper works, one that is truer to the things that viewers in the 1960s believed art could do. I maintain that Schneemann held the actant as just one of many possibilities—that she performed the dissipation of "onto-theological binaries" in her live works so that we might consider the terms *actor, resource,* and *commodity* as shifting and contingent.[11] Her intensive, expanded drawing process helped scaffold this argument, since she herself used the paper page to explore state changes, literally *making with paper* by capturing images but also repurposing them through embodied observation.

Schneemann's conceptualization of what it meant to make and be made with paper proved to be both immediately controversial and ultimately extremely successful. *Illinois Central* would become the most frequently performed live work of the artist's career. But when Schneemann traveled to the MCA in late January to finalize preparations for this site-specific live work there, she discovered she'd been thrown out of the show.[12] After inviting *Illinois Central* to be part of the exhibition *Made with Paper,*

Jan van der Marck, her friend and the museum's curator, approached her apologetically at the exhibition's opening preview event. Van der Marck informed her that the exhibition's underwriter, the Container Corporation of America (CCA), had requested that *Illinois Central* be withdrawn from *Made with Paper*'s checklist. According to van der Marck, the problem lay with the museum's trustees, who had demanded the removal of any trace of Schneemann's participation, and, with little explanation, dismissed van der Marck from his position there later that month.[13]

The reasons for the withdrawal are unclear and reveal a peculiar inconsistency in the Container Corporation of America's history of sponsoring modern and contemporary cultural initiatives in the postwar United States.[14] At first the CCA, interested in extending its market share into the community of contemporary art viewers, sponsored the production of Schneemann's work, *Illinois Central,* by contributing fifteen reams of typing paper free of charge to the performance, affirming the exhibition's intention to position paper as "the medium of ideas."[15] The established artist, known for her performance work *Meat Joy* (1964) and her film *Fuses* (1967), had been an MFA student at the University of Illinois Urbana-Champaign ten years earlier. Her arrival at the MCA was part of *Made with Paper*'s gathering of locally specific but internationally celebrated talent and signaled her "favorite son" status.

Things changed, however, after the reviews of *Body Collage* hit the press. Despite Schneemann's claim that the work was "basically a development of landscape sensations" that used paper as a structural material, the CCA's attention seems to have fallen on the artist's other purpose, unstated but later made explicit.[16] Through a performative construction harnessing the complete life cycle of paper, Schneemann wanted to compare the Illinois landscape, cleared of trees by American agribusiness, with escalating environmental devastation in Vietnam.[17] Indeed, shortly after Schneemann released photos of *Body Collage* to press outlets, the CCA's Department of Information Services sent her a letter inquiring about the content and production details for *Illinois Central.* The work fell into the trifecta of live, anti–Vietnam War, anticapitalist countercultural projects which the Department of Information Services most overtly disliked.[18] And despite the Container Corporation of America's longtime patronage of American arts and design, this was not quite the face of paper—a product now virtually omnipresent in the booming consumer economy of the 1960s—that the company had had in mind. The Container Corporation withdrew its offer to contribute free paper and forbade *Illinois Central* from showing in the MCA's main exhibition space.[19]

To show solidarity with Schneemann's predicament, her friend Ray Johnson mailed her a collage he'd fashioned from one of the performance flyers (fig. 12). The collage shows van der Marck frolicking next to Schneemann's body, a dandy covered in his own paper costume of dollar bills, a broker for the museum's economic interests, dressed up in the benefits of its growing market valuation. Here Johnson makes an important point: that all materials are most definitively *not* the same. But the controversy over *Body Collage* did

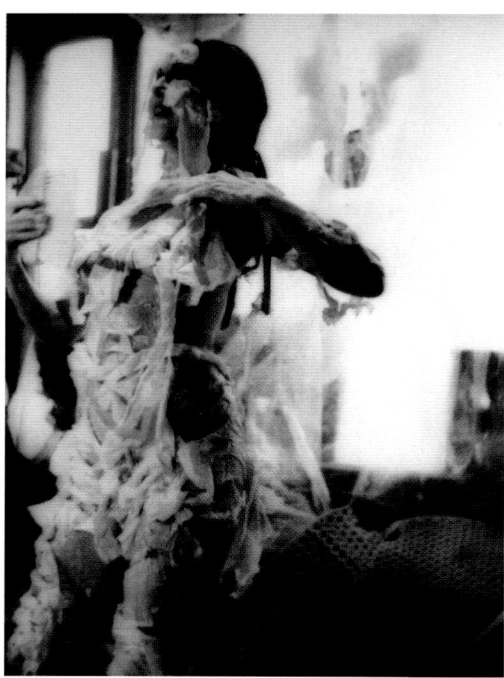

not center directly on its political or even economic critiques: rather, critiques focused on the project as monstrous and ruinous. Visible within these critical responses are numerous ways that Schneemann ruptured paper's "clean" honorable identity by introducing lived experience into the planned obsolescence of pulp products. Her aim for *Body Collage* was "not simply to collage [her] body" with materials. Rather, she wanted "to enact movement so that the collage image would be active, found, not predetermined or posed," and to refigure materiality in a way that could bring to the forefront the problems and possibilities of decay, both human and inanimate.[20] It is this instability, grafted onto Schneemann's physical form, that paradoxically helps "particularize" her body and self "to expose and challenge the masculinism embedded in the assumption of 'disinterestedness' behind conventional art history and criticism," as Amelia Jones has put it.[21] A film still of the performance shows the artist not posed but *paused,* as the camera's glancing shot captures her body midgesture like a life drawing model—touching her newly adhered paper garb with her left hand, with a paste brush held in her right (fig. 13). She is exuberant, her shoulders thrown back in a wide, birdlike arc. Small irregular fragments of shredded white printer's paper, donated by a local print shop, cling to her body by virtue of the flour and molasses and, when the molasses soon proved insufficiently sticky, store-bought wallpaper paste.[22] The brush used to apply the adhesive (and the costume) is still in Schneemann's hand, which she raises in midgesture, as though to pat down any errant shreds before running and bouncing through the space.

Fragmented materials could and should provoke physical exuberance, which itself was inseparable from thought. As if to punctuate this argument, the figure with outstretched arms from McDarrah's photograph appears

Wild Waste

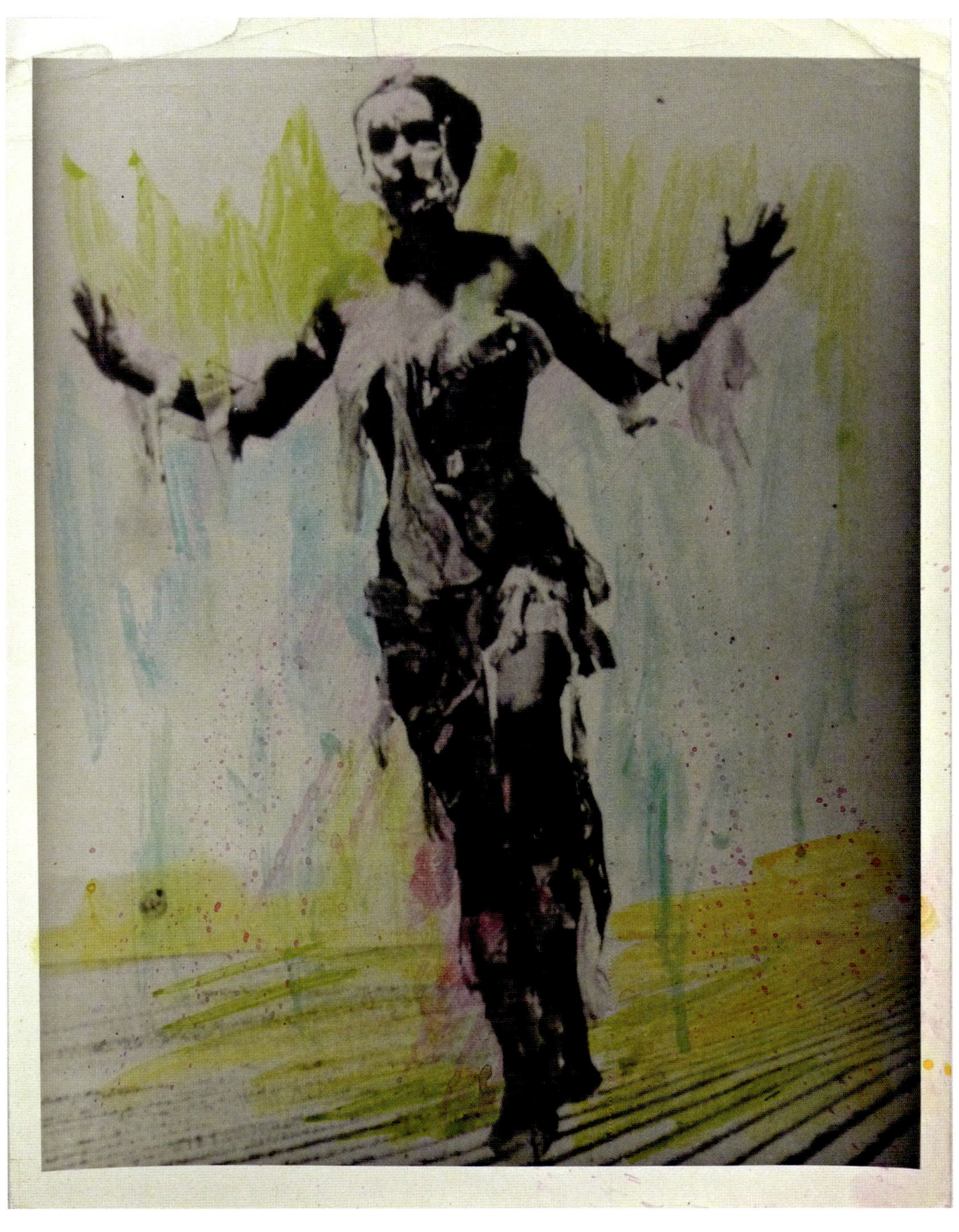

Fig. 14 Carolee Schneemann, *Illinois Central Collage,*
1967/1979. Hand-colored digital print, 16¾ × 13¾ in.
(42.5 × 34.9 cm).

throughout the life and afterlife of the work. In 1979, Schneemann took a cutaway of *Illinois Central*'s collaged flyer and colored over it with diluted paint (fig. 14). The resulting image, with its vibrant strata of green, blue, and magenta-purple that follow the horizon line yet also trouble the differences between sky and ground, stages a reckoning between the art history of collage and the art history of such gestural media as drawing and painting. In modernist aesthetics, both of these practices were associated with mental dexterity. The artist's uniquely clever mind could isolate drawing and painting as pure, two-dimensional phenomena, a task more intellectually challenging than the intuitive physical dynamics of sculpture. Similarly, collage practices served to generate a distrust of images and thus of image economies, by distancing pictures from their referents. When artists cut up pictures and repaste them together for a collage, they liberate pictures from narrative or factual representation, so that "the [artistic] materials function as signs for . . . experiences and not representations of them," as Rosalind Krauss has written.[23] In *Illinois Central Collage,* we are called to attend not just to the picture's flat surface but to its physical connections to other kinds of matter: soil, trees, and, yes, garbage. And so Van Gordon Sauter's misapprehension of the artist's paper-covered body, set alongside the initial cancellation of *Illinois Central,* do much to demonstrate the dominant art historical constructs against which Schneemann's work spoke: the idea that drawing is an iterative, progressive way of capturing the world—a purely intellectual exercise, a journey toward clarity—and the argument that the female nude is somehow part of nature and therefore immanently possessable to image makers.

In McDarrah's picture, reproduced in both the *Village Voice* and the *Chicago Daily News* (see fig. 1), visual metaphors between flesh and wildness accrue: her body really *is* made abject, monstrous, *a mess.* The clusters of paper, alternately dampened by the adhesive and curled, dry, against her body, ensure that her movements will come with their own uncomfortable sensations—brittle, crunchy, and, as she squints through all the matter, blind. The scrap-costume festoons the body as much as strips it. Its masses of paper and glue give Schneemann the look of a body with its skin both augmented and flayed, but also of a woman's curvaceous form whose disordered garment barely clings to her flesh. The artist had long been interested in feminist art histories that included goddess worship, and so this combination of precarity, ecstasy, and violence was no accident.[24] The collaged matter on her body converts Schneemann into Benedict Spinoza's purposefully loose concept of an extended thing, in which all matter, including bodies, are an extension of divine energies.[25]

Seen in this way, this photograph, itself an object reproduced on paper, then becomes a tautology of the material and its potential to both *sign* and *act:* a yarnlike strand of paper dangles from Schneemann's left arm, harmonizing with the patterns of the photographs and paper cutouts taped to the window behind her. The 1979 version of this image extends this argument

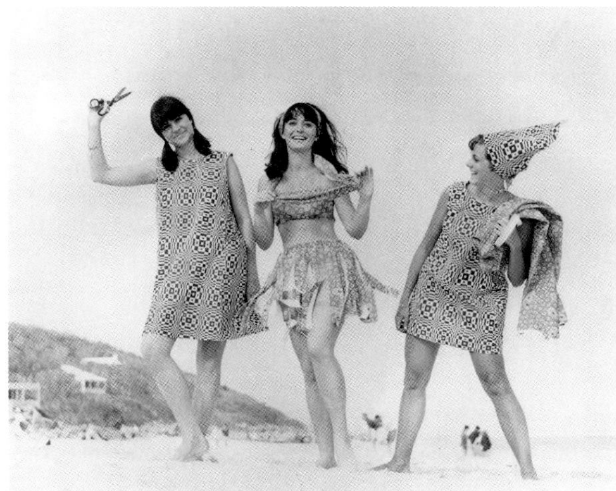

and makes it atmospheric. The colored strata show that paper's true origin point is the supply chain, where pulp and other raw materials "seep and ooze out of their containers in quantities beyond measurement," as Nina Wexelblatt and B. Jack Hanly have put it.[26] It is paper's end stages that bring each permutation of this artwork into being, not its smooth, blank beginnings. Instead of capturing, supporting, or fixing the body, this sketch's dynamism lies in the body's ability to animate its support, rather than the other way around.

Schneemann's body steps out of the paper that is meant to bind it. Here is her principal act of disruption, one that would be echoed in other ways in the fuller presentation of *Illinois Central*. I am reminded of Laura Mulvey's argument that representations of the female form are always pushed into a symbolic order, where they can refer only to castration, lack, or, as Mulvey puts it, "[woman's] image as the bearer of the bleeding wound."[27] Mulvey's thesis now forms a well-known feminist adage about images: that the body speaks *before* its existence as material. Schneemann, too, gestures to this problem, particularly in the ways we wrestle with "placing" her materials. Paper becomes a textile, provisional and partial, grafting to the body as easily as rhetoric grafts to an object. It alters the viewer's perception of Schneemann's emergent frontal posture. Her conventionally attractive body is transformed into something quasi-monstrous—a garbage Barbarella.

Although *Body Collage* predated the American adaptation of the French adult comic character in *Barbarella* by fourteen months, Schneemann's play with costume contrasts with the throwaway fashions and futuristic garbage-culled designs that dominated the mid-1960s.[28] Reed Crawford's Dollar Princess hat, for instance, an allover plastic head covering decorated with foil milk tops, ignited London's fall fashion week in 1966.[29] That same year, corporations such as the Scott Paper Company began offering paper dresses, woven with nylon fibers for added durability, for sale as promotional items, meant to be worn only a few times (fig. 15). These designs fashioned an image of paper and plastic as youthful and cosmopolitan—a material virtually synonymous with the new technologies that could support a society of class-neutral luxury. They were in demand among readers of the fashion magazines that embodied the same cycle of luxury and consumption as the dresses themselves.[30] The dresses, in particular, were meant to promote brand loyalty and solidify the brand identities of disposable products such as pies (which came in a throwaway tin) and Campbell's soups (which came in a can). Scott Paper's ad, in which young women frolic in paper dresses on a Bermuda beach, underscores the strange temporality of paper in the post-war moment. One model holds up a pair of scissors to augment or change the designs of the ebullient op art–patterned garments—they are infinitely durable, infinitely malleable, until the moment they are no longer needed.

Schneemann's collaged paper project, underscored by drawing, contributed something different. It illuminated the supply chains in which all materials are entangled, many of which are gendered. *Body Collage* introduced the possibility that materials might be *alive*—in early 1968, when ecological discourses around garbage had not yet taken life in popular imagination—and that they originated somewhere and produced serious effects. This chapter presents several paths that Schneemann charted, in recuperating and reusing materials, toward a feminist position on science based in drawing's potential for active, engaged observation. Archival records from *Body Collage* and *Illinois Central* show how paper in multiple states functioned as a simultaneously world-building and destructive material. In positioning paper this way, Schneemann did crucial work in responding to New Left philosophers who called for new approaches to science in the 1960s—approaches that rejected scientific observation as an isolating and instrumentalizing way of examining the world.[31] The German American philosopher Herbert Marcuse, for instance, proposed that true liberation could only come from "a science and technology free to discover and realize the possibilities of things and men in the protection and gratification of life, playing with the potentialities of form and matter for the attainment of this goal."[32]

She also forged a path for ethical feminist material reuse. In 2009, the feminist theorist Karen Barad remarked on the ways that "matter is figured as passive and immutable; at best it inherits a potential for change derivatively from language and culture," a comment that was in step with Mulvey's critiques of images of women written thirty-nine years earlier.[33] It was also a position that Schneemann shared.[34] By 1967, Schneemann had been lamenting for years about the negative critical reactions that she received for making her body an "extension" of her painting and drawing constructions.[35] Like Barbarella's costumes, the scraps in Schneemann's work became inseparable from the titillating possibility of their displacement; when placed on a woman's body, critics saw only potential for denuding. Indeed, one false step in *Body Collage* and the scraps could come completely off their ground of flesh and glue. But the scraps also cited paper's vulnerability to rending and decay—a quality it shares with flesh, as Schneemann's beloved precursor Antonin Artaud has noted.[36] The shreds disrupt the conflation between surface and picture plane that is central to modernist art making, taking the lens's artificially closed space of fantasy and throwing it open.[37] Both the body and its materials are acting within this picture. With its forward stride, Schneemann extends the photo's foreground, using flesh as a hinge between the ground of the image and the ground of her body. Her flesh, holding paper as both collage surface and artistic ground, is the center of a set of entanglements—entanglements that inspired the "exploded canvas" of *Illinois Central* and its "metaphorical arena of sensory juxtapositions."[38] While paper is not exactly on equal footing with the body, each entity occupies its own striving and causal place in an ecological system.

PRODUCT, SHREDDED

Schneemann's interest in ecological systems was copresent with a massive increase in disposable paper and packaging in the United States. It is impossible—indeed, it was impossible for the sponsors of *Made with Paper*—to miss the aching divide between Schneemann's art and the aims of the exhibition. Referring to paper as "the medium of ideas," Paul J. Smith, one of the exhibition's organizing directors, established the exhibition's objective: to frame pulp products as omnipresent, culturally cosmopolitan, and infinitely adaptable. In a catalog essay, John Massey argued that paper's primary role in the world was catalytic: paper was a receiver and conductor of great ideas. According to Massey, these great ideas should achieve one thing: "the conversion of the natural wealth of the world into distributable form."[39] The installation's layout was composed of corrugated cardboard modular sections designed by the CCA's in-house packaging designers. The bulk of the installation materials had been donated by several corporations, including DuPont, Monsanto, and of course CCA (fig. 16). The show

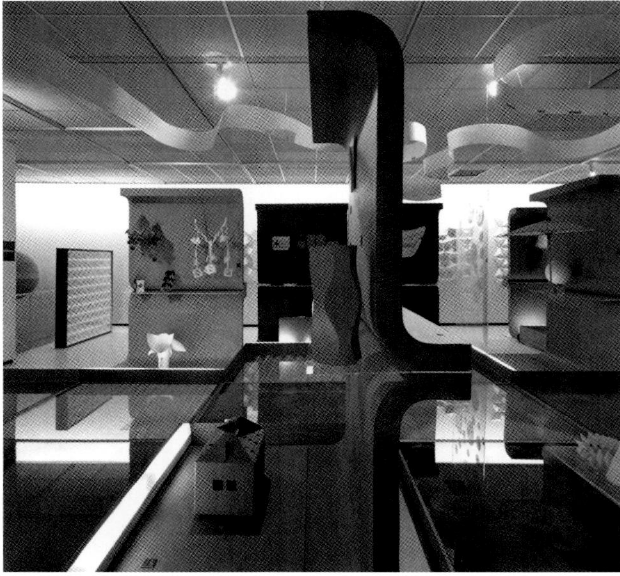

Fig. 16 Entrance to the *Made with Paper* exhibition at the Museum of Contemporary Art Chicago, 1968, including corrugated cardboard display panels and paper floor tiles.

featured artists and works that, according to Smith, expressed "the qualities of paper," and the panels helped to make *paper art* synonymous with *paper products:* the walls featured ambitious molded paper cones and displays of freshly rolled corrugated cardboard, as well as large displays of paper packaging and bales of wastepaper (fig. 17). Viewers were offered paper slippers to change into, along with the opportunity to stand on a glass panel balanced atop patterned corrugated cardboard, to showcase the cardboard's strength. Implicit to the exhibition's premise was the Keynesian economic theory that a material could do anything in a single-use state and should be produced new for consumers in unlimited quantities.

The display also included traditional paper costumes and textiles fashioned by, as the catalog put it, "native peoples," providing an illusion of globalism through primitivist appropriations of non-Western forms.[40] Viewers could buy large paper bibs for keeping their bodies clean at mealtimes; the men's version mimicked a striped business shirt, the women's a dress bodice with a sweetheart neckline.[41] *Made with Paper* followed immediately on the heels of another exhibition, *Dan Flavin: Pink and Gold,* that had offered visitors yet another permutation of paper's future: they could purchase a catalog and watch it print automatically on an IBM 402 accounting machine (fig. 18).

For the Container Corporation of America, paper was compatible with emerging postwar exhortations to perform, both in the home and in the workplace. But for Schneemann, whose interdisciplinary works all began with dozens, sometimes hundreds, of drawings, the drawing was a

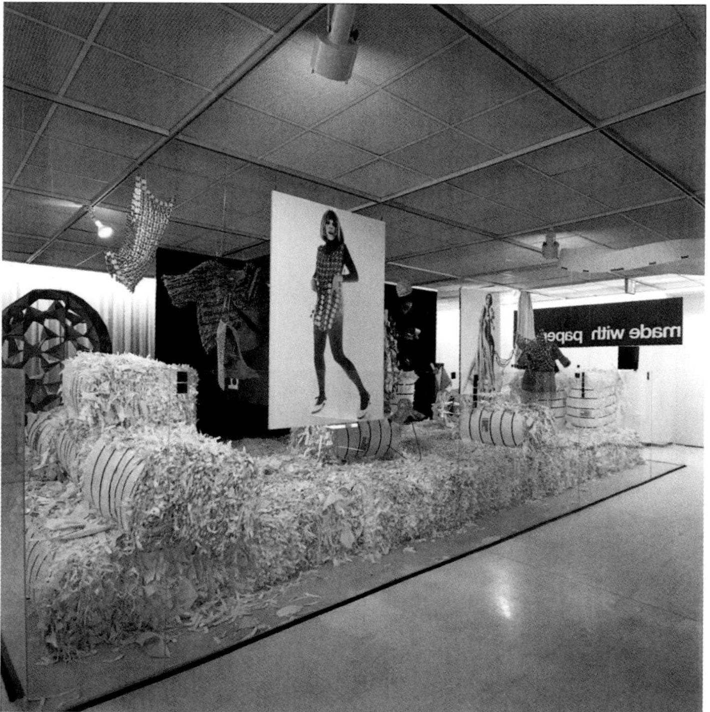

Fig. 17 *Made with Paper* exhibition at the Museum of Contemporary Art Chicago, 1968, with paper dresses pinned to the ceiling with monofilament wire above a display of bales of shredded paper.

Wild Waste

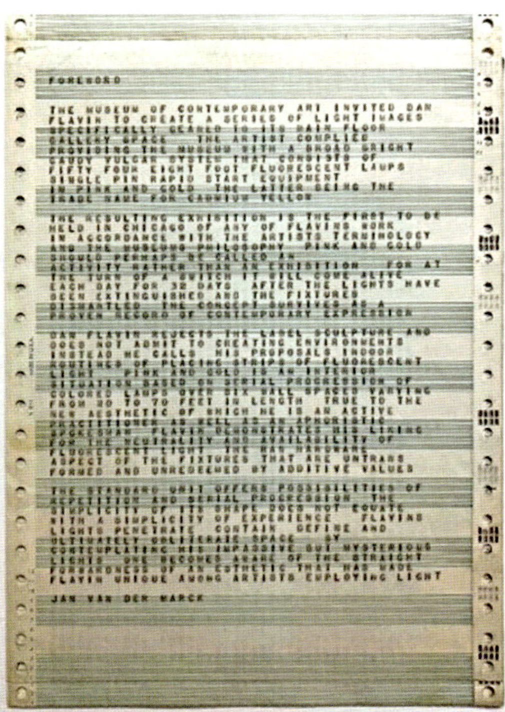

FOREWORD

THE MUSEUM OF CONTEMPORARY ART INVITED DAN
FLAVIN TO CREATE A SERIES OF LIGHT IMAGES
SPECIFICALLY GEARED TO ITS MAIN FLOOR
GALLERY SPACE   THE ARTIST COMPLIED
PROVIDING THE MUSEUM WITH A BROAD BRIGHT
GAUDY VULGAR SYSTEM THAT CONSISTS OF
FIFTY FOUR EIGHT FOOT FLUORESCENT LAMPS
SINGLE PIN RAPID START EQUIPMENT
IN PINK AND GOLD   THE LATTER BEING THE
TRADE NAME FOR CADMIUM YELLOW

THE RESULTING EXHIBITION IS THE FIRST TO BE
HELD IN CHICAGO OF ANY OF FLAVINS WORK
IN ACCORDANCE WITH THE ARTISTS TERMINOLOGY
AND THE MUSEUMS PHILOSOPHY   PINK AND GOLD
SHOULD PERHAPS BE CALLED AN
ACTIVITY RATHER THAN AN EXHIBITION   FOR AT
THE TURN OF A SWITCH IT WILL COME ALIVE
EACH DAY FOR 32 DAYS   AFTER THE LIGHTS HAVE
BEEN EXTINGUISHED AND THE FIXTURES
DISMANTLED   THE CONCEPT SURVIVES AS A
PROVEN RECORD OF CONTEMPORARY EXPRESSION

DAN FLAVIN REJECTS THE LABEL SCULPTURE AND
DOES NOT ADMIT TO CREATING ENVIRONMENTS
INSTEAD HE CALLS HIS PROPOSALS INDOOR
ROUTINES OF PLACING STRIPS OF FLUORESCENT
LIGHT   PINK AND GOLD IS AN INTERIOR
SITUATION BASED ON SERIAL PROGRESSION OF
COLORED LAMPS OVER SIX WALL SPACES VARYING
FROM 40 TO 70 FEET IN LENGTH   TRUE TO THE
NEW AESTHETIC OF WHICH HE IS AN ACTIVE
PRACTITIONER AS WELL AS AN APHORISTIC
SPOKESMAN   FLAVIN DEMONSTRATES HIS LIKING
FOR THE NEUTRALITY AND AVAILABILITY OF
FLUORESCENT LIGHT   THE MAT MEMBRANE
ASPECT OF THE FIXTURES THAT ARE UNTRANS
FORMED AND UNREDEEMED BY ADDITIVE VALUES

THE STANDARD UNIT OFFERS POSSIBILITIES OF
REPETITION AND SERIAL PROGRESSION   THE
SIMPLICITY OF ITS SHAPE DOES NOT EQUATE
WITH A SIMPLICITY OF EXPERIENCE   FLAVINS
LIGHTS PENETRATE   CONTAIN   DEFINE AND
ULTIMATELY OBLITERATE SPACE   BY
CONTEMPLATING HIS IMPASSIVE BUT MYSTERIOUS
LIGHTS   ONE BECOMES AWARE OF THE STRAIGHT
FORWARDNESS OF AN ESTHETIC THAT HAS MADE
FLAVIN UNIQUE AMONG ARTISTS EMPLOYING LIGHT

JAN VAN DER MARCK

Fig. 18 Foreword to the catalog for *Dan Flavin: Pink and Gold* exhibition at the Museum of Contemporary Art Chicago. 11 × 8½ inches (27.9 × 21.6 cm).

particular and "very insistent" mode of experience, as playful and loaded as the CCA's bibs were clean.[42] Many of her working drawings are collaged from small scraps of paper, done in many locations on a napkin or a hotel stationery envelope, and transferred onto a different support to be retraced with differently colored pens or markers. The figures and sketches that she drew, and the paper supports onto which she collaged them, worked together to trigger her visual memory as they activated multiple spaces and temporalities. In ushering various places visited (and attentions paid) to the fore, drawings on paper were unruly objects that could violate the confines of the studio—and thus outperform or even underperform the modernist fantasy of universally flexible paper products.

A collaged flyer that Schneemann created in 1964 shows drawing as not just a "medium of ideas" but a mutable extension of an environment, convertible into liquid capital at any moment (fig. 19). The flyer announces the sale as both an exhibition and an environment of interrelated objects whose distinct properties were in dialogue with the four classical elements of earth, wind, air, water, and fire. Its title also gestures to the nineteenth-century industrialist practice of the fire sale—offering deep discounts on merchandise after it had incurred smoke damage following a fire.[43] Here we can spot a few precursor ideas for *Illinois Central,* such as the channel of torn white paper laid over black-and-white reproductions of her photographic series *Eye Body.* The white space directs the viewer's attention to the "flow" of collaged text like a spotlight or a ticker tape. Further, latent within the poster is a counterhistory of art *as capital,* one that has long been

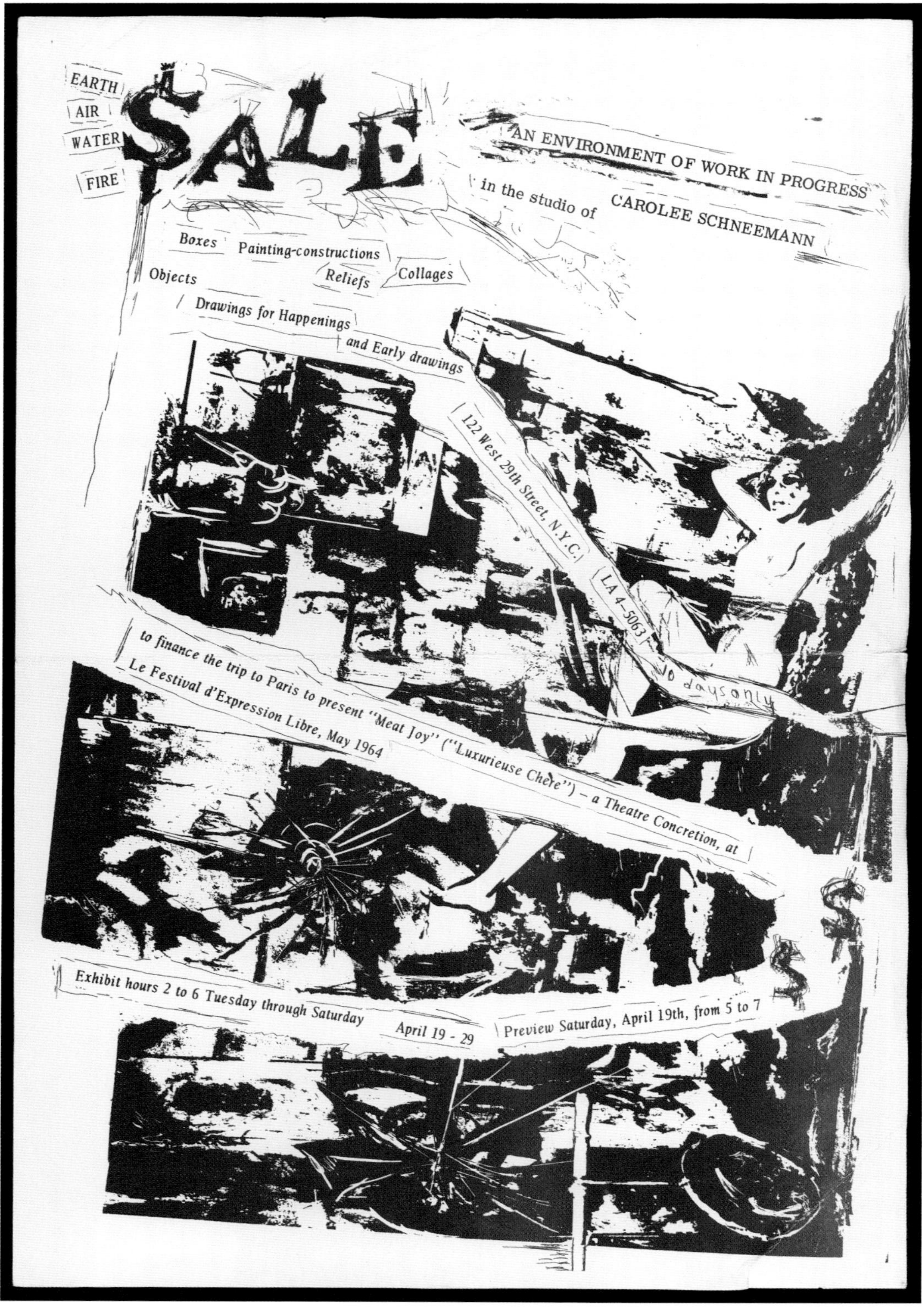

Fig. 19 Flyer advertising *Sale: Environment of Work in Progress,* April 1964. Carolee Schneemann Papers, Getty Research Institute.

a leitmotif of twentieth-century modernism and beyond. Schneemann portrayed her own studio materials as fungible with one another when her financial situation forced the sale of her assets. Each object, material, and category had inherent value, and with luck they would add up to the price of her ticket to Paris, which she needed to perform at the Festival of Free Expression that spring.[44] It is worth noting that the market for drawings in this decade was only barely beginning to emerge, led by male painters and sculptors whose discrete works were already commanding high prices. Robert Rauschenberg had had a solo exhibition at the Whitechapel Gallery in London in which drawings had been prominently placed.[45] Schneemann, however, insisted that this interest had not yet spread to the broader community by the mid-1960s and that no visitors to her studio asked to see drawings until she proposed it to the Berkeley Art Museum in 1973.[46] In advertising a "fire sale" of performance ephemera, she positioned drawings as living, yet liquid things whose state changes were just as interesting as finished paintings or sculptures.

The Museum of Contemporary Art's rejection was consistent with other institutional reactions in the mid- to late 1960s against Schneemann's feminist film and performance works that cast the nude body as a material in live, multimedia art.[47] Her film project *Fuses,* developed between 1964 and 1967, was the subject of numerous venue shutdowns and police raids because of its representation of mutual sexual pleasure between Schneemann and her partner, James Tenney.[48] That the MCA's exhibition space at 237 East Ontario Street had been the former home of the *Playboy* headquarters mattered little to the CCA, but it gives their anxieties about Schneemann's applications of paper an ironic cast.[49] Publishing nudity was apparently different from staging it as a metaphor in a live work. Still, van der Marck persisted on Schneemann's behalf. He secured her an "immense, filthy abandoned loft" on Wells Street to stage the work, four icy blocks from the MCA's home on Chicago's emerging gallery row.[50] The local fire department closed the loft down after the performance's second night, and the museum moved the production to a public television studio on Chicago's North Side. They gave attendees no notice of this change.[51]

When the museum revoked its space and the CCA withdrew its resources, Schneemann felt disrupted, "lost without a sense of scale."[52] Her kinetic theater projects were deeply engaged with their sites, from preparatory sketches to multimedia plans.[53] She had planned to select her performers from strangers passing on the street nearby, whose ways of moving casually in the world complemented her ideas and sketches. Instead Schneemann had to refashion the entire work, starting with its multimedia score that plotted the precise positions of her performers in relation to the materials and seated audience. In her hotel room, the artist produced a brand-new score, charting its six multimedia components—bodily gestures, lights, projected slides, sound, film, and air-blowing machine—in ballpoint pen on the back of a mass-mailed flyer for the MCA. This handwritten chart would later be typed out and would change its order four times as Schneemann received more invitations to stage it in other locations (fig. 20). All told, *Illinois Central* was the most frequently performed live work of the artist's career.

Absent the 7,500 sheets of typing paper to clothe her performers, Schneemann also had to recalibrate her performance materials, adjusting for the lack of uniform paper that the CCA had promised to provide. She walked the Chicago streets searching for local materials to reuse. Ultimately, she was rescued by the finance industry: the Illinois Savings Bank donated twenty bales of shredded canceled checks and other financial records for use in the work. Schneemann would recount later that her most performed work was brought into being by "Illinois trade representing millions of dollars."[54]

This bears repeating: the work's reincarnation was occasioned on the backs of the recently expired, shredded remains of the circulation of capital. Just as drawing had brought together chance and intention in *Body Collage,* the shredded checks in *Illinois Central* fused the market economy's fantastic promises with the real material consequences of trade. The paper made no distinctions between resources and remains. It was the dissolution of this very boundary that allowed Schneemann to mobilize the dry, dissolving shreds and crumpled planar sheets within larger circulatory systems of land, waste, pollutants, media, and capital—a broad constellation that artists and the public were just beginning to scrutinize.

Named after the main train terminal in Chicago's transit system, *Illinois Central* was one of three works Schneemann created in the late 1960s that used paper to explore the intersection of human and ecological systems. It lasted between forty and sixty minutes, depending on how long the audience participated in its open-ended components. The artist's revised score used wastepaper both as a projection surface and as costume material in the work, embedding references to numerous transport systems and supply chains throughout. Audience members negotiated these pathways in different ways, as its multimedia components linked such disparate entities as trees and hogs as sources of energy and bound them to the same production pathways as commercially produced paper. This arrangement began, crucially, with the work's architecture. Paper shreds and added butcher paper were piled together on the sides and in the center of the room to create a complete, flexible environment. The loft's walls were collaged with large strips of torn white paper, with layers of crumpled paper piled where the wall intersected with the floor—a feature that some audience members would have had to sidestep, or at least reckon with, when they entered.[55] Schneemann said that the paper elements were crucial, as they created a "texturally active" projection surface for a series of slides mounted to a projector at the center of the space.[56]

The performance's sound and lighting components extended her ecosystemic vision. As the six performers entered the space, their body positions and movements were responsively timed with a soundtrack of

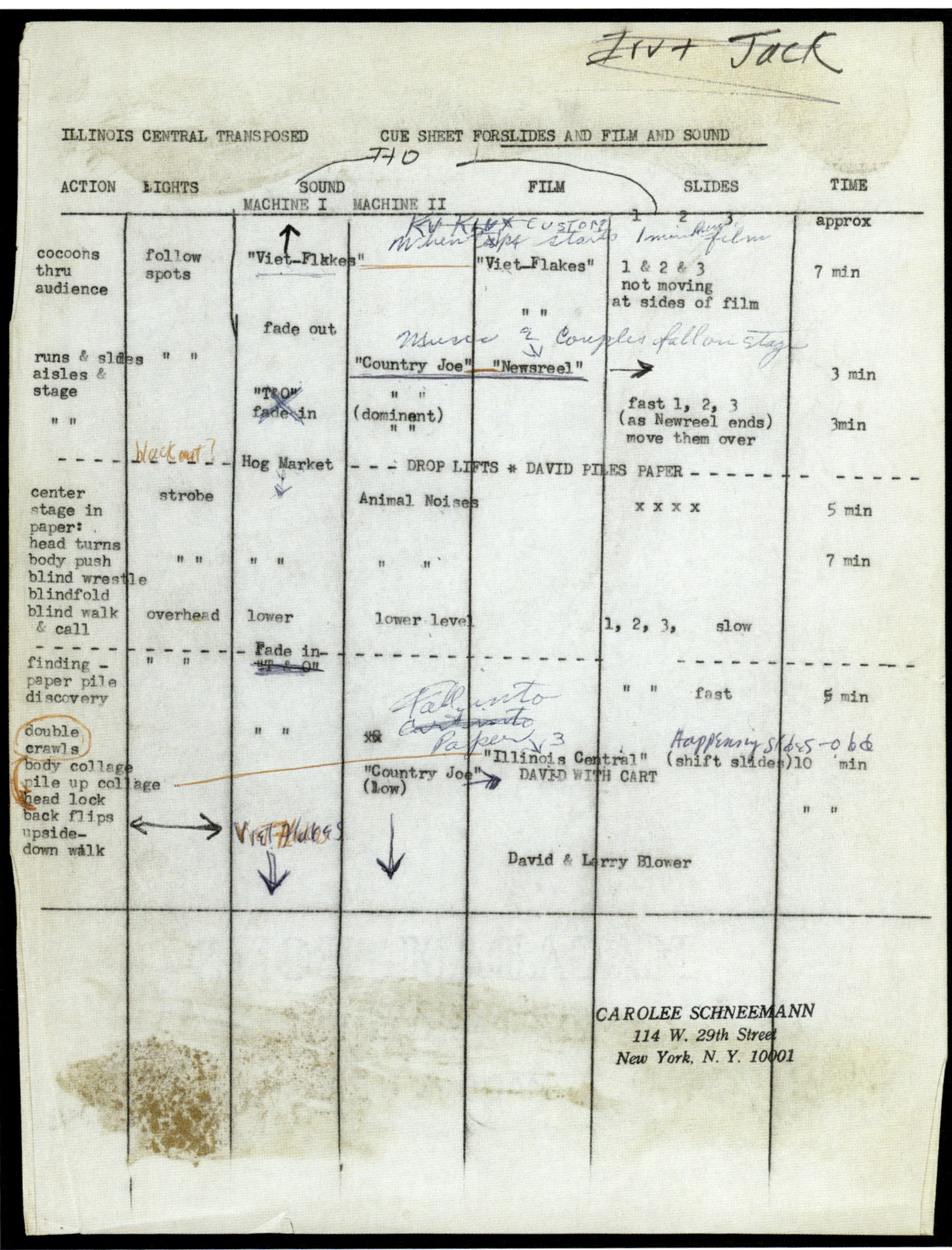

ACTION	LIGHTS	SOUND MACHINE I	MACHINE II	FILM	SLIDES	TIME
cocoons thru audience	follow spots	"Viet-Flkkes"		"Viet-Flakes"	1 & 2 & 3 not moving at sides of film	approx 7 min
runs & sldes aisles & stage	" "	fade out	"Country Joe" "Newsreel"			3 min
" "		"TOO" fade in	(dominent) " "		fast 1, 2, 3 (as Newreel ends) move them over	3min
- - - -	- - - -	Hog Market	- - - DROP LIFTS * DAVID PILES PAPER - - - - - - -			
center stage in paper: head turns body push blind wrestle blindfold	strobe		Animal Noises		x x x x	5 min
	" "	" "	" "			7 min
blind walk & call	overhead	lower	lower level		1, 2, 3, slow	
- - - -	- - - -	Fade in	- - - - - - - -			
finding - paper pile discovery	" "				" " fast	5 min
double crawls body collage pile up collage head lock back flips upside-down walk		" "	Paper "Country Joe" (low)	"Illinois Central" DAVID WITH CART	(shift slides)10 min	
				David & Larry Blower	" "	

Fig. 20 Redrawn and retyped score for Carolee Schneemann, *Illinois Central Transposed,* 1968. Carolee Schneemann Papers, Getty Research Institute.

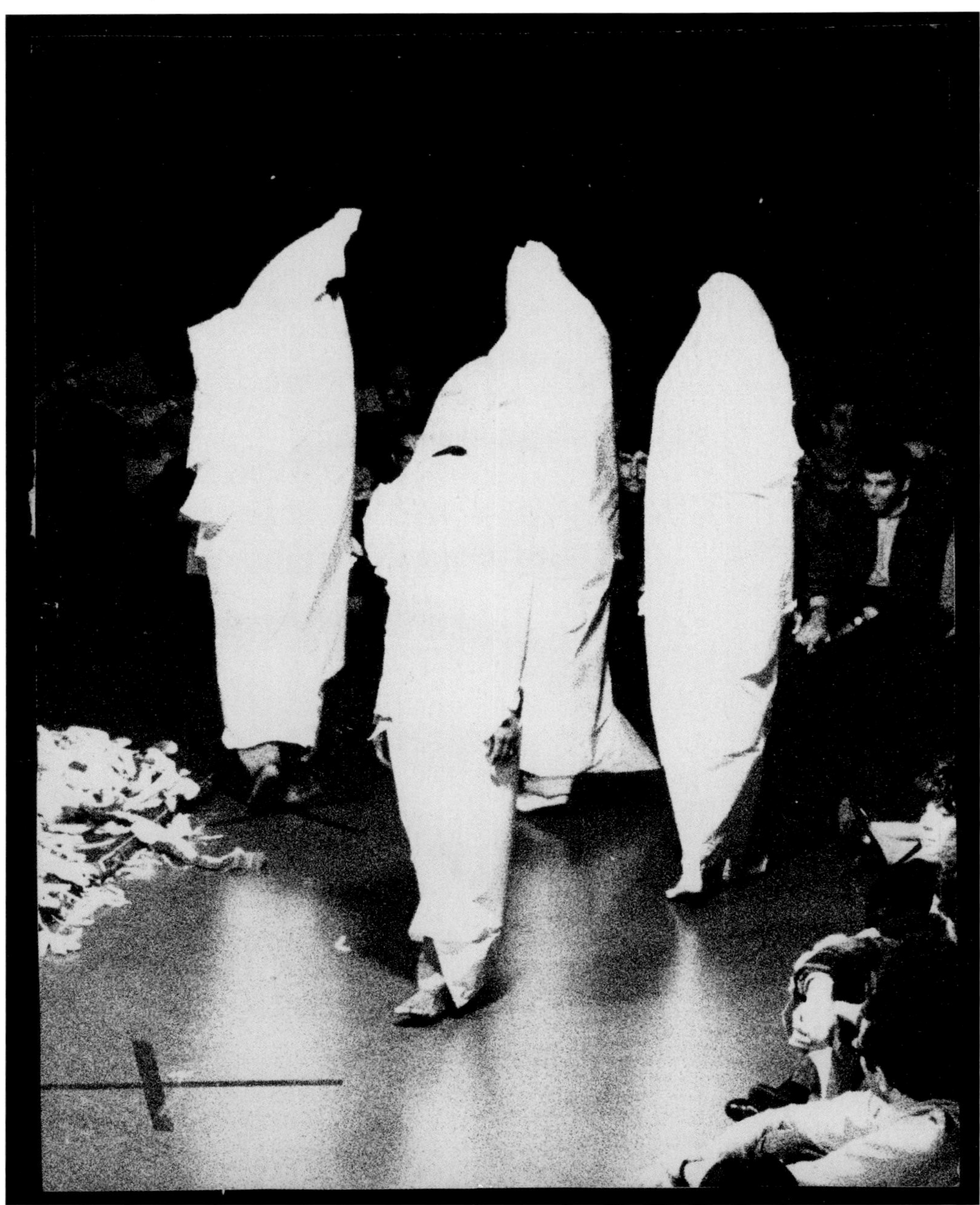

recorded train sounds, which also cued a lighting technician to run a spotlight intermittently over their bodies. The lights, much like the cameras for *Illinois Central*, generated a template for visual apprehension that was intermittent, fragmentary, *sketchy*. They highlighted each body's surface as the states of their paper costumes changed. Later in the work, they would execute parts of the score as a recording played of livestock radio reports from Illinois farm country.

In the opening sequence, animal bodies and their sensoria were on full display. Two photographs from the opening section of the performance

     Wild Waste

show the participants entering the space wrapped in a layer of butcher paper, the details of their bodies obscured by its opaque white sheets (fig. 21). These pictures narrate the performers' evolving negotiations with the material: if the performers obey their fragile costumes—if they restrict the pendula of their gait and curl their feet up from the floor with enough care— they can find their way to their places, marked in the photograph's lower left quadrant with a black tape X. They might tilt their heads at an obtuse angle to glance down at the tape; the first and third performers attempt this. They might follow Schneemann's directive to stiffen their fingers like antennae and brush them against one another's bodies in space. Strobe lights designed to be responsive to their sounds and motions disorient the performers further. In her stage directions, Schneemann recommended that the performers echolocate one another using guttural voice calls but forbade them to use intelligible language to communicate.

After feeling their way to their positions, and in time with the responsive strobe lighting, all six performers burst out of their fragile bindings in collective metamorphosis, tearing their paper exoskeletons so that they spread, winglike, out from their bodies. The photos show them first scattering and running—Schneemann's wings stretch blurrily out in the photograph from the "neutral" overalls that she selected as costuming because local ordinances forbade them from performing nude in public—and then reassembling in the staging area in pairs (fig. 22).[57] Paper anatomy appears here as a playful quotation of enfleshed parts, but ones that create real challenges, nonetheless. The body becomes a fungible unit subject to various pressures, an actant sensitive to other actants, a system of moving parts comparable to other biotic and abiotic matter.

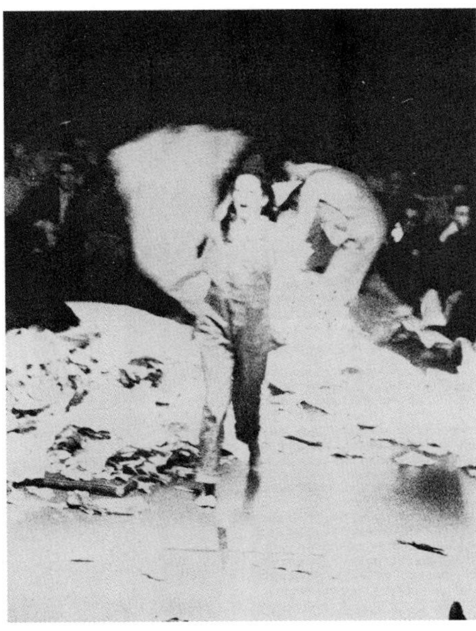

Fig. 22 Carolee Schneemann, *Illinois Central*, performed January 28, 1968, at the Museum of Contemporary Art Chicago.

Scavenged and perishable materials have a storied history within postwar art movements. They have long been cast as lively or fascinating in different ways, often in direct relation to the viewer's experience as a distinct, bounded body. As Branden Joseph and others note, Schneemann's approach to materials was especially "quasi-biological" and arose from her experience creating multimedia art that activated the senses.[58] "I am after the interpenetrations and displacements which occur between various sense stimuli," she wrote in her notes in 1965, "[as well as] the interaction and exchange between the body and the environment outside it; the body as environment, for the mind . . . where images evolve."[59] And as a multimedia artist whose circle included experimental filmmakers, film theorists, poets, activists, and members of performance movements such as Happenings, Schneemann inserted herself into a moment in which street trash often appeared next to high-tech materials acquired through art-commerce collaborations. Her partner, James Tenney, had had a residency with Bell Telephone Laboratories from 1961 to 1964, and she had participated in pop artist Claes Oldenburg's notorious immersive environment *Store Days* in 1962, in which she played a kind of throwaway commercial object herself, "balanced on a small shelf" and stabbing the wall with a knife.[60] Scavenging both new and postconsumer materials was de rigueur for American artists in the postwar period and came with the firm conviction that the artist's gesture and the external object would inform and build on each other—and thus illuminate the commercializing conditions that encompassed both modern life and modern art.[61]

Those in Schneemann's circle, including Robert Rauschenberg, Allan Kaprow, Jim Dine, and Dick Higgins, all found liberating potential in what Kaprow called "plain debris": either surplus industrial products or postconsumer waste, jettisoned from the structured moments of their original use and thus loosened from aesthetic or social hierarchies.[62] He himself had used newspaper and cardboard in works such as *Apple Shrine* and *Words*. As Liz Kotz has pointed out, "A new form of 'object' becomes available" in art practices of the 1960s, "an object that both is and is not understandable as sculpture, an object whose frame of reference is to the everyday consumer object, to the cheap, mundane and nearly ephemeral stuff of daily life, and not to any overt figurative, commemorative or hieratic sculptural model."[63] Kaprow's practice often began as a kind of bricolage of used consumer objects, hunting in secondhand shops and inside waste streams for "objects of every sort."[64] This led artists to solicit corporations or local businesses for excess products, which they then reorganized into components for interactive performances or sculptures. Schneemann's first major performance work, *Meat Joy,* in 1964, had relied on fifty pounds of meat donated from local butcher shops when she staged it at the Festival of Free Expression in Paris.[65] In her mixed-media sculptural work before 1967, her works incorporated broken umbrellas, cast-off motors, plastic painter's tarp, rubber snakes, and factory tubing, which turned each studio setup into a laboratory for comparing different kinds of mobility and motility. When Rauschenberg moved to Captiva Island, Florida, in 1970, he repurposed his own cardboard moving boxes to make sculptures, having already taken interest in the "constant irrational juxtaposition" of objects and materials in New York City from both commercial and postconsumer sources.[66]

Perishable matter such as food or yard clippings also appeared in multimedia performance works, and emphasized the speed at which consumer products quickly became waste, aligning these products with the temporalities of modernity, or "the nameless sludge and swirl of events," as Kaprow put it.[67] He asserted that "the use of obviously perishable media such as newspaper, string, adhesive tape, growing grass or real food" linked art to capitalism's relentless cycles of consumption and obsolescence but also dislodged it from these structures. Kaprow pointed out that "no-one can mistake the fact that the work will pass into dust or garbage quickly," which caused the curator William Seitz to diagnose a "striving" inherent in the work's base matter itself.[68] Materials could communicate this striving in different ways.[69] A broken umbrella could take on an erotic charge, for instance, or chicken feathers could seethe with aggression and displeasure. The debris' plainness facilitated its twinning with anguish, ecstasy, and all states in between.

Seitz's use of the word *striving* shows how the new debris-rich artworks intervened on long-standing philosophical debates about self-determination—a fact that would not have been lost on Seitz, who was the first person to earn a PhD in modern art history at the notoriously conservative Princeton University art history department.[70] Two major past philosophers came up in debates about motion and self-determination in the 1960s: René Descartes, whose work held that human consciousness was irrefutable and could be understood from within, and Baruch Spinoza, who proposed that consciousness was transitive and could be observed through multiple agents acting on one another.[71] These positions reveal an important divide regarding an object's ability to *strive* independent of human action. Descartes described motion as something that an object tended to do (*tendere*) after being handled or pushed in a certain direction, a variation on inertia. But for Spinoza, an object did not so much tend as strive (*conari*) in its trajectories. A ball, for instance, could exhibit its own inherent tendencies to strive and persist, independent of the force that pushed it. This seems to have been Schneemann's designation as well. "Anything I perceive is active to my eye," she asserted in 1963, turning herself into the receiver of a material's energy rather than the other way around. "The energy implicit in an area of paint (or cloth, paper, wood, glass . . .) is defined in terms of the time which it takes for the eye to journey through the implicit motion and direction of this area. The eye follows the building of forms . . . no matter what materials are used to establish the forms."[72] For Schneemann, debris was something more, right from the beginning. This approach unified her interest in natural ecologies amid urban trash systems in a moment at which the line between consumer and postconsumer waste had not yet been made legible. In the late 1960s, trash was still rhetorically connected with networks of postwar plenitude, unless an artist's choices made it mean otherwise. Schneemann foregrounded her use of materials within a vitalist, animistic framework extending from pantheism. Unlike "plain debris," her debris maintained its own agency, even after it had been shredded, folded, or fractured into abject, disintegrated states in a supply chain. This wasn't detritus or junk; it produced its own set of effects independent from the creator's poetic impulse.

Further, Schneemann's understanding of drawing—its status as an unruly, combinatorial, but small unit of creative practice, as well as an essential tool for visualization and optical learning—made such a leap possible. She had no access to life drawing classes at her first undergraduate school, Bard College. Instead, she assembled her own drawing education through a combination of books on early modern and modernist art and as a visiting student at Columbia University in the late 1950s. Fondly, and in the present tense, she recalled professor André Racz's drawing course, where she devoted eight hours a day to drawing: "I just draw and draw and draw."[73] She considered drawings—the product within which drawing's gestures are always implicated—to be part of a living, portable landscape; they could be unplugged, removed from their context, and, as she put it, made into "an image that then might be inhabited."[74] Thus her naturalistic drawings and chartlike projections built the basic structure and order for her multimedia works. She tore up and pasted drawings onto different collage surfaces, letting individual pictorial units take on migratory capabilities across time and space. Her more developed performance sketches use a wide range of drawing materials, including less visible elements of the studio environment such as dirt and bodily fluids. Combined with more traditional mark-making materials including ink, pencil, and watercolor, she experimented with a dynamic understanding of optics in which materials provided different levels of optical and physical resistance. Individual figures or drawings migrated, creating an interchange of vision, touch, and gesture.[75] With active subject matter and material, the eye drew, the mind drew, and the material could also draw. This formulation is similar to arguments about drawing in modernist circles before World War II, led by Paul Klee and others, that drawing was "an active line on a walk, moving freely, without goal."[76] Drawing became an act of shared power: between the optically visible line, controlled by the artist, and the artist's comparatively disorderly materials.

This autodidactic and synesthetic approach to drawing prefigured Schneemann's involvement with Intermedia, a term coined by Dick Higgins that integrated new media, film, and other disciplines and emphasized live performances and festivals. "Due to the spread of mass literacy, to television and the transistor radio, our sensitivities have changed," Higgins wrote in 1966. "We do not ask any more to speak magnificently of taking arms against a sea of troubles, we want to *see it done*. The art which most directly does this is the one which allows this immediacy, with a minimum of

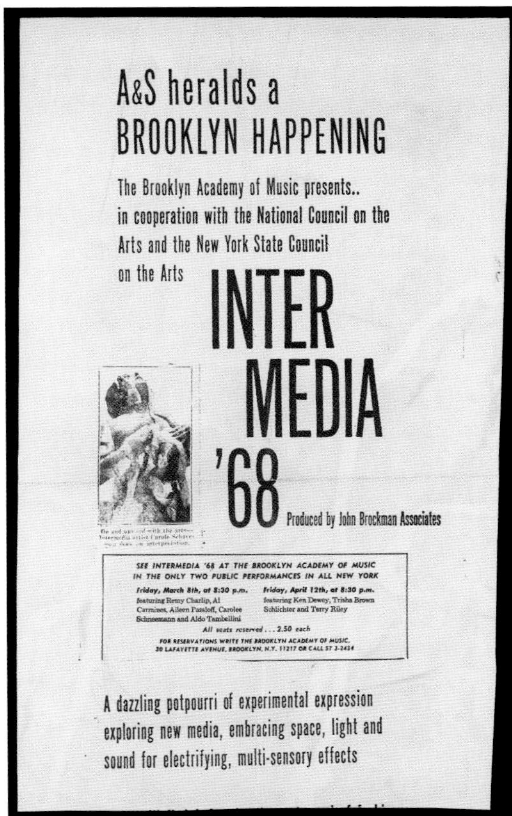

Fig. 23 Advertisement in *Look,* April 16, 1968, for Intermedia '68 festival, illustrated with Schneemann's *Body Collage.* Carolee Schneemann Papers, Getty Research Institute.

distractions."[77] An advertisement in *Look* for Brooklyn's *Intermedia '68* festival shows how easily Higgins's mandate for immediacy could be yoked together with spectacle and how unruly materials could become quickly fixed to gendered schemas (fig. 23). A photograph from *Body Collage* decorates the flyer and depicts Schneemann with an arched back, her hands grazing her chest. The image shows a young woman in a state of ecstasy, roiling in clumps of indeterminate matter, and promises to readers that they, too, can take part in a "dazzling potpourri" of countercultural experiences. Even the most disorderly states of perception were at risk for commodification. As if to concede and forestall this truth, Schneemann began referring to perception as "empathy drawing."[78]

The second section of *Illinois Central* consolidated empathy as its theme. After shedding their paper exoskeletons, participants met in the middle of the space, where they were guided onto a cart by performers that Schneemann called "roustabouts." From here, the participants remained standing on the cart as the roustabouts pulled them back and forth in front of the projected landscape photographs. Schneemann's instructions also required the roustabouts to shine flashlights at the audience. Although their disruptive flashes of light have not been preserved photographically, one can imagine the bodies as vulnerable to the incoming light, superimposing fields and trees on their white shirts, and to the cart's movements.

Part of the scene's construction of empathy lay in its multimedia effects, which blurred the line between livestock, human flesh, and debris—an assemblage that linked science's violent and extractive features with new possibilities for living. This had been a key strategy in her three previous paper-based live works, *Newspaper Event* (1963), *Night Crawlers* (1967), and *Divisions and Rubble* (1967). For these works she sourced most of her materials from near her loft on Twenty-First Street, whose supply chains and waste collection sites were often directly overlaid with one another. New York's SoHo and East Village neighborhoods were an urban grid of rags, rag-processing plants, scrap wood, string, rope, and other industrial castoff materials. Paper posters for events past and present were applied to brick surfaces with wheat paste, often in many layers.[79] When Schneemann published her notes for her performance *Divisions and Rubble* of 1967 in the avant-garde magazine *Aspen* in spring 1969, she emphasized the project's scaffolding made of "natural debris: a rotten mattress, plastic garbage bags filled with leaves, old clothes, food containers, discarded toys, dirty papers."[80] She positioned garbage as powerful and generative, asking viewers to find their way through a maze of "what refuse would be found in immediate vicinity." Her term for the trash's structural scaffolding was "garbage gestalt," an explicit link between postconsumer waste and modernist aesthetic unity. Trash could crystallize artistic form as well as change its surroundings.

For Schneemann, destruction and decay were actions of transformation, rooted in ancient agrarian societies of the past. These actions offered important corrections to what she called the "old wormy white-spirit energy" of contemporary New Left activist movements.[81] She was aware of the Destruction in Art Symposium (DIAS) in London, a major countercultural event that had taken place two years earlier. *Divisions and Rubble*, produced for the related event *12 Evenings of Manipulations in New York*, rehearsed these same ideas.[82] In her essay accompanying *Divisions and Rubble,* she wrote about the ideal ecosystem, one that was "a rural agricultural ancient delicate organically balanced society which had no garbage—consumed without waste, without exploitation; so integrated that its very waste became nourishment."[83] Vision and touch were causal agents, acting in concert with organic waste materials to dissolve the ontological and boundaries between them.

In asserting this idea, she also challenged the persistent mechanistic approach to "the environment" espoused by her contemporaries in Happenings and new media. Allan Kaprow and Dick Higgins and other makers who connected with such corporate-sponsored art-tech initiatives as EAT (Experiments in Art and Technology) imagined nature as a series of machines, ideally to be evacuated of their metaphoric potential via rigorous interrogations and relevant to contemporary urban intellectual frameworks only insofar as natural phenomena functioned as well-oiled mechanical objects. Buckminster Fuller's popular book *Operating Manual for Spaceship Earth* of 1969 encouraged readers to develop an "awareness of the generalized principles underlying all special and only superficially-sensed experiences" so that they might employ those principles in "rearranging the physical resources of environment" to solve world problems.[84] Schneemann had sent Fuller's work to several friends by the last few months of 1967.[85] Many artists and other makers in her milieu aimed to liberate science and empirical knowledge from the totalizing, technophilic, and colonial frameworks to which it had been yoked since the Enlightenment.[86] *Environment* was the hinge around which discussions of the individual's relationship to their surroundings could rotate. At times used synonymously with nature and at other times used to articulate permeable boundaries between an individual and the rest of the world, this emergent, unsettled term helped artists create (and reckon with) issues of enclosure and permeability—things made urgent because of the increasingly violent realities in American geopolitical affairs.

Just as natural environments had become models and thinking tools, so, too, were "media environments" becoming a way to understand modernity's effects within ecosystems particular to human beings. An issue of *Aspen* on the media critic Marshall McLuhan, published in spring 1967, advocated for "a knowledge of the way media work as environments," positing that media configured their own sets of borders and boundaries, with varying effects on individuals' physical and mental health.[87] When Richard Schechner wrote about Expo '67, Canada's centennial celebration and World's Fair in Montreal, he highlighted "film and still-image environments" that "serve[d] as background for performers and as independent performing elements."[88] An issue of the *Drama Review* would be published in spring 1968 on environments and experimental theater; an issue of *Aspen* published the preceding fall consisted of Schneemann and several contemporaries discussing their use of ecological science in their work.

But at this moment, Schneemann was joining the chorus of thinkers who were taking this theoretical construction of environment—that is, a system bounded by walls or screens, with specific sets of effects—and positioning it in dialogue with the notion of being *outside,* "in nature," and synonymous with ecology rather than a psychosocial construct that was reliant on an architectural envelope. In Allan Kaprow's work *Overtime* of 1968, for instance, Kaprow set up two hundred feet of snow fencing across a rural stretch of New Paltz, New York, and moved the fence into different positions while setting off flares all night. The work was dedicated to the artist Walter De Maria, who was also making large land-based artworks that called the viewer's relationship to the earth into question. Kaprow's goal was to "de-charg[e]" the metaphors associated with nature, transforming the land's material components through collective labor. The Canadian Yugoslav scholar Darko Suvin reviewed *Overtime* in 1970 arguing that it sought to deconstruct the "age-old metaphor of the old dark wood. . . . [The wood instead] turns into a humanly-mapped grid, a surveyed space complete with food, light, and communication." Suvin reflected on, and reified, Kaprow's interest in pastoral themes by focusing on the then unusual theme of out-of-door space: "Its nonurban character is due to Kaprow's personal propensity for the bucolic—most authors of Happenings work in an urban environment, where metaphors are less easily identifiable in terms of the cultural tradition," he wrote.[89] In a moment when avant-garde art was mostly associated with urban centers, Suvin's response illustrates the pervasive—and vexing—critical coupling of nature with the pastoral.

Efforts to shift makers' perceptions of the natural world as something other than metaphor were mixed. Some architects in Schneemann's circle, such as Christopher Alexander, used the patterns in nature as inspiration for cities or other built forms but distanced themselves firmly from actual trees.[90] Manfredo Tafuri wrote about photography's potential to change our perception of the composition of our environment but left out its botanical or zoological particulars.[91] Other endeavors, such as CASE, the Conference of Architects for the Study of the Environment, which Schneemann's friend Kenneth Frampton first organized in 1964, barely mentioned botanical forms, rural supply chains, or soil.[92]

SOIL

Within this gap, numerous opportunities arose for artists to engage in experiments with the *actual* matter of nature. Conventional art historical narratives credit earthworks artists for reintroducing soil and dirt as subjects proper to contemporary art, but feminist body artists such as Schneemann and Ana Mendieta also took part in these debates by deconstructing the genre of landscape—by getting their hands dirty, literally and figuratively. Schneemann was trained as a painter and began her career at a moment when performance, video, and minimalist sculpture were ascending, thus posing an existential threat to painterly praxis. She referred to her hybrid and multimedia projects of the 1960s, in fact, as "an existential grief worked out on a beloved corpse."[93] In laying painting to rest and mourning its failures, she also used it as an important ground of her practice. "As a landscape painter, you can only fail," she recalled, "because whatever you're looking at is completely changing. The light changes, the wind changes, the colors start drying too slowly, too fast, you have to pee, a storm might turn up. It's very exciting, invigorating, and enveloping. When I got into indoor space I wanted [to retain] some aspect of that enveloping activity."[94] If landscape painting's constant surprises made it a risky practice, that risk was infused with rigor—it could train the artist to accept and assimilate shifts in one's surroundings.

This had been the case since her undergraduate training at Bard College in the mid-1950s. One of Schneemann's favorite teachers there, the German poet and philosopher Heinrich Blücher—a temporary faculty member at Bard and the husband of Hannah Arendt—emphasized in his courses that human beings could never know the world through scientific observation alone. Working without lecture notes of any kind, he always began his "Foundations of Western Philosophy" course by discussing the pre-Socratic philosopher Heraclitus. Blücher challenged Heraclitus's two-thousand-year-old claim that "there is a rational order of things that is also a natural order of things." Blücher's longue-durée argument resonated with students and faculty, a generation defined by mass media and technological innovations but sobered by their attendant genocides and mass migrations. Within modernity, Blücher admonished, science had become "a battlefield between man and nature, a battle that is being fought to the death, a battle where man must prove really and finally that he can rule nature, the whole of physical being, by one mathematical formula."[95] As the technophilic enthusiasms of the Cold War gave way to postwar countercultures agnostic about technology, skepticism cropped up around the idea that systems and formulas could distill or manage the world.

Schneemann's attention fell on the landscape and the nude body, two systems familiar to painters. Unlike Blücher, Schneemann made copious notes, drawings, and copies of other artworks to move back and forth between these two genres. She used the act (and the materials) of drawing to knit together other artistic processes that, for her, merged thought with action and self with world. One of Schneemann's earliest works, painted while she was living in South Shaftsbury, Vermont, follows this line of inquiry, as it was among Schneemann's first paintings that explored the human figure. At this time Schneemann was in the process of escaping Bard, where she was attending on a full scholarship but would soon be expelled for "moral turpitude." The title of this work, *Three Figures after Pontormo* (fig. 24), references a drawing of three nude figures by the Italian mannerist painter Jacopo Carucci da Pontormo (fig. 25), which the Florentine artist produced when he was around twenty-six years old. Schneemann was eighteen when she made the painting. Her canvas obscures two human forms, one on either side of the central axis of the middle figure, within a sea of brushstrokes both thickly applied to and partially scraped down from the canvas. As the central form runs down the middle of the painting, it has the potential to anchor it; instead, it generates a sense of swirling, like a DNA's double helix.

Some of these choices reveal her dialogue with Pontormo's approach to figure and space, especially with the elder artist's desire to "give spirit to a figure . . . and yet place it on a flat surface."[96] This quality is evident in the red chalk drawing, which shows three models posed on boxes in the artist's studio, each crowding close to each other but layered concentrically away from the viewer in space. In *Standing Male Nude*, the seated figure's head on the left side of the drawing has clear but variable borders, forming a red chalk corona around the head and face.[97] If Pontormo had followed the usual order of Renaissance one-point perspective, the figure on the left should be receding into space, but instead the artist's red chalk outlines on the lower torso and head make it spring into the foreground. The two figures closest to the picture plane look fused. The art historian Janet Cox-Rearick would call them "academically posed," in an attempt to parse the artist's layered, idiosyncratic approach to the human figure.[98] The art historian Daniel B. Rowland had a different opinion, declaring in 1964 that "[Pontormo] has rejected the Renaissance image of the self-sufficient man acting in a rational environment

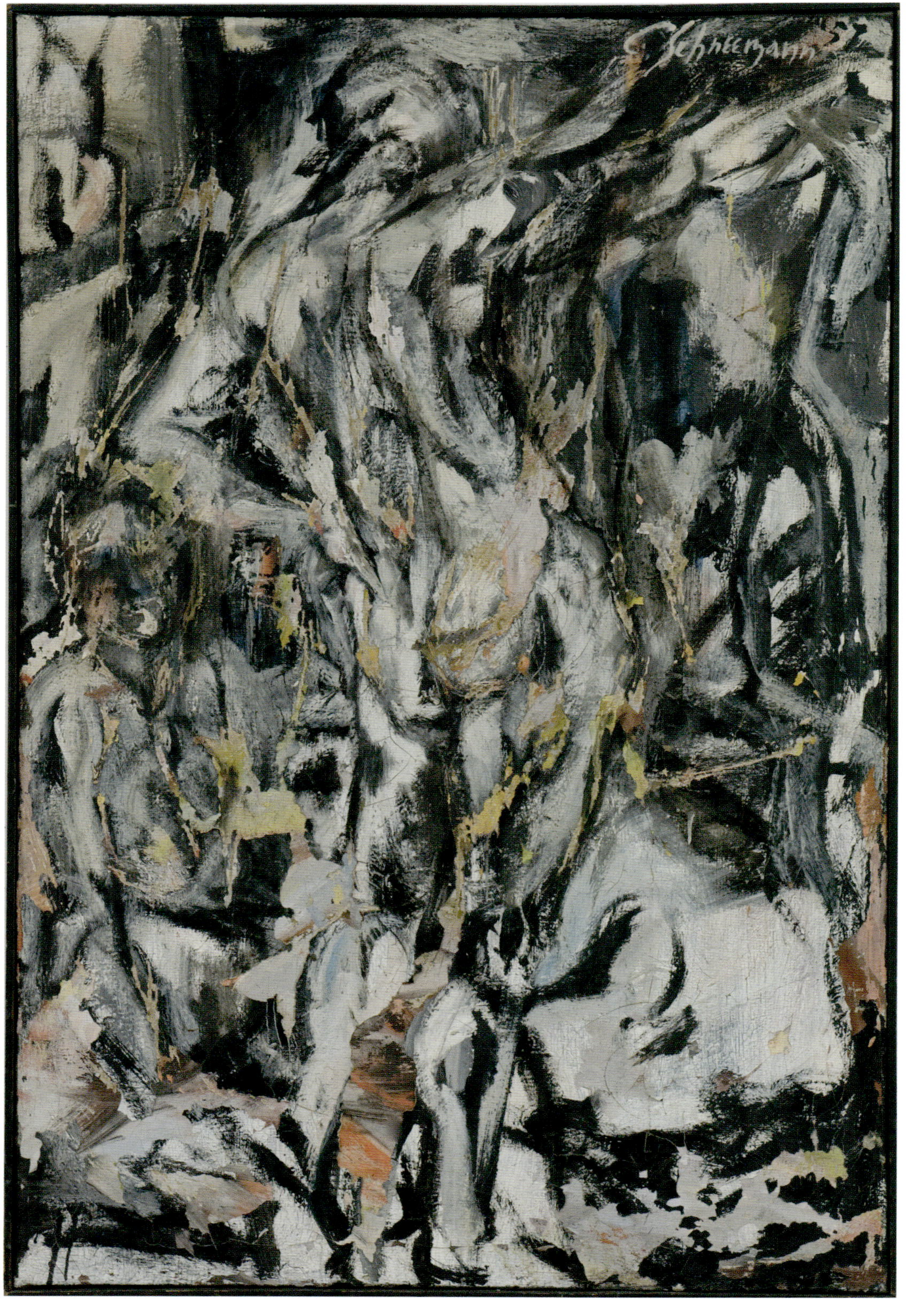

Fig. 24 Carolee Schneemann, *Three Figures after Pontormo*, 1957. Oil on canvas, 46½ × 31½ in. (118.1 × 78.7 cm).

   Wild Waste

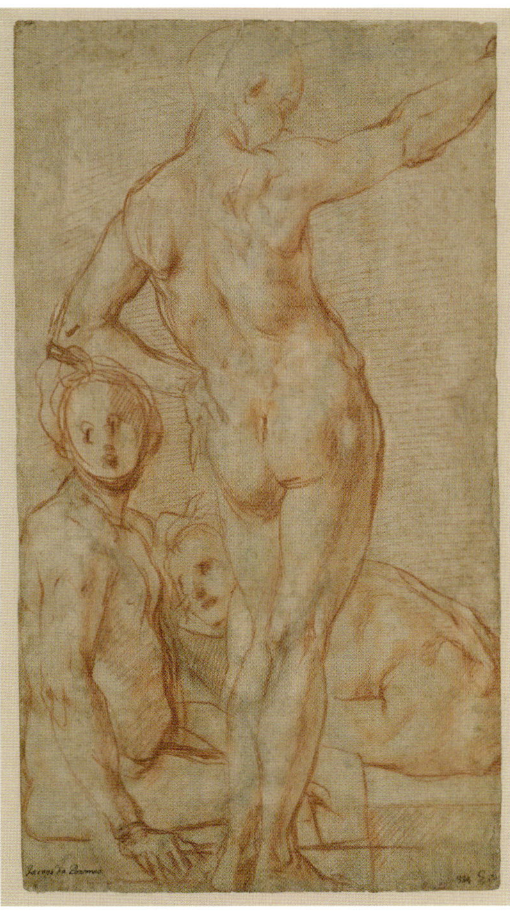

Fig. 25 Jacopo da Pontormo, *Standing Male Nude Seen from the Back, and Two Seated Nudes,* ca. 1520. Red chalk on paper, 15¹⁵⁄₁₆ × 8¾ inches (40.5 × 22.2 cm). Morgan Library and Museum.

which he can understand." To Rowland, Pontormo's figures "seem to float in a kind of neutral world unaffected by the ordinary law of gravity. . . . The environment has almost ceased to exist, and all that is visible is a few fragments which fail to fit together in any coherent pattern."[99] Just as Pontormo's delinking of bodies from their environment had long made him a historiographic problem in art history, so, too, did he arouse the interest of other artists.

But this red chalk version of the drawing was not the true template that Schneemann used for her painting. Instead, she used an image from an exhibition catalog of 1953 from the Royal Academy in London (fig. 26), reproduced with the title *Drawings by Old Masters.* Drawings such as this one by Pontormo were newly circulating in printed books and in small traveling exhibitions in the 1950s when cultural initiatives sought to make the art historical canon more accessible to nonelite American viewers. Such drawings helped her develop enough familiarity with representing the human figure to abandon landscape painting in the late 1950s for figure painting and performance. But this drawing was photographed before the extensive repairs to its verso and recto in March and April 1954 by the Morgan Library's conservator Minna Horwitz, which made its lower quadrants look smooth and

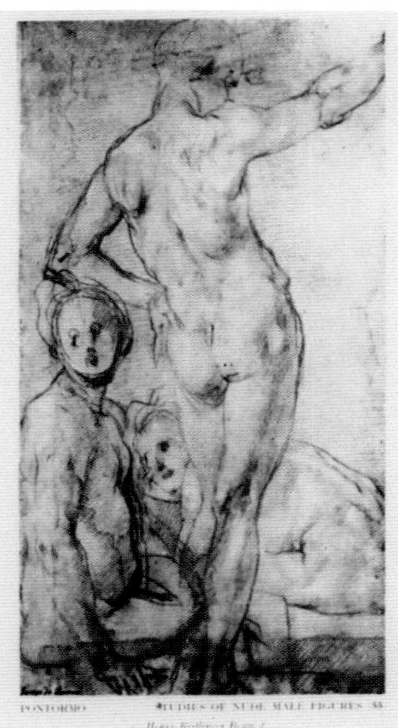

Fig. 26 Reproduction of Jacopo da Pontormo drawing, *Drawings by Old Masters*, Royal Academy Diploma Gallery, 1953.

clear. Here, by contrast, the dark shading at the bottom of the image is a layer of old, darkened glue that affixed a strip of linen to the back of the drawing, changing the shape of the surface of the paper enough to make it legible in the catalog photograph.

Schneemann's composition, then, registers some of the drawing's topography that has since been repaired out of existence. The bars at the bottom of Schneemann's composition and the patchy paint in the lower left quadrant indicate how closely she looked at the reproduced drawing. (In these early years she often worked with her eyes closed, attempting to both see and feel the image's makeup.) In the painted version, bodies melt into the landscape, interfering with the viewer's ability to discern the second and third figures, as well as foreground and background.

Horwitz's conservation project in 1954 clarified this drawing. We can see more clearly that the models are sitting on boxes and that their weight is distributed according to gravity onto solid forms at the bottom of the composition. The illusion of abstract grouping, of floating in space, is curtailed. But in the black-and-white reproduction, much of the visual energy of the drawing rests on the way that body parts are fused and joined. Schneemann clearly found inspiration in the section of the painting where the left figure's head appears fused to the central figure's body, as though the two forms mutually generated each other. In fact, Schneemann eschews foreground and background, instead looking at the forms as though they were floating in a liquid substrate. This effect is complicated by the fact that the canvas in fact supports two distinct layers of material—the top painting, which Schneemann painted mostly in grisaille and blue tones, and the layer underneath,

  Wild Waste

which was a discarded landscape painting that she had developed from an old picture of Robert Frost's historic home in a neighboring town in Vermont. To make the two surfaces commingle into one, Schneemann scraped and peeled back the top layers of paint with her hands and a single-blade razor.

This canvas enacts an exchange between one set of data and another, mediated by what might be called drawing only in the most expansive sense. We move from an image bank to an image ecosystem. The straight razor cut, for instance, bridges several techniques—Schneemann employed it here as an outline and contour strategy but also used it as an archaeological tool. She worked away at the surface, scratching out the volumes that appeared to her through the drawing using a subtractive method—two lower legs here, an elbow there—to make one image into a catalyst for the other's development. The body's components do not coalesce for the viewer because they are bounded by lines; they instead carve themselves through and upward, a product of shared energies among the tool, the materials touching it, and the bodies latent within the image. Such combined energies hazard an account of the body as implicitly linked to landscape because of its base matter that can be changed or melded and evince Schneemann's commitment to "disciplining vision" through material, as the art historian Kristine Stiles has put it.[100] Take the section in which the largest figure's arm intersects with the head of the second figure, an accidental Siamese twinning that happens in the original Pontormo drawing and thus proves the fragility of depicted space. Schneemann detected this and sought to literalize it in paint.

Three Figures after Pontormo explored paint's potential to supply a dirty substrate for line. Its duologue with the young mannerist artist provokes us to consider two realities, one historical and one theoretical. The first is the artist's transition from working primarily in landscape to taking an interest in the human body. Doing this required her to assemble a vocabulary for the human figure very much on her own, drawing from life but also from reproductions, to construct her own canon in the absence of the live figure. To make this canon, Schneemann turned to what she had: in this case, reproduced drawings—drawings that, unbeknown to her, would soon be repaired—in a catalog for an exhibition at the Royal Academy in London. In her intervention, the depicted figures were inseparable from the passage of time, as they were transmitted from an aging red chalk image to the exhibition catalog's pages to the difficult topography of her own scraped-down paintings.

Theoretically, this is an exercise for the eye that involves a palpitation across the surface—empathy drawing literally writ large, a game of recognition that makes no part of the image any more or less available to vision than the other. Looking at pictures in this way helps to unite two seemingly incommensurate ideas about viewership: that matter structures what we see and that looking is structured and constituted by cultural norms. In this painting, made a decade before the naturalization of second-wave feminist aesthetics, we can see what Laura Mulvey, Judith Butler, and countless other theorists recognized as the "cultural vacillations of vision": the way that bodies, particularly female bodies, are declared by authority figures to both spell out and obey concepts of gender or sexuality—things that seem immutable but in fact have a clear archaeology.[101] As these figures emerge out of the past and within matter, it is the drawing out of the body into both time and space that helped create a new approach to seeing.

It is also not an accident that the young painter was layering her own old material to deemphasize the flat plane of the canvas, so that each image layer in the scraped-down painting could "come through the figuration."[102] In *Three Figures after Pontormo* and many of her later projects, detritus does the work of creating new forms in space. Each component of *Three Figures* demonstrates the potential for materials to generate their own biology. Her own biography and art-making practices are implicated within this biology also, in the same way that art's histories are made available to us through a rich, loamy (and often managed) topsoil of value, critical support, and canonicity. Each actant has its own set of biological effects, so vigorous that they come through the canvas, literally *coming through* the figuration. The painting thus reveals a combination of individual agents: Pontormo's imagination; the cumulative damage to his red chalk drawing, reproduced on the book's page; Schneemann's discarded work, flipped to a new orientation; and the painting itself as a living, enfleshed body in a constant state of change.

Consider this in relation to Leon Battista Alberti's proposal that all order comes from line and his exhortations to artist-designers to prioritize line to create life and structure. Schneemann was aware of the one-point perspective that Alberti and Filippo Brunelleschi discussed in their writings, and that it came into being through the artist's projective vision. Her interests in Renaissance perspective reached their apex in her 1968–71 film project, *Plumb Line,* which used the geometries of the split screen and the horizon line to work through the dissolution of her relationship with the composer James Tenney, her partner of thirteen years.[103] According to Renaissance art and architectural theory, the shape and style of all buildings "depend[ed] on lineaments alone."[104] But, as *Plumb Line* would go on to demonstrate, form is imperfect, as is vision. It has the ability to misshape things; as Schneemann put it, "Projection deforms perception of the female body."[105] Where intellect might be the sole driver of form in Renaissance theory, Schneemann's feminist scientific approach concedes to the challenges and vagaries of observation, as form develops in the process of attaching itself to intermittent, ongoing, and even snatched moments of looking. Vision generates its own order. Matter's wildness ensures that we will get what we need.

Despite this shift from landscape to body, landscape remained a critical part of Schneemann's oeuvre. It appeared in the form of dispersed matter—land that had been broken down into its constituent parts of dirt, pulp, trees, and branches—rather than in romanticizable scenes. A preparatory drawing made for an earlier live work, *Water Light / Water Needle* of 1966, uses dirt to simulate three-dimensional space on a flat page (fig. 27). In this drawing Schneemann mapped out a plan for six performers to navigate

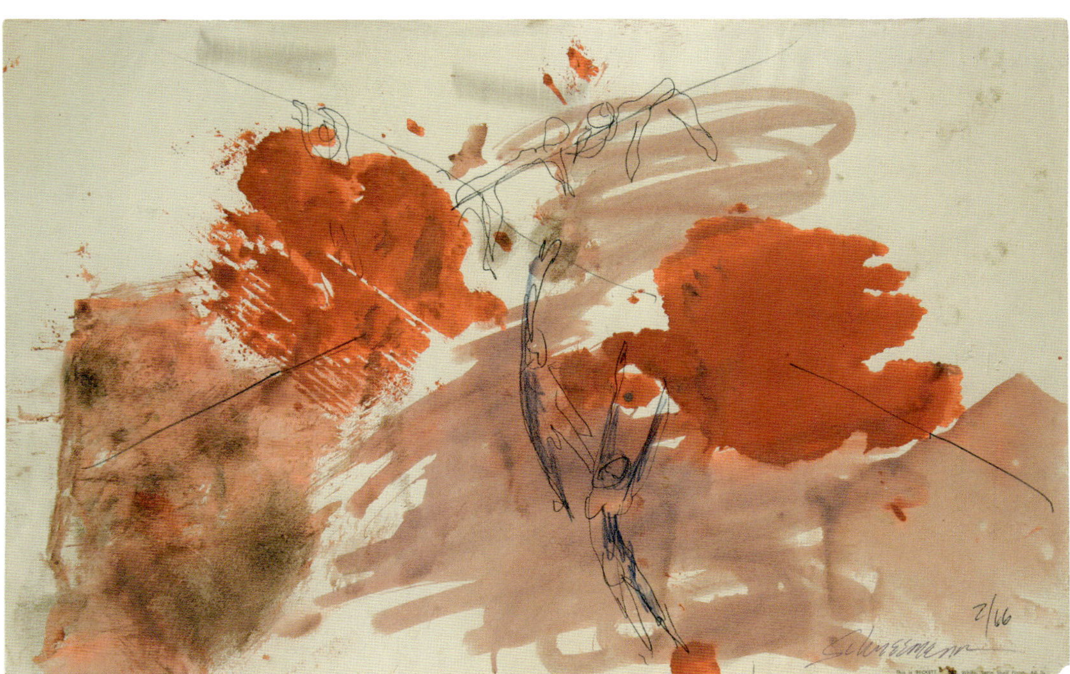

Fig. 27 Carolee Schneemann, *Water Light / Water Needle*, 1966. Watercolor on paper, 12½ × 20 in. (31.8 × 50.8 cm). Menil Collection.

their way across heavy lines of rope strung through the performance space. The pen-and-ink passages in the drawing show performers clambering and swinging across two perpendicular rope lines that do not touch the edges of the page. Five human figures walk and tumble along the bisecting lines, illuminated and sometimes obscured by clouds of watercolor paint in pink and red. Their shading and volume come from ballpoint pen and studio dirt as much as they do from paint—widely available materials that are most present to the artist when working, whether drawing, painting, or writing.

The figures are integrated within (and made equivalent to) the gaseous structures that the ink, watercolor, and crayon mediums help co-create.[106] Five gleeful figures in the center are shaded in blue crayon, darkened by pink and red watercolor clouds. The pink clouds in the lower right quadrant demonstrate watercolor's simultaneously liquid and singularizing qualities. A smoky gray shade tinges the pink paint that disperses across the center and bottom of the page, shading it in a scribble, as though the brush were a centrifuge shaking off the black pigment. Brown stains of studio dirt in the lower right corner create a similar chromatic contrast; dirt is both pigment and resistance, an embrace of the many resistances that the body—and hand—encounters in the world. Though the stain looks gaseous, its density structures the picture rather than disrupting or damaging it. The paper sheet changes, too. Instead of a blank space readying itself for an account of its maker's actions—or inactions, or even redactions, as Schneemann's friend Robert Rauschenberg had introduced in his *Erased de Kooning Drawing* of 1955—it becomes a plane that registers the generativity inherent in befoulment. The mythical, terrifying "bleeding wound" to which Laura Mulvey refers is suddenly present and alive, its castrating absence inverted into a mark-making agent.

This was not a staging of paint *as* dirt, as postwar modernist artists such as Jean Dubuffet had done in the 1940s to debase the human body and mock the constitutive materials of culture.[107] It was not a polemical statement about the arbitrary valuation of paint and graphite in modernist art making, as Robert Rauschenberg's *Elemental Paintings* had been.[108] Rather, this was an expansion of matter's role in image-making, staged through the physically and socially fertile space of the support. Dirt could articulate contours, changing the page's flat plane and illuminating paper's origins as a shapeless, friable mass. The layers of damage in a Mannerist drawing could emerge through the cotton weave of a canvas. Later, in her artist's book *Parts of a Body House Book,* she would use menstrual blood as a printmaking medium, with her own body acting as the print matrix. Lost, discarded, or externalized materials could collapse modern capitalism's persistent binary of user and product.

By incorporating grime into the typically human-generated space of drawing and printmaking, Schneemann also threw light onto the ways that matter, when yoked to an outflow state such as garbage or menstrual bleeding, possesses a power that is a direct function of the fears and anxieties attached to it. Matter is "the site at which the feminine is excluded from philosophical binaries," to use Judith Butler's turn of phrase.[109] Butler reached this conclusion by considering one of her own predecessors, the feminist linguist and philosopher Luce Irigaray, who exposed philosophy's long history of dividing material qualities by gender using language and symbolism: "phantasmatic notions of the feminine" are linked to materiality, while authorship and autoreproduction are understood as mythically masculine.[110] Perhaps this is why the two passages of studio dirt feel like a guide for how to look at the rest of the picture, a new set of possibilities for following befoulment. In its current, worn condition, the paper loses its integrity at the edges, reflecting its years of being stored in Schneemann's personal archive and thus its function as a well-loved private object.[111] The dirt points our attention toward the page's state of decay; in Jane Bennett's words, it models "a materialism in which matter is figured as a vitality at work both inside and outside of selves, and is a force to be reckoned with without being purposive in any strong sense."[112] Instead of looking at the signs of wear as evidence of inherent vice—a term in art conservation for an artwork's tendency to fall apart due to its material's intrinsic vulnerabilities—we might search for *more* exhaustion in the candy-colored swirls of watercolor or for *more* grime to disrupt the author-material binary further.

TREES

The third phase of *Illinois Central* focused on one of paper's least processed components, the tree. "The central imagery of this work is The Tree," she affirmed later—but also the terrifying ways that agriculture removed and

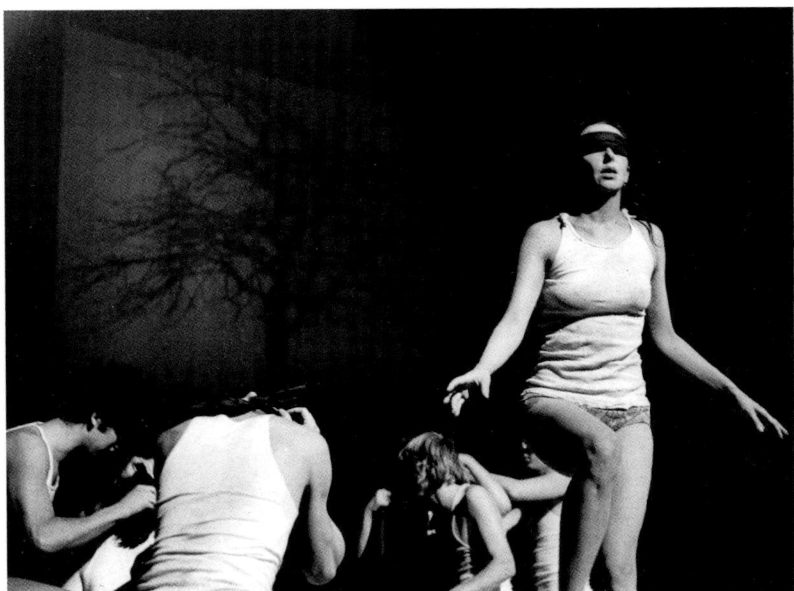

Fig. 28 Carolee Schneemann, blindfold removal in *Illinois Central*, 1968.

transformed trees, which led to "the absence of the tree as characteristic of the Mid West landscape and the transformation of the tree into paper."[113] To literalize *Illinois Central*'s tree thematics, the performers gathered in front of projected slides of trees and midwestern landscapes. Occasionally they entered the beam of the slide projectors, and their bodies became the ground for the projected images. Blindfolded, they were instructed to find the pile of shredded bank checks at the center and sit in it, surrounded by the audience (fig. 28). This entanglement among different image-states, species, and materials was purposeful: Schneemann aimed for what she called "a complete exposure of the body, being naked, being covered in glue, collaged with paper, remnant of tree, becoming ourselves 'tree.'"[114] Many of the slides were taken from her former professor Art Sinsabaugh's photographs, which she had encountered while studying with him at the University of Illinois Champaign-Urbana in 1960. Sinsabaugh, who had studied with the Hungarian photographer László Moholy-Nagy at the New Bauhaus School in Chicago, is best known for using a large-format "banquet" camera to produce twelve-by-twenty-inch negatives of American landscapes. He cropped his negatives dramatically, so that they produced sweeping views. Of particular interest for Schneemann were Sinsabaugh's long, horizontal landscape photographs of central Illinois, which she reported were the truest to her memory of this region during her three years living there. *Midwest Landscape #34* (fig. 29), which captured row after row of industrially tilled crops, used orthogonal lines to project the space of the picture into the viewer's actual space. The rows, arranged in one-point perspective, yoked together the geometry of classical perspective with the standardized and seemingly limitless row-hoeing of industrial agriculture, done by tractors and combines since 1903.

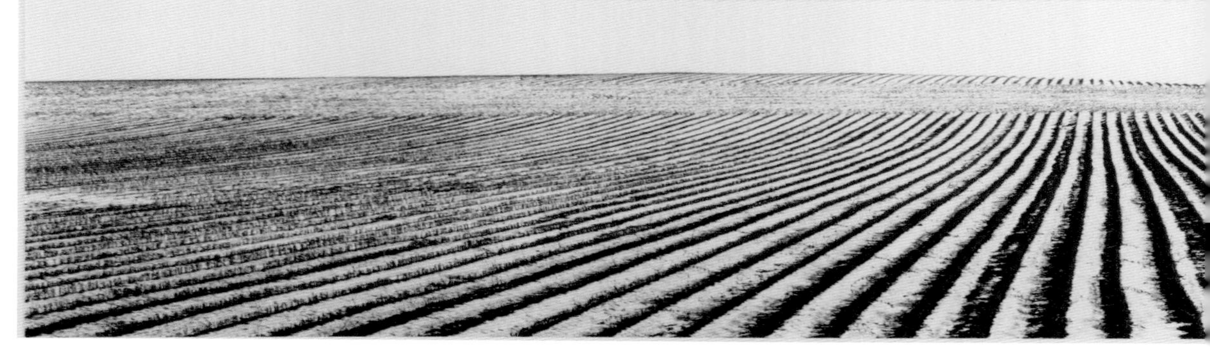

Its horizontal sweep so enchanted Schneemann that she used it as the "ground" for her clip art poster advertising the event (see fig. 11). Seen together with a collaged photograph from *Body Collage*, the crop rows' vertical sweep fuses Renaissance one-point perspective with the development of mechanized agriculture. Schneemann has written of her graduate education at the University of Illinois as being marked by the landscape's irreparable changes in the face of industrialization. "The trees once marking the boundaries of small farms were cut down as if an effluvium," she wrote, "inviting soil erosion, floods, destroying natural cover, the ecology of wild life." She found a parallel between this destruction and "the destruction of the intensive, traditional farming in Vietnam," which was leading to the ruin of indigenous agricultural systems there.[115]

As the daughter of a country doctor Schneemann had worked on rural farms growing up, which gave her an unvarnished experience of agricultural labor—as well as a uniquely distanced perspective on binary gender. "If you were mowing and haying in the field all day long, you just jumped in the river," she recalled in 1998. "Nobody was thinking about what sex you were. You were red and stinging with the heat of the hay on your skin and in your nose. And you looked at each other like lively exciting animals."[116] Animals and animality appeared in *Illinois Central*'s performance score. In the work's middle section, performers took on the role of livestock as a "roustabout" figure walked around the space, blindfolded the participants, and led them all onto a cart. Gently but firmly, the cart wheeled participants around the space as the audience watched. They fell over in the cart, which must have been troubling for the audience. In some moments, the blindfolded performers looked impaired; at other times they were stimulated by their other four senses. Their bodies shifted from (being perceived as) creatures to objects of fascination to human beings in need of rescue.

Schneemann offered some clarification on product cycles in a letter to her friend Daryl Chin in 1975, in which she reflected on ecological themes in her work: "For a pantheist like me it all runs and streams together—city life holds one experience, one fragment of an organic cycle in strange relief, cut apart, thrown into a beam of light, seen as a thing on its own . . . feathers belong to chickens, I wipe my ass with a sacrificed tree, I know how

      Wild Waste

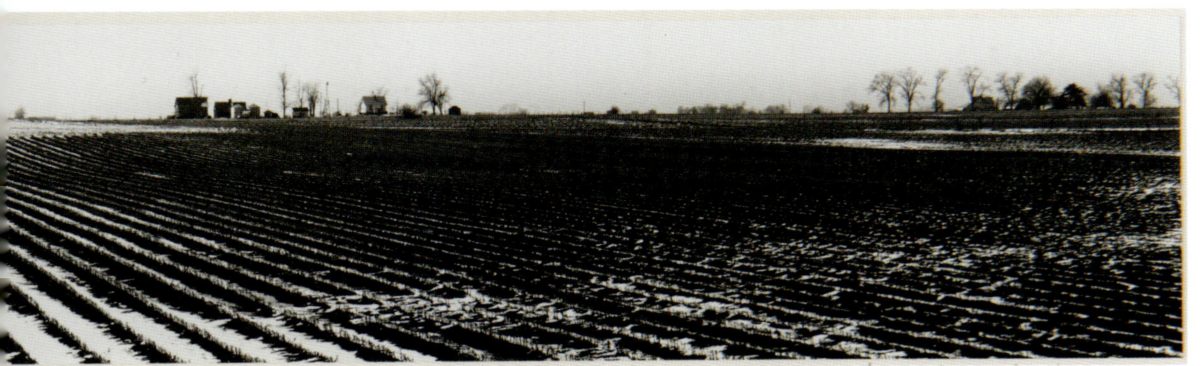

much grain made that hunk of hamburger get to the plate, how many days of sun before the lettuce matured (and how and with what it was sprayed & dosed commercially . . .).”[117] This systemic thinking, in which plucked chickens, crop dusting, and grain overproduction all constitute an ongoing, lively calculus of the everyday, echoes the ecological theorist Rachel Carson, who imagined natural spaces as teeming with unnoticed life in her writings on ecology in the postwar period. Carson's groundbreaking book *Silent Spring*, published in 1962, captivated artists and writers by framing the landscape as a register of different energies, each of which was legible to those who dared to take notice. “The natural landscape is eloquent of the interplay of forces that have created it,” she wrote. “It is spread before us like the pages of an open book in which we can read why the land is what it is, and why we should preserve its integrity. But the pages lie unread.”[118] For Schneemann, human users and their inanimate daily products such as food and paper were immanently knowable but constantly shifting—connected through luminous chains, with each supply chain bringing forth uniquely destructive effects.

WASTE, AGAIN

Just as Rachel Carson made the case for nature's availability, so Schneemann leveraged natural materials to make her performers physically and emotionally available to one another. This connectedness—or the “running together,” as the artist put it—was literalized in the final twenty minutes of *Illinois Central,* when the six performers invited the audience to paint their bodies with glue. Immediately afterward, they jumped into the pile of shredded checks in the center of the space, rolled in the pile, and began to touch one another (fig. 30). Their touching wasn't just limited to brief moments of contact; they joined together in pairs and formed different linking shapes with their bodies (fig. 31). A small ink drawing by Schneemann shows one of the linked figural shapes that she plotted beforehand, complete with written instructions that helped her “configure” the “exact image” that the performance would create (fig. 32).[119] An upright stick figure holds the upturned legs of another stick figure who appears to lean mostly

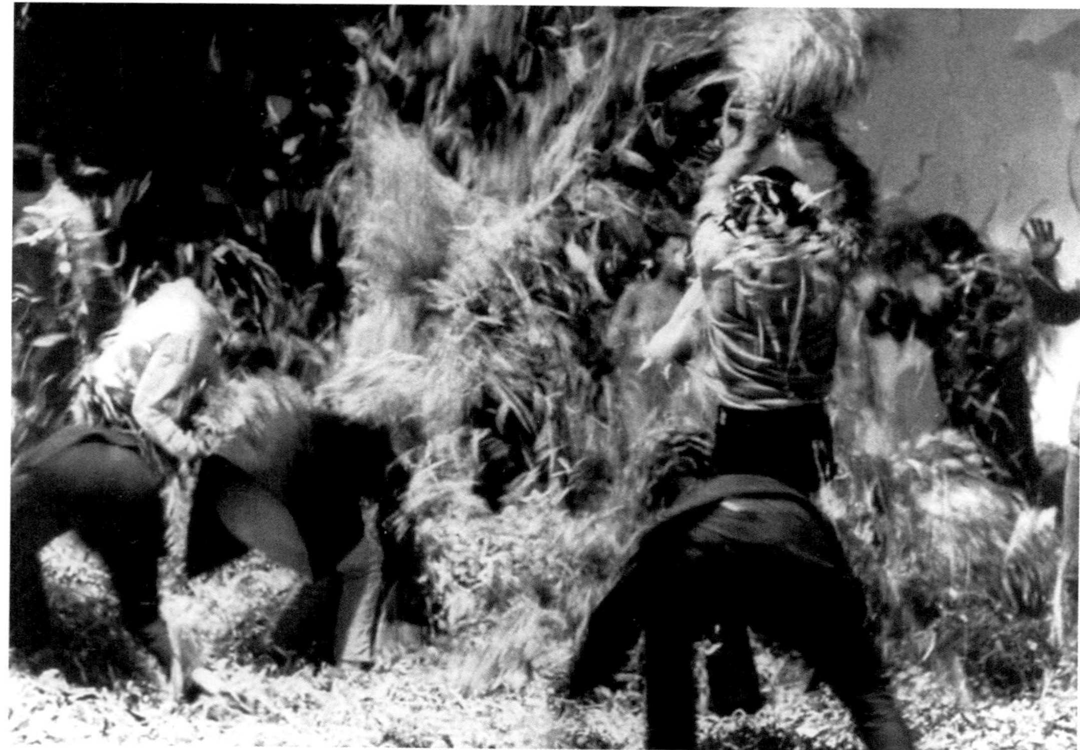

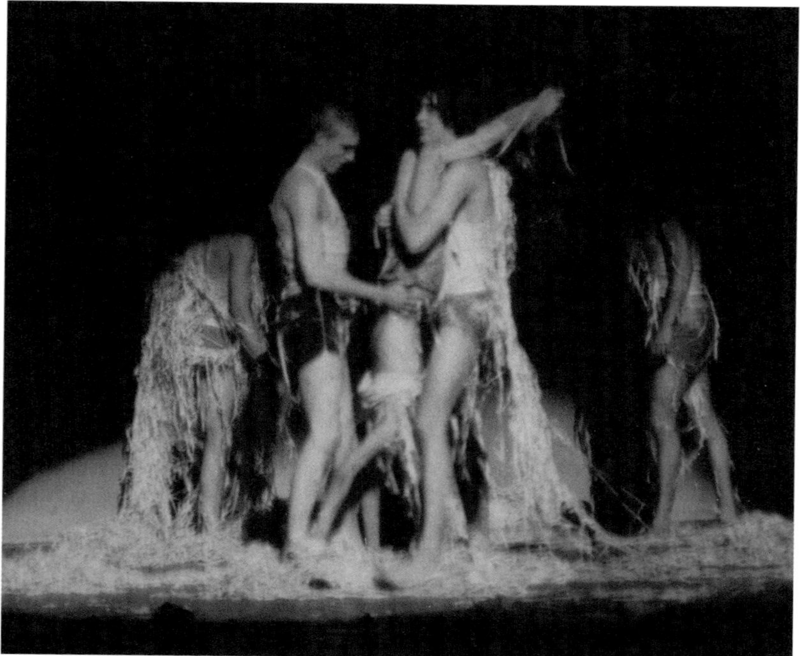

Fig. 30 Carolee Schneemann, *Illinois Central Transposed,* March 8, 1968. Performance at Brooklyn Academy of Music, NY.

Fig. 31 Carolee Schneemann, *Illinois Central Transposed,* March 8, 1968. Performance at Brooklyn Academy of Music, NY

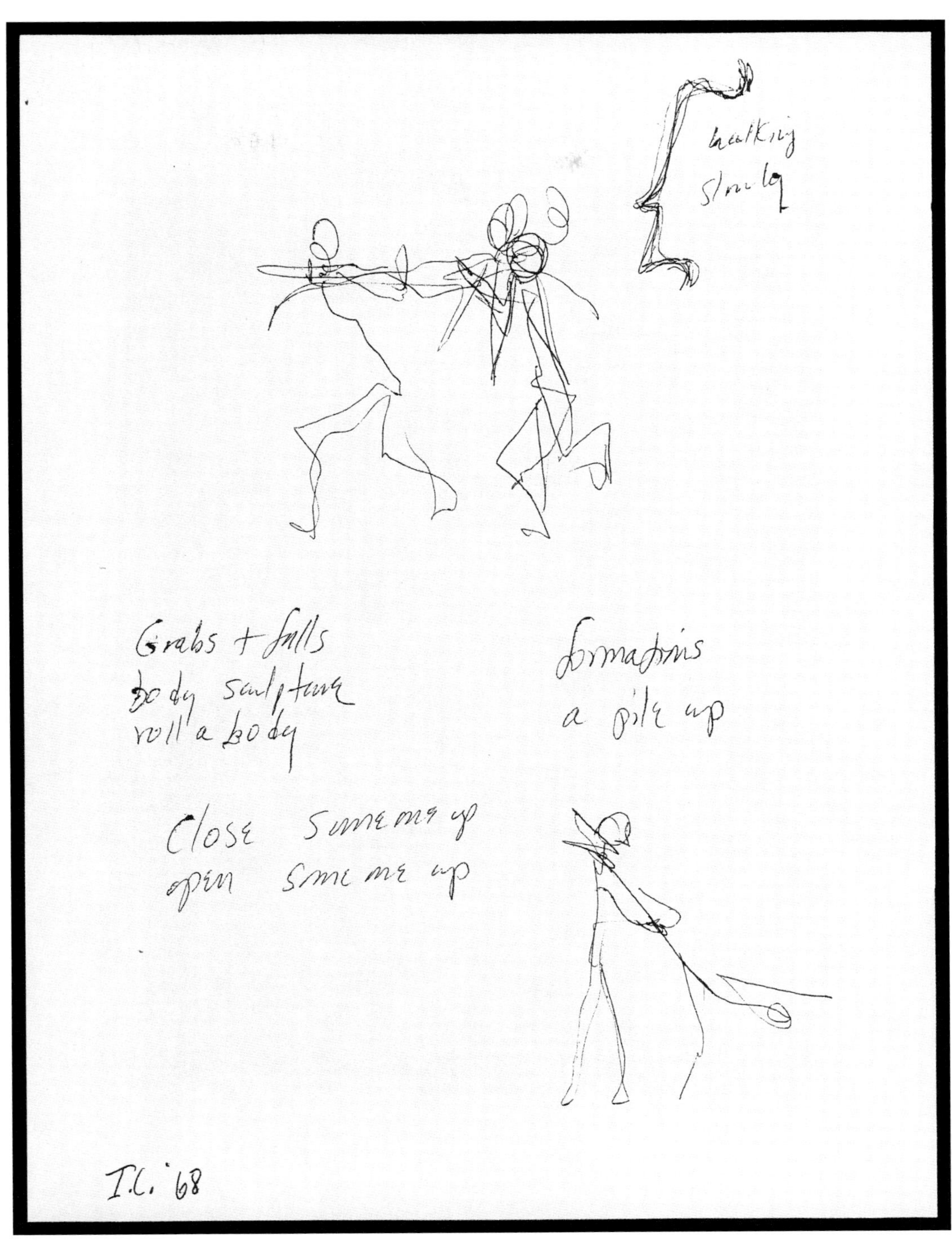

walking
slowly

Grabs + falls
body sculpture
roll a body

formations
a pile up

close some me up
open some me up

I.C. '68

Fig. 32 Carolee Schneemann, notes and sketches for *Illinois Central*, ca. January 1968. Carolee Schneemann Papers, Getty Research Institute.

on one hand in an upside-down position. Brief instructions are written next to the figures: "close someone up," "open someone up," they exhort, addressing both the artist and the performers of the work.[120] Reading the photographs alongside the drawings reveals how central they are to establishing an ethos of mutuality and exchange for the work.

Here, the tension between *Illinois Central* and *Made with Paper* reached its apogee: between Schneemann's use of paper to interpolate social and environmental violence and *Made with Paper*'s framing of paper's plenitude as an endless stream of single-use objects. Throughout her career, Schneemann sought to show that the bodies and lands that the United States sought to destroy were real. And so the tree and the shreds became a signifier for other, equally vulnerable, nongrievable lives in 1960s geopolitics: the Illinois plains shorn of trees to make room for industrial agriculture and the Vietnamese citizens being attacked with petrochemical-based weapons. The shreds, when positioned next to the tree forms, addressed the violence that the United States was perpetrating against the Vietnamese people during the Vietnam War's twelfth and most savage year.

By the time *Illinois Central* came into being, Schneemann and many other artists were reconsidering the ways that materials could shape and change the body, even from the inside out. She had written to both the Dow Corporation and Playtex in 1965 and 1966 asking for free plastic wrap and bras for her performance works. But 1967 saw a massive protest in Chicago against the Dow Corporation because of its role in manufacturing chemical weapons in the Vietnam War, and Schneemann became more involved in public conversations criticizing corporations and their role in the military-industrial complex. Dow was then manufacturing Agent Orange, which was defoliating vital mangrove forests in Vietnam's Mekong Delta and other waterways. By that year, Dow was also the main manufacturer of Napalm B, a mixture of gasoline, benzene, and polystyrene that formed a volatile chemical weapon and could be packed into canisters and dropped from an aircraft from above.

Napalm attracted considerable criticism in the press for the physical pain it caused when deployed: it acted like liquid fire on the skin, clinging to the body and burning off layers of flesh or melting flesh into clothing. Just six months prior to *Illinois Central*'s first performance, Schneemann took part in a series of public protests in New York's SoHo neighborhood organized by the activist group Angry Arts against the War in Vietnam. Almost all the images reproduced for flyers and posters at the Angry Arts events came from an article written that year by William Pepper in *Ramparts* magazine, "The Children of Vietnam." The article focused on the devastating effects of the war on children (fig. 33). It described the conditions under which the children lived, emphasizing that many of the refugee camps were built on large garbage mounds.

"The Children of Vietnam" was so popular that it was reprinted as a stand-alone pamphlet, with an added foreword by the famed American

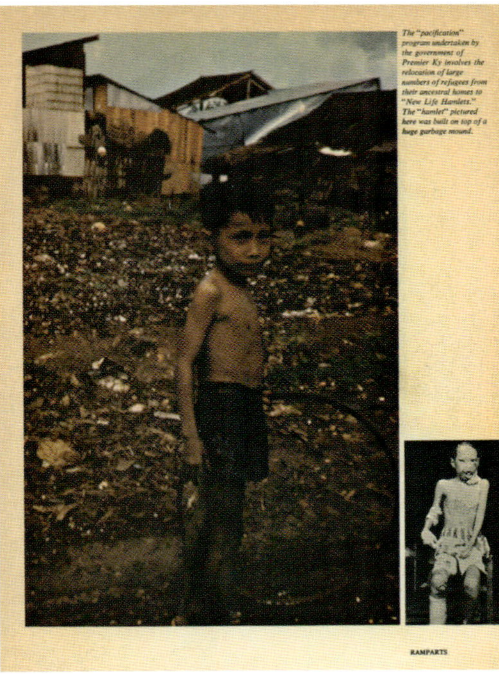

Fig. 33 Page from William Pepper, "The Children of Vietnam," *Ramparts,* January 1967.

pediatrician Dr. Benjamin Spock. The article's numerous references to bodily damage and children's suffering made it a touchstone for activists seeking proof of the Vietnam War's wastefulness and the Vietnamese people's vulnerability to American aggression. Unflinching photographs of scarred or injured children were juxtaposed with healthy children playing with garbage in hastily constructed refugee hamlets. In one caption, a triage nurse confesses, "I never left the tiny victims without losing composure. The initial urge to reach out and soothe the hurt was restrained by the fear that the ash-like skin would crumble in my fingers."[121] Evoking precarious physical states—such as damaged skin on the verge of disintegration—was just one of many ways in which bodies were rhetorically and politically mobilized in terms of wastes and externalities in the Vietnam era.

Paper became central to antiwar protests in 1967 because of precisely the qualities that it shared with flesh. A sheet of paper is vulnerable to all kinds of injuries: pull it apart, and it tears; crumple it, and it yields to a clenched hand or any pushing force. Four months after *Illinois Central* debuted in Chicago, nine people in Cantonville, Maryland, would be convicted of burning draft records using an outdoor fire laced with homemade napalm. Father Daniel Berrigan, one of two Catholic priests who had taken part in the action, wrote a written statement from prison that would become a sarcastic refrain for social activists: "Our apologies, good friends, for the fracture of good order, the burning of paper instead of children, the angering of the orderlies in the front parlor of the charnel house."[122] The poet Adrienne Rich responded to Berrigan's elegy with her own poem, "The Burning of Paper Instead of Children." In it, she concedes to paper's inadequacy as a material for transmitting ideas, distancing written language from actual bodily harm: "I know it hurts to burn. There are flames of napalm in Catonsville, Maryland. I know it hurts to burn. The typewriter is overheated, my mouth is burning. I cannot touch you and this is the oppressor's language."[123] As entire populations became imbricated with waste, paper was a powerful metaphor—a stand-in for precious flesh.

Destroying a paper environment thus became a homeopathic gesture, rehearsing the human devastation in Indochina by destroying the problematic structures that treated Vietnamese bodies as cheaply as the magazine pages upon which they were printed. In short, paper exposed the image's economies and ecologies of violence and also deconstructed them. Through its use of materials, *Illinois Central* mobilized debates about escalating violence between the United States and Vietnam, *highlighting* the problem of the environmental devastation there. To dive into and wear the shredded checks—themselves a product of deforestation—was to participate in and become a part of commerce's unmanageable waste products. The shredded paper's jagged, shaggy material qualities also worked to shift the numbing effects of photographic images in the news media.

In 1969, Schneemann expressed frustration in an interview with how mass media spectacularized violent news. "What people really want is *tactile information*, to be in touch with their physicality, to be able to communicate, and to grow, to touch one another and be touched," she told the filmmaker Gene Youngblood. "We get all this information and there's absolutely no way to react. You're reading some horror in your newspaper while eating your doughnut. And if you were a natural animal you'd at least scream for fifteen minutes or chop the sofa into bits."[124] This kind of volatility is evident in *Illinois Central*'s shaggy conclusion because the paper, when worn, implicates the body as a flexible and malleable image surface. Shredding the paper and otherwise disrupting its surface made the projected images in her performances more friable. In so doing, the performers deconstructed the very things that are used to control human beings in mass media contexts. If newspapers turned readers into desensitized consumers of America's violence against the Vietnamese, the paper made the performers vulnerable in real time. The paper touched them and could even hurt them, but it could not be ignored or set down—a perfect counterpoint for news and mass media, in front of which we might feel "touched" or "struck" by something but without a way to respond in kind. True to this ethos, viewers were invited to join the performers and jump into the mulched paper pile—a union that constituted the conclusion of the work. However, many of the audience members were shy about painting themselves instead of the performers. As *Illinois Central*'s final lights pulsed across dozens of bodies covered in amorphous scraps of paper, the chance to transform into anything—much less "natural animals"—faded in kind.

I suggested at the outset of this chapter that science studies can help us think through the implications of Schneemann's contributions. Not only did she perform the ways that human beings and materials are bound up in natural cycles, but she also centered drawings not just as the product of the artist's creative mind but as volatile actants in a larger, constantly changing system. In many ways, her work responded to new challenges about how we see and experience our surroundings—challenges that were gaining ground in the nuclear age and that undermined Immanuel Kant's assertion that materials are purely mechanistic: "We cannot even think of living matter as possible. (The concept of it involves a contradiction, since the essential character of matter is lifelessness, inertia)."[125] *Body Collage*'s and *Illinois Central*'s critical reception helps us understand exactly what was in play in this moment in 1968, just as American industrial paper was being reevaluated, and a mere three weeks before the violence of the American-led Tet Offensive in Vietnam would become global news. Schneemann's shredding of materials, coupled with the fracturing of the photographic image, implicated industrial capitalism in the transformation of native landscapes both at home and abroad. In fashioning her own feminist ecological framework, she demonstrated how the daily and even cursory parts of artistic practice hold within them complex considerations of nature, labor, and the environment.

CHAPTER 2

Off the Record

William Anastasi's Stenographic Body

In the summer 1968 issue of *Arts Magazine,* the critic Gregory Battcock addressed William Anastasi's work in a review, "Four Artists Who Did Not Show in New York This Season." In reverent terms Battcock described a proposal that Anastasi had made for a room-sized work at New York's Museum of Modern Art (MoMA), *Canvas Wall,* which MoMA had rejected. Anastasi wanted to record a short sixteen-millimeter film of the walls in one of MoMA's galleries when they were cleared of all other art. Then, in the darkened space of that same gallery, he would project the film onto the blank walls he had just shot. *Canvas Wall* would inscribe the wall's surface as a point of interest, but one devoid of visual incident—compelling because excluded. As the wall provided a support for the projected moving image, so too did it supply raw material for the film itself. Battcock's review praised the artist's ability to animate the wall's surface qualities, and thus to create innumerable possibilities of out of very little. "The observer is left with nothing. Or perhaps, with everything," he marveled. "Almost anybody disgusted with the hypocrisy, distortion and reaction characteristic of the modern world is bound to find Anastasi's idea worth, at least, considerable speculation."[1]

For Battcock, looking at a surface and seeing nothing—or, conversely, seeing everything—was an antidote to the misreading of data and the telling of lies. Artists and critics alike in the mid- to late 1960s saw exciting possibilities for the work of art's environment to act as a surface or a medium, to direct attention to art's nested situation within many types of spaces: art, film, room, mediascape, world.[2] That same summer, Anastasi continued making two series of works on paper that, like *Canvas Wall,* did not show in galleries but probed other interior spaces. One was the *Pocket Drawings,* which converted the space of a pants pocket into a drawing space (fig. 34). To make the *Pocket Drawings* and his concurrent *Walking Drawings,* the artist drew on the sheet with a 6B or 8B pencil during his walks across New York City or while sitting still in public spaces, the paper adapting to both the shape of his hand and the fabric of his pocket. The works shared similar features to a private sketchbook—namely, the ability to condense the continuous panoramic scope of individual viewing within the repeated small

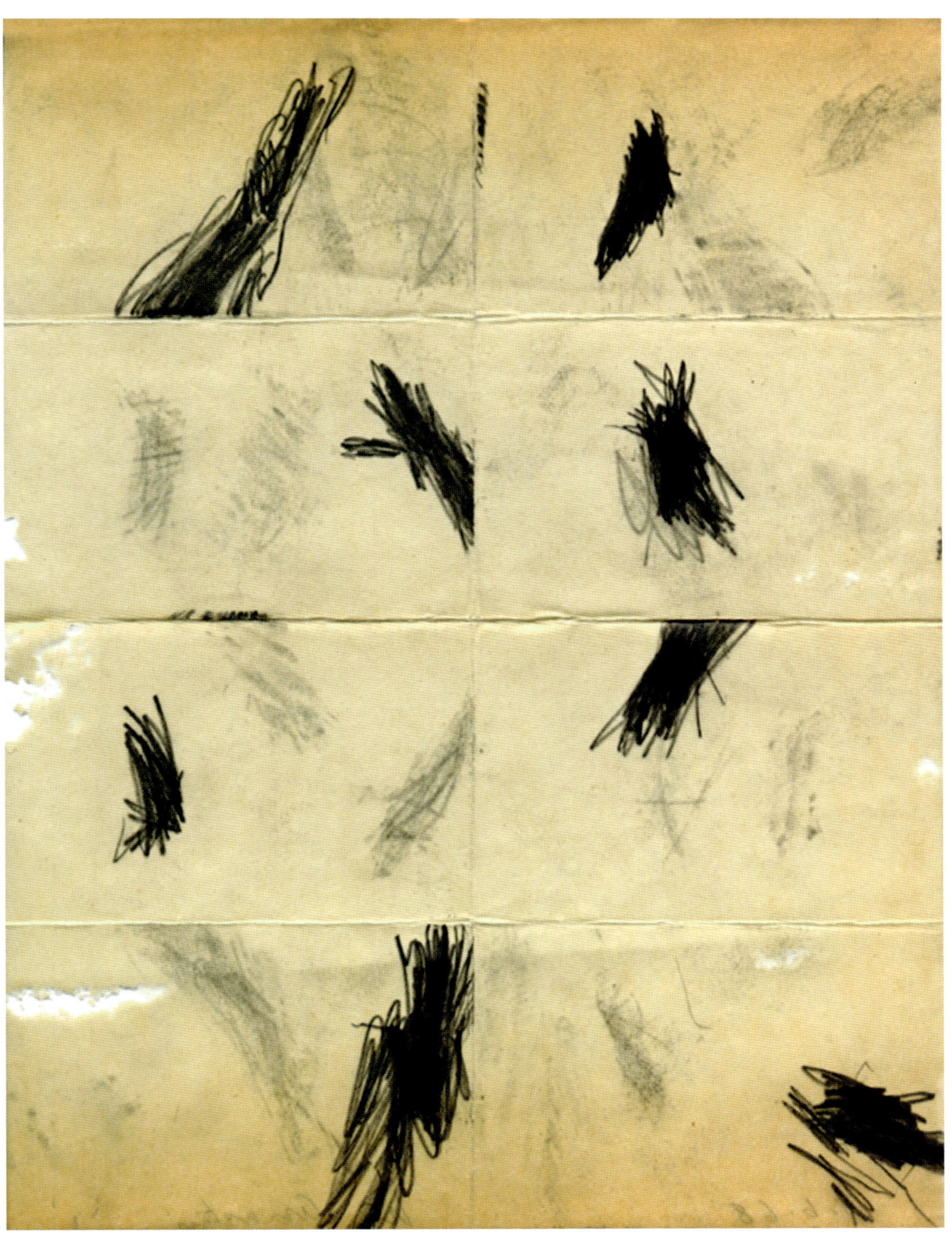

Fig. 34 William Anastasi, *Untitled (Pocket Drawing)*, 1968.
Pencil on paper, 14 × 10⅞ in. (35.6 × 27.6 cm).

scale of the page—but Anastasi didn't look at the drawings while he did them. Instead, he looked straight ahead while he sat or at his surroundings as he walked. Like the filmed surface texture of the wall in *Canvas Wall,* these folded papers exposed the many possible glitches in the human gaze.

These drawings, hidden from the artist's sight, were not exhibited publicly until the mid-1980s. Their marks convey a liveliness that only occasionally overlaps with sentience; in this one, the looped masses float inside the paper's folded edges as though inhabiting a strip of celluloid. The surface— the outermost boundary of a thing, and a space where observation is understood to begin—becomes not just a bonded home for choices and marks but instead a set of material relations that alerts us to the very conditions under which appearance, disappearance, and distortion become possible. This all takes place through obstructing the artist's gestures rather than highlighting them: fold a piece of paper in half, then fold it in half again. In dividing the paper into smaller cells, the surface assumes an ever-smaller scale, with some pleats folded away but still present. As the material yields under your hands, more and more paper rectangles become temporarily unavailable to sight, perceivable only through touch. One might then begin to recognize the matter around the paper as similarly variable, even volatile. In playing with this bit of unsighted space, one might feel compelled to take notice of not just its exterior but also, as the Spinoza scholar Gilles Deleuze described, "the pleats of matter that surround living beings held in the mass."[3] Another untitled drawing by William Anastasi, dated the same year as *Canvas Wall,* uses this very play between folds and sightlessness to record the city dweller's chance movements in public space (fig. 35). The work uses a sheet of transparentized paper folded in half three times and tucked into a pants pocket, then unfolded, taken out again, and put back in at undetermined intervals while the artist went about his daily activities. The result is a semitransparent surface that has been folded, unfolded, flattened, and then folded again many times, which registers a series of small yet disciplined gestures.[4] It was as if they were recorded to be forgotten, to evade the status of such well-known modern art axioms such as *message, sign,* and *gesture.*

The artist's body is implied; we fill it in. Yet the cosmic, expansive quality of the page remains—held in relation to the closed act of reaching into the pocket, which is itself layered within a larger public negotiation of urban citizenship. Spinoza, who sometimes speaks in the twentieth century through Deleuze, proposed that each body was part of a vast ocean of material interactions and "requires a great many other bodies, by which it is . . . continually regenerated."[5] And indeed, as this chapter attests, the assemblages of paper, environment, and gesture that Anastasi created in his drawings provide a template for both visualizing and experiencing data while foreclosing on the possibility of mastery. His method leveraged the position of the amateur scientific investigator, by then robust among late modernist artists, and overlaid the pink-collar practice of stenography to

    Off the Record

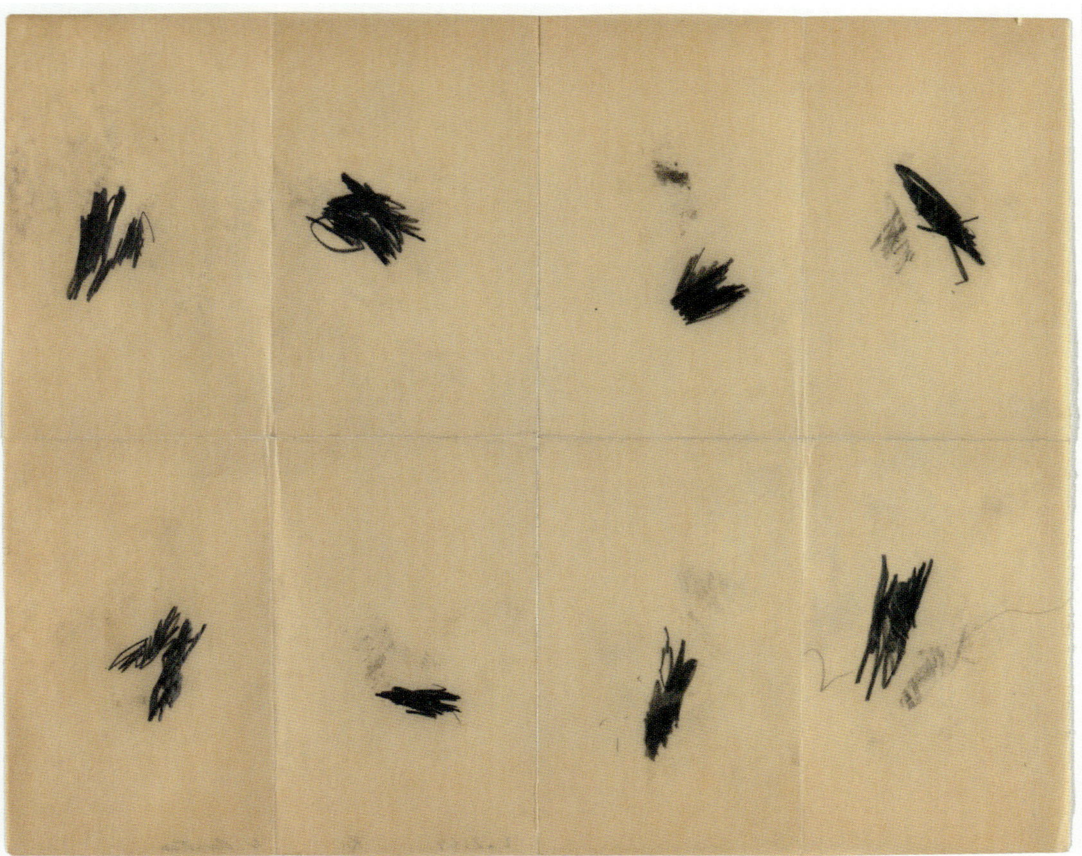

mix inscription with transcription, to advance the idea that one mark was as good as any other, regardless of the impulse or entity that generated it. The results accorded everyday life the status of something empirical. Paper, after all, holds a singular power to mediate real-time events and record them as data. In seeing a page creased with folds and bearing the marks of an ordinary event, we unpack its past actions in an "urge towards [perceiving] some vacuous definiteness," as Alfred North Whitehead called it, and *undermine the processing of the information.*[6] We thus enter a situation in which we can see and feel pure data—deposits of intelligence not yet subject to discourse—at the same time as traces of actual events and occasions.

This chapter attends to two of Anastasi's drawing series created in the 1960s and 1970s, the *Pocket Drawings* and the *Subway Drawings*, that used paper to disrupt conventional readings of data that the printed page might otherwise solicit. The series demonstrates a growing concern with the body's enmeshment within a set of mechanized, predetermined conditions—such as professional training, urban infrastructure, or language itself—that place individual persons within grammars of classed and gendered behavior. Anastasi, an untrained artist, found the physical handling of data and language particularly attractive. But his questions about the interfaces between the body and the mechanized world were also vital for other

Fig. 35 William Anastasi, *Untitled (Pocket Drawings)*, 1969. Pencil on two sheets of transparentized paper, 10⅞ × 14 in. (27.6 × 35.6 cm) each. Museum of Modern Art, New York, Gift of Sarah-Ann and Werner H. Kramarsky.

artists and movements with whom Anastasi was in dialogue and sometimes collaboration, including Fluxus, minimal, and conceptual art discourses. In my analysis, anti-Cartesian theories of embodiment take notes from feminist phenomenology to consider the ways that different bodies inscribe and transcribe in different ways. Since the pocket and the subway are both microenvironments that accord men more abundant freedoms than they do for women, it feels germane to reflect on the ways that an environment, especially an urban one, accrues and transfers meaning—not just through Anastasi's work but in any instance where a city is traced and used as a co-creative force. Ultimately, these two series, with their simultaneously empirical yet impaired use of space and place, created evocations of data that struck at the core of emerging conceptual concerns: what possibilities might arise from tracking the body within an automated, bureaucratized, gendered world?

Stenography provides the focal point for my analysis, and not just because it helps to reveal Deleuze's pleats of matter or Spinoza's other bodies. I position stenographic practices—some done on paper, some done with the body or the filmic medium as in *Canvas Wall*—as significant to the postwar artistic practices that eventually consolidated into conceptual art. In using a stenographic approach to representation, Anastasi adopted a stance that was different from the practice of publishing one's notes, as Marcel Duchamp had done to great fanfare in 1966, or from other critical stances that early conceptual artists took in relation to writing and language. It allows us to imagine the body's daily habits as full of possibilities, while also being conscious of how those habits, those mannerisms, become reduced to mere data. Roughly a dozen years after the *Walking Drawings* and *Pocket Drawings* created newly mobile relationships between the individual artist and her surroundings, the *Subway Drawings* shifted the work of recording and transcribing onto Anastasi's body within the context of a moving machine—a body that is prone to unconscious adjustments in response to its environment. This somatic approach relied on a thoughtless but nonetheless purposeful way of navigating public and private space, in line with the writings of Maurice Merleau-Ponty, whose text *Phenomenology of Perception* had been newly translated into English in 1962 and whom Anastasi encountered in dialogues with Robert Morris and John Cage.[7] But Anastasi's interpretation of phenomenological ideas was distinct from his peers, most of whom had graduated from art schools. In their physical execution, the *Pocket Drawings* and *Subway Drawings* anticipate (and engage with) more contemporary theories of habit and knowledge.[8]

Postwar capitalist society was defined by the kind of habits and habitus that Anastasi embodied in his drawings: the walking, subway-taking, movie-going, professionally progressing, newly skilled earning classes, people who constituted the economic and social foundation of modernity. These new workers were just as likely to ride the subway to work as they were to work with transcription technologies or listen to recorded music.

Off the Record

Anastasi has spoken of the transcriptionist, the subway, and the atomic bomb as parts of an interlinked system, calibrated to transmit goods, services, and information with ease.[9] In particular, his investigation of stenography within a broader range of recording technologies reveals the subtle ways in which mechanical and bureaucratic structures serve to simultaneously mediate and distort modern life.[10] As an everyday, middlebrow, and often invisible version of a translator, a stenographer relied on a visual language—shorthand—to reorder spoken sound, and so necessarily faced a good chance of error. By positioning the stenographer and other modes of transcription as simultaneously precise and error-prone, Anastasi's drawings expose important tensions between amateur and professional, or between active discernment and passive tracing, that were central to emerging discourses on conceptualism in the 1960s.[11] In Anastasi's drawings, the page is a proving ground with no proof: a field both for performing iterations of a practiced craft and for surrendering expertise to chance. Its surface unlocks a new way of reading what Joshua Shannon has called the period's "complicated relationships to facts, to evidence, and to science."[12]

Anastasi's lack of formal training in art proved little impediment to his professional success in this decade. By 1969, the thirty-four-year-old Anastasi, who had worked as a masonry contractor and brickwork salesman until 1962, was well on his way to becoming a well-known, commercially successful artist. Anastasi's works on paper—the *Walking Drawings,* as well as larger pieces of tar paper smeared with plaster—were what first attracted interest from the gallerists Betty Parsons and Virginia Dwan.[13] Starting in 1966 he had four solo exhibitions of sculpture and photography in rapid succession at the Dwan Gallery—exhibitions that placed him squarely within that gallery's trajectory as an emerging hub of minimal and conceptual artists.[14] Begun as "some kind of therapy" for the artist in the late 1950s, helping him to "forget [himself]" and "forget art history" in a calisthenic exercise, the drawings continued when he moved from Philadelphia to New York.[15] They were made in these city spaces with Anastasi's attention focused on the street in front of him as the marks accumulated on the page in the pocket's interior. Anastasi has maintained this practice using the body's centrifugal motion to generate visual incident, with variations in positioning and setting, for six decades. These drawings now number in the hundreds.

Anastasi displayed all the *Pocket Drawings* as a grid, unfolded. With its snarl of marks gathering at the center of each cell, *Untitled (Pocket Drawing)* incites many metaphors. Each evokes a burst, but also the puzzling paradox of visualizing any process: we see the energy of formation and potentiality while anchored within the boundaries of serial form. As with many grids, too, the small variations between sections invites comparison and sequencing between one another: biological samples on microscope plates, nineteenth-century chronophotographs in the style of Eadweard Muybridge, even illustrated narratives of stellar death. Repeated, they

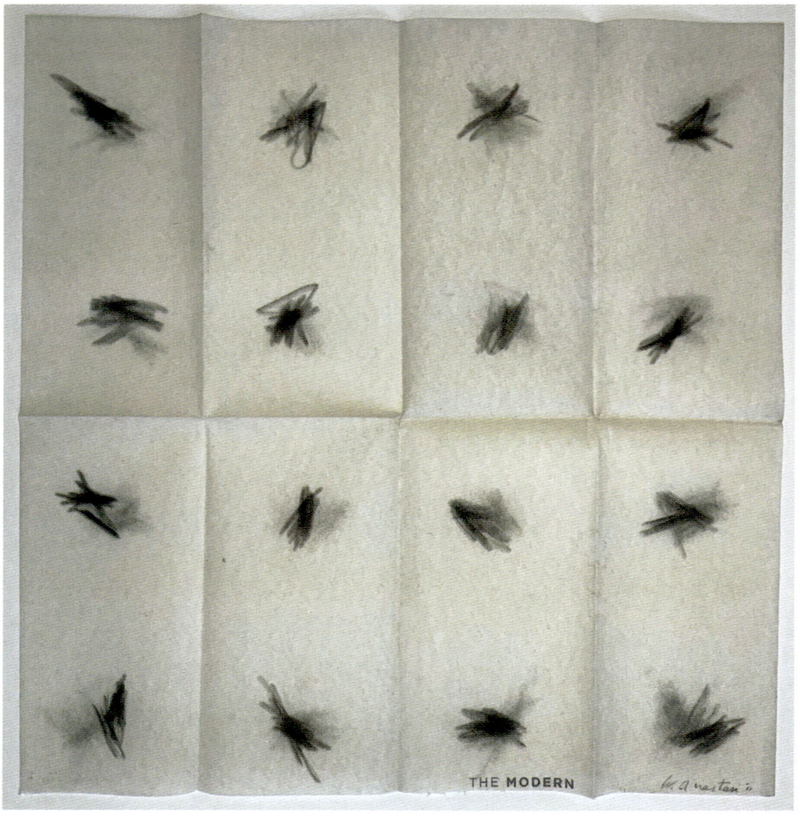

Fig. 36 William Anastasi, *Untitled (Pocket Drawing)*, 2008. Graphite on paper towel from the Modern restaurant, 16⅞ × 16⅞ in. (42.9 × 42.9 cm).

aggregate from a series of singular moments into a broad record of ongoing habit. This habituation is mutual: the paper is habituated to its new, folded shape just as the hand becomes habituated to the pocket in which it rests. Laid across the grid with a consistency that reflects the repetition of everyday travel, the marks condense into a trope even as they individuate themselves. One thinks of semiotics, of semantic significance, even of classification. If the *Pocket Drawings* were meant to be soothing and private, rooted in but also escaping the psychology of personhood, *Untitled (Pocket Drawing)* at the same time gives a sense of the empirical—a test sheet registering the most quotidian components of being a body in the world.

Anastasi made these unsighted drawings within various situations: on the street, in movie theaters, in concerts, but always with the same approach. He couched them within the behaviors that were expected of average citizens in urban spaces: avoiding eye contact with others, for instance, or concentrating on one's own activities to create a semblance of privacy. But as much as they track different occasions, they do not provide any narrative record of experience. Another pocket drawing, this time created forty-nine years later, in 2008, shows no discernible changes in technique to distinguish it from a much older one (fig. 36). Once again, the creased paper grid hints at the standardization that we associate with scientific readouts. Its napkin support makes the object feel ordinary, even fugacious—a napkin, after all, is only useful for a short time—but the signature at the bottom right corner evokes myths of individual artistic expression, and the mystery and authority of the archive. Anastasi produced this work on a napkin, which, as Robert Morris and Andy Warhol had already noted by 1969, was a cliché of the spontaneity of the artist's individual authorship.[16] Yet the artist also chose this napkin intentionally, because of its semantic and textural differences from drawing paper. The Modern, the restaurant at MoMA, wove its dinner napkins with cotton fibers, which occludes the napkin's creases when unfolded.[17] "The Modern" appears at the bottom of the sheet as though it were a title, its definite article a pun on both the evidentiary potential of titles and the branded banality of modern art. Insofar as this drawing is *modern,* it dares us to discredit it, since its preservation, sale, and display further establish Anastasi as a mature artist. Making, eating, valuation, and forgetting all transpire in the same place.

It is compelling, then, to ask what exactly we get out of looking at these works and how this might intersect with the organic, mobile experiences that go into their making. Anastasi chose paper as the substrate for this component of his practice, but he admits that "[at first], I didn't take them as seriously as I did my other drawings. I really thought drawing was drawing, and subway drawing was something else."[18] This aside prompts us to consider not only the drawings' host of references to standing and sitting, note-taking and dictation, scratching and being bored, writing and rubbing, but also what those things conceal. As he tracks and documents his movements blunted by fabric or darkness, he provides a barrier between his work and the gestures, clothes, and mannerisms that provided the grammar for an individual's personal brand in a nuclearized capitalist West. By appropriating a distracted state and applying it as a method for drawing—the form of private expression most fiercely scrutinized by historians and connoisseurs—Anastasi creates with these papers an almost parodic relation with sightlessness. Enlightenment philosophers imagined that blind people held key insights into how vision worked because their other sense faculties became sharper in compensation for their lost sight.[19] Anastasi's occlusions are in some ways no less romantic. In acting out seemingly uncalculated behaviors and always remaining at a distance from expertise, Anastasi may well have demonstrated that parody—or is it fear and wonder?—might be the very thing for which the confusion, inexpertness, and inexactitude make space.

Like Schneemann's supply chains, Anastasi's explorations of his immediate environment found an ideal partner in paper's malleability and portability. Anastasi understood paper as the material vehicle for recording a series of habitual, and continually inexpert, gestures—gestures that challenged positivism in their very irregularity and through which he could project visions of an unpredictable future that included nuclear annihilation. Whereas the paper dresses by Scott and other corporations harnessed a seemingly inert, bureaucratic material to promote fantasies of spontaneous movement, Anastasi promulgated the paper surface as a plane that could simultaneously register the rote facticity of gesture and material through its inertness while opening the sensing body to the material world. By making unsighted drawings within different parameters, either in his pocket or balanced against his body, he conflated writing surface with apparatus, formulating flawed, "dumb" movements into a loose, sensitive, and generative methodology, drawn from Duchamp's conception of the artist as an *appareil enregistrant,* or recording device.[20] In so doing, Anastasi constituted his body as so many particles of matter, like the radio static, tape-recorded white noise, rubble, and nuclear dust that were gaining visibility within Cold War human-nonhuman assemblages. Most important, Anastasi's drawing together of blindness, obtuseness, and amateurism constituted a repetitive countermethod—a form of "calisthenics rather than aesthetics," as the artist has called it.[21] In a moment when questions of personal identity began to merge with the inevitability of nuclear disaster, they illuminate the problems of rational systems within Cold War scientific and bureaucratic discourses.

PRACTICING AMATEURISM IN 1960S NEW YORK

At first blush, Anastasi's drawing practices correlate with the broad trend in 1960s conceptual art that the artist Ian Burn called deskilling, in which US artists responded to postwar commodity capitalism by distancing themselves from the physical execution of their art and rejecting modes of making that required rigorous training. But as Burn has shown, we might also examine this refusal of training as simply a commitment to a new and different mode of knowledge.[22] Anastasi put a great deal of effort into making drawings, a culturally coded practice, quotidian and effortless—a reflexive response to regular activities such as walking and riding the subway. His deskilling was in fact a way of *probing knowing rather than refusing it,* of recognizing that the most uncalculated reflexive behaviors could be observed and analyzed by others, each one becoming minute data points for how one might be judged socially or legally. Once again, the *Pocket Drawings* serve as a working example. The marks in the untitled drawing of 1969 (see fig. 35) do not have the loose potentiality of scribbles, the sense that the artist is gathering together a point that eventually may be made. Instead, the graphite shows small, jagged passages of lines that evoke scratching an itch or boring a hole. The paper's edges are worn down from being carried, but only slightly. An entanglement as well as a support, the page helps demonstrate that these gestures are not natural gestures; they are generated by an encounter that the artist has trained himself not to parse fully. The fidelity of Anastasi's effort is not in question, but the data—the pencil marks—do not show anything. Instead, the drawing reveals the mandate of intelligibility that culture, with its many institutions and codes, heaps upon unprocessed phenomenological experience. We might test this out for ourselves, in our historical moment where we doubt that raw and unprocessed experience is possible. Within the matrix of the cloth envelope of Anastasi's pocket, the blank recording surface bent like a textile in accordance with his body, and the jagged, randomly generated marks, one seeks a modicum of what Walter Benjamin calls *translatability*—that something is meant to be voiced or shown.[23] And, in fact, the action has generated the terms of its translation. In an interview in 2014, Rachel Nackman asked Anastasi, "When do you decide that you will pull out the paper, unfold and refold it?" Anastasi replied, "That's hard to answer, because it's not as though I decide. In other words, I'm not consulting the drawing and saying, 'Is that enough?'"[24] The timing of his folding and marking is coordinated to the impulsive decisions made by his body, which corresponds with its environment to create a system of materials all its own.

Anastasi's uncertainty about whether he *consults the drawing* is crucial here. To consult the drawing directly would subject the paper to the same boundaries and responsibilities as the modern self. Seen through a Spinozan lens, however, his method assigns agency to present forces, regardless of whether a subject generated them. A close encounter with the pocket drawings, then, elicits two key insights into our own moment rife with questions about authentic artistic skill and artificial intelligence. The first is that deskilling in contemporary art reflexively demands a focus on community, as Jacques Derrida, Margaret MacNamidhe, and others have long noted.[25] The other, possibly more obvious but no less exciting, is that deskilling can serve as the grounds for renegotiation of the terms for artistic skill, to give more nuanced names for the role that more-than-human entities play in artistic practice.

In the *Pocket Drawings,* the page is an especially interesting more-than-human entity since it teeters between an archive, an agent, and a tool. Although composition books and other bound notebooks increased in popularity in the 1960s, Anastasi seldom used them. Like Jackson Pollock and his friend Sol LeWitt, he gravitated instead toward white or cream wove paper.[26] LeWitt in particular fed this compulsion, trading pads of drawing paper with Anastasi up until his death in 2007.[27] The drawing pages he used rarely corresponded in a systematic way to the scale of his own body; instead he used the highest-quality paper he could get. Unlike Schneemann's exhortations to herself and artists to use the cheapest, most accessible paper she could find for sketches, Anastasi's connection to the notebook was largely conceptual and performative: the possibility of a blank sheet of paper stood in for infinite potentiality, as well as an assembly of data qua data.

The drawings record the details of physical ambulation, moment to moment, within the artist's surroundings. In 1962, Anastasi moved into an apartment on Eighth Street between Avenues C and D on New York's Lower East Side, which at that time was a low-priced neighborhood of mixed Puerto Rican and German Jewish immigrants.[28] In his early years in New York, Anastasi gave little thought to what kind of art he would produce. The son of Sicilian immigrants and a divorced father of three, Anastasi, by his own admission, was driven first by a desire to move on from his work as a "bricklaying apprentice and owner of a masonry-contracting firm." "Artist" had an aspirational cast to it; he remarks that his mother told him it was the highest vocation for which he could strive.[29] The activity that provided him with a stable framework for this ambition was drawing, which is something he had done "almost every other day since childhood."[30]

Anastasi wove drawing into his walks to and from his jobs in sales and service management and to silent film screenings at MoMA. He worked as a restaurant manager and as a door-to-door salesman selling photographic portrait packages for Olan Mills and books for Doubleday Press. These jobs were regimented—measured by footsteps taken and dollars earned—and contingent on maintaining a charismatic warmth and ease.[31] His drawings, by contrast, were unstructured. He made them on small and portable sheets of paper that he could fold and place in his pocket. The minute differences of his body placement forced his hand to adapt to change; it was a hijacking of early modern theories of creativity, posited by Leon Battista Alberti, that located drawing in the mind rather than the body.[32] The timbre and length of each line were determined by the roominess of the pocket on his blue jeans or work slacks. After walking and drawing for a bit, he would refold his paper, like a notetaker or a clerk folding a sales receipt, and start again. Later drawing series transcribed the physical experience of other daily tasks. He made the *Constellation Drawings* of 1962 and 1963, for instance, while listening to music, and the *Subway Drawings* (1975 to the present) harnessed the motion of the New York City subway to generate pencil or pen marks onto a paper that he balanced on his lap. In these situations, he adapted the act of drawing to accommodate his travels, which shaped his lines according to his environment, the fit of his garments, or restrictions on his proprioception.

Marcel Duchamp popularized this model of the sightless producer when he asserted that there was no earthly reason why a blind man could not become an artist—a claim that interested Anastasi greatly.[33] The *Constellation Drawings* and *Walking Drawings* were shaped not just by Duchamp's popularity among New York avant-gardes of the 1960s but by his immersion in the downtown New York milieu of minimalist sculptors, Fluxus performance artists, and avant-garde musicians influenced heavily by the chance compositional methods of John Cage and the allover compositions of the New York School. His first exhibition at the Washington Square Gallery, at the southwest end of Washington Square Park in Greenwich Village, included drawings and paintings of Donald Duck, an image the artist could draw from memory—reference-less, if not sightless—as well as early versions of a series of sculptural works made from torn cardboard and brown paper (fig. 37). He called his Donald Duck works "automatic drawings," a nod to the automatic drawing technique that the abstract expressionist painters had themselves taken up from surrealism as a therapeutic technique.[34] The Washington Square Gallery was an organ for an especially

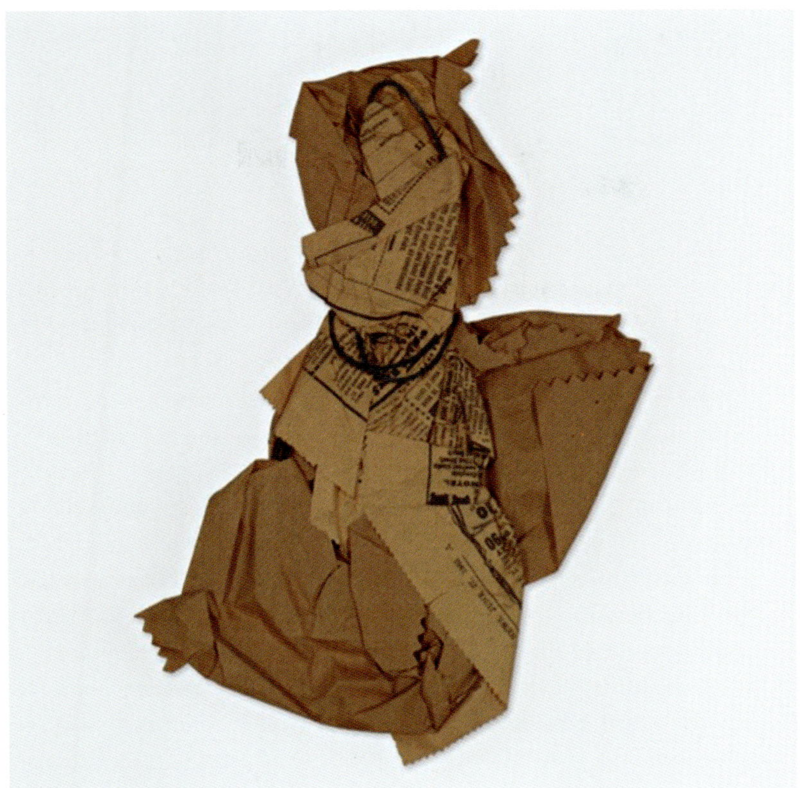

Fig. 37 William Anastasi, *Brown-Paper & Wire*, 1965. Mixed media, 14 × 11½ in. (35.6 × 29.2 cm).

heterogenous group of makers, including international Fluxus performance artists deployed side by side with works by such abstract expressionist painters as Cy Twombly in exhibitions including the Perpetual FluxFest in November 1964. The six-block radius surrounding Washington Square Park that abutted SoHo's industrial fabricating spaces and cold-water studio lofts was, as critic Lucy Lippard put it, the "Wild West," and Anastasi formed his practice based on an entire community that celebrated uncalculated gestures before the rigid lines between artistic movements had been established.[35]

Anastasi's attention was drawn not just to the uncalculated but to the unordered. He often invokes a quotation by Heraclitus in his interviews: "The most beautiful arrangement is a pile of things poured out at random"—although Anastasi's preferred translation ends with "a pile of random sweepings."[36] It matches the affinity for disorder, seepage, spillage, and entropy that Anastasi shared with many other artists of this moment, including the artist Robert Smithson, who invoked a version of this quotation in his essay "A Sedimentation of the Mind" (1968). Anastasi and Smithson knew each other, but not well; the gallerist Dick Bellamy had introduced them. Like Anastasi, Smithson executed numerous works on paper in the 1960s such as *1000 Tons of Asphalt* in 1969 and *A Heap of Language* in 1966 (fig. 38).[37] There is a significant difference, though, in Anastasi's and Smithson's use of the quotation. Consider Smithson's recourse to Heraclitus, quoted here in full:

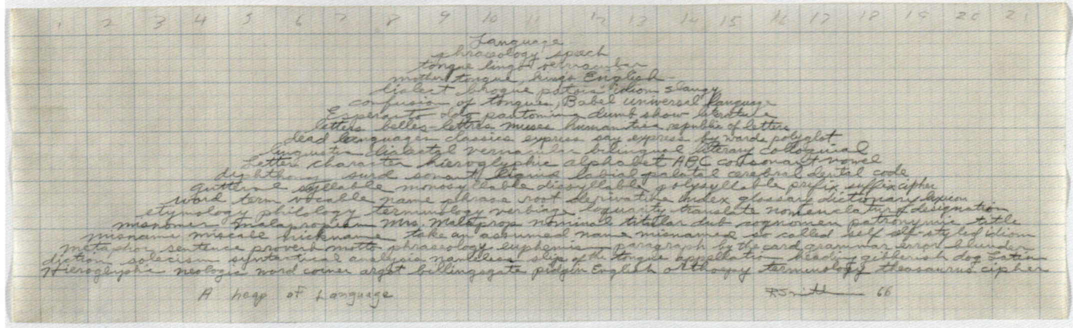

A sense of chaotic planning engulfs site after site. Subdivisions are made—but to what purpose? Building takes on a singular wildness as loaders scoop and drag soil all over the place. Excavations form shapeless mounds of debris, miniature landslides of dust, mud, sand and gravel. Dump trucks spill soil into an infinity of heaps. The dipper of the giant mining power shovel is 25 feet high and digs 140 cu. yds. (250 tons) in one bite. These processes of heavy construction have a devastating kind of primordial grandeur, and are in many ways more astonishing than the finished project—be it a road or a building. The actual *disruption* of the earth's crust is at times very compelling, and seems to confirm Heraclitus's *Fragment 124,* "The most beautiful world is like a heap of rubble tossed down in confusion."[38]

Anastasi favors a janitorial version, orienting Heraclitus's chaos more closely to the scale of the body, to gesture and to sweeping. Anastasi's output, which spans fifty-five years, stages new relations between the human body and its immediate surroundings, unlike Smithson, whose land art projects relied on vast quantities of space and matter drawn from beyond the architectural envelope.[39] In his unsighted drawings, Anastasi stays close to the body even as he departs from it via a meditative state; Smithson, in contrast, uses the space of the page in his drawings to imagine vast piles of matter and language and then concretizes this idea by using representative imagery.[40]

Like Smithson, Anastasi was interested in language and its representation, often in the form of random sweepings, a topic he experimented with through numerous personal transcription technologies during the first two decades of his career. He played with phonograph needles and tape recorders and collaborated with court stenographers on stenotype machines, often using them for recording his (or each other's) actions. In so doing he, like many artists of his generation, obscured the sources and values of aesthetic meaning. His drawings, meanwhile, shifted the work of transcription away from his supposedly skilled hands and onto his body, which responded insentiently to his various environments and situations, making his reflexive bodily movements the sole source as well as the transcriber of his ideas. He rigorously trained himself to do the drawings, but the goal of his training was to draw effortlessly, "like breathing."[41] He established a set of quasi-ecstatic, meditative strategies that shifted decision-making power onto trains, sidewalks, clothing, and urban infrastructure. In so doing he probed questions not just about agency but about professionalism: did the experience, qualifications, habitus, or practice of the artist somehow alter the quality of the mark? Anastasi was an untrained artist who had formerly trained to be a contractor, and his sculptural work occasionally alluded to his construction skills.[42] His drawing practice, however, helped him reconcile two emerging identities: one as a dedicated, ambitious artist and the other as an amateur conceptualist—this latter position being the standard one in emerging conceptual practices but nonetheless requiring standardized behavior.

In the 1960s, many artists in Anastasi's circle embraced everyday tasks and gestures as source material for their work. The sculptor Robert Morris and the choreographer Yvonne Rainer, who lived in the same studio building as Anastasi from 1964 to 1968, stand out in this regard. Rainer created task-based dances that were built around repeated bodily movements that "required no skill or little energy" but found her earliest experiments frustrating because it was difficult to make them look unremarkable within a timed dance performance. "Every time [an] 'elbow-wiggle' came up, one felt like applauding," Rainer recalled.[43] Morris, a sculptor, sought to make sculptural objects that "[broke] the tedious ring of 'artiness' circumscribing each new phase of art since the Renaissance."[44] The kinetic painter Carolee Schneemann, another neighbor, produced performance works with groups of individuals whom she found on the street, individuals who might be "eating [their] soup in a beautiful way" but lacked the established vocabulary of the trained dancer.[45]

By embracing stupidity and rigidity, to use Anastasi's terms, the drawings exposed the grace of the body negotiating an organized system. It is interesting that Anastasi began referring to his own sculptures as "dumb art" and his drawings as "old-fashioned work" around this time, a move that seems to anticipate, and refuse, the possibility of being romanticized.[46] A dumb artist is not even intuitive; they promise no secret revelations, as would the romantic model of the "naive" artist. Anastasi's method is likewise distinct from the "fast thinking" that Donald Judd discussed in his reviews from this period, in which an artist might articulate, with light and rapid effort, a possibility for arranging a quickly perceivable whole out of many parts.[47] Instead of completing a vision, Anastasi was simply—to borrow John Cage's phrasing—an "empty glass into which anything [could] be poured," as at home in the studio as in the subway or on the sales floor.[48] Anastasi's frequent intellectual sparring with Morris in this period makes his framing of himself as "dumb" even more interesting. Whereas Anastasi was well versed but self-taught in literature, philosophy, and art history, Morris had a graduate degree in art history; Anastasi therefore positioned himself in opposition to the art history and formalist criticism that Morris often disavowed through parodies and strident polemics.[49] To invoke the French philosopher Jacques Rancière, Anastasi developed such an intuitive, comedic approach to works on paper because of his desire to "experiment . . . with the gap between accreditation and act."[50] In Anastasi's drawings, paper was a material across which experience and knowledge could quickly converge.

Paper was central to Anastasi's appropriation and simulation of experimental methods because it helped him to mobilize the methodological inconsistencies of the amateur, a title he magnified through his engagement with art centered on other professions in which he was obviously, glaringly an amateur, particularly stenography. Amateurism was a popular position in modern and postmodern avant-gardes, and it often overlapped with note-taking and record-keeping. Marcel Duchamp had transposed the *flâneur*'s aimlessness and indifference in relation to the urban landscape by distilling it into the sculptural readymade. In 1966, Duchamp published his notes, *The White Box (A l'Infinitif)*, the third of three volumes over a fifty-two-year period. They were distributed over 268 pages, often in interchangeable order (fig. 39).[51] Note-taking and its public display were a research method for a nascent form of "playful physics," an attempt to bring art's emotionally charged qualities into relation with rigorous standards of science and measure.[52] But these standards must also be flexible, distant, even indifferent to socially constructed notions of what a professional scientist should do. Duchamp held that artists should avoid professionalization at all costs and that there were "two kinds of artists: the artist that deals with society, is integrated into society; and the other artist, the completely freelance artist, who has no obligations."[53]

Such amateurism emerged as political in postwar neo-avant-gardes, whether grounded in agitprop politics or within abstract expressionist resistance to fixed categories.[54] Rancière, who in 1968 broke with his mentor

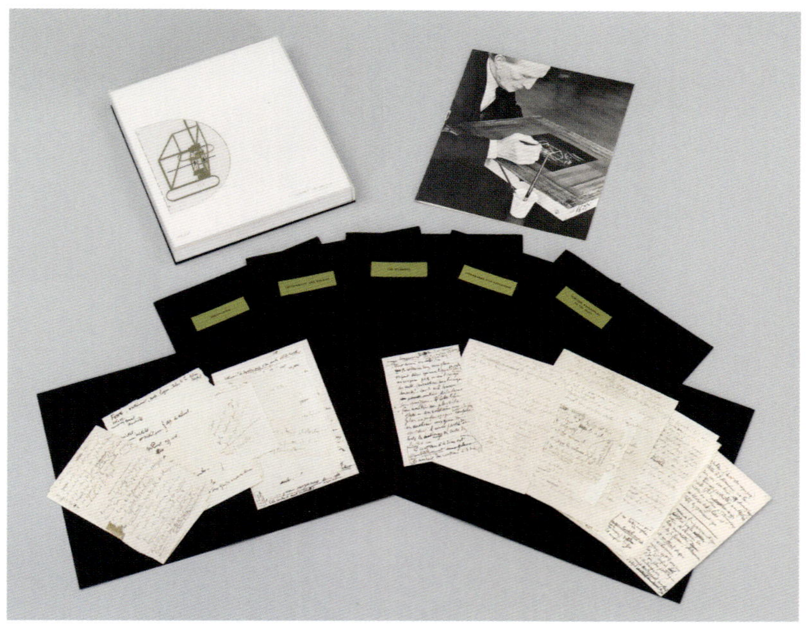

Fig. 39 Marcel Duchamp, *The White Box (A l'Infinitif)*, 1966. Mixed media, box (closed): 13⅛ × 11¼ × 1½ in. (33.3 × 28.6 × 3.8 cm). Edition: 145/150. Whitney Museum of American Art, New York; purchase, with funds from the Postwar Committee, the Grace Belt Endowed Purchase Fund and the Richard, and Dorothy Rodgers Fund.

Off the Record

Louis Althusser's modernist polemics on the matter of spontaneity, located amateurism firmly within the realm of theory as well as politics. Amateur thoughts and practices could "sideline the authority of specialists" by "re-examining the way the frontiers of their domains are drawn at the point where experience and knowledge intersect."[55] The amateur is free to defy known taxonomies, replacing unifying theories with explorations of the gaps between intellectual propositions. "I have imitated, parodied, certain professions," Claes Oldenburg wrote in his notes published in *Artforum* in 1966. "Now I am beginning to parody the scientist and the inventor (something like that is what Duchamp did all along)."[56] True to his dialogue with the elder artist, Oldenburg released *Notes in Hand* in 1970, an artist's book that condensed his ongoing collection of pressure binders full of notes (fig. 40). The book's cover shows Oldenburg scratching his arm with his left hand, an arch reference to the titular "Hand" holding the notes. The photograph linked Oldenburg's thoughtless, intellectually vacuous, even boorish gestures with the uncalculated quality of the handwritten material inside. On one side of each page of the book were early sketches, notes, and illustrations; on facing pages, Oldenburg decoded the material for the reader. At the end of the book, there were notes on which pages were developed into final projects.

Scholars have framed Anastasi's works on paper in terms of their surrealist lineage, positioning his speculative, seismographic drawings as a reworking of automatism—an attempt to transcribe past surrealist tactics into purely physical, rather than psychic, terms.[57] But rather than seeking to record an event, which lay at the center of surrealism's fascination with machines and machine politics, Anastasi's tactics might be seen as part of a larger examination of work and agency in the downtown New York art world of the 1960s, when amateurism, liberation, and chicanery were playfully explored even though hard-nosed professionalism was necessary to succeed in the gallery system.[58] Skill was at the forefront of artistic discourse in the Vietnam War era. Julia Bryan-Wilson and others have explored the implications of the terms *work* and *worker* for artists during this decade, pointing out that artists grafted different kinds of labor onto their respective practices, often in performative ways, extracting social and professional benefits as a result.[59] Anastasi's contemporaries such as Robert Morris and Carl Andre did this through tactics that, as Bryan-Wilson puts it, "connected art to work while also removing artists from labor's specific class formations."[60] Anastasi's approach to the unique forms of nonagency inherent in stenographic work and my analysis of it here suggest a different valence, instead asking: What are the ethical stakes of an artist quoting professional behaviors at which he was quite adept but were outside his social milieu? If the British artist Roy Ascott was correct in his assertion that "to attempt to unravel the loops of creative activity is, in many ways, a behavioral problem," might we not see the performance of classed and gendered behaviors as a way of working through certain anxieties about professionalism?[61]

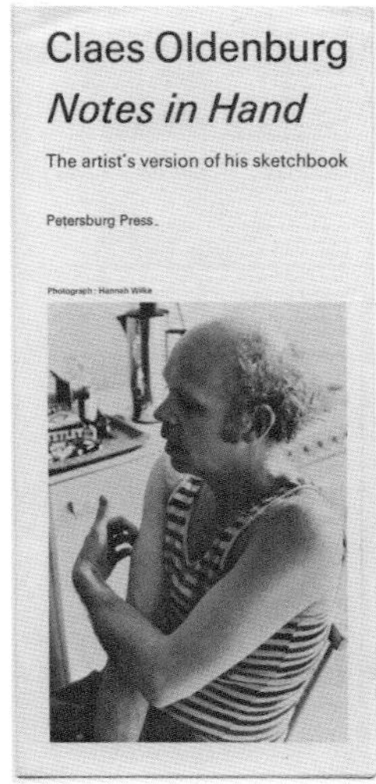

Fig. 40 Claes Oldenburg, *Claes Oldenburg: Notes in Hand, the Artist's Version of His Sketchbook*, 1970. Offset-printed, accordion, black-and-white, 8¼ × 3⅞ in. (21 × 9.8 cm), 6 pp. Edition size unknown, unsigned and unnumbered. Paula Cooper Gallery.

The idea that embodied actions undergo specific semantic processes to become behaviors had an entrenched history, both within the New York art world and within linguistic and social sciences. Ever since Harold Rosenberg had called for "a new kind of criticism" in 1952, "one that would distinguish the specific qualities of each artist's act," the stage had long been set for the commodification of specific artists' techniques.[62] Anastasi's own choices sometimes fell under this rubric, as when Gregory Battcock discussed the artist's work once again in a 1970 *Arts Magazine* article. By this time Battcock's fandom extended beyond *Canvas Wall* to more of Anastasi's wall pieces, asserting that "the earliest forms of painting involved 'paint' applied to a surface directly, as in cave paintings, or frescoes." In turning to the wall, Anastasi was "rediscover[ing] issues that were pertinent to the origins of painting, and [that] had to be rediscovered in order to clear up the aesthetic tyrannies that make up our modern art heritage."[63] The article legitimized Anastasi, Frank Stella, and other contemporary artists by comparing their choices with the existing art historical syntax, and it attached

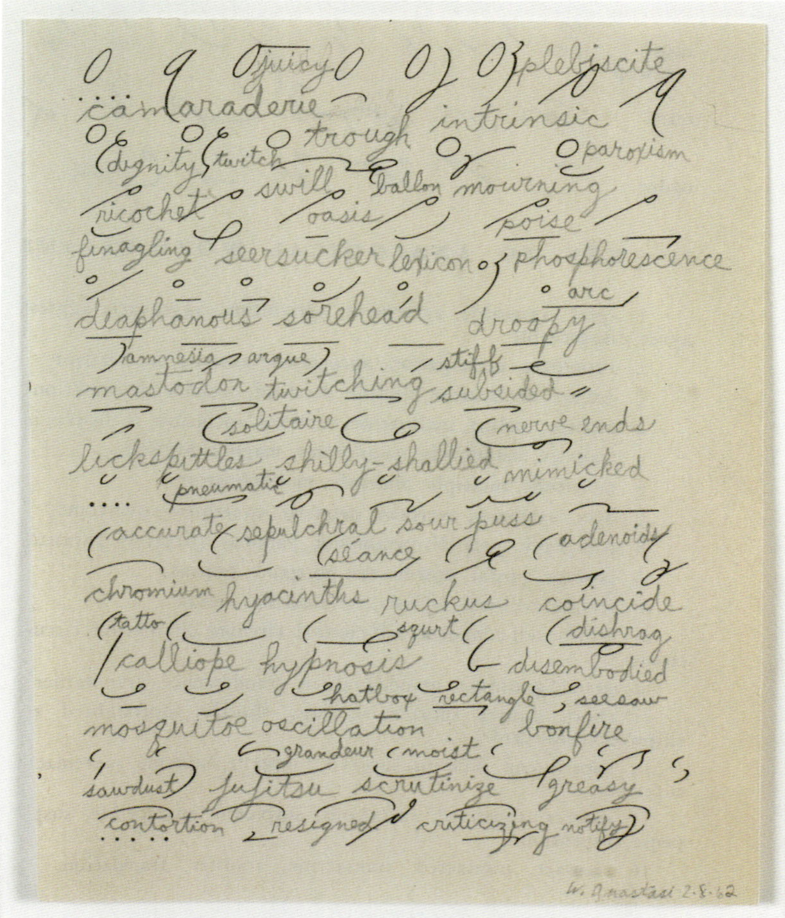

Fig. 41 William Anastasi, *Word Drawing over Short Hand Practice Page*, 1962. Graphite on found paper. Sheet: 5⅞ × 4⅜ in. (14.9 × 11.1 cm). University Museum of Contemporary Art, UMass-Amherst.

 Off the Record

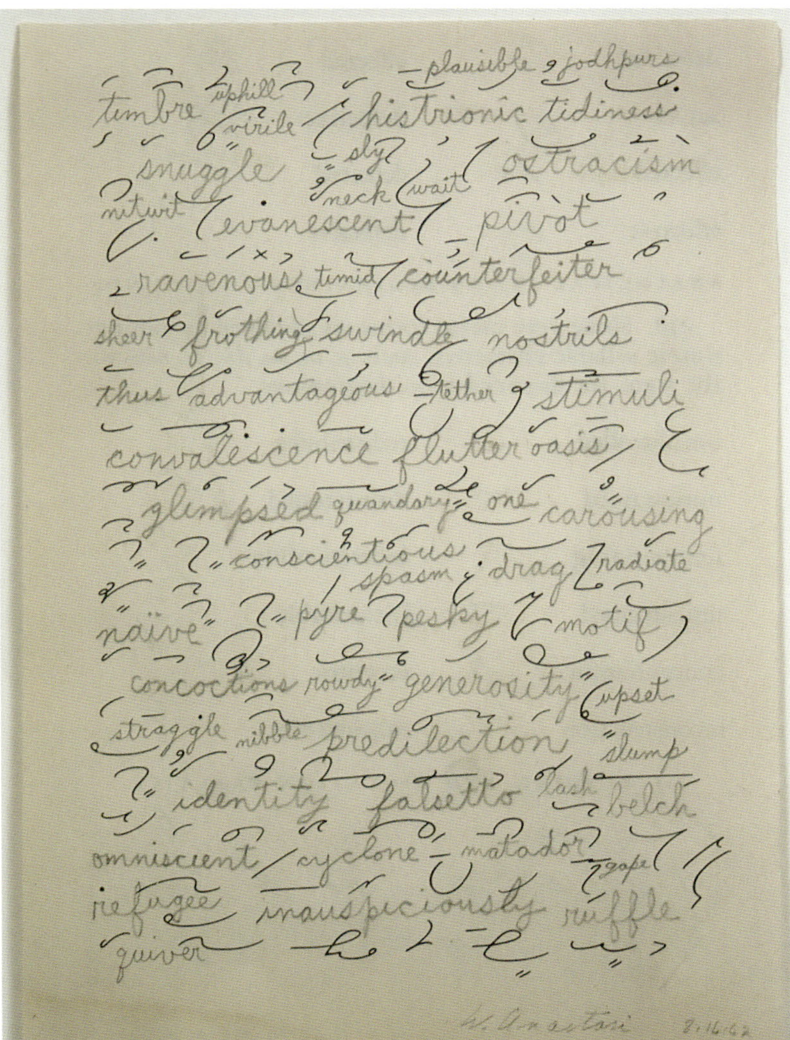

Fig. 42 William Anastasi, *Word Drawing over Short Hand Practice Page*, 1962. Pencil on found paper, 11½ × 10¾ in. (29.2 × 27.3 cm). Pennsylvania Academy of Fine Arts, Gift of Sarah-Ann and Werner Kramarsky.

the seemingly novel notion of art's environment to the absolute longue durée of painting itself. A gesture could innovate, or it could rediscover; either one was ripe for consolidation.

This context is worth considering in relation to Anastasi's early explorations of the highly sensitive, rigorous, and aural approach to language typified by professional stenography. Two drawings on found paper produced in 1962 tamper with the professional skill of transcription (figs. 41, 42). Using a practice page designed for professional stenographers, Anastasi penciled a series of words between the lined exercises, adapting his word choices to the available space on the printed page. Here the artist takes the found papers as a ready-made exploratory space and attempts to adapt to the pedagogies that its printed surface provides: writing in his own English handwriting between a set of symbols that stood for spoken words. Stenography is a phonetic way of transcribing sensory data that requires vocational training: a stenographer writes down words as they are heard,

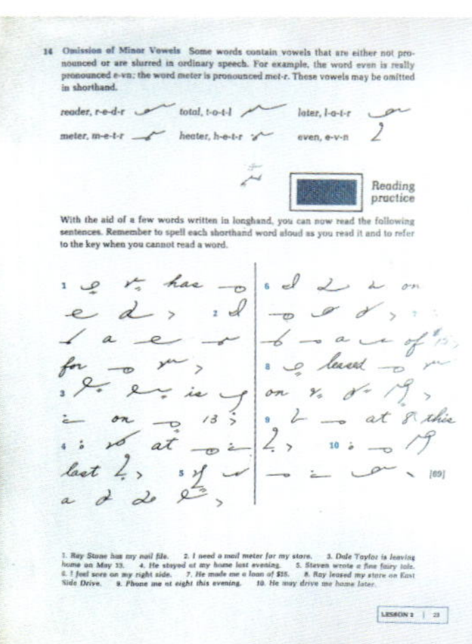

Fig. 43 Illustration of reading exercises in *Gregg Shorthand, Diamond Jubilee Series,* 2nd ed. (New York: McGraw-Hill, 1971).

dropping the silent letters in each word to make a compact approximation of it using symbols.[64] Exercise books for stenographers used written drills to build transcription speed (fig. 43). Anastasi could not read stenographic forms, so the two drawings convert a rigorous training space—the space of a profession he did not practice—into an arena for casual, ad hoc exploration. Anastasi recalls that, for him, the practice pages presented a spatial puzzle: unlike his later *Walking Drawings* and *Pocket Drawings* on blank paper that he felt free not to consult, some spaces were "begging" for larger letters, while other parts of the page were so compact that he had to use his own shorthand to make them fit (such as *squrt,* in the lower middle register of fig. 41).[65] His cursive words are rich with consonants and diphthongs— the sounds that stenographers listen for in order to choose which symbols to write—which detaches them from their denotative meaning and renders them auditory forms. *Lickspittles, chromium, amnesia:* these words constitute a worthy stenographic drill in themselves.

In conceiving the page as a puzzle that anyone might work out, Anastasi offers a Rancièrian approach to paper, as a surface synonymous with both knowledge and experience simultaneously. For most artists, paper was an undeveloped space bursting with possibilities; it was also a display space for synthesized knowledge, acquired through skills and drills. It was common, in fact, for observers of neo-Dada and early minimalist works to discuss them in terms of the exercise. The critic Eugene C. Goossen romanticized this component when discussing minimalist artists in 1966 referring to Carl Andre's "Platonic . . . beauty of lathe, ruler and square."[66] By 1970, so many artists employed ready-made materials to be thrown away later that the critic Lucy Lippard frequently spoke of "conceptual demonstration."[67] But Anastasi's hacking of stenography pages shows us that the exercise is marked by the categories that coalesce around its repetition, including gender, as well as its distinct material entanglements. As someone repeats an exercise, their professional or physical capabilities develop. Practice becomes codified work; behaviors become manners. Anastasi anticipates Rancière's

Off the Record

formulation by exploring some kind of gap—that between consolidating guesses into beliefs, between a problem and the steps needed to solve it.

Continuing to scan these shorthand practice page drawings invites still more thoughts about the exercise book and the space for writing that it creates. Here, the page is a register of learned gestures and also the way out of them; the paper charts the ways that the world trains the body to move. The exercise book's continual leaves, some filled and some unfilled, show the architecture of the learning process through the matrix of individual experience. They are of no consequence to anyone but their maker and the reflection of the larger structures for learning and thinking of which they are a part. We watch speech joining a wider "world of thoughts, or a sediment left by our mental processes," as Merleau-Ponty puts it, with paper as the organizing field—the ground for Heraclitus's random sweepings.[68] Learning takes on an atemporal quality as well as a spatialized form, one repetition after another, which Anastasi negotiates by yielding to it. He appropriated a space that was not designed for him, something that is supposed to reach a skill to someone else. By trying out this exercise, Anastasi allowed it to change his work and subtend his growing community of artist interlocutors.

By yielding—that is, by sensing and responding to the paper field's putative desire for more or fewer letters—he overcomes the resistance inherent in any new project. William James argues that yielding to overcome resistance is a form of habituation—a parallel learning process that is situated between physiology (the question of the body's mechanical functions), phenomenology (the problem of how the body learns of a space as it unfolds through that very space), and social theory (since habit also encompasses habits of mind). To approach the spaces and apparatuses of writing "exercises" enjoined the notion of *habit*—which, in numerous philosophical traditions, is understood as rote, mechanical, and unconscious thought—with *habitus,* which various thinkers in sociology describe as a learned set of social behaviors developed in response to the conditioning of a particular social group.

Beginning in the nineteenth century, habit was seen as psychological; it went hand in hand with taste.[69] Essays and compendia by numerous US authors between 1945 and 1965 accelerated this connection, analyzing the habits of social classes to identify, target, and prioritize certain ones over others. In addition to the cultural historian Russell Lynes's much-reprinted essay of 1948 "Highbrow, Middlebrow, Lowbrow," which explicitly linked habit with habitat, these texts ranged from legitimate sociobehavioral studies (such as Alfred Kinsey's *Sexual Behavior in the Human Male* and the books and symposia that followed) to behavioral surveys meant to make American consumer habits legible to a curious public and professional marketers, such as Leo Bogart's *Age of Television: A Study of Viewing Habits and the Impact of Television on American Life.* Anastasi, who came of age after abstract expressionism's focus on the expressive self, distrusted all psychoanalytic frameworks for analysis; he refers to his work as "phenomenological rather than psychological."[70] His ideas find closer kinship in the work of the philosopher Catherine Malabou, who contends that habit is not only a way of adapting the body and the self to external stimuli but also a field for reversing active and passive energies in order to process changes in our surroundings.[71] Everything from turning a lock into a key to mastering portfolio presentations constitutes habituation, and the merest beginning of solving those problems—inserting a key for the first time into a lock, for instance—habituates not only human behavior but the lock as well. Each time, the lock gets easier to open, the exchange of energies functioning at the material as well as the physiological and social levels.[72] This analogy is apt because of the way Anastasi places more emphasis on allowing other kinds of agency to come into play when he makes drawings; he made these works to "forget himself," to evade the very notion of the fixed self and conditioned behaviors, and he used stenography precisely because he could act as an agent of transposition.[73] In the *Pocket Drawings,* the act of *walking,* itself a conditioned behavior, neutralized a purely psychological interpretation of habit.

The gendered connotations of professional stenography are also worth considering. By 1930, 95 percent of trained stenographers were women.[74] In the bureaucratic culture of the postwar United States, the stenographer was continually associated with her omnipresent notebook or typewriter—as Friedrich Kittler put it, "the conversion of a profession, a machine, and a sex."[75] Even after the publication of the Diamond Jubilee shorthand textbooks in 1949, which made shorthand easier to learn, the stenographer was engaged, omnipresent, and servile, but also at constant risk of making errors. Marcel Duchamp's invocations of stenography, newly in print in the 1960s, would have illuminated for Anastasi the libidinal, liminal potential of servile collaborators.[76] In fact, in an essay of 1917 in *The Blind Man,* Mina Loy also mentions stenography as a tease directed at women in Dada and surrealist circles; women were sometimes treated as stenographers and told to take dictation at parties.[77]

Anastasi deploys stenography as an emblem of this kind of professionalization. Where he finds that fusion creatively productive, others, including Susan Sontag and Jacques Derrida, have prodded more directly at the reductive qualities of such stenography. Sontag, for instance, argued against strict mimetic representation in art, referring to it pejoratively as "atomistic visual stenography." To Sontag, stenography denoted rote copying, just as it denoted representation and professionalization for Anastasi. It was amateur, hackneyed, and indicative of a retrograde view of American culture. Sontag's essay "America, Seen through Photographs, Darkly" (1977) about the poet Walt Whitman positions him as the impetus behind a uniquely American approach to picture making. She argues that Whitman's poetry, particularly *Leaves of Grass,* approaches American life as an array of ordinary, singular, but all equally interesting subjects. His poetry worked to eliminate the value judgments that divided aesthetically worthy subjects from unworthy ones. Whitman believed that "the majesty and beauty of the world are latent in any iota of the world," and Sontag notes that American photographers of the twentieth century labored to capture the beauty of ordinary subjects, such as city streets, immigration offices, and tenement buildings.[78] Although Sontag uses the word *stenography* only once, and pejoratively, she mobilizes the term in a way that speaks uncannily to Anastasi's project. She attributes the stenographic transcription of reality to a maker's innocence and naivete—she all but calls it dumb art—but also compares it to meditation. She called Whitman's verses "a psychic technology for chanting the reader into a new state of being. . . . They are functional, like mantras—ways of transmitting charges of energy." For Sontag, stenography was passé—a representational method that implied that "no moment is more important than any other moment; no person is more interesting than any other person."[79]

For Derrida, stenography is a pliable and codependent form of writing that "links you, like a leash in the form of an umbilical cord, to the paternal belly of the State."[80] He quoted Friedrich Nietzsche's Fifth Lecture to introduce this idea, which I also quote here: "The student listens. When he speaks, when he sees, when he walks, when he is in good company, when he takes up some branch of art: in short, when he lives, he is autonomous, i.e., not dependent upon the educational institution. Very often the student writes as he listens: and it is only at these moments that he hangs by the umbilical cord of the university."[81] Here again is the notion of power and autonomy measured against an institutional standard which the writer-artist can either exit or enter. When we *take notes,* we are servile, shifting to the framework of an actor being given notes by a director. The note is taken as a direct result of the unyielding standard-bearer's gesture, the director's guidance handed out—guidance that has generosity at its center. But there is a reason that one would imitate a rote notetaker or even a pen itself. By highlighting the human-object assemblage that operates below the standards of autonomy that uphold and constitute a modern, liberal, thinking person, by bypassing the university in favor of the autodidact and the wayward stenographer, Anastasi posited knowledge as something that emerged imprecisely. Through the exchange of sensory data, habit, reflex, and chance (rather than from the diagnoses of trained experts), experience and knowledge create fertile gaps between themselves, thus making possible what Erin Manning has called "the intuitive process for activating the relational composition that is life-living."[82] To reject professionalism is not to reject knowledge; paper is a democratic and democratizing medium on which anyone can represent experience and knowledge.

Deferring to the page's lack of proof creates space for all objects, particularly those put into circulation as art, to isolate and denaturalize the things we imagine to be inherent or spontaneous. The art historian Alex Potts has observed that sculptural impulses of the 1960s "unhinge tactility from plastic form" in numerous ways, "as if to make the imagined felt encounter with it simpler and more real."[83] Similarly, Laura Hoptman asserts that drawing can also foreground directness and naturalness, as "the most direct and unmediated method of catching the creative process as it happen[s]."[84] While Anastasi's unsighted drawings seem to do this, he also delinks the creative process from an individual self even as he repeats the individual's snarly, scratchy, atomized symbolic language. Paper becomes central, then, in interrogating what constitutes an instrument, what's a tool, and what's an environment. Much of Anastasi's work does this by harnessing or parodying several things that ultimately register on the page: the writing implement, the recording machine, the speaking voice, and the acting body. This parodic mode scrambles his own position as an originary speaker, thus formulating a critique of expertise and skill. Unlike Potts's or Hoptman's assertions in which an object is progressively stripped of its affectations or structural affiliations to facilitate a more "real" encounter, Anastasi follows the critiques of language theorists such as Derrida, who locate language and writing as uniquely tactile and also structural, full of complexities at their core. "Natural writing is immediately united to the voice and to breath," Jacques Derrida tells us. "Its nature is not grammatological but pneumatological."[85] He contrasts this with formalized symbols such as the alphabet, which have a stenographic function: "[Romanized letters] hold meaning in a narrower, stricter place."[86] Derrida's words provide ample foregrounding for Gordon Brown's comment on Anastasi's early work, in 1963: "Anastasi remains an artist because his work is never quite the same as nature," he said, "even if the variation is small, and because he accentuates certain appearances."[87]

Anastasi's drawings are not diaristic notations, but they can be seen as a kind of training diary, akin to a stenographer's practice notebook. Like stenography, the drawings involve a sensitivity to the sensation of perception in a phenomenological sense (fig. 44, see also fig. 35). Stenographers

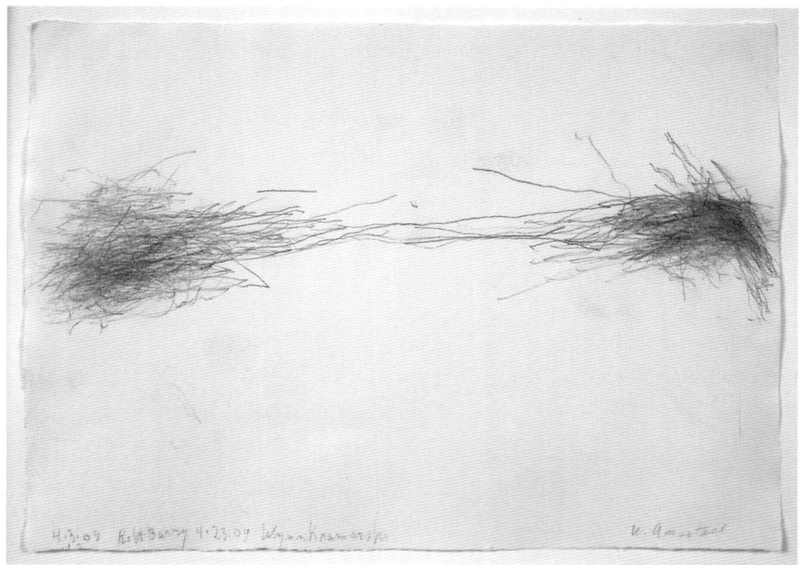

Off the Record

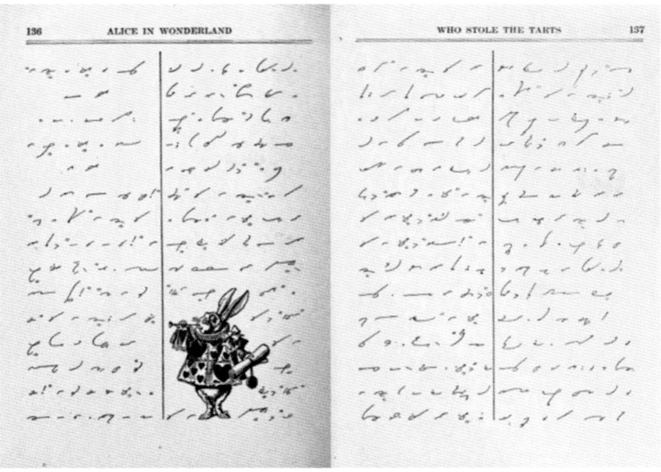

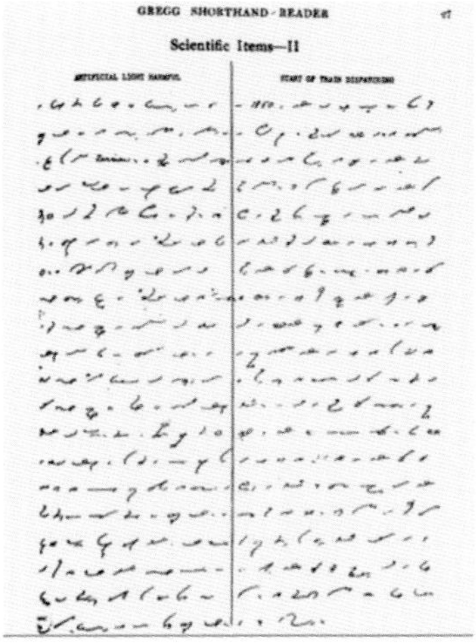

have to know how to listen; they must resist certain impulses and hear spoken words only as sounds that trigger muscle memory. Stenographers, like the various recording technologies Anastasi used in this period, repackage data, but inevitably the represented data contain variations because of human error. This is why many of the educational materials for stenographers are based on simulating the materiality of "real" books and magazines (fig. 45); they emphasize the behaviors associated with reading (such as turning pages and looking at long sections of text) in order to associate stenographic note-taking with these physical processes. When the training materials then shift to steno format in succeeding pages, stenographers would read and write as smoothly as in standard type (fig. 46).[88]

In the drawings in question, the training diary leads to facility in the artist's chosen practice but never quite leads to mastery. We might view his amateur stenographer-scientist model as a calculated engagement with, and distance from, the problems of language and other practice protocol. Anastasi did not use the tools of provisional artistic production particularly earnestly; he considered his blind drawings less "serious" than conventional artistic drawing that moves toward a plan, diagram, or prototype. Rather than using the surface of the paper as a support for thought, he instead leverages it as an encounter with the physical world, implicating both the idea as well as the rest of the artwork in the entanglements of medium. Alchemies occur; something can bend or transform from liquid to solid, and one thinks about the world anew. As Rancière notes, amateur politics allows passersby and idlers to connect "any two points on a topography," pulling numerous wanderings and daydreams into consideration "as a world," matching Deleuze's and Spinoza's desire to see the world as arbitrary points joined together through thought.[89] An inventory of Anastasi's use of other tools—mostly amateur recording technologies at the center of their own enthusiast communities in the postwar period—shows how he explored the physicality of the world as ardent admirer of science, as a technocrat with analog tools.

Fig. 45 *Alice in Wonderland,* published in *Gregg Shorthand* (New York: Gregg, 1919).

Fig. 46 Translations of scientific articles in steno format from *Gregg Shorthand Reader* (New York: Gregg, 1912).

There are key differences between learning, recording, and imitating. Anastasi's interest in paper as a catalyst for interdependence rather than individuation had its roots in his early exposure to mass-market cultural forms. In 1951, at the age of sixteen, he was stricken with polio and bedridden. To ease his convalescence, which resulted in permanent injury to his shoulder, his father purchased a three-speed record player as well as 78-RPM recordings of canonical classical music.[90] The artist has conceded that he has little visual memory and that the experience of sitting and repeatedly listening to Columbia Records' compilations of Beethoven, Rachmaninoff, and J. S. Bach interlaced the production of visual art to the experience of listening to music.[91] While listening, he would draw. Alan Solomon wrote in 1967 that "today's young artists are more at home with the Beatles than with Beethoven," but Anastasi, for all his lack of formal art training, used classical music as a structuring element in several of his drawing series from this decade; his *Constellation Drawings* series was based on Bach's preludes and fugues in *The Well-Tempered Clavier*.[92] Such records did not just form an ambient "soundtrack" to his formal vocabulary; rather, the entire constellation of Anastasi's studio practice was steeped in the visual and material culture of the postwar everyman. His interests in existentialist philosophy, anglophone literary modernism, and, occasionally, High Renaissance aesthetics map closely onto the larger grid of intellectual preoccupations and habits of mind that by the 1960s had migrated from avant-garde circles to lay enthusiasts.

While selling encyclopedias, the self-taught artist began collecting survey textbooks and heavily illustrated art historical volumes, which were marketed in the late 1950s and early 1960s as ways of converting the average reader's aesthetic curiosity into the aesthete's firm and crystalline world of established knowledge. Each produced with more than one hundred color plates, the volumes ranged in topic from the two-volume *Flemish Painting* to the Taste of Our Time series that included *Claude Monet.* The Italian publisher Skira was particularly prolific in this decade (fig. 47).[93] Skira's powerhouse lay in its rehearsal and analysis of Old Master paintings and in

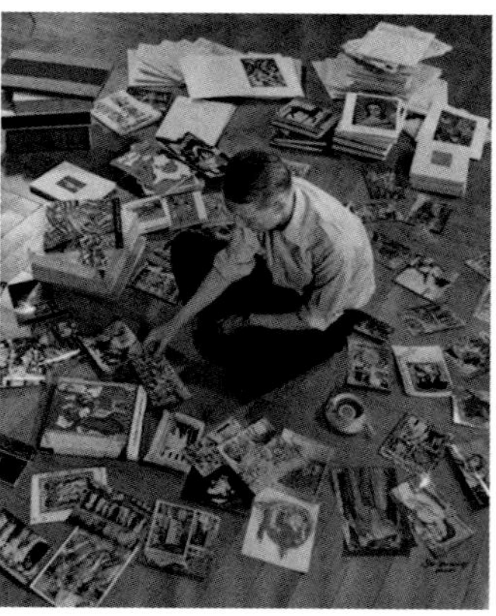

Fig. 47 Skira Publishing photo of Alberto Skira, ca. 1930s, circulated ca. 1960s.

large, color-illustrated compendia of "modern" masters that illustrated and mapped the tradition of largely Western art for US readers. Prentice Hall, a publishing company theretofore disengaged with art books entirely, had by 1958 extended its specialty in "technical books" to volumes about pottery, cave paintings, and ancient Rome.[94] Harcourt Brace followed suit, employing the literary scholar Roger Shattuck to write a chronicle of French avant-garde groups in the first quarter of the twentieth century, *The Banquet Years*. Offered at the not-insignificant cost of $7.50, Shattuck's emphasis on Alfred Jarry, Guillaume Apollinaire, Erik Satie, and Henri Rousseau would have buttressed Anastasi's growing interest in the corner of the French avant-garde that trafficked in pseudo-factual speculative fiction. One reviewer in the *Nation* called this flood of illustrated volumes "Everyman's Museum," "a small gallery of art to be held in the hands," opining that "the twentieth century mind and perception are scaled to accept the part for nearly the whole."[95] Anastasi cut these up, pasting them all over his space. We might call these books a collision and entanglement with the *matter* of learning rather than texts in the epistemological sense. Duchamp's *Boîte-en-Valise*, which was on view in William Seitz's exhibition *The Art of Assemblage* at MoMA in 1961, affirmed this formulation by displaying small printed copies of the elder artist's readymades on the wall just above facsimiles of the published notes, which were set upright in a stack like so many books or records.[96] It would make sense for Anastasi to explore material networks of expertise, teaching himself about a subject as well as instrumentalizing and capitalizing on the dynamics of knowledge.

Not coincidentally, this was a moment when artists' multiples were beginning to ground the art object in the material culture of truth, attribution, and proof and away from the uniqueness and medium specificity of modernist painting and sculpture. Consider Anastasi's work *Incision* (1966), for example. The work's title references what it is empirically—an incision cut into the gallery wall in the rectangular shape of a painting or drawing, or even a circle (fig. 48). Blank and open-ended, it is at once a drawing, a cut, and an articulation of the object-driven terms of Western art. Its cuts and handwritten certificate of authenticity (fig. 49)—both references to writing—explicitly map the pathways that unite paintings, legal documents showing authenticity, and drawing. Again, it siphons aesthetic terms away from those discernible through the sense of sight, asking instead: Does a work of art require detail or even substance to be interesting to the viewer? How can we benefit from meditative contemplation free of details? Unlike similar wall-works in this period, such as LeWitt's wall drawings, *Incision* is almost always executed by the artist. This work is *of the wall;* it is an action done *to the wall;* it displaces the notion that an artwork should be *on the wall*—much like *Canvas Wall* would be a few years later. It is a sketch or an evocation just as much as it is a concrete, empirical set of steps that set out a new axis for looking, interpreting, and attributing value. It *cleaves* in both senses of the word: it parodies the "easel picture" that Rosalind Krauss

Fig. 48 (left) William Anastasi, *Incision*, 1966. One cut made in a specified gallery wall. Sol LeWitt Collection, Chester, CT.

Fig. 49 (above) William Anastasi, certificate of authenticity for *Incision*, 1966. Sol LeWitt Collection, Chester, CT.

so stridently criticized as a component of Clement Greenberg's modernist doctrine, and it also satirizes the monochrome and minimally detailed work of the mid-1960s designed to critique medium specificity; the critic Grace Glueck even referred to a similar work of Anastasi's the following year as "[an] exercise in gag Minimal."[97] It circulates between owners by way of a handwritten certificate of authenticity.

The certificate is part of Anastasi's effort to track and legitimize the work; whoever has possession of the certificate also has possession of *Incision* itself. It is not usually displayed alongside the incision, but in this case the certificate tells a story of its own: Anastasi's crossed-out handwritten text shows *Incision*'s transfers of ownership between 1966 and 2001. In 2001, Anastasi's longtime friend conceptual artist Sol LeWitt acquired the work, and LeWitt's studio assistant accidentally tore the certificate to pieces while making a photocopy of it. Anastasi, delighted at this chance occurrence, taped the certificate back together, allowing it to perform as a legally binding document and proof of the material's fragility. Anastasi's authority to certify things operates, much like Duchamp's, at a distance from professional authority.

These early works synthesize the experience of growing up in an immigrant household whose advancing prosperity was woven into the postwar building boom. His parents were bilingual; his mother had immigrated from North Africa in her childhood, and his father immigrated from Sicily. His father owned a bricklaying business where Anastasi worked starting at

Off the Record

age of twelve, and the artist now attributes some of his early works' formal qualities to the daily experience of this bricklaying business.[98] Virginia Dwan recalls seeing, in his studio on 113 Greene Street, an untitled work consisting of two rows of limestone concrete bricks that, in the construction trades, are typically piled systematically to create a rigid wall (fig. 50). Everything about *En Route,* from its title to its compact, tabular form, shows a slippage with its ostensible referent as a wall or boundary. The work is a rectangular prism, *bozzetto*-like, much smaller than a wall but perhaps en route to becoming one. We can easily get around it. Anastasi referred to *En Route* as "an *objet trouvé*," one that evoked his memories of participating in construction work before abandoning it for contemporary art.[99] This work is, in fact, a strange transcription of sound or film: solid, ineffable, yet displaying an absence of architectural containment, uncoupling the architectural envelope from markers of Western capitalist progress.

Anastasi's indifference to the paradigm of the finished building found kinship with his community's interest in molecular assemblages: things invisible to the naked eye, deploying themselves through the uncontained space of air.[100] In several such works from this period, paper became both a space for diagrammatic (and therefore abstracted) traces of experiences, and also a material fact. Anastasi's *Constellation Drawings* of 1962 harness such an operation, when he made random marks on a white page while listening to the arias and fugues of Bach's *Well-Tempered Clavier,* noting that the results pleased him because of their resemblance to the "random sweepings" of the cosmos. Robert Barry, whose apartment was close to Anastasi's and with whom he has shared a fifty-year friendship, produced conceptual artworks using such invisible forms of matter as inert gases, which structured themselves around mundane forms of connection like telephone calls and traveling to post office boxes. In his work *Inert Gas Series / Helium, Neon, Argon, Krypton, Xenon / From a Measured Volume to*

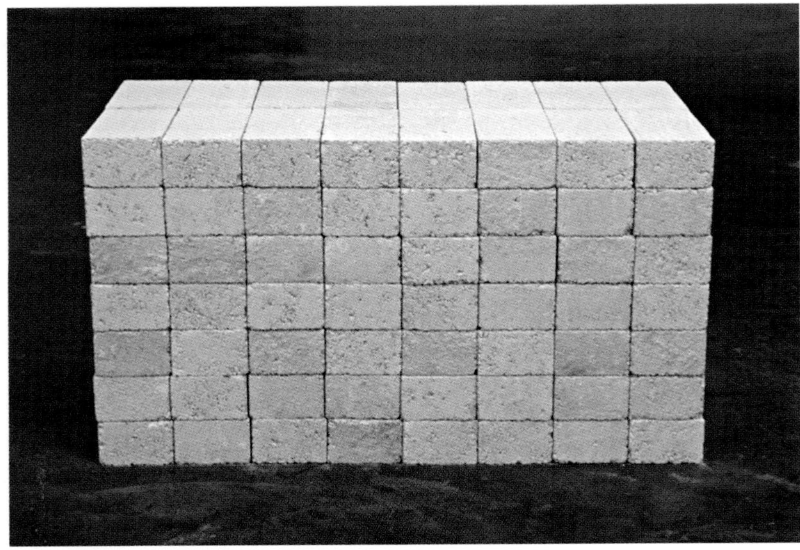

Fig. 50 William Anastasi, untitled brick piece (*En Route*), 1964. Concrete bricks, 16 × 29¼ × 15¼ in. (40.6 × 74.3 × 38.7 cm). Collection of the artist.

Fig. 51 Robert Barry, poster advertising *Inert Gas Series / Helium, Neon, Argon, Krypton, Xenon / From a Measured Volume to Indefinite Expansion,* 1969. Letterpress, sheet: 35³⁄₁₆ × 23⅛ in. (89.4 × 58.7 cm). Published by Seth Siegelaub, Los Angeles; printed by Alphabets Unlimited, Hollywood, CA. Edition of 600. Museum of Modern Art, New York.

Indefinite Expansion (fig. 51), of 1969, five vials containing one measured volume of noble gas each were dispersed at different unspecified locations and documented through photographs. The gases, known as "noble gases" because of their ability to diffuse easily into the atmosphere while maintaining their molecular structure, had no visual imprint or visual record of their acting on (or effecting) the world. These gases spoke to anxieties related to the atomic bomb, when fallout from a sudden Cold War skirmish could disperse into the air at any time. The work was not mounted in a gallery; the address that Barry printed on the poster was a post office box, and the telephone number was connected to a recorded message that described the work. No physical evidence remained of the act; the image here is Robert

Off the Record

Barry's poster advertising the work. The poster's unbroken white surface satirically mimics the much more crowded everyday space into which the invisible gases were released. Here, like Marcel Duchamp's invocations of "illuminating gas" and "love gas" earlier in the twentieth century, material is instantly absorbed by its surroundings, but its effects on the viewer happen within the realm of the social. Although the *tracing* of the work took place along various social and media pathways, such as using the telephone, the gases that composed the work's performative locus existed in no specific place after their release except in their documentation.

A RECORDING DEVICE FOR PUBLIC SPACE

Anastasi's twenty-seven-year friendship with John Cage nourished his interest in drawing and even provided catalysts for new series. In 1965, Virginia Dwan hosted a fundraising exhibition and asked Anastasi to contribute a drawing to it. Anastasi offered a small sketch of a poured-paint work, the only drawing he ever sold in Dwan's stable. At the time, she and Anastasi were planning their first exhibition together, a series of sound sculptures that the artist today describes as "everyday utilitarian objects that 'remembered' the last sounds they had made before they were retired and claimed for [the] exhibit."[101] The works consisted of a deflated rubber tire, a record player, and other objects with their own "natural" sounds recorded on a tape recorder that was then embedded inside the object itself and played as part of the gallery installation (fig. 52). These assemblages were grounded explicitly in the mutually constitutive sensory experience of sound—yet another evasion of vision, foregrounded in the voice of the object that was then snatched away to the silent gallery. They also suspended the labor the objects perform and render them as documents, as paper functions. Dwan told Cage of Anastasi's interest in recorded sound sculptures, and Cage asked to meet the younger artist.

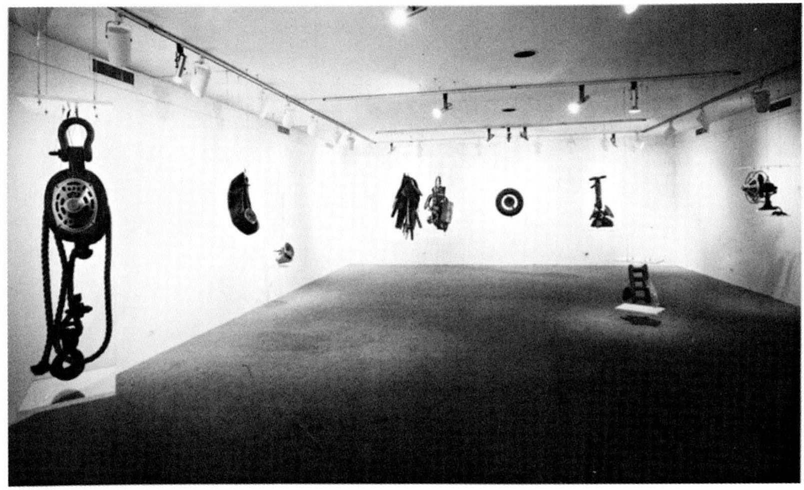

Fig. 52 *William Anastasi: Sound Works* at Dwan Gallery, 1965. Virginia Dwan Gallery Archive, Archives of American Art, Smithsonian Institution.

When Cage visited Anastasi's studio, their conversation fell on the sound sculptures, with Cage taking time to listen to the individual voice and recorded ambient sounds of each object. The elder artist put the work firmly into the terms of nonhuman collaborations that intervened on the environment, making compositions that literalized the "polyphonic" mode of picture-making that Greenberg had described a few years earlier.[102] Cage suggested that "the sound of a glass jug smashing against a cinderblock—about three seconds in duration—would be an ideal percussive staccato to the sound of a pneumatic drill digging up a section of Broadway, which lasts for several minutes."[103] This is another notable use of "environment" that draws together all objects and makes them equal; *Women's Wear Daily* called the sound sculptures "a myriad of ordinary tools and utilitarian accoutrements of our time," cheekily including the office radiator in the list of noted objects.[104] Since listening is also a transcription technology, it feels relevant here to scrutinize Anastasi's longtime investigations in sound art through these early works. Even the reviews' cursory observations about the works, and Cage's pronouncements about their nonhuman liveliness, are surface investigations into the connections between writing and listening and how they are mediated by the page, which is an extension of the environment *elsewhere.*

Cage and Anastasi's friendship was immediate, lasting, and mutually generative. They discussed hermeneutics in literature, particularly the work of James Joyce. Speculations flew; they proposed new literary precursors for Joyce's book *Finnegans Wake,* which captivated them with its "neologistic multilingual puns": the Italian Dominican friar and hermetic occultist Giordano Bruno, perhaps, or Enlightenment philosopher Giambattista Vico, who advocated for "capriciousness and chance" rather than Cartesian theories of reason.[105] A prime ingredient of their rapport was sound, figured as a mode of knowledge-construction, with the document at the center of the operation. Rather than showing an already existing knowledge system, paper is implicated in the construction of knowledge itself, creating a space for portmanteau and other wordplay.[106] Not coincidentally, conceptual artists were also beginning to explore the materiality of language, perhaps also as an arm of phenomenology; the Dwan Gallery hosted a monthly language-themed exhibition as well as the mostly paper-based *Scale Models and Drawings* in January 1967. Anastasi's drawings were not included in these exhibitions, which shows how difficult their categorization and exegesis really was. They were uncoupled from the plans and other project prototypes that made artists such as Robert Morris, Mel Bochner, Claes Oldenburg, and Christo into art-design stars. They invited hermeneutical engagement but were organized around a squirming, bending body that could change spaces and defer to machine movement.

Anastasi's works on paper developed around two distinct axes of sociality in the 1960s and 1970s as these decades progressed: the gallery and the subway. Anastasi committed to producing *Subway Drawings* regularly in the late 1970s on weekday train trips from his apartment on Eighteenth Street to Cage's loft on 137th Street on his way to and from their daily games of chess. Anastasi entered the train at the Twenty-Third Street station, using the local AA or CC lines, whose stops were more frequent than the Express; both the AA and CC stopped at the 135th Street stop at Saint Nicholas Avenue in Harlem, which was the closest to Cage's loft. The trip usually took thirty minutes each way.

By the 1970s, white flight from New York City's urban core had led to rapid decay of public infrastructure, and the subway was a site of frequent mechanical problems and labor struggles. A systemwide transit worker strike, which lasted twelve days in January 1966 and made front-page news, set off a string of other public-sector worker strikes.[107] The strikes' ensuing gridlock set the tone for newly elected mayor John Lindsay's ongoing struggles with labor and anti-gentrification activist groups.[108] Meanwhile, concerns about crime intensified, and the subway's poor lighting and limited visibility were front and center to many users' complaints. Vision and legibility were key to protecting against theft, but also to distinguishing between the data of daily experience and identifying threats. Even after the strike brought improvements in worker salaries and attempts at renovations were made in the mid- to late 1960s, the aging system and cars were the source of frequent complaints for years to come. When the Grand Central end of the Times Square station was improved with orange, blue, and white tiles (the colors of New York City) in late 1966, people remarked mostly on the lighting renovations that illuminated the previously shadowy spaces. As one waitress interviewed said, "I think it's a grand improvement, the walls all bright and shiny, and the lights. Oh, it's never been as bright, even outside on a sunny day." A crew member commented, "All of the crews like it, they like coming to a brightly lighted, clean-looking platform—they can see the waiting passengers better. Most of them are nicer to look at now, because they, too, look brighter."[109] But in May 1970 when an empty GG train crashed head-on into a GG train going the other direction, the public's faith in the New York City transit system reached an epic nadir. "An understaffed, partially dilapidated and poorly maintained subway system endangers the safety of its four-and-a-half million daily riders," one anonymous commentator insisted. "The system is old. . . . Service interruptions are far too frequent. Many station stops are [still] dirty and grim."[110]

The subway as a space—with its "salt and pepper mob" of users who were expected to behave indistinguishably from one another, its advertisements that solicited riders as though they were all one audience—proved a fertile laboratory for introducing "dumb" and blind stenographic practices.[111] It revealed to Anastasi that the permissions and affordances of everyday existence in New York's public spaces were ineluctably contingent on race, gender, and class. Some riders were noticed on the subway and in other public spaces; others were not. Cage observed Anastasi making the *Subway Drawings* several times and at one point noticed a group of teenage boys mocking Anastasi's methods. Anastasi was enormously pleased with this, though Cage exclaimed angrily, "They were laughing at you—the idiots!"[112] New York City was also a battleground for racially charged police practices in the 1960s, with the Congress of Racial Equality (CORE) and the city's Civilian Complaint Review Board highlighting the tensions within the New York Police Department and their policies of arresting African American and Latinx-signifying youth in public spaces.[113] Anastasi's proximity to Washington Square Park made him privy to this and concentrated these lessons for him in a particular incident in 1967, in which he was arrested for defending a young Black man being accosted by the police. Anastasi's usual route through Washington Square Park brought him into contact with the scene, and when he saw the man—later determined to be underage—punched in the face by several New York City police officers, Anastasi followed them to the Sixth Precinct police station on West Tenth Street. He approached the police clerk to make a report as a witness to the case, only to find himself detained by the police involved in the original incident. "I spent the night in jail," recalls Anastasi, "and after that everything became clearer to me."[114]

Although Anastasi's brief imprisonment shattered the promises of anonymity inherent in public space, the subway's mechanical unpredictability sustained the *Subway Drawings*. Since no transfers were involved and the artist usually visited Cage during off-peak subway hours, the artist made his way to a seat, closed his eyes, and opened a drawing pad and balanced it on a board on his lap. Then, holding a pencil at a ninety-degree angle from the board, he rested the pencil against the paper and allowed the movements of the train to create the lines; a recent video still shows that this geometry has stayed the same for decades (fig. 53). He did not guide the pencil in any direction, ceding bodily and creative control to the train. On the way to his

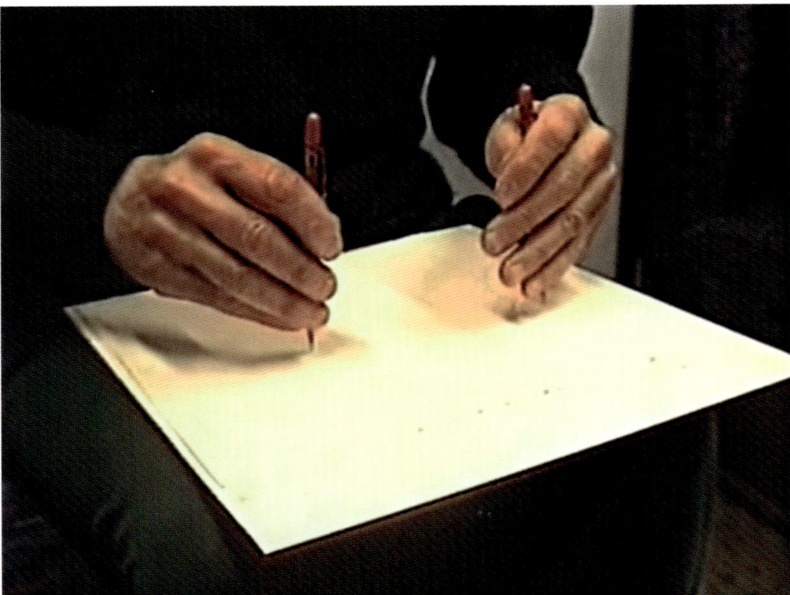

Fig. 53 Video still of William Anastasi making a subway drawing, Copenhagen-Holte train line, 1999.

     Off the Record

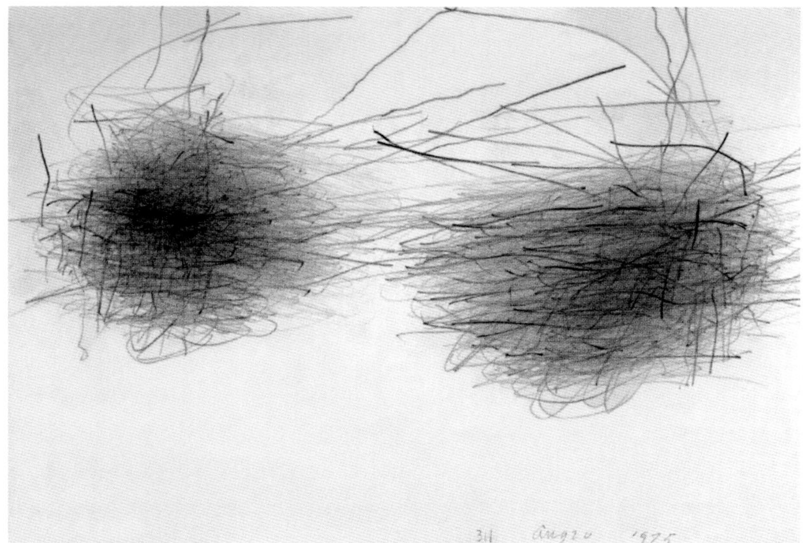

Fig. 54 William Anastasi, *Without Title [Subway Drawing: 3:14 Aug 20, 1975]*, 1975. Pencil on paper, 7¼ × 11 in. (18.4 × 27.9 cm). Collection of the artist.

destination Anastasi held the pencil in his right hand, and on the return trip, his left, thus splitting these works' compositions into two masses of pencil lines. Anastasi continues to make them to this day and has shifted his practice to work ambidextrously, producing the right and the left sides simultaneously.

The *Subway Drawings* show a seismographic (indeed, stenographic) relation to the train's stops and motions (fig. 54). One can see the sharp, wide-spanning lines that register the places where the train's aging brakes ground to a stop. When the train bounced, Anastasi's drawing tool made small skips. Lines crawl across the page but also fan out in every direction from two different centers. There are some variations between when Anastasi first started using this method in the 1970s and his more recent *Subway Drawings*—namely, Anastasi graduated to larger sheets of paper and began using firing-range headphones to block out surrounding noise—but for the most part, it is difficult for the untrained eye to place them in order of their creation date. They illustrate the vast and beautiful differences between each iteration of a single habitual experience; anticipating Derrida, they invite us to equate repetition with potentiality rather than with closure.[115]

Anastasi uses his body to develop a craft and mechanism for drawing, but this craft is never too well developed or skilled, lest it attract the epithet of "slick art" so derided in conceptual circles.[116] He creates his work out in public, against the physical affordances that structure one's everyday phenomenological negotiations with space: subway seats, cars, wheels, and so on.[117] The video still is instructive here, revealing how Anastasi trains his body to rest capably within the vehicle that is his collaborator. They can be stopped and started according to the artist's preference in the moment, switched out for other drawings and returned to later, and are ultimately named after the journey that facilitated their completion.[118] An untitled subway drawing of 1975 shows the result of the recorded marks

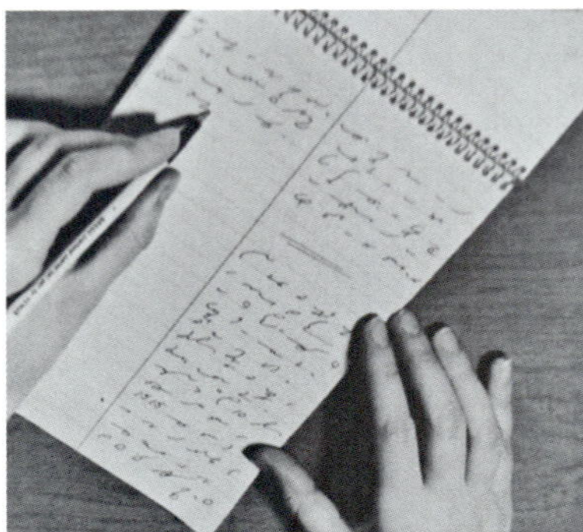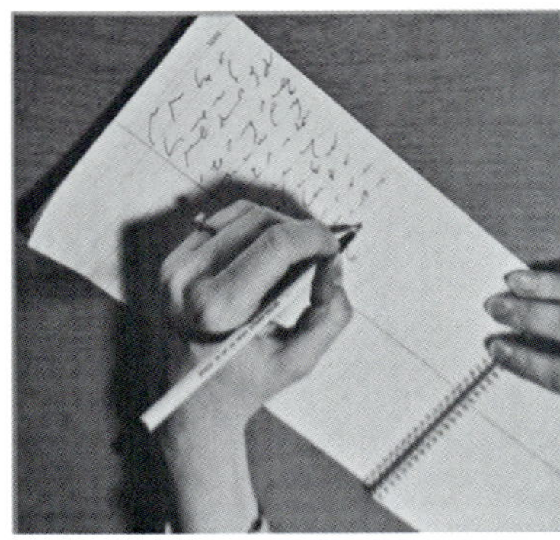

Fig. 55a–b Stenography exercise using a steno notebook, *Gregg Shorthand Fundamentals,* Diamond Jubilee Series (New York: McGraw-Hill, 1963), 24.

from several trips, with the top layer completed in a softer lead pencil than the lines beneath it. In the work of a professional stenographer, writing is also frequently bilateral; the steno notebook is divided in the middle by a vertical line so that the notetaker need only write short phrases at a time, instead of long lines of content (fig. 55a–b). Drawings like this one concede to the existence of a lived binary within the body but reach toward a state in which such binaries lose their moral weight.[119] They are a graphic representation of the trivial, of someone disciplining themselves to push past their boredom threshold, but more crucially, they model the ways in which all skills develop in collision with other conditions.

A closer look at the stenographic instructional texts is revealing here, as it shows the disciplinary practices that helped transform the human body into an efficient conduit for spoken content in modern capitalism. Duran Kimball's book *Business Shorthand* (1900) describes the ideal position of ease to prepare the hand for the effort of writing (fig. 56): "The hand should assume its easiest position on the table, the position it would take natu-

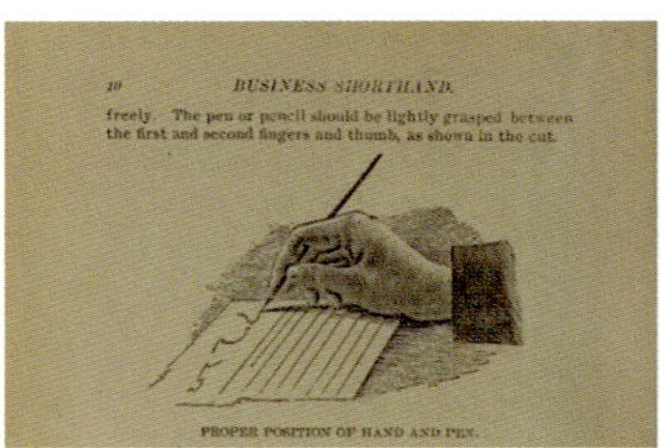

Fig. 56 Illustration showing proper position of the hand and pen, Duran Kimball, *Business Shorthand: Presenting a Method of Swift Writing for the Use of Amanuenses and Reporters* (Chicago: D. Kimball, 1900), 10.

Fig. 57 "Automatism," in Roger Cardinal and Robert Stuart Short, *Surrealism: Permanent Revelation* (London: Studio Vista/Dutton, 1970).

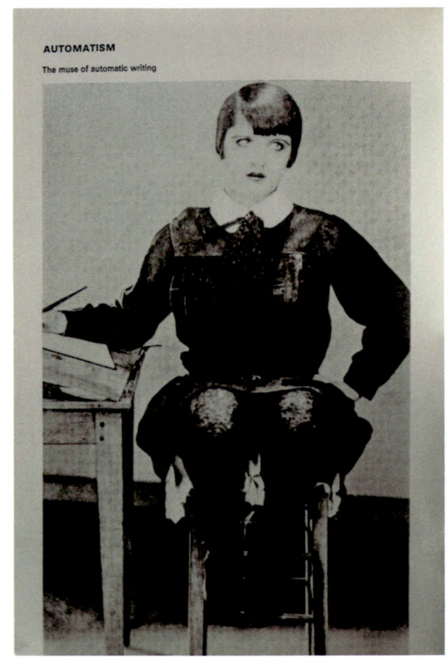

          Off the Record

rally if dropped upon the table in a moment of rest, without thot [*sic*] or restraint, the knuckle of the fore-finger uppermost, the third and fourth fingers curved under the palm to form an elastic support to the hand and steady its movement across the paper. The wrist should be slightly raised, so that the hand may move freely."[120] Anastasi's hands, by contrast, do not assume an easeful position for writing; instead, they grip the pens with five fingers, as though they were walking sticks (see fig. 53). He retains some control of his body by eschewing writerly control, using the pens to calibrate his body position so that he always remains upright, back straight, abdominal muscles engaged but not tense. Occasionally he taps the page, as his body translates its surroundings precisely but unintelligibly. This is not a grip of practiced dexterity, nor is it showcasing the pliant body that André Masson and Salvador Dalí described in surrealist automatic writing sessions in which participants were "bound to their chairs by an ingenious system of straps, so that they could only move a hand in a certain way."[121] If anything, this resembles the surrealist automatism described in the popular literature of the 1960s and 1970s, whose authors focused on reverie and wonder.[122] In 1971, the art historian Roger Cardinal described automatic writing as an ecstatic state, a "passionate manifestation of lunacy" (fig. 57).[123] But while Anastasi's "lunacy" might seem evident here (the other train passengers clearly notice his nonnormative behavior), it is in fact subtly controlled.

READING WITH STENOGRAPHY IN *YOU ARE*

The sole performance work in Anastasi's career challenged the value placed on skilled gesture as a marker of credibility and instead used stenography to "read" gallery visitors. The artist proposed a new live work, *You Are: John Cage, One of Three Narrators on Three Successive Evenings, 8–9:30 PM*, to the Museum of Modern Art, but like *Canvas Wall* the previous year, his proposal was rejected. Then, in 1977, curator Alanna Heiss invited Anastasi to conceptualize the work for the Clocktower Gallery, formerly the Institute for Art and Urban Resources, an alternative space inside a nineteenth-century former architectural firm in Lower Manhattan (fig. 58).[124] *You Are* included a narrator, a stenographer, and a court typist. On the opening night of *You Are,* Anastasi closed his eyes and instructed the narrator—the narrator was his friend John Cage—to describe each person who entered the room. The stenographer then wrote Cage's description in shorthand and handed it over to a courtroom typist, who translated the shorthand back into Roman text. Anastasi chose collaborators of both genders. Two more narrators were rotated into the space on the next two successive evenings, so the three narratives were different each time and the stenographer's account removed them even further from the original speakers. The project distanced the individual from how they were perceived in social space, using stenography and translation to show the possibilities for multiple ways of recording, describing, and documenting. Data collection becomes liberating rather than a flattening out of the senses. The audience entered the room and slowly came to know that they were being described, leading to a documentation of the gallery space that was inseparable from multiple relations with the audience. At the end of the performance, we still know little about the participants or the viewers in the room. Cage goes on the record with his observations, but we only have a limited sense of what, or who, we are. The stenographer, court typist, and Anastasi himself also participate in recording these observations and transcribing them onto paper—paper that then becomes an analog of public space as well as a literal part of the wall.

You Are is different from the earlier drawing projects, offering a putative illumination of character even as it shuts that possibility down. But paper remained at the center of these operations. It opened new possibilities for performing notation and representation. Activated as a private mode of pathway building that was weighed down by modernist freight, Anastasi's public, self-referential and very mobile drawing practice disrupted numerous modernist topoi including that of the flâneur. In helping Anastasi negotiate spontaneous moments of contact between the body and urban space, paper's planar flexibility made it a model of both economic and physiological mobility. Paper activated both these things at once by employing habit, which reverses the energies of active and passive, of dark interiors and illuminated exteriors.

By engaging with transcription technologies, both analog and electronic, Anastasi inserted himself into dialogues about recording techniques and artistic agency, extending them beyond the surrealist template. His drawings and performances complicate the relation between aesthetics and social class, creating space for a form of know-how that was powerful and mobile precisely because it could appear inexpert and thoughtless. To walk with Anastasi was to witness a constantly shifting set of entanglements, each one keeping expertise at bay. Just as each mark was as good as any other, so no mark (or agent, or entity) was qualitatively better. The workers and operators of modern urban infrastructural machines, for instance, are the agents behind modernity's magic, but they were also beings that reinforce the social order. We are weak against machines, but we control them nonetheless; they shape our behaviors and vice versa. In demonstrating the codependence of subject and object, his drawings allowed class and identity to stand out as peculiarly inert while the objects of classed designations—like people and buildings—swirled with activity. The drawings ultimately showcase the body's vulnerability to vibratory forces, departing from Anastasi's modernist precursors in extraordinary ways. Paper becomes a canvas wall, operating in concert with the probing, yielding, habitual activities of body within world.

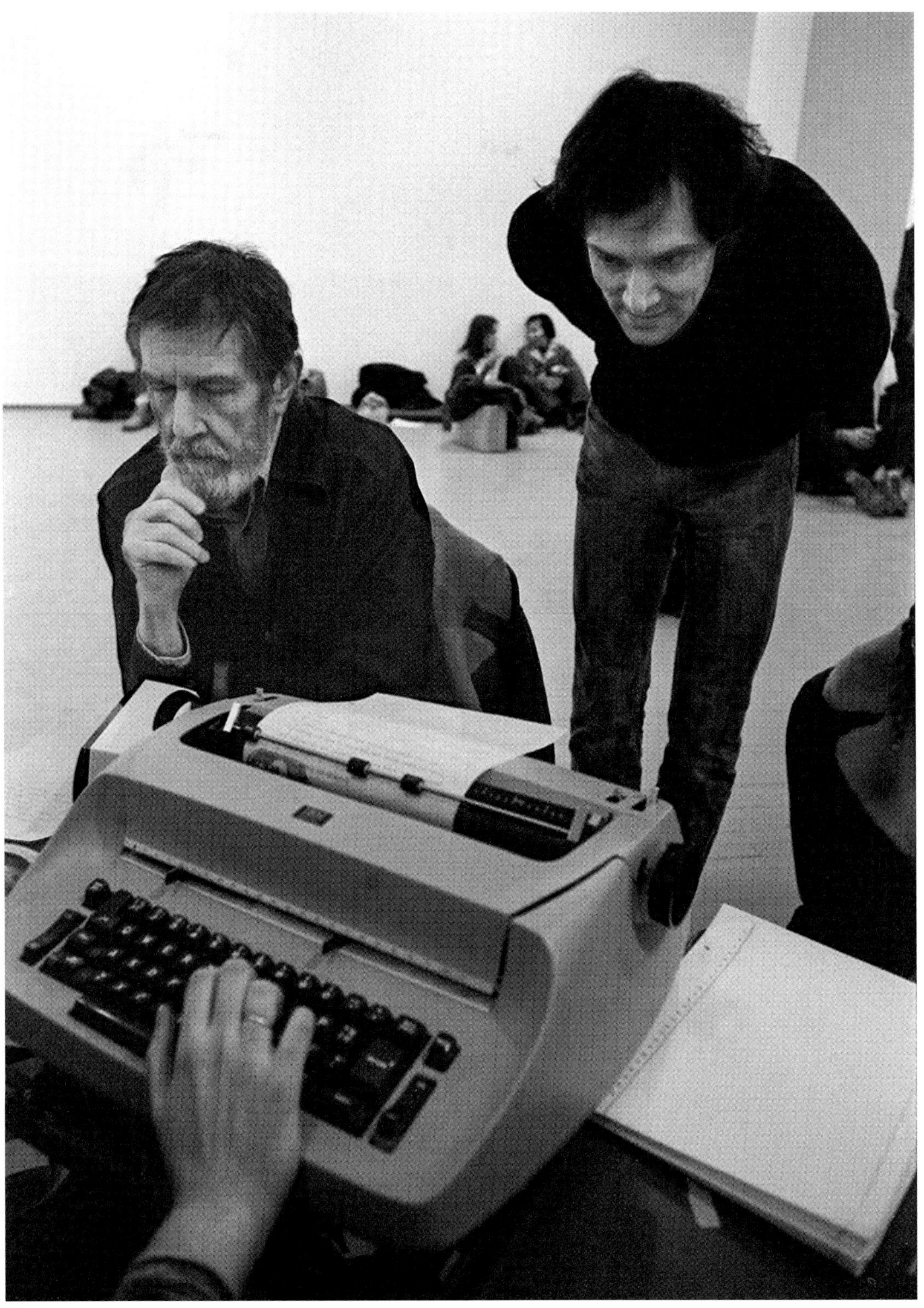

Fig. 58 William Anastasi, *You Are,* 1979. Performance with John
Cage, a stenographer, and a court typist. Clocktower Gallery, inside
the McKim, Mead and White Building, Lower Manhattan.

CHAPTER 3

Cutting into Things

Richard Tuttle's Complete Functions

The impulse to look transversally, delicately, or even askance at Richard Tuttle's untitled paper cubes of 1964 is always close at hand. Each of the three-inch paper forms has different shapes cut recessively into its interior (fig. 59). Instead of continuous lines and planes creating a smooth surface, as with a cube generated by a geometric formula, these are cubic forms carefully modified. Each distinct shape houses the empty space of other shapes. The spaces become presences. (Are they entry points? Exits?) While working at the Cooper Hewitt Design Museum library in the fall of that year, Tuttle produced this series of ten cuboid forms in paperboard, the same type of paper he had used for paste-up work on his college yearbook.[1] Unlike the careers of Carolee Schneemann or William Anastasi, Tuttle's passage from student to blue-chip gallery star began when he was young; the paper forms were featured in his first solo exhibition at Betty Parsons Gallery in Midtown Manhattan in 1965 when the artist was twenty-three years old.[2] Unlike Morris's performance sketches, they are not lost to the archive; people saw them readily and immediately. They were placed all together on a pedestal at waist level, and the gallery encouraged viewers to hold them in their hands.

Their portability likely fascinated Betty Parsons, the gallery's director, who had just hosted *Toys by Artists,* a group exhibition of thirty-four small works by Andy Warhol, Ruth Vollmer, and others.[3] The critic Robert Pincus-Witten said that the boxes had "an oddly infant-like thrust" compared to even the smallest works in the galleries that season.[4] Indeed, their scale recalls mock-up experiments and spaces of preparation: the yearbook's typesetting room, the sculptor's studio, the designer's drafting table, or even, to ratify Pincus-Witten's claim, the classroom or playroom. A longer pause in front of these sixteen objects might extend their references even further. Each one is three inches per side, almost five times larger than a single die, but small enough for the fingers to graze the sides if placed in the palm of one hand. Some of the boxes have shallow shapes recessed into their surfaces so that a finger, if small enough, could press all the way inside them; on others, the shapes went all the way through the cube. They could be stacked in different permutations. The curator, Marcia Tucker, would

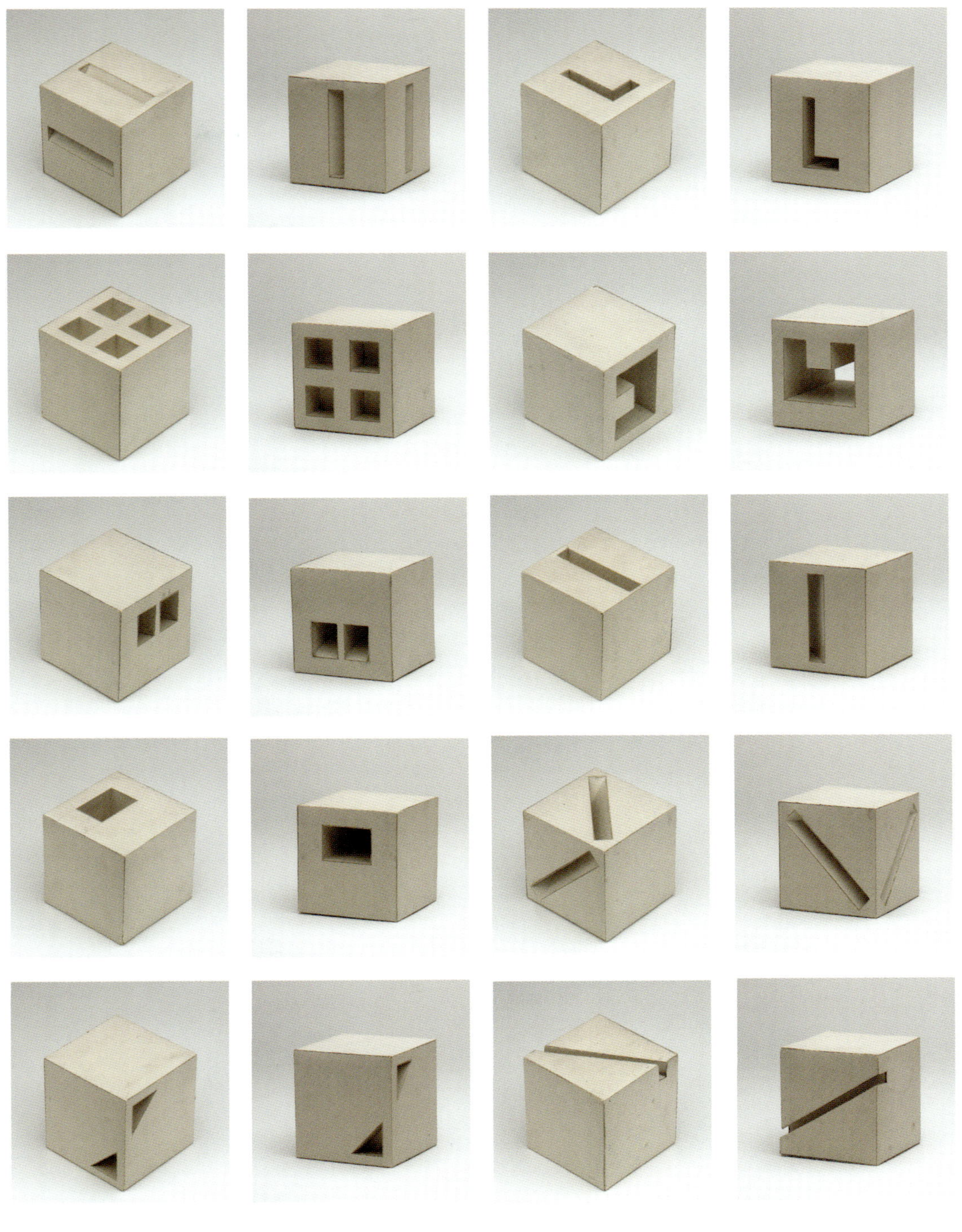

Fig. 59 Richard Tuttle, untitled paper cubes, 1964. Cardstock,
each: 3 × 3 × 3 in. (7.5 × 7.5 × 7.5 cm). Moderna Museet, Sweden.

reference them when she wrote eleven years later that Tuttle's work "is 'felt' rather than 'understood,' and lends itself to a powerful, often transcendental physical assimilation rather than to verbal analysis."[5] She asserted this in her catalog essay for Tuttle's retrospective exhibition in 1975 at the Whitney Museum of American Art—an exhibition so panned by critics for its spare and unprofessional presentation that Tucker was fired from her position there. Nevertheless, Tucker's choice of words anchor the work's physical assimilation to a unique form of perception, a cutting to the heart of the matter that starts with a reach and can be realized in the vaguest flicker of a grasp.

The works deploy linked concepts of inviting and cutting, wholeness and occlusion, delicacy and power. Like Tucker, the artist has described the *Paper Cubes* in terms of both feeling and seeing, citing their *see-through* qualities as evidence of their transparency of concept. "The best of the 'white boxes' have the most clarity," he wrote in an artist statement for the critic Barbara Rose, as she prepared to include these works in her eponymous early essay on minimalism, "ABC Art," of 1965.[6] His quotation marks around *white box* are a wry joke on the box form, whose popularity in the New York and Los Angeles art scenes that season was undeniable.[7] Andy Warhol had exhibited his *Brillo Boxes* at the Stable Gallery one month earlier (fig. 60); the Green Gallery had mounted a show that April of Robert Morris's wooden boxes that he had used in collaborative dance performances; and Sol LeWitt's open wooden grids appeared for the first time in a group show that Dan Graham organized at the Kaymar Gallery in September.[8] Works like these coincided with the near ubiquity of cardboard boxes and paper packaging in postwar consumer culture.

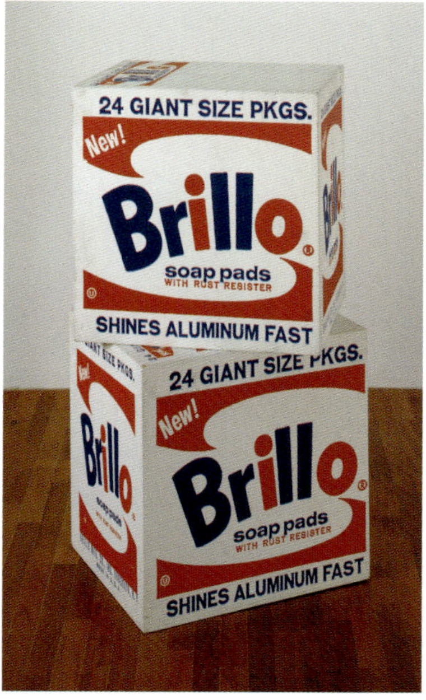

Fig. 60 Andy Warhol, *Brillo Box*, 1964. Synthetic polymer paint and silkscreen on wood, each 17⅛ × 17 × 14 in. (43.3 × 43.2 × 36.5 cm). Purchase, Museum of Modern Art, New York.

  Cutting into Things

For artists, the box proved to be both a wellspring and a receptacle—not just for art's newly charged relationship to supply chains and everyday life but for the questions it raised about fixed or closed spaces in general. Multiple "box shows" sprang up in contemporary art galleries in New York and Los Angeles. The Irish art critic Brian O'Doherty, who in 1976 would publish a series of articles called "Inside the White Cube: Notes on the Gallery Space," organized his *Box Show* at the Byron Gallery on Madison Avenue in February 1965, observing in his notes for the catalog that the white cube "seems to side-step time into a more or less fixed state."[9] In exhibitions of avant-garde art in the first half of this decade, the box could make genealogical arguments about premade and ready-made forms, as had Marcel Duchamp's *Boîte-en-Valise* in John Weber's *Boxes* show in Los Angeles in February 1954; or allude to the icon and the shrine, as Dan Flavin's boxed light works had in March 1964; or evoke metaphors of the vagina, called a *box* in 1960s parlance, as Eva Hesse's drawings and box-shaped *Accession* sculptures did later in the decade.[10] But, though formally similar to the projects of his contemporaries, Tuttle's paper cubes were different, both in their scale and in their mode of address. First, their size implies that they can be picked up and shifted from one hand to another—"almost weightless," as Tuttle himself noted—rather than lifted with both hands, as one might a moving box or a suitcase, or reached into, as with the cages or operant conditioning boxes common to postwar laboratory experiments. Second, the recessions in their surface—we might call them *cuts,* given the stray pencil lines in some of their corners that mark where a sharp blade would divide the plane of the paper— simultaneously affirm that surface and create new space from it. The final work would condense the literal cuts in the boxes' moment of making with the constructed cuts in the finished product. And perhaps most important, the cubes foreground this surface-extending quality as a mode of learning.

Learning to cut a cube out of stiff paper is a surprisingly delicate affair. Tuttle's boxes appear to be guided by cuts—cuts that would have been physical in the construction stage and ended up as designed lines by the final iteration. A maker would need to imagine the design as comprehensive and anticipate how the cuts would come together to create forms of their own. Though Tuttle was a philosophy and literature major as an undergraduate, he also studied for a semester at the Cooper Union and absorbed lessons from its design and science faculty. Perhaps this is why Tuttle's work privileges the material of the mock-up, which a conventionally finished artwork rarely reveals, even as it solicits athletic looking from the viewer. The little boxes have an open-ended, instructional quality: now *you* try. A second version of Tuttle's untitled boxes that he made in 1969 even shows thin ridges of tape at the edges (fig. 61). The entire formula is made available to us, the willing witnesses, the sidlers, the close observers. Just as it grounded someone's body in the act of doing, so, too, could it plug another person into the same function (fig. 62). His cuts are not pure or eternal; in fact, they establish a kind of posterior moment for purity.

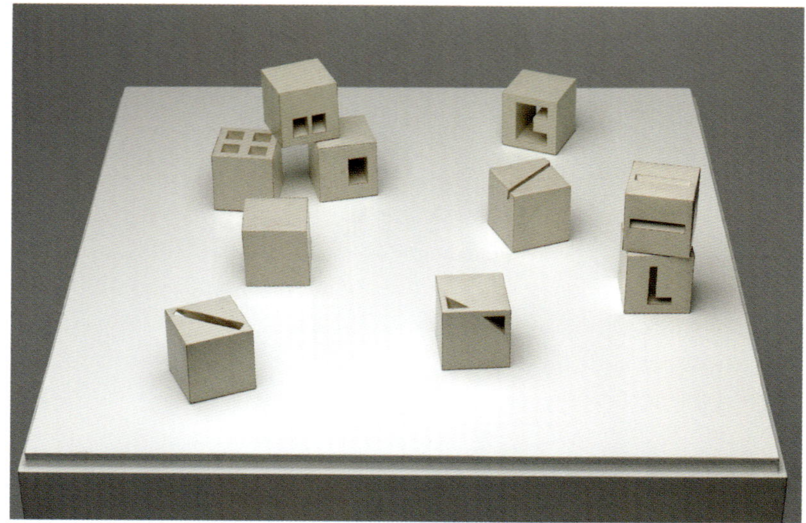

Fig. 61 Richard Tuttle, untitled paper cubes, 1964. Cardstock, each: 3 × 3 × 3 in. (7.5 × 7.5 × 7.5 cm). Moderna Museet, Sweden.

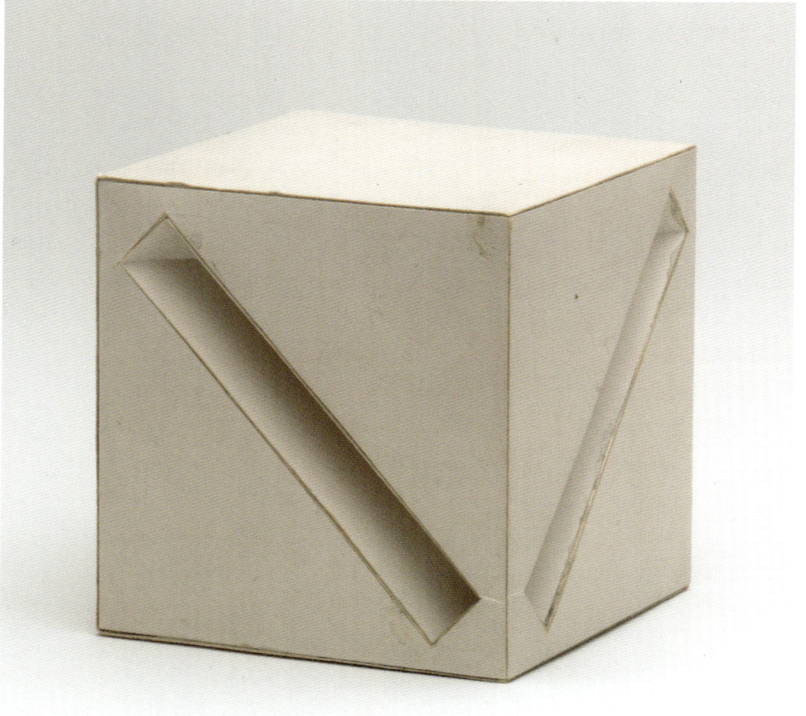

Fig. 62 Richard Tuttle, single paper cube, 1964. Cardstock, 3 × 3 × 3 in. (7.5 × 7.5 × 7.5 cm). Moderna Museet, Sweden.

　　Cutting into Things

In the six decades since Tuttle's meteoric launch into the art world, the embodied, organic, and continually unfolding qualities of his art have attracted widespread critical discussion—and even rancor, as in the case of his retrospective exhibition at the Whitney in 1975. As this chapter will attest, Tuttle's abundant engagements with paper in the first decade of his career not only nourished these organic qualities but were also linked with calls in the late 1960s to reexamine the notion of revolutionary social change and the human body's scaled role in that change. As an essential, yet hidden, connective part of the design-painting-sculpture nexus, paper was pedagogical. Tuttle's projects in this decade all share an inquiry into paper's key role in teaching and learning, particularly with respect to the possibilities for the human body's many different biotic and social relationships with space. Rather than obviate the artist's hand, which many of his minimalist predecessors made a priority, or make himself present in his work through indexing his own labor, Tuttle's cutting- and paper-based projects put forward possibilities for objects themselves to oscillate in and out of volition and embodiment. His projects from the 1960s probe the idea of what it means to have a body, and to derive power from the commingling of other bodies. This included metaphorical bodies—bodies of letters, the body of evidence, the body politic—and all the limits that the word *corpus* implies, both necessary and arbitrary.

What follows is a narrative of several key bodies of Tuttle's work that have drawing and cutting at their core. Tuttle's many modes of cutting into materials challenged established notions of what was, and wasn't, an object, at the very moment that social and political power was being discussed in terms of scale and objectification. And although certain aspects of Tuttle's work and writings encourage an object-oriented way of thinking—namely, his belief that an artwork's material is vibrantly alive and sets our relations to it through a radically destabilized order—traces of humanistic thinking in Tuttle's practice invite a more complicated way of sitting with Tuttle's work from this volatile part of the 1960s. Spinoza, whom Tuttle loved, provides theoretical scaffolding here and will help map the artist's interests across several centuries of philosophy on agency. Spinoza posited that all bodies were part of a connected system that also included ideas and things. The body was simply one instantiation of this connected system, "a mode or created form which expresses in a certain determinate manner the essence of god." Because all bodies held connections to both an infinitely powerful spiritual presence as well as to the larger world, any attempt to differentiate worldly phenomena demonstrated that "all the explanations commonly given of nature are mere modes of imagining."[11] This monist position—the belief that all phenomena were the same and that human intellectual activity created unnecessary divisions that were secondary to the true nature of the phenomena themselves—resonates in interesting ways with paper's generative role in Tuttle's art practice. He used it as a space for sketching and notetaking, as a tracing surface, and as a material for making models.

It was a collaborator for producing anything but also a site where boundaries and divisions came into being. There was something *located within* the paper substrate for Tuttle, then, that encouraged the cut as a form of intervention, an intervention that resulted not in closure, premise-making, or empiricism but in uncertainty and change. My analysis proceeds from Karen Barad, Alfred North Whitehead, and Baruch Spinoza—not just because Tuttle admired the work of the latter two theorists but because each of them shares an interest in the border or boundary as a mode of expansion and intimacy rather than merely division. As interlocutors, these philosophers can help chart a path into the large-scale injustices that undermined democratic order in the postwar United States while cleaving close to the scale of Tuttle's potent, yet often small, *things.*

Scale was something that artists in this moment were determined to relearn. By the end of the decade, Tuttle's work firmly centered paper as a cheap, casual, and critically important material, pulling from both the rapidly expanding New York gallery market and from subcultures trading and selling papers and drawings, from psychedelic concert posters to artist's multiples. And insofar as his artistic profile and gender allowed him to pass through spaces as disparate as galleries and military hospitals and use them to his advantage, his paper-based work illuminates media histories of the long 1960s that both embraced and bypassed dominant markets—in other words, they trace multiple shortcuts through the art world. He was in Tokyo during the student uprisings, for instance, and was part of the marketing of paper multiples to new global buyers during the fourth and fifth documenta exhibitions, in 1968 and 1972, respectively. His paper letters and touchable objects were supported precisely because they could be understood as both mystical and charismatic, auratic and distanced.

I deliberately engage Tuttle's paper projects as flowing into and referring back to one another, in keeping with the artist's abiding interest in forestalling orderly trajectories for his artistic process. Tuttle often made studies and sketches of his works after they were finished, thereby demonstrating drawing's potential to cut into history, rehearsing it selectively, and reproducing it imperfectly. They are the sort of drawings that make us not want to make art history out of them. I narrate these cuts and their effects as they coalesce into the paper octagons of the early 1970s. But the basic tendency is that Tuttle would first draw, then cut up and sew together from paper templates. Occasionally he would make sketches of these works after they were finished and pass them off as preparatory studies, subverting a clear narrative of progression from idea to archive to exhibition space. The artist also published and gave away instructions for mass-producing his sculptures with ordinary household items, addressing the readers as *you* and encouraging them to trace their own forms and shapes first on cardboard or on cloth the way a dressmaker might. His written instructions even implicated the writing surface—"I used paper like this that I'm writing on, but cardboard is to be better if it is to be used over and over"—to highlight the cleavage between individual communication and repetitive craft substrates, between thinking alone and making again and again.[12] His instructions allowed new works to be recut from old templates, so that the same gestures could generate ideas anew.[13] All these interconnected projects combined cutting and drawing with learning. They situated drawing as both a generative and destabilizing force, a force that "cuts together and apart [a] complex set of multimodal constituents," to use the feminist philosopher Karen Barad's turn of phrase.[14] Tuttle's work is an example of Barad's "agential cut": it is a matter not of rending two things apart but instead of holding together two things purportedly separated.

The term *agential cut* also helps to outline artists' understandings of repressive Cold War conformity politics at home and colonial conflict in Vietnam as "cut from the same cloth," as historian Christine Knauer has put it.[15] Tuttle's projects, called "process art" or colloquially "stuff art," offered a way of processing the ecstatic promises (and stunning gendered and racialized exclusions) contained in discourses of the 1960s.[16] Both the Cold War and the Vietnam War mobilized an extraordinary impasse between a belief in the democratic humanist project (of which Tuttle has long been a proponent) and in emergent, noumenal, nonhuman ways of being.[17] As Eve Meltzer, Alexander Alberro, and numerous other scholars have noted, the concept of *system* was a guidepost that artists used to deconstruct the banal, colloquial "system" at home and to understand the plasticity and variability of such other systems as scientific naturalism, positivism, and nationalism.[18] As debates about school integration and military conscription became topics of public scrutiny, cutting became not just a physical act in the postwar United States but a mode of bureaucratic violence, as authorities such as George Wallace, who blocked the University of Alabama's Foster Auditorium doorway with his own body to prevent Black students from registering just a few months after Tuttle graduated from college, cut off opportunities to grow and thrive. Elders exhorted young men to cut their hair and referred to people fond of pranks as "real cut-ups."

Cutting is also a form of drawing, one that generates division and disrupts the flow of systemic formations. It corresponds to, and makes visible, the inherent ambiguity of line: that it joins but also separates. Additionally, cutting and tracing are bodily acts, incorporating the space outside a material and including it as part of a new, larger pathway. We might even say that such cuts guide the body—prompting Tuttle's observation in 1968, when bodies were busy chipping away at social hierarchies on a global scale through student protests, that "art is discipline and discipline is drawing."[19] Most importantly, the cut implies an opening beyond itself. It is an act of material and metaphysical jury-rigging, capable of extending space. In collage, cutouts of cloth or paper stage absences or disruptions; in narrative genres such as film, the cut frees a storyteller from attachment to linear time. In design, it is the first step toward making a new shape. In presenting the ways that Tuttle's work was informed by philosophies of learning, including speculative mathematics, I reveal here how cutting held a fundamentally different set of possibilities than did institutionalized schemes made manifest through technological networks or bureaucratic institutions. Tuttle was enamored with democratization and the common household items that mass production made available, yet the kinds of cuts he made drew attention to the imperfections of systems and the odd intimacies they might sustain, rather than to their anonymity or uniformity.

LEARNING ABC ART

By the end of his education at Trinity College in 1963, the artist was aware of these systemic imperfections and more. Having found "little outlet for doing any creative work" at Trinity, he sought out a series of art world luminaries as mentors, many of them queer- or gay-identified. He befriended the artist Agnes Martin, who introduced him to gallery owner Betty Parsons, and was given a job the same day. He sought out Samuel Wagstaff, a curator at the nearby Wadsworth Atheneum in Hartford, who taught a reading course for Trinity alumni called "Looking at Modern Art."[20] In his course lectures, Wagstaff praised the elder artist Jackson Pollock's ability to express "not a world of forms but a world of forces, energy, restless passion, fluidity, motion, speed, rhythm—energy made visible."[21] Amid mounting discourses on bodily immediacy and bureaucratic blockage, Wagstaff also organized the exhibition *Black, White, and Grey* in January 1964, an exhibition of twenty-one artists whose monochromatic work would eventually be canonized as modernist orthodoxy, an exhibition Tuttle saw. Minimalism, or "literal art" or "ABC art" as it was called in this moment, was beginning to crystallize as something literal, in "real space," that denied the valuation of such basic principles in art history as narrative and the human figure. The show distilled artworks down to their chromatic and formal essence—a stance that intrigued and aggrieved critics in equal measure.[22] This part of the decade fomented a cultural universe where one might toggle between "literal space" and "forces and energy," between action and concealment—a situation that arose in part due to the discursive mobility that queer artists, who were selectively visible as such, helped create.

Wagstaff and Tuttle took trips to New York and attended Intermedia, Happenings, and pop performances as well as gallery shows of painting and sculpture.[23] At this moment, the private actions of the studio, previously yoked to abstract expressionism's confessional dynamics, were becoming public through live performances that incorporated the human body.[24] The art critic Harold Rosenberg discussed abstract expressionist painters including Mark Rothko, Willem de Kooning, and Jackson Pollock—Pollock's drawings had been exhibited at Betty Parsons while Tuttle was working there—as artists who "went up to [the canvas] with material in [their] hand to *do something to* that other piece of material in front of [them]."[25] Jasper Johns, arguably more Tuttle's contemporary than Rosenberg, abridged this

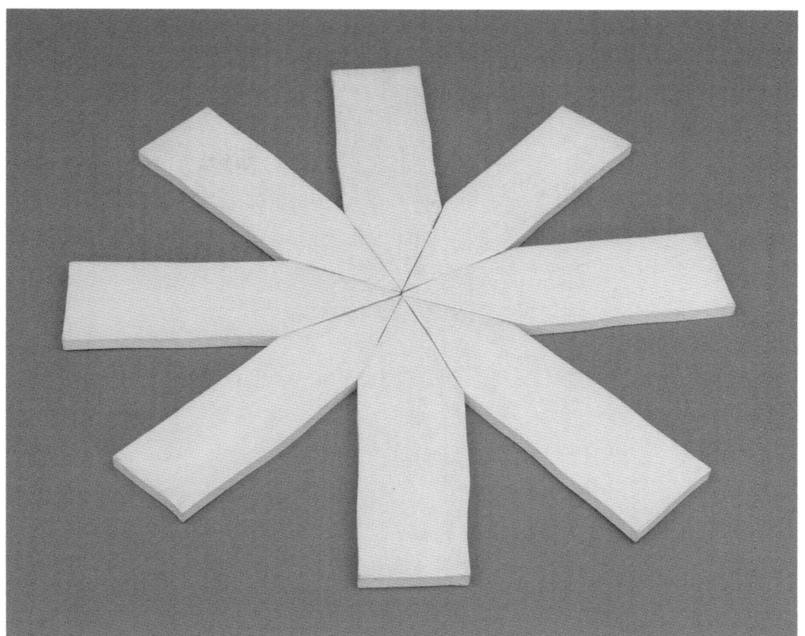

idea when he wrote in his notebook in 1964, "Take an object / Do something to it / Do something else to it. [Repeat.]"[26] The trouble was, Rosenberg immediately called on critics to attend to these human actions and to develop a connoisseurship of gesture and behavior—"a new kind of criticism, one that would distinguish the specific qualities of each artist's act."[27] Although Tuttle cut into his earliest works with scissors, in some ways reflecting the object-verb dynamic that Rosenberg and Johns had praised, his cuts did not constitute *action* in the Rosenbergian sense. Returning to the second image of his paper cubes, one notices how the objects' yielding to action turns them into sources of action, as they maintain an intimate scale with most bodies (see fig. 61). Each cube lies on the pedestal in a chance arrangement, ready for the next viewer to pick it up and manipulate it. With spaces visible where the paper sides have begun to come apart and some pencil marks that remain, the objects show their minute differences from one another. They trace the famed line from Spinoza's *Ethics* that Tuttle would invoke decades later: "If all things follow from a necessity of the absolutely perfect nature of God, why are there so many imperfections in nature?"[28]

Tuttle's interest in imperfections extended into his series of plywood sculptures that followed (fig. 63). These took on numerous abstract shapes and were made using a specific formula: make a paper template, then trace that template onto plywood, then cut the plywood into its main shape, then create its thin sides so that it would stand out in low relief from wherever it was installed. These sculptures could be installed on the wall or the floor, positioned close to one another or drifting apart. Occasionally, a sculptural form might reappear but in a new permutation, in a separate drawing or in a printed book, and inspire new possibilities for these shapes' orientation

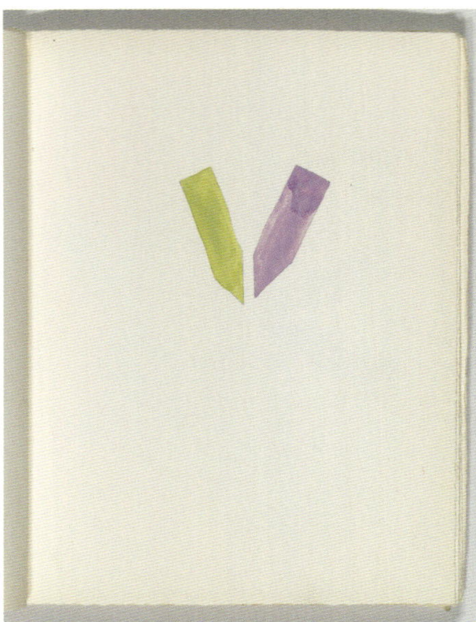

Fig. 64 Richard Tuttle, *Sparrow*, 1965. Twelve drawings in a bound book. Book: 8³⁄₁₆ × 6¾ × ⅜ in. (20.8 × 17.1 × 1 cm); sheet (each): 8¹⁄₁₆ × 6¼ in. (20.5 × 15.9 cm). Ed. 25. Whitney Museum of American Art, New York; purchase, with funds from the Wilfred P. and Rose J. Cohen Purchase Fund.

(fig. 64). The art historian Anne Wagner has referred to this cutting and drawing together, one coming after the other, as "perfectly paired."[29] Agency, once again, comes from the cut; but in this instance, the time it takes the viewer to perceive the work is instantaneous compared to the artist's multistep process of cutting out a paper template, tracing it onto plywood, using a band saw to re-create the original line, and grazing the edges of the plywood while painting its surface. This multistep process is not completely visible, but the organic and imperfect qualities of the finished sculpture indicate the changes in methods, or gestures, over time—a change in apparatus, as Karen Barad might understand it. "If the apparatus is changed," Barad has written, "there is a corresponding change in the agential cut and therefore in the delineation of object from agencies of observation."[30] Just as Spinoza also invites us to do in his *Ethics,* we look at a boundary line and immediately lose a sense of where the circumscription starts or stops. Once more, a connection arises between sculpture and drawing, with paper leading the way because of its ability to mediate both, a pathway for dressing further and further down. As Tuttle put it in 1972, "I started out making thick wood pieces and they got thinner and thinner. They turned into cloth. And now I am doing paper."[31]

These arguments about scale—that something small and unruly could prompt a breaking free of an entire system—repeated themselves across numerous treatises on the natural world and natural behavior in the 1960s and 1970s, which affirmed the idea of the small cut leading to paradigmatic shifts. Many texts of the time invited readers to meditate on the impact of small things, among them E. F. Schumacher's *Small Is Beautiful: A Study of Economics as If People Mattered* (1973), Frances Moore Lappé's *Diet for a Small Planet* (1971), and Charles Reich's *Greening of America.* Reich's book was in dialogue with Rachel Carson's *Silent Spring* insofar as

     Cutting into Things

it offered counterexamples to prescriptive, top-down conceptions of "the environment," incorporating a broad range of behaviors and philosophies that reduced the scale of human activity and simultaneously magnified the importance and impact of small-scale interactions. A key text of US countercultures in the 1960s and 1970s, *The Greening of America* diagnosed the absolute appropriation of culture by capitalist politics as a problem of reframing and reconstituting our understanding of the scale of human intervention, inviting the reader to consider the magnified consequences of individual choice.

The book's author, Charles Reich, came from a progressive New York City medical family and taught at Yale Law School for fourteen years before coming out as gay and moving to San Francisco in 1974. He felt that the heavy hand of the state, including the policing of individuals' (and particularly young people's) bodies, could not be remedied by traditional methods of legal debate, politicostructural change, and the drafting of new legislation. Reich used his preprofessorial experience working at white shoe firms in New York City as evidence that any large system, however organically managed by individual persons, would inevitably develop or move into new and dangerous forms of violence when it handed over the bulk of its doings to nonhuman logics. Like Carson, Schumacher, and Lappé, Reich saw technological networks as being in contrast to and a danger to natural ones, acting in destructive, "pulverizing" opposition to "the landscape, the natural environment, history and tradition, the amenities and civilities, the privacy and spaciousness of life, beauty, and the fragile, slow-growing social structures which bind us together."[32] The sole alternative to capitalist technology's spread beyond human intervention was revolution; one that was driven by the restless, unedited energy of youth culture and would fashion "a new and enduring wholeness and beauty—a renewed relationship of man to himself, to other men, to society, to nature, and to the land."[33] For Reich, vast social shifts were the "final act" in a much larger and more meaningful theater of smaller acts occurring in relation to nonhuman forces made legible through enhanced means of observation.[34] Ultimately, the prefigurative politics of 1960s countercultures—*be the change you want to see in the world* was a frequent exhortation on signs and T-shirts, paraphrased from an early essay by Mahatma Gandhi—asked human beings to engage in the largest of social problems through the everyday, and even intimate, lens of their own bodies.[35] Actions like looking, gesturing to other beings, "doing things" to objects, and even digestion could be newly learned and produced, with the rest of nature and society clustering around the acts themselves.

The mathematician and philosopher Alfred North Whitehead also left a significant impression on Tuttle; one of his first paintings when he moved to New York featured quotations from Whitehead, painted over, on the back of the canvas support. Whitehead's work on speculative thinking as it intertwines with material experience drew curious artists into the philosophy of science. In the 1950s, Whitehead was frequently invoked in meetings of the Club, an abstract expressionist venue in New York, and by the early 1970s, lectures at the Yale School of Art, Philadelphia Museum of Art, and Smithsonian Institution linked him to postwar theories of perception.[36] Whitehead's book *Science and the Modern World* (1925) was a popular text for undergraduate literature and philosophy courses in the late 1950s.[37] Widely read in the nuclear age but written a generation earlier, the book discussed the cultural aspects of scientific discovery through the framework of process philosophy, a field of study devoted to analyzing the shifting and dynamic modes of human experience. Its affordable Mentor paperback editions (1949 and 1963) included an endorsement by the American pragmatist philosopher and educational theorist John Dewey on the cover. In general, Whitehead argued through his oeuvre of philosophical writings on science that experience was everything; we are brought into being *in relation with* the world. It is also extremely difficult to interrogate experience, so we cannot rely on fixed concepts to do it. "Bifurcating," or dividing the world (nature) into separate categories of mind and matter, is also a risk. Nature is generative, "a continuous stream of occurrence," so any theory must be arrived at through the direct experience of nature.[38] Instead of depending on structures or ideas that could repeat from experiment to experiment, the thinker should rely on more abstract, flexible methods.[39] It is speculation, Whitehead claims, that helps us to transcend rigid formal schemes, so all thinkers must devote themselves to what he calls speculative reason—a "speculative understanding for its own sake."[40] Unlike most US scientific writers in the first half of the twentieth century who wrote of the light of reason that illuminated scientific problems, Whitehead argued that clarity of discovery was inseparable from the things we hold in "dim apprehension," which shaded off "imperceptibly into unidentified feeling."[41] Feeling was a castoff of perception. Whitehead often spoke of perception's failure to clarify feelings and affects, and as a result, both things were often bound together in the actual practice of observing the world.

Speculative reason is an apt term to apply to Tuttle's cubes, constructed paintings, and, later, cloth pieces, which were in dialogue not only with the new geometrically driven and minimal artworks in Lower Manhattan galleries but with Parsons's own cube paintings and sculptures—Parsons was another selectively concealed member of the queer avant-garde herself.[42] Tuttle would continue to explore smaller works, which affirm what his friend Agnes Martin referred to as human beings' futile pursuit of mastery. "You find out that failures are inevitable. You can't even draw a straight line, you know that," she said in 1974.[43] Speculative failure differed significantly from minimalism's unadorned geometric forms that distanced themselves from the expertise of the artist's hand—as Barbara Rose had put it in "ABC Art," minimalism represented "a downgrading of talent, facility, virtuosity and technique" and a "concomitant elevation of conceptual power."[44] Because Tuttle was so interested in broad philosophies of the natural, of process, and of innateness, he created possibilities for small gestures to disrupt

     Cutting into Things

both power and perfection. These small cuts cleave together and separate disparate phenomena simultaneously. His objects could almost become mobile instead of mobile—or could deploy Tuttle's idea that paper was "place, without location"—and therefore could conduct themselves through the world because they invited curators, scholars, art handlers, conservators, and even the artist himself to adapt to the material's tendencies and vulnerabilities.[45] They rendered the object porous to its environment.

Tuttle, reflecting the broader societal movements of his generation, had spent time transitioning into and out of various spaces of regulation and enforcement. He had a brief stint as an air force trainee in 1964, a few months before he was hired at the Betty Parsons Gallery. "It seems like all my friends are against this, but I know it is right no matter what happens," he wrote in a letter to Wagstaff, as he settled into Lackland Air Force Base in San Antonio, Texas, for the first eight weeks of drills that would form the foundation of his communications and electronics training.[46] Although he "didn't think [communications] was [his] talent at all" at the time, Tuttle's induction into this specific arm of military service saved him from being drafted into active combat.[47] At the time, the US Air Force's communication program was chronically underfunded, and the military in the early 1960s devoted substantial attention to addressing critical deficiencies in avionics, data processing, devices, communications, and radar.[48] A priority in 1963 was to strengthen the Defense Communication System, or DCS, a centralized, long-haul, point-to-point communications network that was being converted from a collection of discrete US communication systems.[49] Its three main platforms were a worldwide US military telephone system (called AUTOVON), a punched card and teletype data storage system (AUTODIN), and a worldwide secure voice network (AUTOSEVOCOM). Tuttle's voluntary enrollment was unusual. Many would-be draftees during this part of the Vietnam War defected; Jerry Garcia had been honorably discharged from army training just three years earlier for unreliability.[50] Lackland, where Tuttle was stationed, had begun "studying psychological testing for prediction and assay of personal proficiency and adaptability," to maintain social hygiene among trainees and prevent just such defections.[51]

Military basic training is basic in the sense that it refines human behaviors that, within most conventional family and education structures, were uncalculated habits. Within eight weeks those habits are to be groomed to conform to military standards of order, efficiency, and hygiene. Such grooming became well known to the 2.2 million draftees who would be called to serve in Vietnam after the United States' escalation of forces in Southeast Asia after 1965. The training emphasized bodily and social protocols deemed necessary to maintain capacity for combat. Eight weeks of sleep deprivation formed the backdrop for daily physical exercises and homework. Procedures ranged from banal (folding clothes, making beds with hospital corners, ensuring that socks were pulled high enough to cover the ankle) to mechanical and grim (timed drills to assemble a gun). Calisthenics, rope challenges, and drills on marked concrete pads all disciplined the body and reinforced hierarchies, which officers underscored by "harassing" trainees, according to Tuttle's letters.

This strict monitoring and circumscription extended into the trainees' living environments more generally, which irked Tuttle. "Texans have an impressive way of hiding anything good to see," he wrote to Wagstaff. The Alamo, a "good building," could "hardly be seen." His comments reveal both his association with the sense of sight as a conduit to free thought and the physical and psychological opacity inherent to the air force and Lackland's overall project. Controlling space inevitably suppressed details. Here it turned both trainees and officers into calculating opportunists and left the body, the psyche, and the architectural envelope almost completely shorn of detail. They were occluded in plain sight, subjected to erasures of various types. This neat folding of clothing, the athletic competitions, and the calibrations of mitered hospital mattress corners were, at their core, procedural exercises "all about psychological breakdown."[52] After intentionally failing the air force's required personality test, Tuttle was removed from the training in the program's seventh week, placed briefly in the psychological ward of Lackland's hospital, and discharged honorably later that year.

The artist's stay in the military hospital gave him access to the building's new occupational therapy facility, which provided him with "wood, clay, paints, weaving looms and all the tools imaginable."[53] He has since spoken widely about art's role in health and how health should include acts of making that imbue the individual and the material with an ability to enhance each other. Since working with materials is a relational act, artistic materials have health-promoting effects because of their ability to modify human experience.[54] Suzanne Hudson, too, has outlined the importance of art therapy programs for the formation of the modern American artistic subject, noting that art therapy programs for children and veterans purported to draw out the latent and lively creative force that itself formed a particularly nuanced angle of postwar creative communities.[55] Art therapy provided traumatized citizens with a happier and more productive life, free from the strictures of professional training.[56] Within the context of military regulation of the body, then, Tuttle found two modes—latency and withdrawal—that distilled themselves in his drawing-based works. The air force prioritized universal uninterrupted communication, but Tuttle's experience of not making the cut prompted him to relearn to engage the world on a different scale.

PERCEPTION AND POWER

In ceding to imperfections, accidents, and even laziness, Tuttle allowed his iterative methods to transfer from material to material. In the spring of 1967, he began making paper templates for shaped cloth sculptures that could be hung on a wall or placed on a gallery floor. After drawing, he would lay the paper template down on a loose length of canvas, cut the shape along its edge, and then machine-sew its sides. He then immersed each one in a tub of hot water infused with powdered Tintex fabric dye. This soft cotton was the painterly canvas's floppier cousin, whose weave was designed to absorb pigment, fold, and collapse. His actions to produce these works were all variations on drawing: cutting, tracing, hemming, folding, with each act occasioning mobility in the maker as well as the material. Paper, too, was a textile and a pliant teacher, stiff enough to support a blade's bite but yielding quickly to cutting. Its many affordances were the very things that led the user through the lesson. The critic Robert Pincus-Witten noted when he visited Tuttle's studio that both the cloth octagons and the early paper octagons that emerged from them "may be affixed limply to the wall, like garments."[57] When Tuttle was making the cloth works, he frequently transported them in a bindle-style roll on his back; sometimes he brought them to galleries wadded up or tucked carefully into an old leather Gladstone duffel bag rather than in a flat portfolio.[58] When these details come to light, more questions arise: What *are* these things? Are they *things* in the sense that Martin Heidegger speculated on in 1967, capable of being "*this one*," standing firmly in space and time?[59] Are they pets, are they friends? Is the wall part of the work or something with which the work is in dialogue?

In throwing the ontology of his works into question, Tuttle draws together the binaries of agency and yielding. Tuttle frequently uses the word *vitality* in relation to his work, along with other terms that express an active, powerful charge, such as *fulmination* and even *pregnant*.[60] Critics in this period, however, tended to highlight the latency or hesitance in his cut and paper sculptures and to borrow from semiotic methods to call them "symbols of a shy but strong spirit," "cunning and sensitive[e]" objects whose "quavering" contours possess "an air of indecision."[61] Emily Wasserman called them "withdrawn," "personal [and] idiomatic," but noted that they manifested a seemingly paradoxical "concern for the sensuous."[62] By disclosing his works' material irregularities, Tuttle made their apparent guilelessness and vulnerability a source of power.[63]

Relatedly, Pamela Lee has observed that Tuttle uses materials that fold, bend, and spring back, thus "begging the question" about primacy: the primacy of three-dimensional versus two-dimensional art practices, as well as the primacy of the artist's role as the sole cause of the artwork.[64] As a literal disavowal of causality, the artist wrote a short essay in 1969 that was a recipe for how one of his cloth octagons might be reproduced, which put him into the role of instructor, dilletante guide, or even chef. He sent the essay to Wagstaff, who was then cocurating an exhibition, *Other Ideas,* at the Detroit Institute of Arts (DIA), that included the cloth pieces. Alongside Seth Siegelaub's *Jan 5–31, 1969* in New York and Lucy Lippard's *557,087* in Seattle, *Other Ideas* was a breakthrough exhibition of conceptual art and included short artist biographies mimeographed from hand-annotated

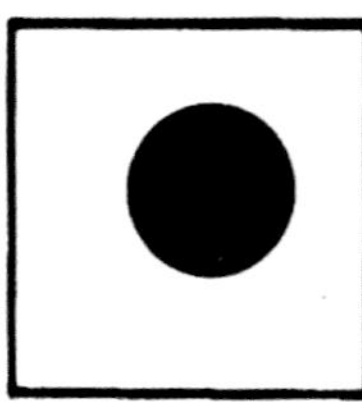
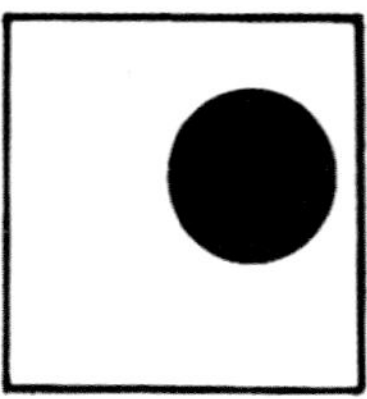

sheets. Tuttle's chosen action was "duplicat[ing] your cloth piece a thousand times," a concession in the second person that also became the de facto title of the essay. To dye the cloth works, Tuttle instructed, "just follow the directions on the package. . . . I do not want an even dye, because the color, too, is at best approximate, so if the piece is turned once or twice—that should do it." The following paragraph, however, provides a shortcut for opting out of the handmade aspects of the project: "If this sounds like too much work, just forget it: I won't be disappointed. . . . If I were you, I would take the piece to a manufacturer and say 'make this.' They probably would do a terrific job and you won't have to worry about it and the 'piece' would be, what they made."[65] Committing to the analog work of sewing might seem to be a counterstrategy against minimalism's cool distancing from the artist's hand, but this was in fact another way of shrugging off authorship: languorously giving away the formula to anyone who might be interested.

As Anastasi had proven with communication, perception could cut slyly into and out of the realm of empirical fact. The 1960s also saw substantive changes in intellectual and artistic approaches to visual perception. Vision as a pure sense, rigorously divided from other senses, was by 1967 at the end of a long denouement. More and more artists began to take perception as an aesthetic target in their works, and numerous texts on the psychology of perception asked readers to consider the ways that their vision was socially constructed.[66] The German film theorist and psychologist Rudolf Arnheim's published *Art and Visual Perception: A Psychology of the Creative Eye* in 1954 and reissued a substantially revised edition in 1974. In it, Arnheim contended that the human eye did not measure things as an empirical tool such as a yardstick did. Rather, the eye made "relational observations," as when it compared different phenomena "as properties of the total visual field."[67] It was vision's bodily effects that made perception central to the viewer's process of being in the world. However, Arnheim's exercises paid little attention to the material makeup of what was being perceived; the forces that affixed ink to the printed page or the tensile weave of pulp fibers that produced the leaves of the very books from which his ideas sprung were not central to his approach to exploring perception.

The book's first chapter leads readers through a series of perceptual exercises, asking them first to look at a black circle placed off center in two different square fields (fig. 65a–b). Arnheim probes: *how* do we know that each dot is off-center? Surely it is not because we measure the two things as unique and isolated phenomena. In the middle of the first chapter, he says:

> In what sense can it be said that these forces exist not only in experience, but also in the physical world? Surely they are not contained in the objects we are looking at, such as the white paper on which the square is drawn or the dark cardboard disk. Of course, molecular and gravitational forces are active in these objects, holding their microparticles together and preventing them from flying away. But there are no known physical forces that would tend to push an eccentrically placed patch of printer's ink in the direction of the center of a square. Nor will lines drawn in ink exert any magnetic power on the surrounding paper surface. . . . The artist [therefore] need not worry about the fact that these forces are contained in the pigments on the canvas. The perceived image, not the paint, is the work of art.[68]

In Arnheim's construction, the psychological occasion of perceiving the image—that is, the act of perception—creates aesthetic incident; the material does not. If we perceive any activity to be taking place in a work of art we are looking at, this is because it psychologically configures itself that way. This focus on perception dominated the postwar matrix of Anglo-European aesthetic theory. According to the influential French philosopher Maurice Merleau-Ponty, perception is the one thing that "at one stroke cuts through all possible doubts to stand in the full light of truth."[69] Once again, perception looms large here, eclipsing the power of materials, microbes, particles. Perception constitutes an active cut, one that illuminates. But Tuttle showed, exhibited, and sometimes sold his drawings in ways that brought their everyday and even cursory components into dialogue with the material field with which we (and certainly Arnheim) associate with the page. Many of his drawings happened on watercolor sketchbook paper and on notebooks, the latter of which Tuttle was at first comfortable to tear out and show, in serial order but with frayed edges, to visitors. Their center point varies, but they are always organized to favor the middle of a page, adapting to the notebook's flexible temporality. We could look at one of these or flip through the entire series. We could depart at the middle or at the end. The material is the source of aesthetic incident, especially the moments when our bodies enter the scene and activate it as such. The perceived image and the material are integrated.

A photograph captured by Dorothy Alexander about 1969 puts this flexibility to work, as the shallow relief–shaped sculpture in the bottom third of the picture invites interaction—kneeling, sitting, or standing—in its orbit (fig. 66). Although Arnheim dismissed the idea that an object or picture could contain "magnetic power" and "molecular and gravitational forces," the photograph shows divisions and separation thoroughly undermined.

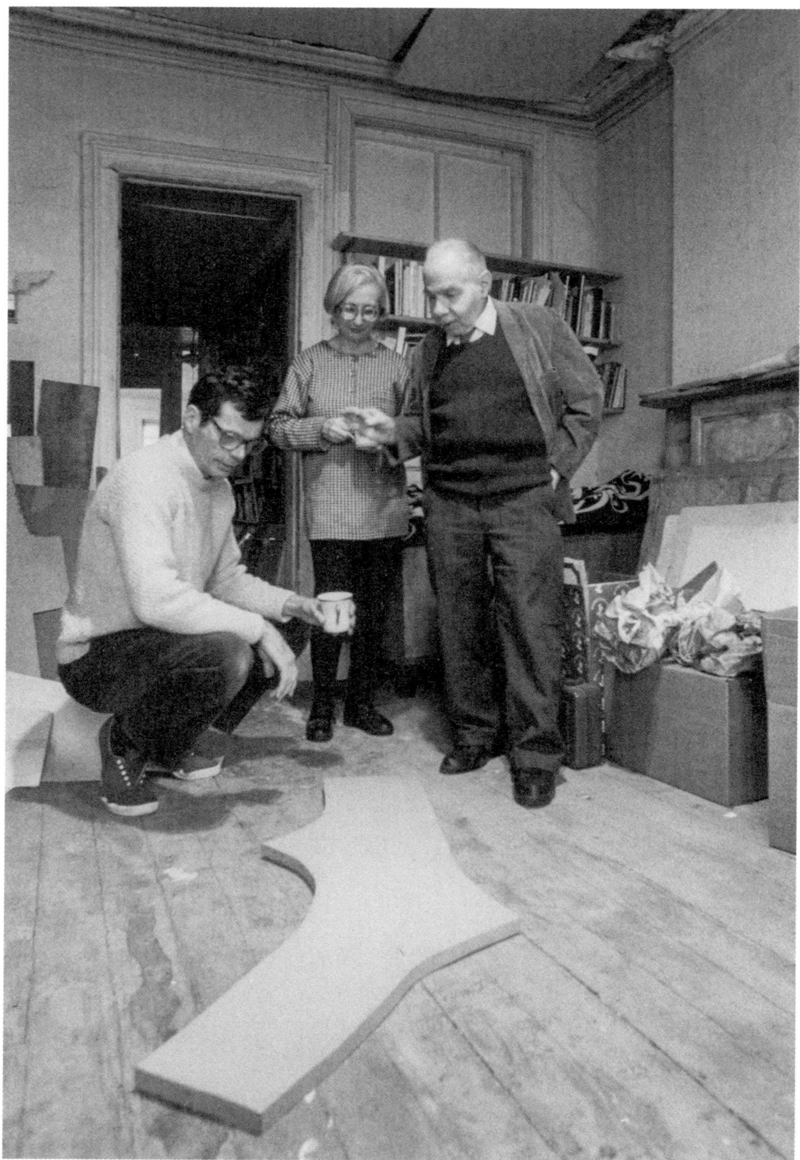

Fig. 66 Richard Tuttle examining a shaped piece with Dorothy and Herbert Vogel, ca. 1969.

The collectors Dorothy and Herbert Vogel behold the artwork while Tuttle kneels next to it.[70] The camera fixes the cluster of friends above the object, but they will have to break their gait if they want to examine it closely. Its edges interject with the wood floorboards' pattern and divert it into a different direction; is this a scrap of road, slipping into space for us or for the bodies represented? The coffee cup in Tuttle's hand creates an air of care and even tenderness, and flattens any hierarchy between maker, collector, and object. Karen Barad's statement that "difference isn't given . . . it isn't fixed" speaks loudly here. The work throws into question the ontological separations between itself and the ground, between painting and drawing and sculpture, between maker and learner and friend. As Barad writes, "Subject and object, wave and particle, position and momentum do not exist outside of specific intra-actions that enact cuts that make separations—not absolute separations, but only contingent separations—within phenomena."[71] While Vogel's eye may wish to align with Merleau-Ponty's claims and cut through all possible doubts, Tuttle's drawing-based sculptures mobilize an astonishing set of material and gravitational forces that make separation contingent. The basic details of the work cannot be separated from its ability to mobilize the other bodies in the room.

Intra-actions such as these can prompt a reconsideration of perception altogether, so that it becomes closely linked to a variety of different types of ability. Merleau-Ponty mentions literal cutting several times in *The Phenomenology of Perception,* particularly when he discusses such nonnormative perceptual faculties as blindness or apraxia. He includes it as part of a series of working gestures, such as a salute, that a patient diagnosed with apraxia might be asked to do in a clinical setting. This patient, who suffers from an inability to recognize and memorize objects, is presented with scissors, cloth, leather, and a workbench. These things combine to form "an open situation, which calls for a certain mode of resolution, a certain kind of work." Space becomes a piece of leather "to be cut up."[72] Those with nonnormative perceptual faculties sense space physically, even speculatively, rather than as a set of prior categories—or as one might do in illusionistic art, "as a category which exists prior to the knowledge of things within it," as Rosalind Krauss put it.[73] For a person with these differences, the body is no more than "an *element* in the system of the subject and his world."[74] Tuttle's acts of cutting, sewing, following templates, and applying pigment are all edge-tracing gestures that allow the body to both create and respond to line. The line becomes, not a concept generated in the artist's mind, but a sudden fulmination—a flash of agency detached from a human subject. It is hardly surprising, then, that Tuttle has discussed these early works in terms of his own cognitive shortcomings, comparing his process making them to a "recognition of a disability."[75] Making objects is a highly disruptive intra-action; it reveals the neurodiversity inherent to most acts of material transfer, a neurodiversity that flourishes in particular when making objects for aesthetic contemplation.

CUTTING INTO ART HISTORY

There is also a social and relational dimension to this intra-active cutting that finds its way into looking and seeing. In conversations with Tuttle, the centrality of his relationship with the Vogels becomes clear. He has many memories of looking at specific artworks alongside them as friends, including, for example, Raphael's drawing *Agony in the Garden,* which he recalls seeing with Herbert Vogel at the Morgan Library (fig. 67).[76] Vogel had taken courses at New York University's Institute of Fine Arts, which emphasized careful analysis of artists' individual choices to reinforce narratives of mastery. Tuttle had been introduced to Herbert and Dorothy Vogel at

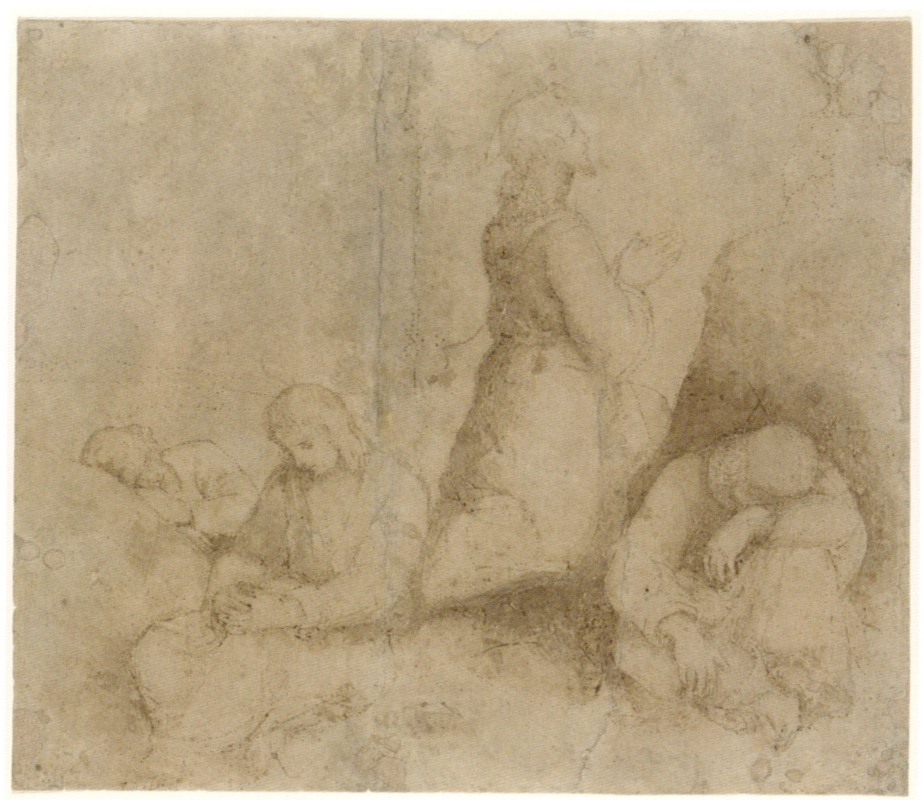

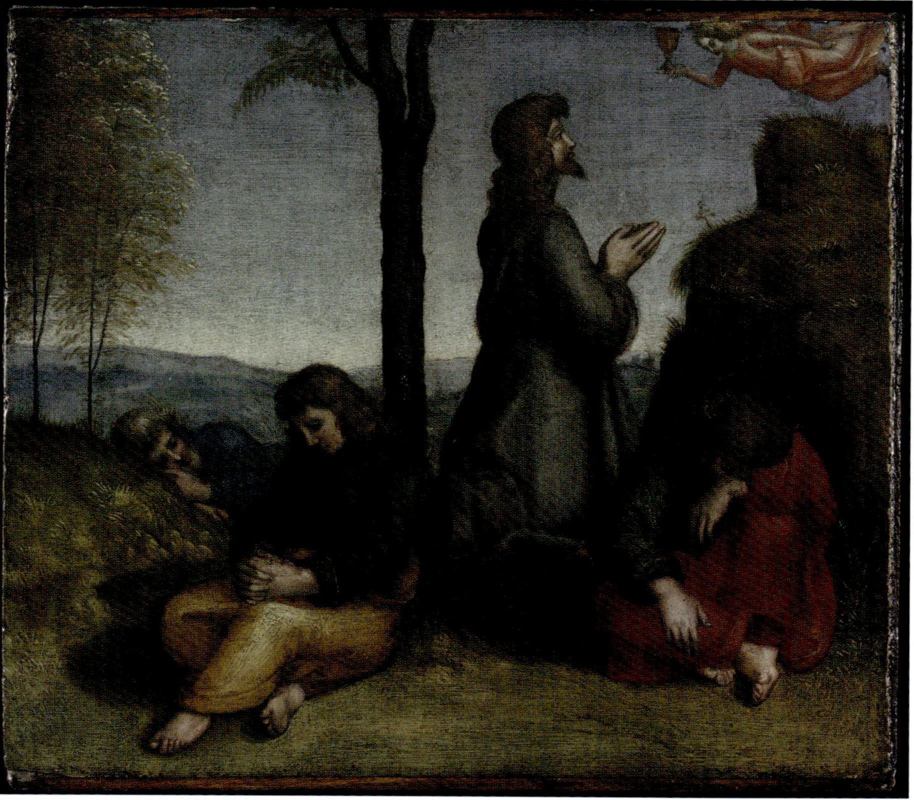

     Cutting into Things

his exhibition in 1968 at Betty Parsons Gallery, *Ten New Works by Richard Tuttle,* and enjoyed walking to and from museums in New York with them in the afternoons, often to compare the drawings of Old Master artists with their finished paintings. *Agony in the Garden* held special interest for the artist because of the way its central tree trunk stood out, firmly drawn and pricked with pounce marks for eventual transfer to a finished painting. The artist's clear delineation of the tree trunk is mirrored in the bright, distinct, solid brown vertical that echoed Christ's upward back in the finished painting *The Agony in the Garden* (1504), splitting the upper quadrant of the composition (fig. 68). "Can we speak of a bifurcated line and a non-bifurcated line?" Tuttle reflected in a poem decades later, referring to Raphael's cuts and pricks left visible after centuries. The tree, which registered Raphael's extra pressure against the paper surface, generated a sense of liveliness that challenged the two friends, cutting through traditional connoisseurly analysis. "Do we look to drawings when we want something really alive?" he continues in the poem, which is written entirely in the interrogative mode. He inquires further: "Are drawings structurally perfect?"[77] A context thus appears for what he called his "self-perpetuating, self-detached and intellectually de-respondent" works in the later 1960s and early 1970s. Developed from the disposable papers that industrial capitalism made possible, they speak to longue-durée concerns about line's power to incise an edge.[78]

The way that Tuttle speaks of the drawings' simultaneous detachment and relationality, not to mention his speculative queries about bifurcation, call into question the direct, causal line between the artist and the object that connoisseurship-driven art history reinforces.[79] Although some writers have examined Tuttle's work in terms of its serial qualities, with productive results, a perusal of his drawings from the late 1960s reveals disruptions, shifts, and cuts in between these serial objects.[80] By late 1967, for example, Richard Tuttle was sketching his sculptures after he had finished making them. In a radical departure from approaches to art and process since the Renaissance, he inhabited the positions of both engaged maker and studious viewer after the fact. While drawing had long been yoked to *disegno,* or the practice of mediating thought through the hand, there is a far sparser record of artists returning to the scene of their own works to study them anew.[81] One drawing, just under eighteen by twelve inches, made of medium-grain manila drawing paper, featured a penciled octagon tilted on its side and filled in with uneven green watercolor. Its title, *Study for First Green Octagon,* deceptively signaled a preparatory *study for* the sculpture to which it corresponded (fig. 69).[82] *Study* also presents an optical illusion on the page: is it foreshortened or really that shape? The octagon is a freehand drawn parallelogram with eight sides of four different lengths, with eraser marks that show the shape's migration toward the center point of the page, reaching it but not quite. If we are to believe its title, it would read as a preparatory drawing of a green shape that later, in its final fabric version, loosened itself from the template of Euclidian geometry. A note at the bottom says, "1 Jungle Green"

Fig. 67 (opposite, top)
Raphael, *Agony in the Garden,* 1503–5. Pen and brown ink and wash, on laid paper; incised with stylus and pricked for transfer, 6½ × 8⅞ in. (16.5 × 22.6 cm). Morgan Library and Museum, Purchased by J. Pierpont Morgan: acc. no. I, 15.

Fig. 68 (opposite, bottom)
Raphael, *The Agony in the Garden,* ca. 1504. Oil on wood, 9½ × 11⅜ in. (24.1 × 28.9 cm). Metropolitan Museum of Art, New York, 32.130.1.

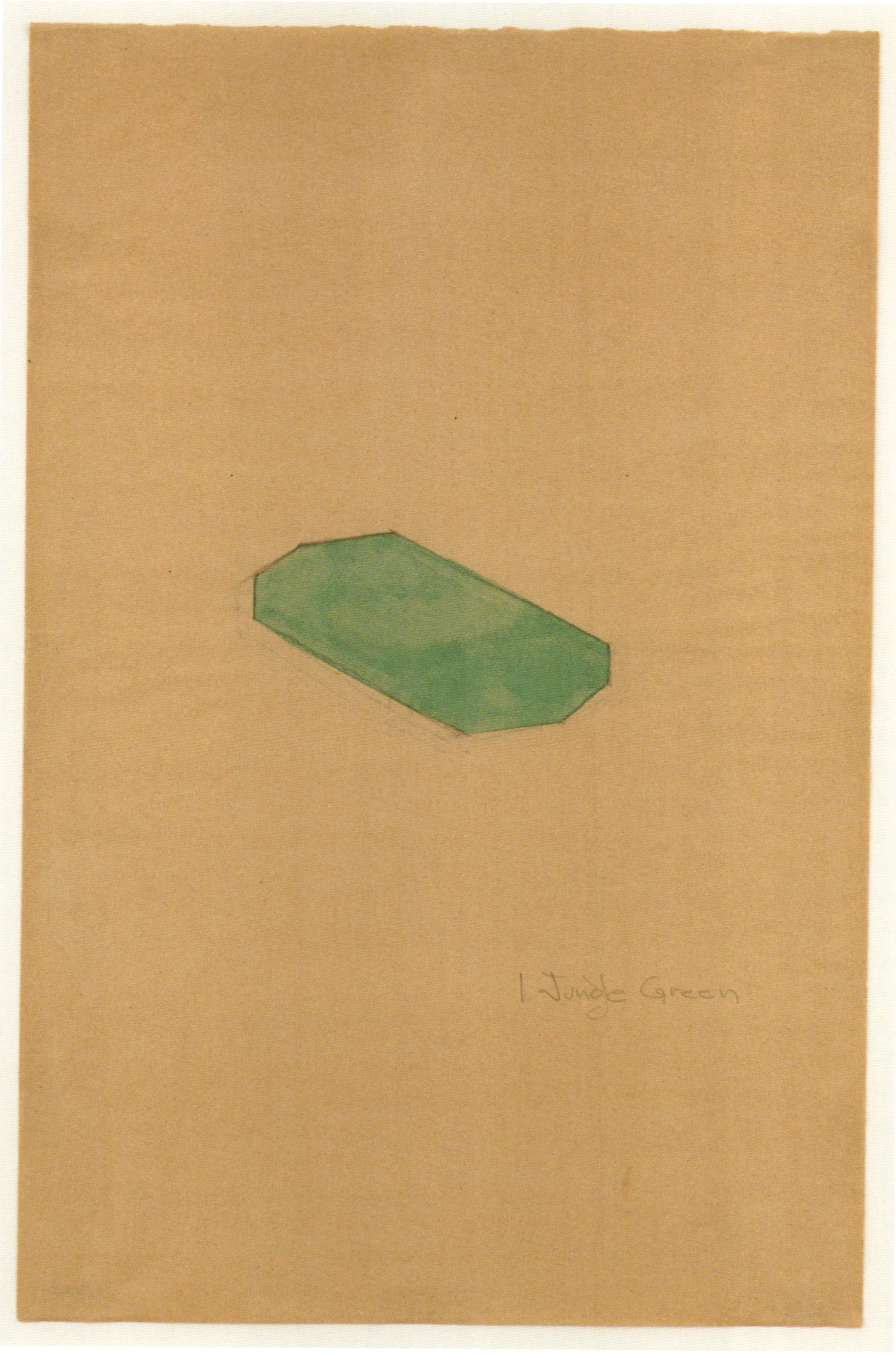

Fig. 69 Richard Tuttle, *Study for First Green Octagon*, 1967.
Watercolor and pencil on paper, 17⅝ × 11⅝ in. (44.9 × 29.5 cm).
Gift of Jock Truman, 124.1974. Museum of Modern Art, New York.

  Cutting into Things

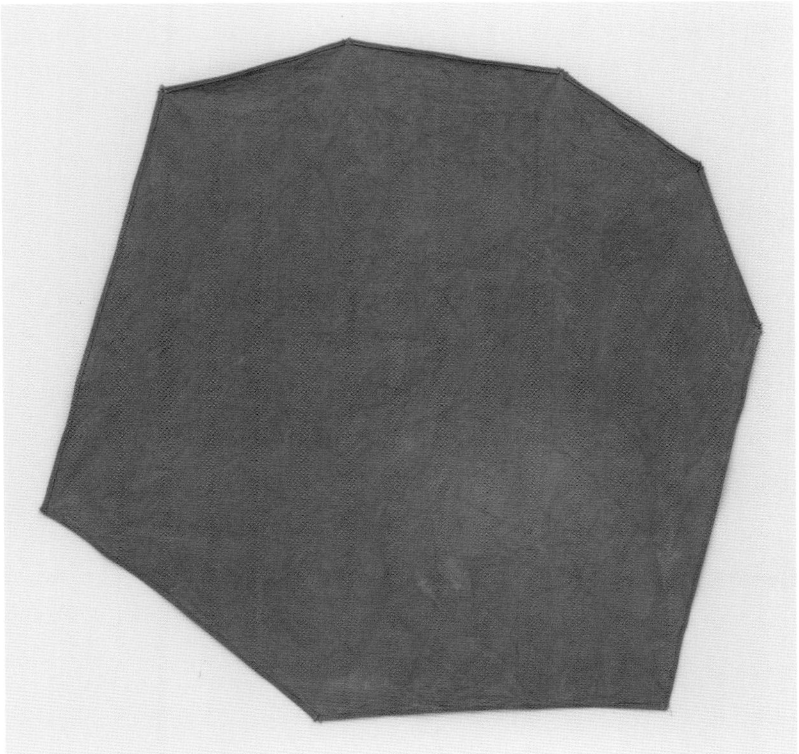

to indicate the shade of Tintex for the final sculpture, like a designer's pitch board, a housewife's pattern book, or fabricator's order form.

Study is in fact a study *of* the sculpture, after the fact. *Cloth Octagonal 2* had been completed months earlier (fig. 70). The fabric octagon, which was shown in Lehigh University's annual exhibition of contemporary American painting that year, has sides of varying length; it came from a previous free-hand pencil drawing of an octagon on a paper template, which was then cut out and traced onto unstretched cotton duck fabric. The artist then sewed the edges and displayed the final shape in no set orientation, either on the wall or on the floor. The drawing is a reflection on the sculpture, and is per-formatively, purposefully out of order. These later "study" drawings are imi-tative; they are a way out of the work rather than a clue *into* it. They subvert the implied hierarchy that makes the preparatory work less complete than its final iteration, but they also carefully maintain a distinct "life" for each of the "states" of the work. Tuttle mentioned in a later interview that the studies were "a joke" that "showed [him] what [he] didn't want to know," making the drawing also into a punch line.[83] It makes us pay attention, in turn, to the artist's opaque reference and casual asides: what *did* he close himself off from assimilating about the sculptures, either voluntarily or in-voluntarily? Subverting the order of things creates ample space for all that has been cut off.

This not-quite-eighteen-inch paper study expands the octagon—the *first* green octagon, as the title reminds us—into ideas and models yet to come, its future inseparable from the provisional qualities of the study. What's more, *Study for Green Octagon* undid the traditional order of the development of an idea: instead of narrating the process of sketch to object, *Study* is a study of the sculpture's future; instead of holding the archival authority of a working drawing, the sketch breaks down the linear narrative of artistic process and implicates paper—the tool of the not-yet-finished—in a faulty evidence trail.

I find Karen Barad's ongoing emphasis on "meaning-mattering" and "differentiating-entangling" through a single "cutting together-apart" especially inviting here.[84] It suggests to me a way to read a material, even molecular history of art objects—to remake art history's relationship with connoisseurship and diagnosis. Many things in *Study* show their effects on the paper surface over time, turning paper from surface into substrate. The watercolor made ripples when it dried on the page, an effect called buckling that makes the paint come forward in three dimensions and stand out as an agent of change, which Tuttle came to like. All material adaptations, even minute ones, became points of interest. He did most of his drawings, which numbered in the hundreds, on notebook paper up until the late 1970s, and insisted that they be hung with the notebook fringe visible after they were sold.[85] Later, conversely, he described the paper octagons simply in terms of their "nature" and shipped their octagonal-shaped paper templates folded up in flat mailing envelopes along with basic directions for installing them that museums and galleries could create variations on.[86] Museums have noted that at least one of the cloth octagons appears to have been sprayed in spots with detergent as though it was a stained shirt or pair of overalls.[87] Indeed, Tuttle said they were "of a nature both free (therefore unnatural) and responsive to social demands (which I abhor)," which inserted them both into and outside the vibrant human social sphere.[88] In the early 1970s he discussed his drawings and wire pieces in terms of their age, sometimes gendering them.

Paper here is not just an exploratory surface that referenced or revealed the art object but also a wisecracking pedagogical agent. In other words, these drawings are real cut-ups, projecting humor into the artistic process through their ability to schismatize its presumed order. Their actions feel quite different from the progressive patterns that even the most imaginative educational theorists (including John Dewey) formulated in the twentieth

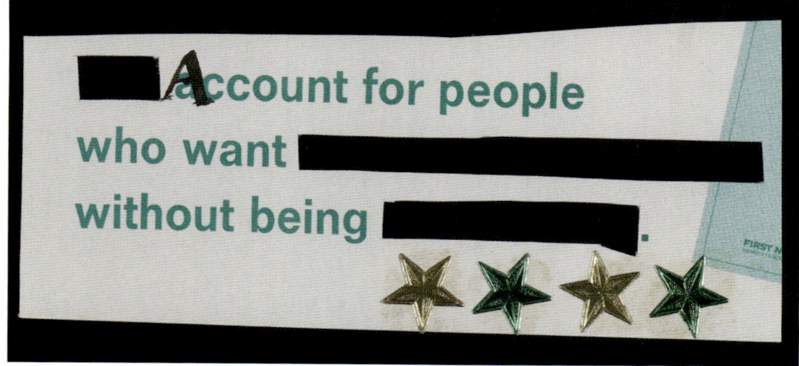

Fig. 71 Richard Tuttle, encoded letter to Samuel Wagstaff with stickers, ca. 1967–69. Samuel Wagstaff Papers, Archives of American Art, Smithsonian Institution.

     Cutting into Things

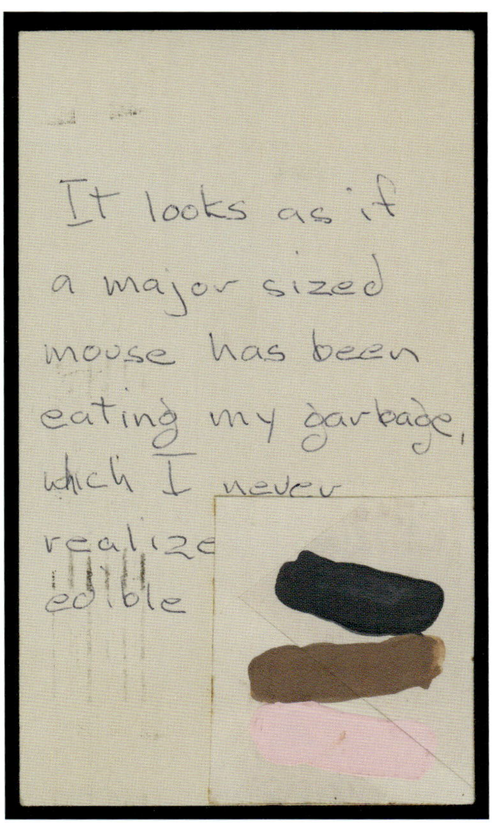

Fig. 72 Richard Tuttle, letter to Samuel Wagstaff with collaged painted marks, ca. 1967–69. Samuel Wagstaff Papers, Archives of American Art, Smithsonian Institution.

century, which placed experiential learning at the center of a larger, beneficial democratic project. Instead, Tuttle has said that "making a drawing is a slipping backward"—a remark that links democracy with the many mistakes necessary to achieve it.[89]

Paper could also cut things off from view. Just as quitting training and faking drawing occasioned important moments for Tuttle as a learner, they also offered other counterstrategies against bureaucratic forces, such as the censor's pen and military exercises, with which he was all too familiar. In the encoded notes that Tuttle sent to Wagstaff between 1967 and 1969, after he had returned from military service and Wagstaff had taken a curatorial position at the Detroit Institute of Arts, disclosure and control are directly overlaid with each other. In one note, Tuttle converts a bank advertisement into a feigned censored military document (fig. 71). Several lines, such as the text that follows "who want," are cut from the page, with only empty space remaining instead of the line. Here Tuttle cuts out a space—a literal absence but also a disruption to the imaginative act of writing—to mimic the black mark of the censor's pen. The other letter has a readable message about a mouse that has suddenly been discovered in Tuttle's Midtown West studio, the top floor of a tenement apartment. The paper's lower quadrant is obscured by three short, brushed lines of paint, wavering against one another like *Sparrow*'s two colored bands (fig. 72). Both letters activate a series of relations between two very different chromatic and formal fields:

the black and colored fields that conceal text underneath them, the presumably neutral background of the white paper, and the white expanse of the everyday notepad. Seen in light of the decade's abiding questions about perception, these little exercises in concealment where Tuttle annexes the power of the censor, where black liquid mimics administrative deceit, come through as very powerful indeed. The ink makes the visible invisible. It attaches a blank boundlessness to human desire ("people who want ___") and mocks the possibility of deriving ordered histories from evidence.

TO DISAPPEAR INTO THE WALL

In 1970 a series of paper octagonals followed from the series of cloth octagons. Tuttle produced twelve of these works, with each work usually constituting a run of one hundred or more octagonal-shaped cut-out forms. To make them, the artist freehand drew a template on white paper in an octagonal shape, cut it out with scissors, and affixed each cutout to the wall of a gallery or private home with wallpaper paste. Since each of the twelve paper shapes could act as the template for many copies, these emerged as hybrids of painting, sculpture, and artist's multiples. His written instructions specify that each paper octagon be affixed to a white wall in any orientation, giving the paper an evanescent effect that highlighted any imperfections in the supporting wall (fig. 73). These paper sculptures, produced in editions like fine art prints and installed with glue like wallpaper, were relatively affordable at a hundred dollars each, and the artist sometimes came to the space of each collector or gallery to install the work himself.[90] In these cases, he would install the paper octagonals after speaking with the buyers, at times allowing the buyers to suggest positions on the wall.[91] In basing their shapes on a cutout template and their placement (and occasionally, their dimensions) on the trajectories of in-person conversations, Tuttle imbricated his own actions (drawing and cutting) within his immediate social and spatial settings. The octagonals turned any space into a space where creativity could happen.

Inexpensive and socially stimulating, the octagonals could be taken to exhibitions such as documenta 5, the much-discussed contemporary art exhibition held in Kassell, Germany, every five years, or folded and put in the mail to European gallerists such as Alfred Schmela, who was establishing rich connections with collectors in Germany and across Europe.[92] They represented a sea change in artist-collector relations at the end of the 1960s and the beginning of the 1970s. Cheap materials such as paper became portable epicenters of the networked social lives of postminimal and conceptual artists. These lives were also highly mediated; artist Lynda Benglis, for example, began filming Tuttle making both these and his wire pieces when he installed them for (and with) collectors Herb and Dorothy Vogel. Tuttle was the first artist whom Benglis videotaped in this way, and she cites the Vogels as significant interlocutors who shaped the works as they were

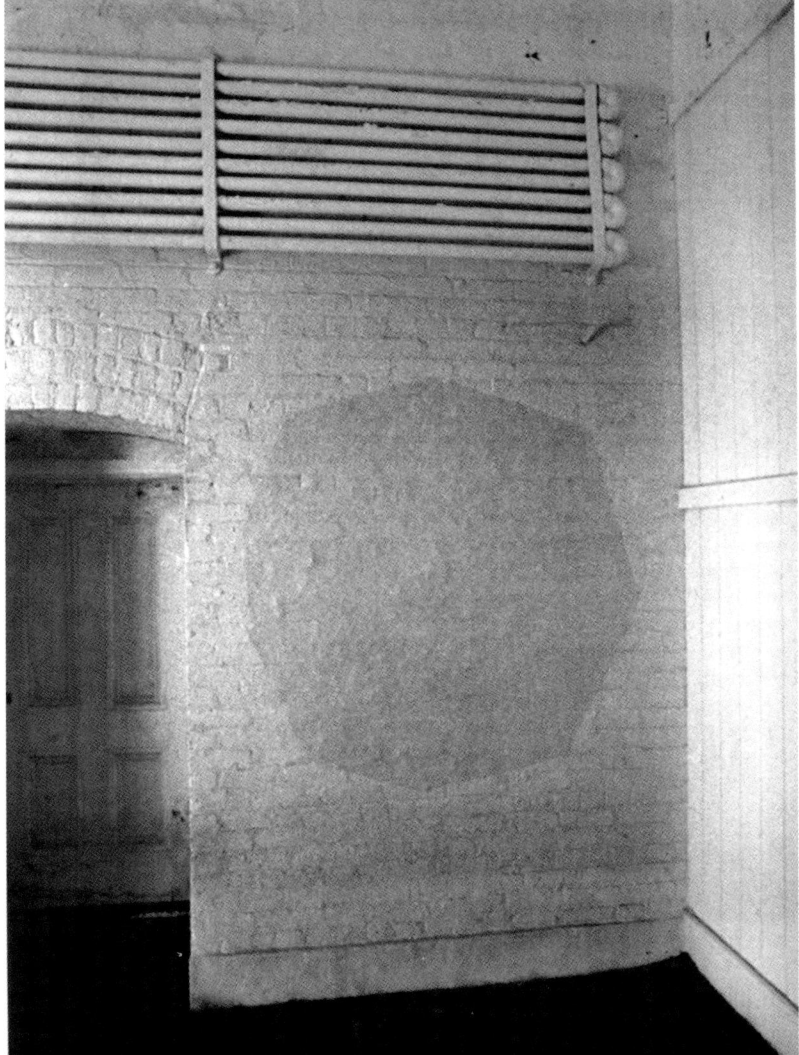

Fig. 73 Installation view of the exhibition *Richard Tuttle* in 1973 at the Clocktower Gallery, Institute for Art and Urban Resources, New York, showing *12th Paper Octagonal* (1970).

made. "People wanted to be collected and also entertained by [Herbert]" when he and Dorothy engaged in the scene," she recalls.[93] She took documents of artists, gallerists, and collectors, first on reel-to-reel tape and later on a small Portapak camera that the Leo Castelli Gallery had given her in an effort to support, catalog, and eventually sell artists' experimental video projects. "I was very interested in what it was; he was doing *something* on the wall," she says of these works.[94] With their barely visible contours, the works "changed the room" and made "deep space magically [expand]" even the smallest display spaces, as another collector remarked.[95] To collect a work of art such as the octagonals changed space in the very same way that Reich imagined: it expanded social possibilities through very small, perceivable differences in one's surroundings.

The cutting and gluing thus generated two modes of instability. The first was an unstable intimacy with the object, whose specific qualities could be sensed only intermittently and imperfectly—a bind that threw the work's ontology into question. "Was it part of the wall?" the collector Flora Miller Biddle wonders in retrospect. "Was the wall part of it? Was it a drawing or a sculpture? Was it sitting atop the wall or was it a white void, like Nirvana or death? With it nearby, the last thing I saw at night and the first thing I saw when I awoke, I seemed to dream deeper, and the day held unlimited potential."[96] The second was a dynamic interplay among the artist, the viewer, and the space in which the work came into being. Drawing and cutting turned the environment into a space of friendship. Perhaps more interestingly, they engaged the functional *components* of friendship, such as conversation, so that each participant could find generativity in any set of coordinates and moments. As participants negotiated decisions together within the optics of the artist-collector relationship, their intimacies and calculations all became discrete risks, as Jacques Derrida has put it, that were "flush with the event, within it and with an open heart."[97] Tracing and cutting encouraged people's spontaneous behaviors within the architectural space by cutting into it and cutting within it, harnessing the total environment before evaporating into it almost completely.

Making a work this way ensured a dynamic ecosystem in which each actor and each element became animated by one another; sometimes literally interdependent—these works could not be removed without being destroyed.[98] If the buyer changed living spaces, Tuttle would come to a new location of the collector's choosing and make and install a new octagonal there.[99] In making the octagonals so reliant on their habitats, Tuttle invited the viewer to understand all art, in the terms established by Whitehead, as being fundamentally inseparable from the changing conditions that support all life. As if in poetic conversation with their vulnerability, there was little chromatic distinction between the octagonals' paper surfaces and their surroundings; the break between the object and its setting and environment is so subtle as to be almost invisible. Douglas Crimp reported that "the works took some time to locate" when all twelve octagons in the series were installed in the imposing main exhibition space of the Clocktower Gallery in 1973.[100]

Tuttle has proposed that this kind of visual indeterminacy creates a "doubling" of the supporting wall. This doubling, in turn, might generate a "non-material 'wall-of-looking'" rooted in the same perceptual flaws and mistakes that Whitehead had championed—that is, a more general space of understanding that helps us understand our own looking conditions.[101] Dorothy Vogel remarked that as the octagons aged, they became more and more visible, giving them a distinct temporality tied to the chemical changes that affect the paper's visibility.[102] As a book ages, it becomes more valuable; as a refrigerator ages, it becomes obsolete and then, after a longer time, a historical artifact. Most important, this quality of simultaneous placelessness and yet binding oneself to a place, as well as the octagons' long exposure time (which was also tied to how long the work's owners lived in the space; if they moved, they could trace and recut a new octagonal from the old), established no clear object-boundaries except those that slowly come to presence after sustained study. Like the labor-forms that they involve—cutting, tracing, and gluing—there is no reason to notice them other than our own curiosity.

Forms of labor such as cutting and gluing prompted reconsiderations of medium specificity and value, and they also incised media hierarchies in modern art. "[The papers] set the limits of a person's appreciation," Tuttle noted to Robert Pincus-Witten in 1970. "They are disposable and not disposable. Even Rembrandts are disposable. It all depends on the limits of a person's appreciation." Like skin, the octagonals were both a barrier and an interface-surface for sensations, but they were also a product. They both contained creative potential and downplayed artistic virtuosity, shimmering into the wall. Tuttle continued in the same interview: "I have a hatred for this white thing. I can't stand the kind of purity that white implies in our environment. But the kind of purity that comes out of the complete electrical functioning of the human being—that's the kind of purity I aspire to. I would really like to be ignorant."[103] Paper seemed to be mediating two conflicting ideas: whatever human beings make and do is a perverted imitation of nature and the body; and although the seer might invest value in anything, according to a given arbitrary value system, there was something necessarily complete about all human endeavors, including art.

Many other artists of the 1960s moment, such as the Supports-Surfaces movement based in Paris, also explored the market economy, with flexible paper, fabric, or latex textiles functioning as interrogations of unfolding postwar plenty. Tuttle's materials, too, held a semantic weight in the twentieth-century United States that is almost irresistible to pick through. Cutting out a drawing and rolling it into a single tube accommodated the easy, unencumbered manner of both the workman hanging wallpaper and the Manhattan designer. Cutting from a pattern was also the purview of twentieth-century Euro-American women, who distilled Puritan ethics of creativity through their thrift and creative know-how. As one popular social hygiene film at the time put it, housewives attracted respect for their "careful planning . . . for further use of what we already have, for *making do* so nothing will be wasted."[104] But whereas Carolee Schneemann had been the object of critical contempt for wasting flour, Tuttle's process attracted praise even as he cut away the edges of the paper. Critics assimilated his practice as uninhibited rather than messy, thrifty instead of wasteful, charming instead of monstrous, sensual rather than erotic. Cuts done by a masculine-bodied person produced an entirely different set of effects.

One photograph from Tuttle's retrospective exhibition in 1975 shows the artist crouching on bare feet, tracing a paper octagonal for hanging (fig. 74). Tuttle kept the paper templates in a set of drawers at home and could either fold them or roll them for transport.[105] The picture shows the variations that might occur on the original during production: the artist

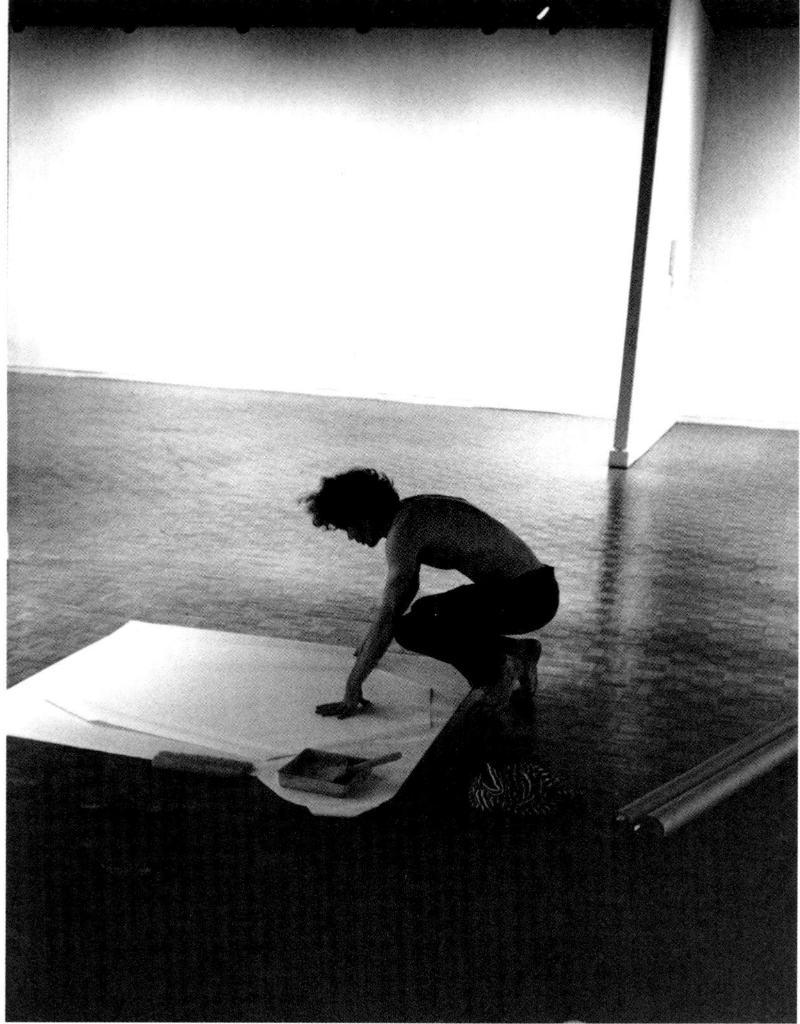

Fig. 74 Richard Tuttle during the installation of *Richard Tuttle,* 1975, Exhibition Records, 1931–2004, box 70, folder 53, Whitney Museum of American Art, Frances Mulhall Achilles Library and Archives, New York. Photograph by Marcia Tucker.

would unfold the paper matrix from a bag or pocket, set a sheet of new paper on the floor, trace the octagon as it sat on the sheet, and cut out the shape with craft scissors. He then used a wheat paste brush to spread adhesive onto the surface of the paper, lift it up, and press it onto the wall with a dry brush, adding more adhesive as he went. All the entities involved will change, even as they adhere to their own true natures. In the picture Tuttle, too, projects a naturalness, both in terms of ease of gesture and insofar as his natural look accords with the countercultural template of the moment. He is barefoot and shirtless, and the wall on which the white octagon will hang lacks nails or other hardware. The cut and naturally curling edge of the paper is visible in the photograph, evoking textiles or wallpaper. Scraps of white paper lie next to Tuttle's cast-off shoes on the floor. On the one hand, Tuttle's actions as photographed appear pragmatic, routinized, rooted in habits of touching and feeling; his hands, draping the paper against the side of the wall, and then casually reaching for the brush in his back pocket, perform a practiced authentic capability and a hermetic concentration that is

Cutting into Things

captivating to look at, even in the photographs. There is a sense that Tuttle is experiencing effortless yet careful expertise and an exploratory process of learning; as Marx might imagine it, this is a form of productive work that is so well organized that it also "gives play to our bodily and mental powers."[106] Here is a body alive with a task. It extends the popular genre of "artist in the studio" portraits to encompass the artist solving routinized, domestic, but nonetheless important design puzzles.

Discussed as *nearly invisible,* then, these tasklike octagonals are imbued with performance, charged with charisma and even erotic energies. Within the artistic and intellectual dialogues of which Tuttle, Benglis, and the Vogels were a part, he was known as "a sensitive, magical person"—Benglis concedes that she was "a little in love with him," as were many people he knew.[107] Sometimes the challenge of tracing, cutting, and gluing an octagonal resulted in an almost dancelike execution for these works, as curator Marcia Tucker observed in the mid-1970s and which some photographs betray (fig. 75). And yet, as Tucker recalled when they installed his retrospective exhibition together in 1975, "The installation decisions were made by Tuttle and me, working together, trying things out, discussing them, making alterations and changes until each piece related to every other piece that could be seen from each possible vantage point."[108] The works and the tasks that created them were a simultaneous avenue into observing Tuttle's individual body and feeling the forces of co-creation that happened between bodies in the moment—another form of cutting-together-apart.

Some critics and curators incorporated these raw-looking, uncalculated works into larger narratives of striving and perfection that aligned

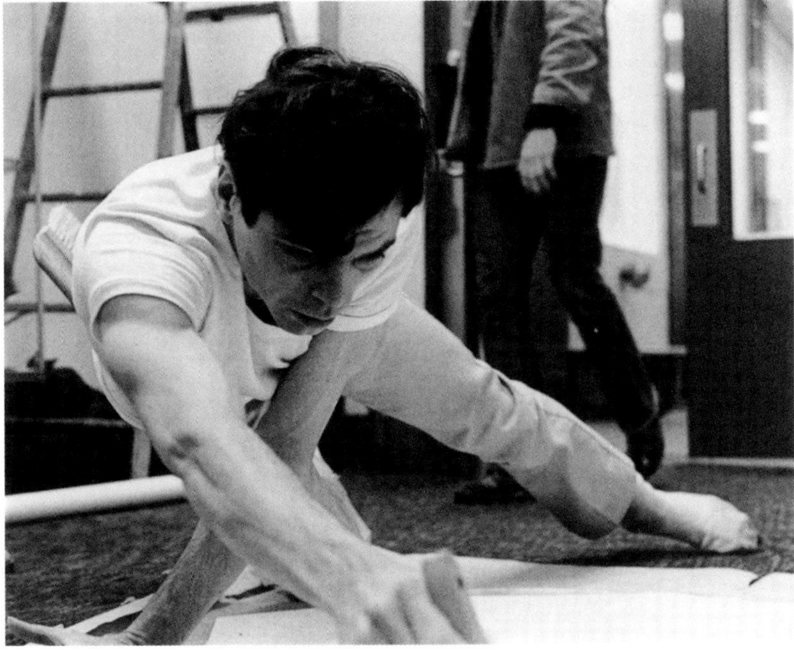

Fig. 75 Richard Tuttle applying starch paste to a paper octagonal in preparation for the exhibition *Richard Tuttle* at Hopkins Hall Gallery, Ohio State University, in 1977.

with global industrial capitalism. By late in the decade, multinational corporations were sponsoring such exhibitions as *Live in Your Head: When Attitudes Become Form* at the Kunsthalle Bern in 1969 in an attempt to link process art with intellectual prowess and generativity.[109] Tuttle was one of sixty-nine artists in the exhibition, which was underwritten by the European division of cigarette company Philip Morris. (The company's sponsorship of cultural projects was no doubt meant to draw attention away from its private in-house research initiatives to make cigarettes nominally less harmful to smokers while still maintaining their palatability. Project False, for example, sought to create a new cigarette filter that was lower in particulate matter but still maintained a flavorful cigarette for the consumer.)[110] The exhibition catalog's introductory statement by the company's president framed the enterprise as oriented toward self-improvement: "Just as the artist endeavours to improve his interpretation and conceptions through innovation, the commercial entity strives to improve its end product or service through experimentation with new methods and materials."[111] In other words, any medium could become the medium of ideas, if it were used iteratively enough. The essay instrumentalized materials categorically, as a function of inner life, of drive and creativity—hallmarks of post–Cold War Euro-American masculinity—with the art object as their natural and necessary product. The artist and critic Scott Burton's essay exploited the anxiety inherent in this masculine enterprise and attributed to the objects a transitive ability to perform this same tension. Burton set Tuttle's work apart from the "torn, flopping, 'anxious objects'" in the exhibition: "The humbleness of Richard Tuttle's wrinkled, dyed, nailed-up pieces of cloth is rivaled only by their grandeur of conception—they have no back, no front, no up or down, they may be attached to the wall or spread out on the floor. Imagine making an object which will maintain its integrity in all circumstances yet which exerts absolutely no demands on its situation."[112]

Tuttle's many series of paper objects thus present a long and complicated case study, one that reveals the often-gendered contours of process and design thinking. By being barely visible and never giving the impression of "improvement," did his works affirm the exhibition's corporate rhetoric or did they undermine it? By cutting into effort, they certainly worked to constitute imperfections and disengagements as powerful modes of breach. Centering imperfections as inherently animating, even pedagogical, was and is a political gesture. Creating art or government is clunky and complicated. We may coordinate efforts to achieve perfection but never approach an ideal terminus; in fact, we subject bodies and the environment to serious damage in order to do it. But the octagonals are more self-sufficient than the uses of print media, news, or capital—they result not in cumulative achievement but rather in momentary mistakes.

These works that were nearly indistinguishable from their supporting wall found themselves in deep accord with mounting tensions about living artists' proper place within museums and galleries. "The whole idea of the museum seems to be tending more toward a kind of specialized entertainment," Robert Smithson wrote in 1967. "It's taking on more and more of the aspects of a discotheque and less and less the aspects of art."[113] Donald Judd's diagnosis was darker still: "Museums patronize, isolate, and neutralize artists. . . . The museums never have much money for contemporary artists but they have money for fancy buildings."[114] The building that supports Tuttle's paper octagonals almost facetiously disappears it. Like a body surrendering to the inevitable, the paper octagon collapses into the building, but its whiteness also implies that, possibly, things could cover it . . . if this were a sheet of paper, traditionally construed. It is certainly the case that mailed correspondence was an inexhaustible source of creativity for the artist and here forms an ideal counterstrategy to the vagaries of institutional display. On small-scaled blank pages throughout this period, Tuttle engaged the complexities of the graphic surface, using clip art, encoded text, and repeated motifs. Letters to friends reveal in frank terms which other artists he was thinking about and occasionally even which exhibitions he was seeing, and these more straightforward disclosures were supported by a playful approach to textual expression. They thus cut into communication, creating a blur between the cause (the agent that draws and writes) and the effect (the thing drawn or written on, or the content).

A letter from 1970 situates these possibilities within the dynamics of written correspondence and mailed print material (fig. 76). In art and literature circles of the 1960s, mail art's position within social life accelerated. The mail artist Ray Johnson also corresponded with Wagstaff, and Tuttle's letters to the curator take a similarly expansive approach to collage forms and other augmentations to the page surface. This letter uses promotional material that Wagstaff had sent to Tuttle from the Detroit Institute of Arts, where the exhibition *Other Ideas* had just been mounted and whose catalog included Tuttle's written instructions included for his cloth pieces. The letter to Wagstaff is written in code, with the message in reverse and each word spelled backward, with each word arranged according to an arbitrary spacing calculus. It consists entirely of an encoded quotation from the DIA members' bulletin:

> Dear Sam–
> The second of our Balcony Shows (Motherwell was the first) opens with light refreshments on the Balcony of The South Wing Sculpture Court Tuesday afternoon from 3 To 6:30, October 13, 1970. The exhibition continues Through November 8. !The Graphic Works of Stanley Mouse!
> The artist Stanley Mouse and a number of his friends will be present. He is a native son of Detroit, famous throughout the United "monster cars"
> –Dick

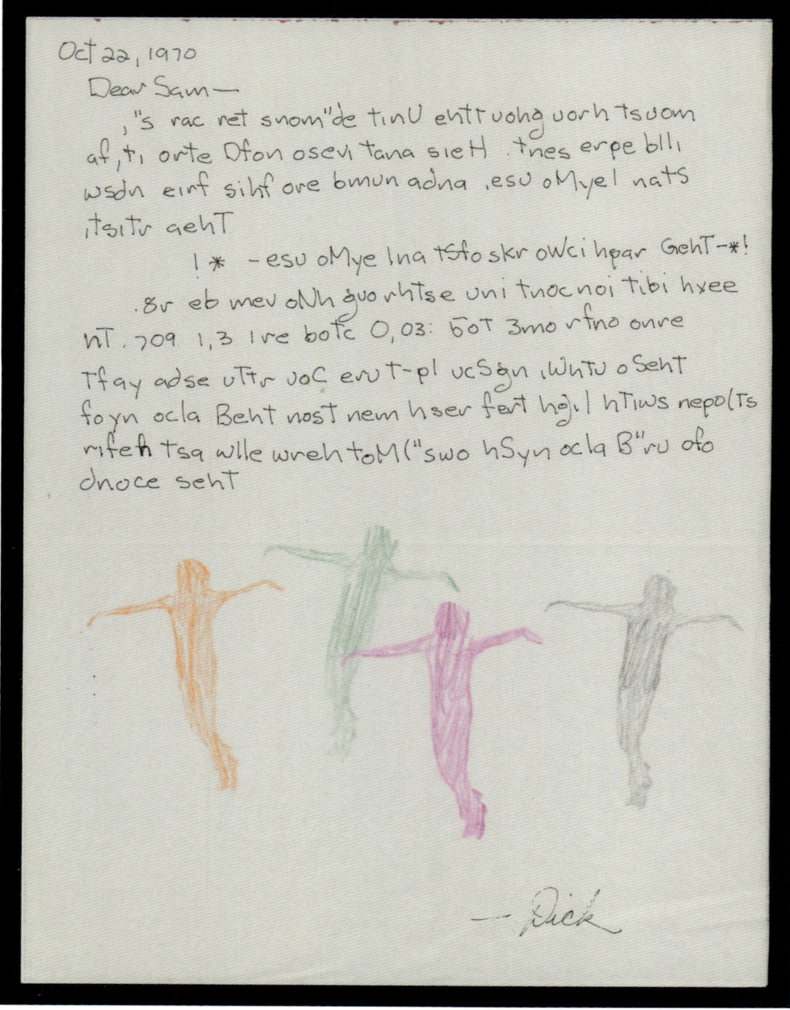

The original text, of course, read "United States" instead of "United 'monster cars.'"[115] (The "monster cars" may have referenced the poster that Stanley Mouse designed for the exhibition, which features a 1946 Buick Super 8 in front of an American flag; this poster was made available through the DIA's Drawing and Print Club.) Introduced in the beginning of the 1960s, museum bulletins were mailed regularly to museum and collectors' club members, inviting them to exclusive events. Wagstaff's tenure overlapped with the founding of the Drawing and Print Club; through such clubs, which were becoming a national trend, museum patrons could pay a modest membership fee in exchange for specially commissioned prints by contemporary artists.[116] Tuttle's letter, with its scrambled and cut-up text, inserts itself into the new trend of courting museum collectors. To cite Smithson, it marks the contemporary museum as a discotheque, but one whose financial commitments led it to graft social opportunities onto its institutional collecting networks. Besides this coded repetition of Wagstaff's museum materials, Tuttle writes nothing else in the letter. It divulges nothing about his daily life but nonetheless requires calculated engagement from its (one very specific) reader. He has *written back, cut into text* in the most speculative sense, mimicking the announcement's signifying content but obscuring it through code.

In disrupting the museum announcement by repeating it, Tuttle's letter pointed not only to emerging debates about the purpose and function of museums in the social body but also the division between high and low art that was beginning to selectively and strategically crumble. Stanley Mouse was a well-known rock poster artist who regularly exhibited in New York and San Francisco, emerging as an artist distinct from the San Francisco rock promotion collective the Family Dog, of which he had been a part. Posters by Mouse and the Family Dog were generally installed in private rooms and homes, and occasionally on telephone poles in other public places, but the exhibition at the DIA in 1970, organized at the behest of Sam Wagstaff, brought their designs to the white walls of galleries in monographic exhibitions. Many of the posters used primitivist fantasies of "natural" native dress and mannerisms drawn from disparate sources such as Indigenous American shamanisms (fig. 77) and tribes (fig. 78), to encourage uninhibited creative impulses that affirmed the Family Dog's core principles of social solidarity. Such impulses were inevitably tied to masculinity. It was correct, even ideal for a man to be shirtless, to have his hair long or disheveled. It must have amused Tuttle to think about collectors being served light refreshments in the sculpture court as they waited in anticipation for Stanley Mouse "and a number of his friends" to arrive.

This letter's graphic surface mobilizes multiple critiques: of the commodification of graphic posters as fine art, ratified by the advancing middle classes' investments in outdoor festivals and removal of physical barriers

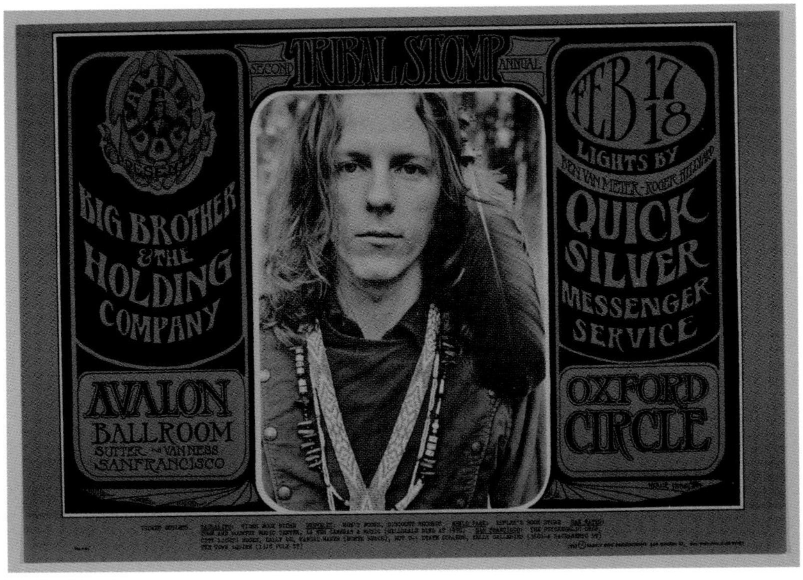

Fig. 77 Stanley Mouse, Alton Kelley, and Bob Seidemann, *James Gurley (Tribal Stomp #2),* 1967. Offset lithograph, 14 × 20 in. (35.6 × 50.8 cm). Published by Family Dog, San Francisco. Sheldon Museum of Art, University of Nebraska–Lincoln, Gift of Charles Wehrenberg, U-6639.1991.

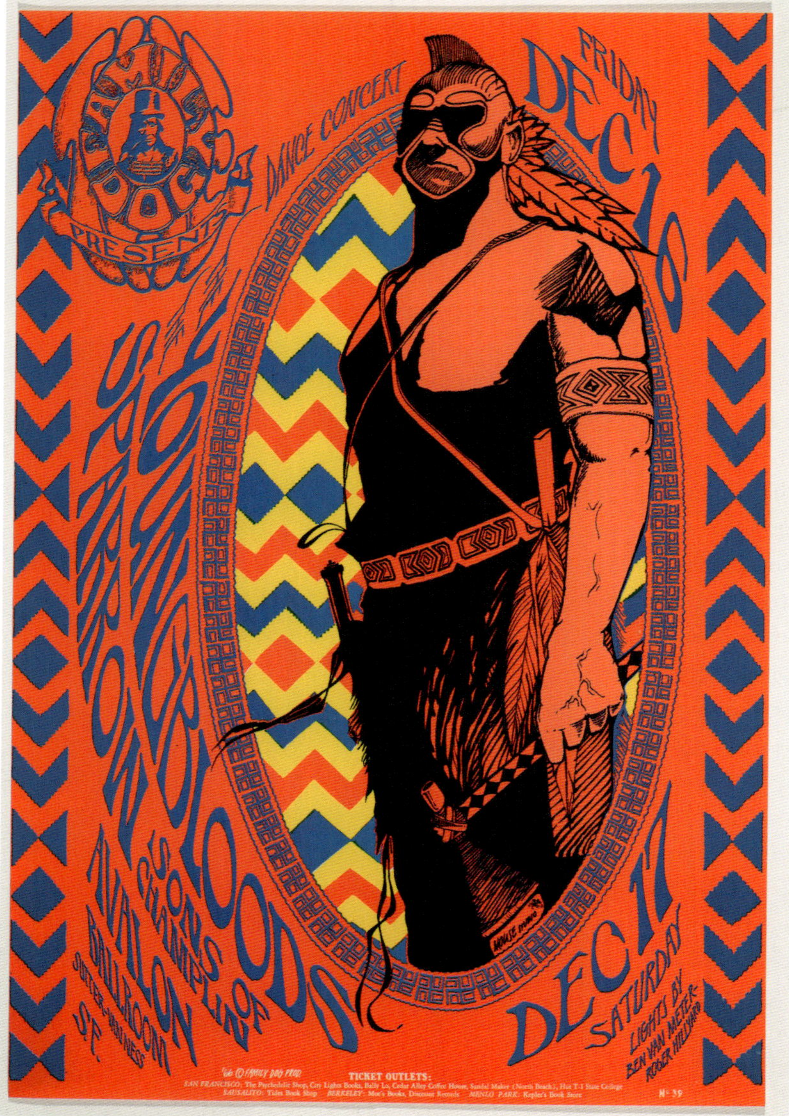

to so-called natural experience. Tuttle's letter helps us see how the market dynamics of the museum transcend hierarchies of media, even disrupt them, at the service of the culture industry, setting terms that exceed the possibility of coarticulating aesthetic and political goals. Paper was not excluded from these affiliations; on the contrary, the lavishly decorated posters performed an important disjunction: of collecting institutions, with their constant appeals to generate new markets for collecting and support, and of the spaces for which such posters were originally conditioned.[117] This is extended further in the letter's second, more behavioral critique of the social conditioning emerging as a central component of museum viewing. Light refreshments, the promise of hobnobbing with the artist and his friends: these staged, artificial, mannered intimacies function as an arm of consolidation of petit bourgeois social habits. They generated no wondrous

    Cutting into Things

wall-of-looking. Their functions were artificial rather than complete, dynamic, "electrical." In letters as well as on the wall, material disrupts both the hegemony of print media and of social scripts, relating the circulation of one to the other.

Tuttle's whimsical use of code exposes the social norms of a rapidly solidifying gallery culture as well as writing's intimacies, its close associations with disclosure. The page is a bulletin board of memory, right down to the tracings of the human figure that deploy across the paper like a rubber stamp. The focus is on the pathways of the media-forms: where were these words and pictures before? Their existence as direct quotations gives them agency, detaches them from aura, even as they perform auratic possibilities, and once again *cuts into* the archival authority of the written page.[118] In this way, Tuttle's account was in line with other emerging artistic projects at the Detroit Institute of Arts and other institutions that concerned themselves with the spaces where manners and habits are allowed to flourish. By 1970, Michael Heizer was designing heavy sculptures to be dragged across the DIA's lawn in random directions; such mark-making acted as another kind of cutting, stamping, and embossing, less intimate but more assertive, that asked: Who or what is an apparatus here? Where exactly might the boundaries of culture lie, if not at the edges of a lawn or at the edges of the museum walls or within a collector's home?

Cut paper proved to be a lively and incisive way to make the transmission of social codes visible. Tuttle's cut-up model boxes, his false study sketches, and his invisible paper sculptures challenged numerous formulas associated with paper and drawing. Within the expanded spaces that these works create, implicit ideas and disclosures are not made explicit, talent is not distilled onto the page. And knowledge is occluded rather than shown. The objects, in their categorically nebulous states, disrupt the postwar and Vietnam-era dreams about information flowing efficiently and unproblematically from place to place. The truth was, in the end, that not everyone had access to ideas; authority figures such as Alabama governor George Wallace proved this by preventing it from becoming so.

"When we can't comprehend or control the major forces, structures and values that define our existence, they must inevitably come to dominate us," wrote Charles Reich in *The Greening of America*. "The public can't be adequately informed about complex issues when news is cut down into staccato pieces of show business and the media systematically deny any fundamentally different or dissenting point of view a chance to be heard."[119] Like Tuttle, Reich felt that structures had to be revealed in all their naked and horrifying complexities and that only the fullest amount of material knowledge could truly engage everyone and anyone. But Tuttle had a different plan for addressing the specific forces that might help us cut into our own staccato habits. "In a materialist society, a lot of people have intimacy problems," remarked Tuttle in 2005. We might take this claim at face value: that the overinvestment in material goods scrambles our ability to form "true" intimate bonds with those objects capable of responding to the extensions of ourselves that we emit. Perhaps we might take it as a negative assertion—that our devotion to the inanimate objects and our investment in the consolidation of our desires, fears, and anxieties (because these things are not reciprocated, Marx tells us, so they only swirl around as deposits) exhausts our capacity to engage in reciprocal, mutual exchange. But, as Tuttle attested further, "drawing becomes a little bit like a pure thing that can stay freer from some of the corrupting influences."[120]

To maintain material flexibility is to thrive. To be small, wrong, or imperfect is to remain perpetually in breach, as Karen Barad and Alfred North Whitehead have corroborated. Tuttle's works created expansive access to art precisely because they were so foldable, so portable. In harnessing the exciting communicative possibilities of line while also cutting against them, in provoking the viewer's intensely human curiosities but also making them the purview of nonhuman materials, Tuttle made an implicit critique of the spaces in which manners and habits are allowed to flourish.

"My generation and I dreamed of this project where art is something that's as available to people as life itself, not something that gets stuffed in some basement," Richard Tuttle has said of the 1960s.[121] For Tuttle, who emerged as a sculptor early in that decade and had achieved international fame by its close, the media of learning and exploration—and his early paper- and drawing-based works that could be folded into duffel bags, recut over and over, and torn from the pages of notebooks—were critical to unstuffing those things that social controls might make unavailable. His broad declaration about the 1960s reflected a politics of abundance and accessibility that did battle with the epoch's simultaneous (and extremely common) rhetorics of exclusion: gendered exclusion, the gatekeeping around what constituted a work of art or an exhibition space, the line between art and its context, and between bodies and the world. Tuttle's interventions of cutting, tracing, and separating readdressed space at an entirely different scale, to show—and to learn for himself—how art could enjoin paper's pedagogical and social functions with its material vulnerabilities.

CHAPTER 4

Prototypes of Empire

Robert Morris Makes Plans

The discovery of the earth, the mapping of her lands and the chartering of her waters, took many centuries and has now only begun to come to an end. Only now has man taken full possession of his mortal dwelling place and gathered the infinite horizons, which were temptingly and forbiddingly open to all previous ages, into a globe whose majestic outlines and detailed surface he knows as he knows the lines in the palm of his hand.

 —Hannah Arendt, *The Human Condition*

There must, it seems to me, be some human activity which serves to break up orientations, to weaken and frustrate the tyrannous drive to order to prepare the individual to observe what the orientation tells him is irrelevant, but that very well may be relevant. That activity, I believe, is the activity of artistic perception.

 —Morse Peckham, *Man's Range for Chaos:*
 Biology, Human Behavior, and the Arts

A few years after Richard Tuttle modeled nonviolent, speculative modes of reasoning for the generation of the long 1960s, Robert Morris would locate violence in the decade's very air and ground. Morris, by then a prominent minimalist artist, received an invitation in June of 1969 to create a work of art on the campus of the University of Puerto Rico at Mayagüez, a university on an island colony that lay at the center of debates on the limits of US imperial control. His collaborative performance with fellow artist Rafael Ferrer created combative visions for state violence by working the connections between thought and extension, between the drawn plan's stretch toward order and matter's uncalculated behaviors in the moment. The performance, titled *Frarmrroreerofibseaterlr* in a scrambling of their names, leveraged the ecological and socioeconomic qualities of materials to take a broad environmental position through an analogy: paper is to throwaway as language is to garbage. A preparatory drawing for the performance shows the Puerto Rican flag hung on the trunk of a palm tree and then plowed down by a bulldozer (fig. 79). Four narrative cells show the bulldozer's stately progress: stick figures gather at the scene to erect the flag, then clap to celebrate it,

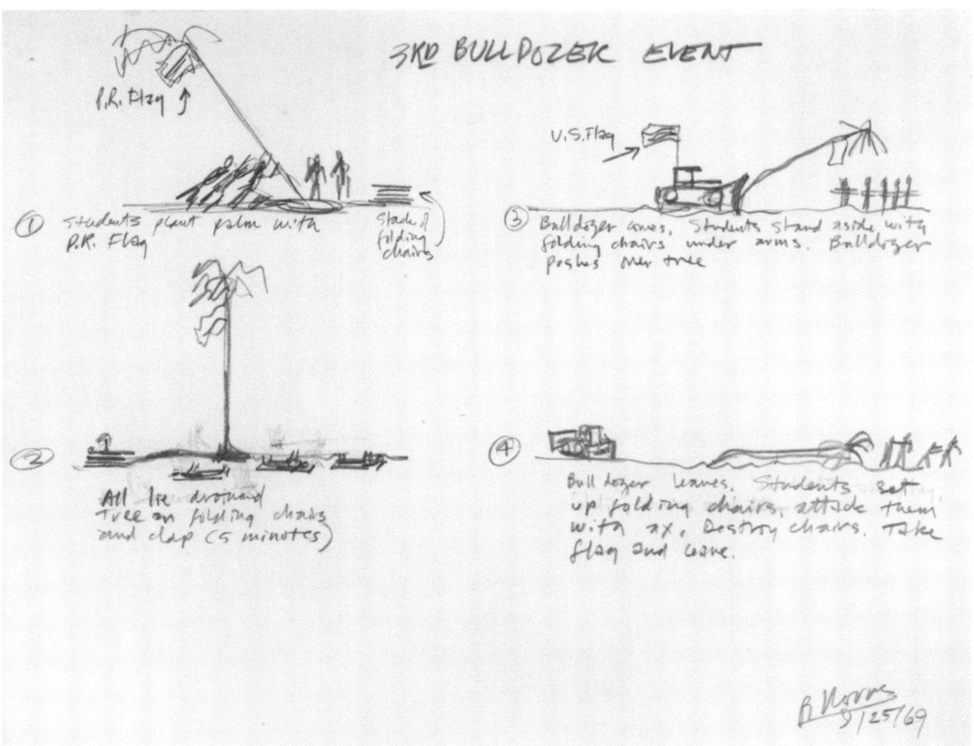

Fig. 79 Robert Morris, *3rd Bulldozer Event,* 1969. Graphite on paper, 18 × 24 in. (54.7 × 61 cm).

and finally watch its demise. This cartoon progression knits together visual references to Puerto Rican and continental American politics, sowing them onto the same soil. The group of graphite stick figures straining under the flag echoes the US Marine Corps War Memorial in Washington, DC, erected fifteen years earlier to commemorate the Battle of Iwo Jima, a final clash in the United States' conflict with imperial Japan at the close of World War II that left 6,800 dead. (The war memorial was itself a copy, modeled after the journalist Joe Rosenthal's Pulitzer Prize–winning photograph, *Raising the Flag at Iwo Jima,* of 1945.) In Morris's version of the scene, however, it is not the US flag erected triumphally but rather the reverse: the US flag adorns the bulldozer that mows down the flag of its island colony, a flag that, under the Gag Law of 1948, had been illegal to fly on the island, even in one's own home, until 1957.[1]

Palm trees feature heavily in the project drawings. They served as both a conceit to Puerto Rico's ecology—palms are "the first to wake up in the mornings and the first to walk down the street" on the island, as the poet Victor Hernández Cruz put it—and to the accelerating Puerto Rican independence movement.[2] Just two years earlier, in 1967, Puerto Rico's New Progressive Party chose the palm tree for its first logo, following a referendum to determine whether to change Puerto Rico's designation as a commonwealth of the United States. The tree's likeness created friction against the legacies of the Gag Law, under which the Puerto Rican legislature had also made it illegal to sing patriotic songs and to organize for independence.[3] Its presence on fabric banners, buttons, and leaflets affirmed it as an iconic symbol of Puerto Rican identity and a recurring motif in the plans for Morris's project.

This chapter considers the sketches for *Frarmrroreerofibseaterlr* as material memory banks, activated as extensions through time and space, to take up Spinoza's term once again. As both a surface and a substrate for logic, this work mirrored the role of paper as the medium of order and bureaucracy, and particularly colonial bureaucracy, as well as empire's tendency to deliver absurd and impossible edicts from afar and thus to enact real physical violence on the colonized landscape. Morris's performance also activated paper's disposability, and the kinships between paper and other forms of scattered matter such as rain and leaves, to undo the medium's ability to trap and fix the body as image. Examining *Frarmrroreerofibseaterlr* this way can shed light on the question of exactly *whose* plans and proposals could be considered visionary in land and antiform art—about who could claim connections to rubble, entropy, and destruction within the art historical canon. This method, which starts with Spinoza and metabolizes Bruno Latour, reveals the ways in which geographic and political centers attach to and detach from their peripheries at will, redrafting the "majestic outlines and detailed surface" of Hannah Arendt's globe into a network teeming with atmospheric actors.

This drawing was one of sixteen sketches that Morris made for the twenty-four-hour performance, which was to last from midnight to midnight on September 2 to September 3. José Enrique Arrarás, the chancellor of the university, had commissioned it along with a permanent outdoor sculpture by Morris consisting of forty uniform shapes in cold rolled steel, to be erected in front of the biology building (fig. 80). Arrarás's invitation to

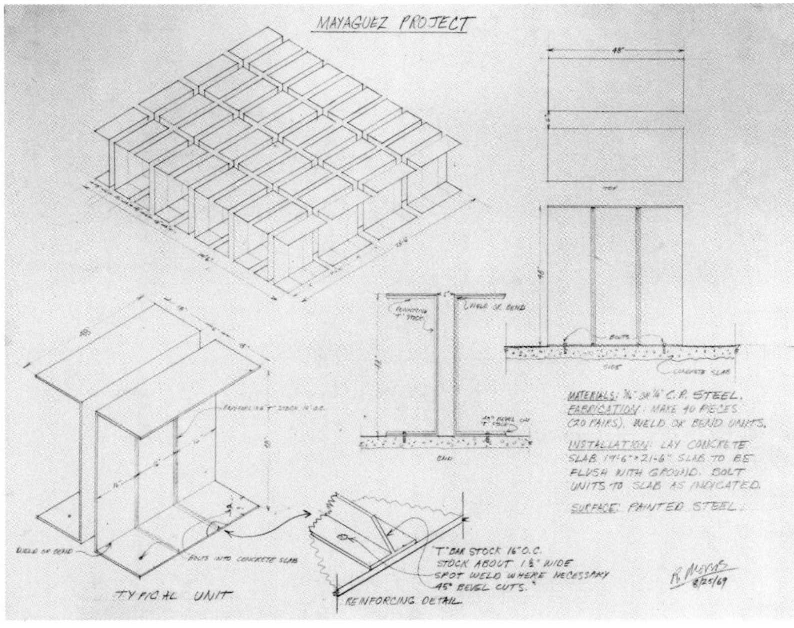

Fig. 80 Robert Morris, *Mayagüez Project*, 1969. Graphite on paper, 18 × 24 in. (54.7 × 61 cm).

Mayagüez evinced a growing institutional appetite at universities for avant-garde art by the late 1960s and included two funded preparatory trips to the island for Morris with the Puerto Rican–born artist Rafael Ferrer. Since Morris had not visited Puerto Rico previously, both Arrarás and Ferrer wanted him "to spend time in the region and study it deeply."[4] Ferrer, who lived and worked in New York and Philadelphia, acted as Morris's ambassador, collaborator, and coparticipant for both of his visits. Flyers and posters on the University of Puerto Rico–Mayagüez campus billed the event as a "gran oportunidad" for the students, one that would surely enhance the permanent sculpture's import and context.[5] However, the performance's execution was so different from the drawings—and so disturbing to the students at this engineering-focused campus—that it resulted in the cancellation of Morris's permanent sculpture.

Unlike the permanent sculpture's fabricated cold-rolled steel forms, the ideas in *Frarmrroreerofibseaterlr* could be used, discarded, or modified according to which materials became available on the day of the live work. Each drawing was quickly executed in graphite, without straightedge or added color, and proposed a different vignette within the timed performance. Each featured numbered and lettered instructions and frequently used a grid to spell out what would happen. The drawings rely on basic Euclidean organizing principles, such as parallel or perpendicular lines, quickly drawn ground lines, diagonal lines, and regular grids. Their layouts toggle between the storyboard outline and the comic strip and use the visual features of these genres to amplify the visual language of public spectacle and advertising. In addition to being bulldozed, for instance, in *U.S. Flag Burial* the American flag is buried at night in a somber ceremony lit by searchlights, laid out in a makeshift coffin built from two layered sheets of plywood (fig. 81). In another part of the campus grounds, twenty trees are planted in a grid of predug holes, with student participants hoisting their trunks upright in a grid that mimicked the serialized geometric forms of minimal sculpture. Another drawing shows a skywriter that was to fly by and write the word *CHE* at 3:00 p.m. (fig. 82). In it, an airplane breezily churns out puffy clouds spelling out the letters C-H-E above a sketchily developed "Mayagüez campus" that sits like an encampment below—an oblique reference to the university's land-grant origins at the beginning of the twentieth century.[6] In some drawings, human participants wear military hats or other costumes.

All the drawings foreground materials with variable and compromised integrity—stones, soil, wet concrete, air—within the white space of the page, with few qualifying details save an occasional horizon line. Each one mobilizes different objects that, when used according to the artists' written instructions, flagrantly overlay nature with machines. Their direct interventions on the natural by the cultural lend a curious dimension to what James Nisbet has called Morris's interest in "ecological composition" in the late 1960s: allowing a work to develop as the combined result of artistic

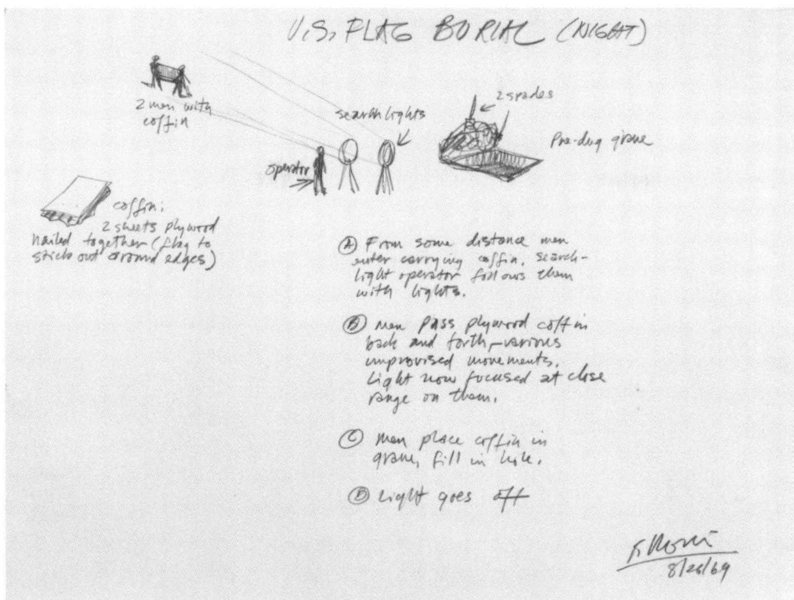

Fig. 81 Robert Morris, *U.S. Flag Burial*, 1969. Graphite on paper, 18 × 24 in. (54.7 × 61 cm).

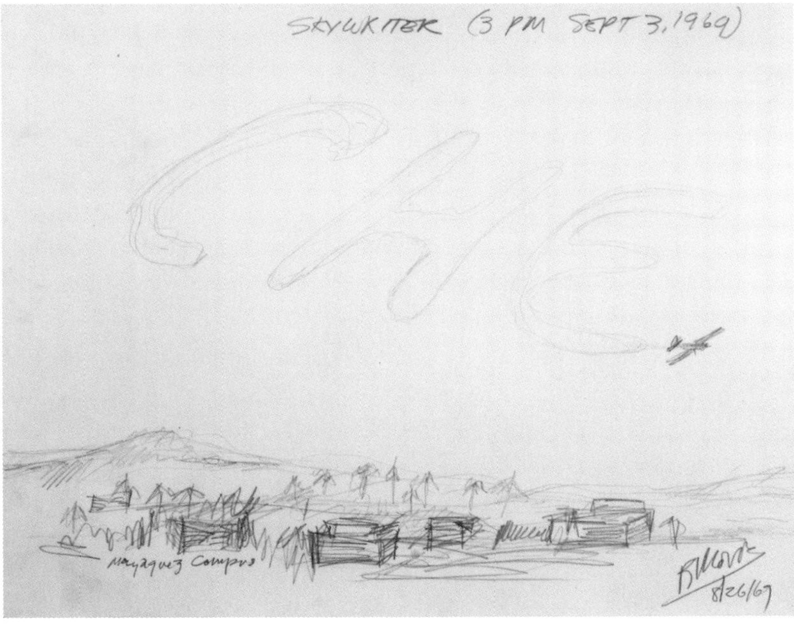

Fig. 82 Robert Morris, *Skywriter*, 1969. Graphite on paper, 18 × 24 in. (54.7 × 61 cm).

choices, the work's material components, and the shifts in its environment over time.[7] The sketches detach land's constitutive matter from landscape, revealing landscape's ties to social control and state violence. Many of these ideas found their way into the final performance; a number did not.

The sixteen drawings on heavyweight drawing paper in Morris's hand are the only extant sketches for the performance work, and they have almost disappeared into Morris's archive. Their relatively light surface markings, except for liquid stains on two of them, betray their lack of circulation. Several medium-specific presentations of Morris's work have included them, but they generally stand apart from his working drawings as a category, and they are absent from the last few contextualizing exhibitions on the subject.[8] As such, they reside both within and outside the history of working drawings, which by the end of the decade were gaining ground as artworks in their own right. Their absence bespeaks an archival and historical silence on artistic views of empire in the 1960s and on US-Caribbean relations, since, in this medium reserved for quick thinking, they perform much about the problem of empire as both a territorial and a textual relation, knit into the fabric of reception, into the atmosphere. Morris exploited the seeming incommensurability between play and plan, maintaining an openness to serendipity, intellectual disinhibition, and utilitarian scavenging.[9]

His paper plans enkindle a larger conversation about the interplay of colonialism and anticolonialist critiques across conceptualism, antiform, and land art, and about the degree to which these artistic movements relied on planning idioms from corporate and university life to flourish.[10] In preparing for this event, Morris and Ferrer approached the campus and the island as a total system. They consulted with civil engineer Henry Gronau Schettini; they discussed what kind of cultural and spatial dialogues their projects could engender; they recruited campuswide for the performance. Morris, a former military engineer, was attracted to Ferrer's interest in chance methods and to his insistence on using local materials in his projects. Ferrer, a trained percussionist, would have been intrigued by Morris's involvement with avant-garde dance and performance idioms. Both artists had recently been featured in several group exhibitions together, at home and abroad. And yet although Ferrer's drawing practice extended before this performance and continued long after it, he separated much of his work's thematics from its material implications, insisting that his antiform artworks "had nothing whatsoever to do with paper."[11]

Morris, in contrast, mapped a clear relation between image and surface. The elder artist would use drawings very differently from Ferrer, as well as from Tuttle: to imagine things that could never be, were never intended to be, and to highlight the differences between his plans' impossibilities and the realities of social and political life in Puerto Rico. "To work with a plan that is pre-set is one way of avoiding subjectivity," Sol LeWitt asserted in 1967 in his pioneering essay "Paragraphs on Conceptual Art": "It also obviates the necessity of designing each work in turn. The plan would design the work. Some plans would require millions of variations, and some a limited number, but both are finite. Other plans imply infinity. In each case, however, the artist would select the basic form and rules that would govern the solution of the problem. After that the fewer decisions made in the course of completing the work, the better."[12] This chapter centers on paper as a planning document, one that harnessed the intentions set down by LeWitt, whom Carl Andre called "our [generation's] Spinoza."[13] The art critic Barbara Rose mentioned prototypes in 1967 when she noted an "interest in mutability" in Claes Oldenburg's work as well as Morris's, Frank Stella's, and Ron Davis's and relayed Oldenburg's desire "to unfold the object and to add to it other qualities, other forces."[14] Prototyping entered conceptual art discourses through systems theory, which emphasized action learning and modeling as central to creative practice. By using a playful, performative approach and by contrasting between different stages of planning— between drawing as a kind of dream on the page and moving objects as a testing format in real time and space—Morris ruminated on state power's profound effects on the body, on everyday life, and on ecological systems and about colonialism's relentless conversion of territory into abstracted forms suitable for exploitation.[15] The contribution appeared to mock public sculpture and land art projects even as they take motifs from them. Public sculpture and land art were tied to the same forms of capitalist development that gained power and traction through paper plans distant from lived realities; the art historian Joan Kee has since noted that they could be "as much logistics as [they were] cloth and metal."[16]

PLANNING TO FAIL

Failure and material instability were default features of both works from the start. The two artists approached their materials in a way that followed and mimicked teleological narratives of development, beginning with damaged, disrupted, or waste-laden supply chains and ending with activated ecological sites. Even the most banal components of *Frarmrroreerofibseaterlr*, such as the supply list, became an arena for accepting and rejecting the conditions of making simultaneously and for testing the boundaries of the defined plan—which, along with notes and notations, had come to constitute important connective tissue between visionary projects and the public gaze. Along with photography, these documents were often the sole preservable component of interdisciplinary projects in the 1960s; with Sol LeWitt's aforementioned commentary widely circulating, those plans could act *as* art and had been included in key exhibitions to disrupt the paradigm of the finished, discrete, commercially appealing art object.[17] Mel Bochner's exhibition in 1966 at the School of Visual Arts in New York, *Working Drawings and Other Visible Things on Paper Not Necessarily Meant to Be Viewed as Art,* gathered notational material from twenty-six individual artists and some unnamed ones, including Xerox copies from pages of *Scientific American,* bound them into four A4 clip binders, and displayed one binder on four white plinths in the School of Visual Art's ground-floor gallery. Two years later, the Bronx-born curator Seth Siegelaub invited seven artists including Morris to participate in *The Xerox Book,* for which they each contributed Xeroxable material totaling twenty-five pages. (Paradoxically, the book could not be produced entirely using Xerox technology as planned, as adding Xerox copying to the binding process was too expensive.) Museums organized collectors' clubs that invited artists to turn

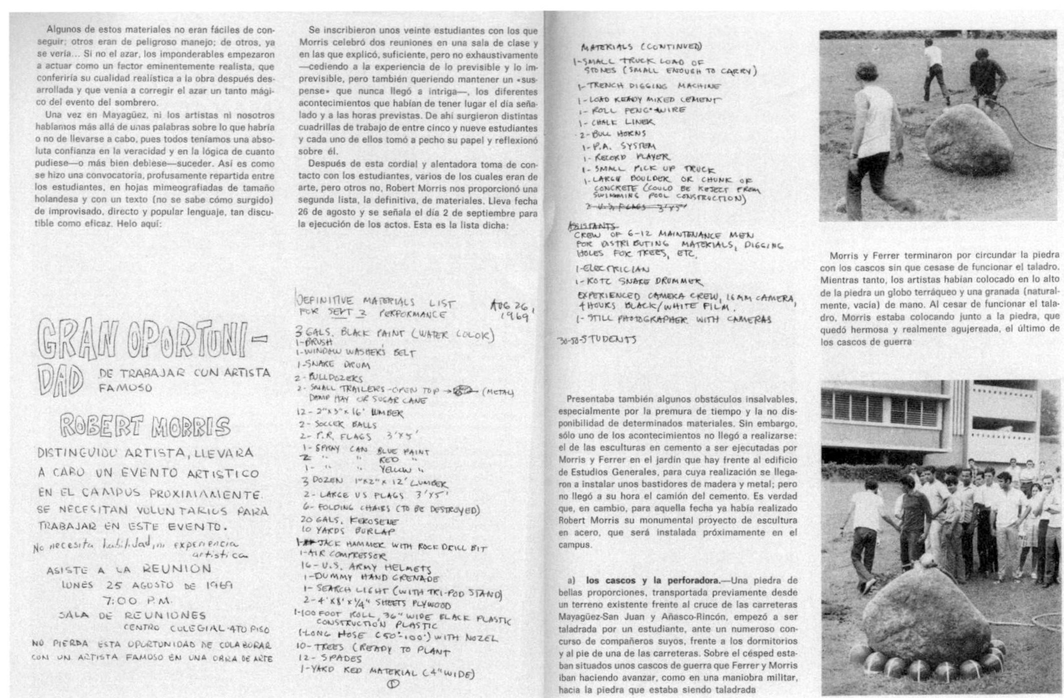

these visionary projects into collectible prints and multiples.[18] Magazines such as *House and Garden, Domus,* and *Casa Vogue* commissioned visionary plan drawings for publication; occasionally they refused to publish the results if the drawings did not meet their expectations.[19] Both the page and the book were accepted in art world discourse as archives of, and conceits to, dynamic change.

Morris's planning documents, however, highlighted a heretofore unconsidered mode of instability: the act of adapting to the materials available from a given context and supply chain. The availability of materials, machinery, and supplies was an acute factor in dividing lived experiences in the continental United States from the Caribbean. At the time, both artists were well versed in using institutional labor to obtain supplies.[20] They were participating in large group exhibitions with substantial institutional budgets, such as Experiments with Art and Technology (EAT), the *Anti-Illusion* show at the Whitney Museum of Art a few months before, and the ongoing Art and Technology program at the Los Angeles County Museum of Art. The president of Athos Steel and Aluminum was supplying Ferrer at the time with most of his materials for an upcoming solo exhibition.[21] But the University of Puerto Rico at Mayagüez was operating under quite different labor and supply conditions, so Morris's and Ferrer's respective artworks became a way to communicate various so-called third world imaginaries and realities, either projected outward or arising from within.

One example was Morris's ambitious supply list, which the artists reproduced on campus flyers to advertise for participants (fig. 83). Gone are the airline pilot and the skywriting aircraft from *Skywriter.* Instead, the list includes two bulldozers, two small trailers, twenty gallons of kerosene, thirty to fifty student volunteers, and an ROTC snare drummer, among other items. Ángel Crespo, the Spanish poet and translator who had been living in Mayagüez in political exile from Francoist Spain, published this list alongside an account of the performance's actual events in the *Revista de Arte,* a monthly journal of art history and criticism that Crespo ran at the university.[22] Crespo's essay chronicled how the final performance shifted due to the availability of supplies and praised the work's "lack of formalism and preconceived ideas."[23] What Crespo alludes to, but does not state explicitly, is that many of the artists' requested materials illuminated the mounting political and infrastructural tensions on campus. The request for a snare drummer was especially layered, a triple reference to Ferrer's extensive training in Afro-Cuban music, to his brief sojourn as a student at the Staunton Military Academy in Virginia, and to the university administration's plans to eliminate its ROTC program due to escalating antiwar and proindependence demonstrations on campus. Pablo Delano's later artwork *Museum of the Old Colony,* an archive begun in 2009, included an image of the ROTC band to showcase the band's use a means of colonial control (fig. 84).[24] Delano shows that sound's dispersion into the atmosphere was the perfect analogy for empire and its effects. As the artists mobilized the planning document as a kind of performance score, ready to deploy atmospheric resistance in sonic form, they revealed that economic and military disparities could take many different material states.[25] The list shows the university's enmeshment within biological and geopolitical conflicts on the island and also presents us with a scrambled supply chain that reflects Puerto Rico's actual conditions, which were distinct from but also inseparable from its tropical ecosystem.

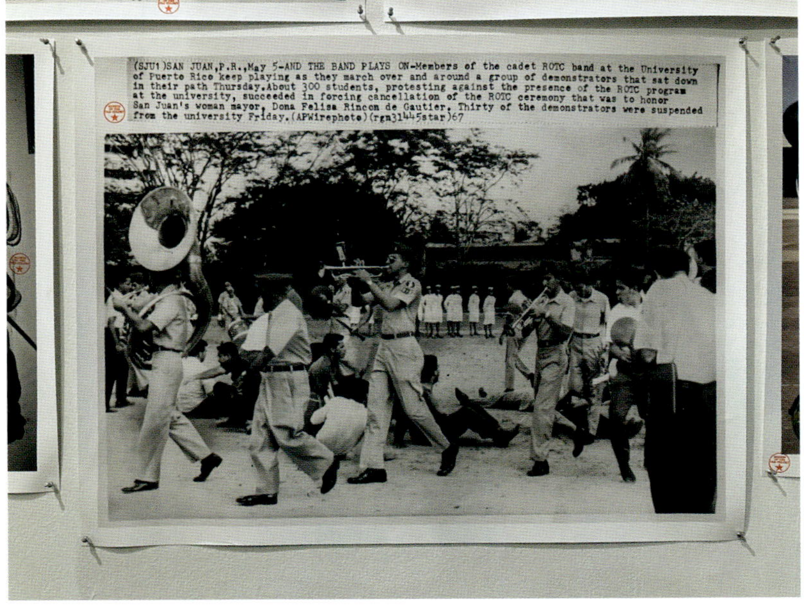

(SJU1)SAN JUAN,P.R.,May 5-AND THE BAND PLAYS ON-Members of the cadet ROTC band at the University of Puerto Rico keep playing as they march over and around a group of demonstrators that sat down in their path Thursday.About 300 students, protesting against the presence of the ROTC program at the university, succeeded in forcing cancellation of the ROTC ceremony that was to honor San Juan's woman mayor, Dona Felisa Rincon de Gautier. Thirty of the demonstrators were suspended from the university Friday.(APWirephoto)(rgn31445star)67

Fig. 84 Pablo Delano, *Museum of the Old Colony,* 2021. Installation, Museo de Arte Contemporáneo de Puerto Rico. Collection of the artist.

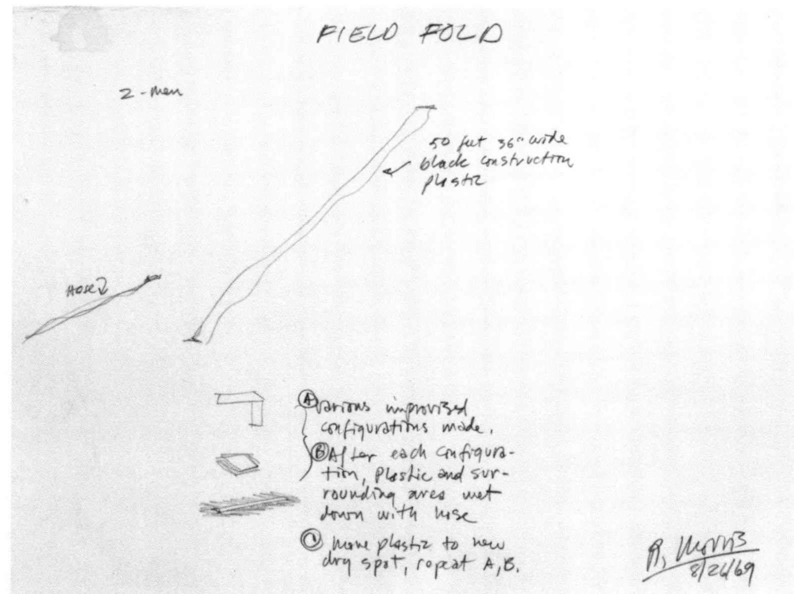

Fig. 85 Robert Morris, *Field Fold,* 1969. Graphite on paper, 18 × 24 in. (54.7 × 61 cm).

One drawing that differed substantially from the performance was *Field Fold* (fig. 85), which was to include two men folding a fifty-foot-long, thirty-six-inch-wide sheet of plastic into different configurations. The men would place each configuration on the ground and use a hose to water the plastic and the area surrounding it. In the drawing, this sequence develops across steps A, B, and C, with new shapes forming, each leaving a negative space of wet ground behind. The drawing seizes on *field* and *ground* as homonymic terms, tied to agriculture and thus generative, while also staging Gestalt psychology's preoccupation with figure-ground distinctions in visual art.[26]

The whole plan was replaced on the day of the performance by Morris and Ferrer pouring gallons of gasoline together onto a large sheet of canvas, then picking it up so as not to spill the gasoline off the edges. In a sequence of photos by an unnamed photographer, this task is tricky and delicate, almost comically so: as Ferrer bends to pick up the canvas, gasoline has already flowed past its edges and stained the blacktop of the parking lot beyond it (fig. 86). In the second photograph, Morris and Ferrer carefully pick up the canvas, leakage notwithstanding, only to have it sag at the middle and gasoline pour out the edge. Their two bodies manage the unruly matter as efficiently as possible, to no avail—the large planes of material are no longer drawn shapes on flat paper. Different variables destabilize their planar qualities: the gasoline's viscosity, the tug of this hand or that one, the speed of each action intervening on Abstract Expressionism's legacies of flatness.

As it develops beyond the drawing, this scene and its materials model the failed pursuit of order. The canvas's foldable flat surface ensures that each human and nonhuman entity involved can persist by means of their own inner telos, or *entelechy,* to use the biophilosophical term invoked by the literary theorist Morse Peckham in 1967.[27] Morris referenced Peckham's theories heavily during this period. He invoked Peckham's work

    Prototypes of Empire

as a "biological foundation" for disrupting binaries between the natural and the artificial. Morris even claimed that "art's function as an adaptive mechanism is as an antidote to the habitual."[28] Understood this way, the plans' limitations engage—and roundly challenge—what Bruno Latour terms the key "optical contrivances" of drawing: perspective, projection, and mapping. Latour identifies such contrivances as key to presenting "absent things" for the viewer: objects and entities such as land and buildings that are not physically there but that perspectival depiction can marshal into being through "translation without corruption." In dialogue with W. M. Ivins, curator of prints at the Metropolitan Museum of Art, and the historian of technology Eugene S. Ferguson, Latour frames drawing as a matter of optical consistency, which is what allows for sight to mediate the translation between a thing in the world and a projected, perspectival thing on the page.[29] The eye, as a guide, reconstitutes the other senses. Linear perspective and chiaroscuro "allow the viewer a momentary suspension of his dependence on

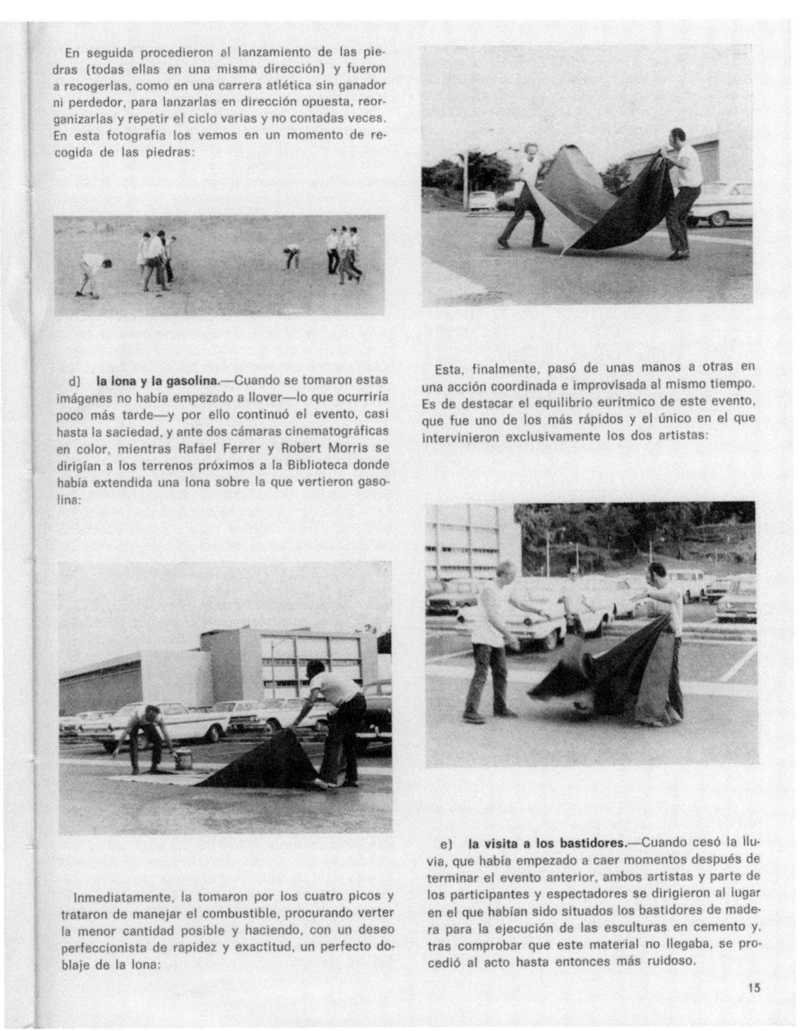

Fig. 86 Robert Morris and Rafael Ferrer performing *Frarmrroreerofibseaterlr*, in *Revista de Arte*, September 1969.

the law of gravity," helping to detach components and free them in space.[30] Notably, the visionary architect-engineer, harnessing a range of disciplinary cues, falls within this same set of optical and material entanglements.

Morris had long been skeptical of such theories, despite his training as an engineer. For the elder artist, it constituted a praxis through which he could loosen his grip on rational systems and orders. In his extensive writings on drawing, he positions himself in "assault mode," fighting his way out of the flat plane of the page. "For me," he said to Rosalind Krauss later, "marking goes on in a hysterical space, a space congealed into that threatening membrane. Claustrophobia."[31] Morris likely refers here to hysteresis, which, in physics, refers to any systemic delay that is caused by the components of the system itself; in other words, the system "keeps a memory" from its past and acts accordingly. As a planning document, the page was a disciplinary order to which the body, which moves about in the comparative richness of three-dimensional space and retains memories of moving and behaving, is always opposed.[32] This hypervigilance about flat space reflects Morris's experience as a military engineer and later as a minimalist sculptor, two contexts where the plan was a means by which the artist met the prescriptive demands of communication.[33] He maintained that advanced art must escape the flat plane entirely, opening instead into the vagaries and vicissitudes of three-dimensional space. Too much dependence on the plan drawing, whose grids Morris claimed were "borrowed from painting's ordering," replicated the enclosures of urban spaces. In a primitivist declaration that would come to characterize land art of this period, he praised the "anti-Cartesian" quality of the Nazca line drawings in Peru, "created for as yet unknown reasons by a culture unacquainted with the enclosing visual grid of urban space." Flatness was "the domain of order"; space, in contrast, was "basically incomprehensible, an absence of things, a nothingness that obliterates order."[34] A prototype that sprung from a plan was doomed to be thought about, made comprehensible, and ultimately constructed according to the limited perceptual data of the maker.[35]

A drawing was not simply digitized ground, as Latour's formulation suggests. Its capacity for modeling the differences among viewpoints, sensations, and experiences of land was powerful and deconstructive. The page was an unstable environment, doubly so in the gendered, classed, and professionalized milieu of artist-designers of the late 1960s. Drawing could signify and summon numerous professional mythologies, from the architect to the general contractor to the almanac-reading farmer to the daydreaming ne'er-do-well to the patron-supported artist. Traversing these boundaries was both subversive and titillating.[36] Morris's and Ferrer's amorphous scenes of boundary-crossing reveal problems inherent in the plan as a construct related to art making. The plan, yoked to the abstract expressionist critical term *picture plane*—a space in which, as Clement Greenberg said in 1949, "art and nature confirm one another"—was simultaneously a viewpoint, a surface, and an ideology.[37]

Morris's invocations of violent uprisings and funereal defeat were also timely. The Argentine revolutionary leader Ernesto "Che" Guevara had been executed in the forests of Bolivia almost exactly two years earlier, ambushed by a CIA-supported military platoon.[38] Martin Luther King Jr. had been assassinated in Memphis the year before, fatally shot through the neck on the balcony of the Lorraine Motel, inciting street protests that the press labeled as violent race riots.[39] Other violences were omnipresent for Puerto Rican residents specifically but invisible to continental US residents. The US military bases on Vieques and Culebra, two islands just off Puerto Rico's east coast, were using the adjacent waterways for ship-to-shore military testing, waste dumping, and air-to-ground bombing. Luis A. Ferré, the island's newly elected governor, dismissed the ensuing protests in Puerto Rico, specifically ones at university campuses, as mere "rockthrowing."[40] Morris's and Ferrer's joint considerations of Puerto Rico were thus enmeshed in larger cultural myths about the tropics, which are both romanticized and stolen under the colonial matrix. Their resulting works at Mayagüez, which drew on themes of plenitude, fecundity, and death, thus reflect an important conundrum in 1960s and 1970s avant-gardes: the difficulty of figuring violence in a world that trafficked in violent representations but also denials of that selfsame violence. It made violence banal, as omnipresent as air.[41]

Violence permeated the terrains and the atmospheres of this moment. I use *atmospheres* intentionally, for it denotes a pervading mood as well as a spatial envelope of vapors. Atmosphere effaces the flat, mapped planes of the Information Age, either physically, like fog, or figuratively, as a political atmosphere that obscures the gathering of information on citizens. It expands indefinitely and permeates space, shaping bodily states and personal experiences; it is felt rather than seen.[42] And while Bruno Latour argues that atmosphere "has now become [the] common condition" for people living in the twenty-first century, his position that "we have no idea how to pursue collective experiments in the confusing atmosphere of a whole culture" was no less true in 1969 than it is now.[43] In leveraging the rapid proposal drawing as a method, Morris could quickly bring puffs of air and the chug of machinery into being while quoting the fears and withdrawals of the post-1968 moment. Attending to state changes, which might range from water to clouds to smoke, could then become a pretext for exploring building materials whose value changed depending on whether they were part of a static sculpture, being moved by human bodies, or lying in a heap of rubble. Envisioning gases and objects in nonhierarchical assemblages of matter through rapid prototyping—assemblages that were made nonhierarchical precisely *because* they were so quickly generated, as their fantastic qualities gestured to the states of cognitive disinhibition typically reserved for the draftsperson—provided a new way into geopolitical power structures broadly and Puerto Rican debates on sovereignty generally.[44]

At the same time, activist commitments to majority-world and nonnativist projects intensified. Martin Luther King Jr.'s Poor People's Campaign of 1968 and his assassination that April had galvanized activist communities in nonwhite neighborhoods.[45] Lucy Lippard reflected in 1972 on the stilted, *retardataire* relationship between activist movements and the emerging conceptual art mainstream of the late 1960s, noting that while "popular/ political culture" often served as conceptual art's inspiration, "that spirit had arrived belatedly in the art world."[46] "We live in a treacherous time," Ferrer wrote of this moment, reflecting on his own position as a Puerto Rican artist in a largely Anglo artistic and political milieu. "The revolutionary is very careful not to do anything that would call for a confrontation between him and the enemy as long as he knows he can't win that confrontation. The revolutionary does nothing that will serve only to unite the enemy against him."[47] It is unsurprising, then, that Morris's and Ferrer's speculative propositions became vectors for anger, resentment, and critiques of power, which then shaped the artist's decision to animate drawing and design within the organic negotiations of live physical performance. This brought out drawing's potential to reflect and refract the corporatized structures that sponsored the then-emerging genre of technological art. These drawings thus served as polemics but also repositories of potentiality, appropriating and highlighting the ethos of plans and projections. The drawn plan created an avenue through which conceptual art could reveal the failings of the capitalist state in graphic and material terms. Further, it was the privileged medium by which to do so, given its designation as the "medium of ideas."[48]

Paper also had profoundly practical connotations for Puerto Rican citizens, as did language. Questions about the possibility of Puerto Rican statehood had led to a public referendum in 1967 that the pro-statehood party boycotted. This left the matter less settled than ever and sparked disputes about the adequacy of paper ballots to mediate citizenship.[49] A plebiscite vote was instituted for Puerto Ricans in 1967, to be held regularly on the question of statehood, which allowed its citizens to register their opinion on whether to remain a commonwealth, become a state, or choose independence. There was no formal commitment on the part of the US government to honor such a request. English-language newspapers and governmental bodies used the term *commonwealth,* which was adopted in the period following World War II to refer to territories that voluntarily maintained US sovereignty over their people. Ballots and literature printed in Spanish on Puerto Rican soil used the term Estado Libre Asociado, or free associated state. As the historian Robert William Anderson stated in 1965, "This ambiguity [may be] a purposeful virtue or a disguised colonial vice."[50] These changes reveal the university embroiled in its own tectonic shift around language: reshuffling its priorities, policing protests and other disruptions to make way for markers and symbols of modernity such as artist residencies and invited projects.

These drawings, then, orchestrate a reversal of the logics of control to which most Puerto Rican citizens were subjected. The drawn scenes

   Prototypes of Empire

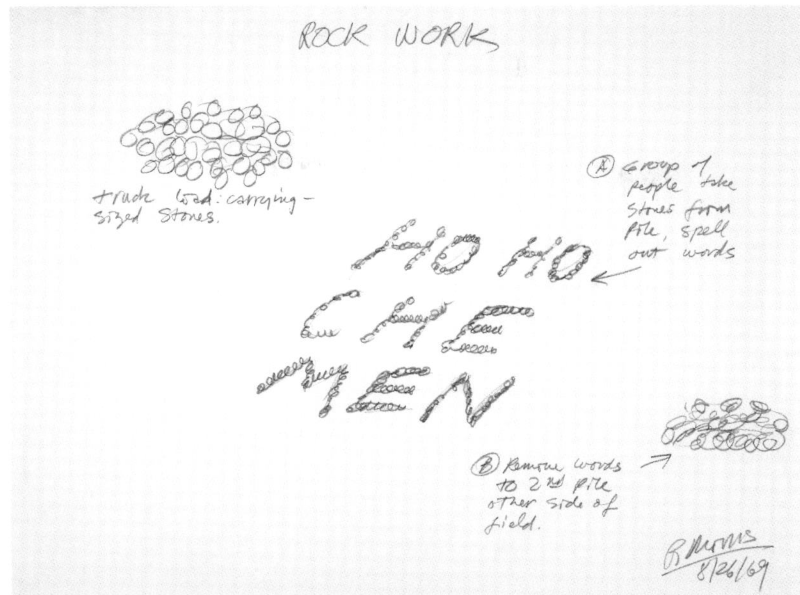

Fig. 87 Robert Morris, *Rock Work*, 1969. Graphite on paper, 18 × 24 in. (54.7 × 61 cm).

construe violence in both general and specific terms, with key words and phrases highlighting major disparities in economic and political power and drawing attention to the distance between the *idea* of the island and its citizens' very real political lives. Some depict modes of surveillance and brutality that were assailing international New Left circles in Puerto Rico, such as aerial flyovers and raids and abductions of leftist activists. Others show manipulations of territory—building construction, land management, and landscape painting—to foreground their oppressive power relations, which distance inhabitants of the space from control of them. Several of the drawings stage these critiques through language and textual commands. In the drawing *Rock Work*, the instructions ask workers to take "carrying-sized stones"—the ideal size for throwing during protests—that had been dumped into a pile from a truck and arrange them in a field to spell out HO HO CHE MEN (fig. 87). The workers would then quickly disassemble the words and remove them to a second pile on the other side of the field. Drawings and plans such as this one were more than just the necessary tools to develop a long-distance project: they were an imperfect but nonetheless generative structure from which numerous possibilities, both probable and absurd, could emerge. Drawings such as *Skywriter* and *Rock Work* make language mutable and insidious, as though mirroring the United States' colonial interests spreading across continents in different juridical forms. The project's rocks and vapors mediate national fears by spelling them out: Ho Chi Minh City is not yet a place but a construct, summoned in news stories and through the popular New Left chant, "Ho, Ho, Ho Chi Minh, NLF is going to win." Che Guevara is central to the work of Latin American left-wing revolutionary politics but also the source of its problematic hero worship. In a moment when militarization and power were distributed across the populations of the United States and Puerto Rico unevenly, and land and territory were becoming increasingly notional—conceptual even—to governing bodies who continued to wage an unending colonial war in Indochina while extracting resources at home, paper plans emerge here as a surprisingly powerful polemic center.

PAPER, NATURAL MATERIALS, AND ECOLOGICAL ART

Morris had explored the concept of material indeterminacy in a seminal essay, "Anti Form," in April 1968. In it, he foregrounded drawing as an important archive of human beings' interactions with wayward materials.[51] To Morris, one of the most persistent and omnipresent problems in the history of art was the hierarchy between maker and object. Art necessitated that the artist give form and order to matter, which then suppressed "what is physical" about it.[52] He hedged that art may never solve this problem because the act of aestheticization constituted a semantic operation separate from the physicality of matter—an assertion that illuminated his struggles with orthodox minimalism in the middle of the decade, when his large, moving sculptures inspired by LaMonte Young and the Living Theatre could be placed in the same stylistic category as Anne Truitt's transcendent rectangular columns.[53] What the artist *could* do, he argued, was mine the process of making itself. And what could be more processual than a planning document whose surface sketched out a provisional set of ideas and whose finer details were yet to come?

Drawings were key to this mining.[54] As Pamela Lee and others have noted, critical conversations in the 1960s repositioned drawing, not as a mere provisional phase of the artistic process, divorced from its final product, but rather as an archive of dynamic interactions with matter.[55] Drawing could be a liminal and highly productive situation in which the materials dictated human discovery instead of the other way around. Morris's career-long experiments with drawing affirm this interest in merging embodied, process-based discoveries with intellectual inquiry. He sought to probe the bifurcated approach to the mind and the body that René Descartes had pioneered in the seventeenth century and that had come under critical scrutiny by the 1950s and 1960s.[56] In *Self-Portrait,* a drawing from 1963, he attached his head to an electroencephalogram machine and thought about himself for as many seconds as matched his height, prefiguring the quantified data of contemporary embodied selfhood (fig. 88). Visible here is a deep interest in all material components (the body of the artist, the mind, modern machines marking up paper, electricity, glass) acting together to co-create the work of art. Paper is not a passive receiver of data but something "very special" whose scale expands according to the task.[57] For Morris, abandoning (as he put it) "preconceived enduring forms and orders for things" could help make way for the most interesting new art, most of which engaged in "the direct manipulation of material without the use of any tool."[58] Drawing would help

Fig. 88 Robert Morris, *Self-Portrait*, 1963. Electroencephalogram, lead, and glass on panel, 74 × 20 in. (188 × 50.8 cm).

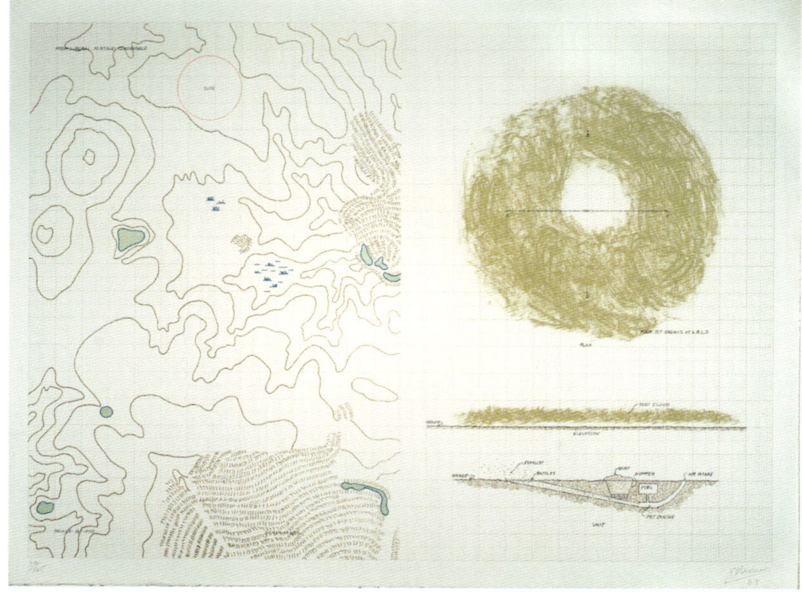

shift his understanding of the plan from one single step in the development of an artist's idea to a "level of transformative representation" that is "metaphysical."[59] Like language, drawing was constantly in formation. Like language, it was both created and practiced, working to constitute reality.

This link between physical entrapment and modernist enclosures underpinned his interest in a broad term, *the environment,* which was also a central construct for the corporatized collaborative design projects of which he was a part (fig. 89). In the last quarter of the 1960s, Robert Morris made a series of project proposals independently of his collaboration with Ferrer, all organized around the simulation of natural processes through mechanical means. Steam, dust, and other particulate matter appear in these drawings, churned out and pumped into the atmosphere by machines buried under the earth. The proposals became a point of difficulty for him, however, because of their repeated failures to be built. He designed his work *Steam* (1967) to pump steam from underground outdoor channels so that it dispersed into the air above ground, but the work was rejected from an exhibition in Philadelphia because it was too difficult to build and maintain.[60] In June 1969, resistance to Morris's drawings reached its apogee when he proposed "an environmental situation" in "any type of landscape," designed to alter and control the local temperature of outdoor space.[61] The project used industrial heating and cooling machines buried underground, with hot and cold air pumped through ventilated artificial rocks, to achieve his somewhat anticlimactic goal of "a little more weather than was there in the first place."[62] The work, which Morris described as an "interface between technology and nature," came into being at the invitation of Maurice Tuchman, the curator and director of modern art at the Los Angeles County Museum of Art, as part of its Art and Technology program, which paired artists with innovative corporations in Southern California. Between

     Prototypes of Empire

1967 and 1971, Tuchman matched artists with aerospace engineering firms, software companies, movie studios, and electric companies, inviting them to move within these industry spaces in the same way that they inhabited their own studios. Lear Siegler was Los Angeles's premier research hub in the private sector for developing missile reentry technology that allowed bombs to pass safely through the earth's atmosphere. With Tuchman acting as a facilitator, Morris sent a detailed research plan to Lear Siegler in September 1969; if the engineers there could help him "solve the problem," he could manipulate the earth and its atmosphere.[63]

Morris's proposal drawings laid out the proposed problem in an invented cutaway landscape, which the machines disrupt and mutate. Sections of the paper are divided into aerial or close-up views, a convention common to proposal drawings of the postwar period and a precursor to the digitized cutaways of the present day.[64] In one drawing on gridded graph paper, a three-quarter view of a giant heater dwarfs the land, which manifests as a small cross-section of terrain at the bottom of the page (fig. 90). A second site view used xeroxed catalog images of Lear Siegler's large-scale heaters and air conditioners, each three to four times the size of the average suburban home cooling system (fig. 91).[65] Forklifts and backhoes would bury them in the earth over a one-square-mile site, with the idea that their pumped vapors would cause a barely perceptible shift in the above-ground

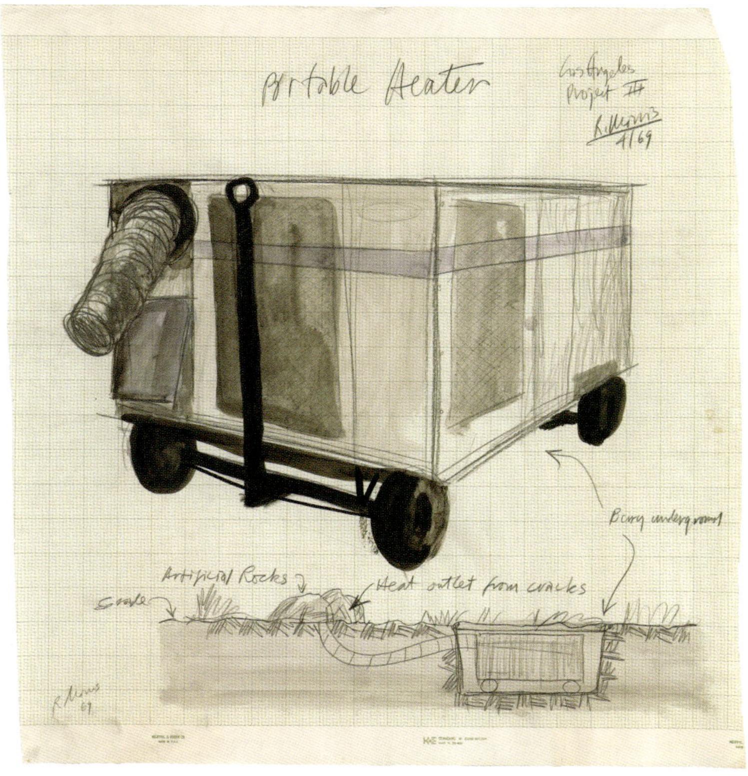

Fig. 90 Robert Morris, *Portable Heater (Los Angeles Project III)*, 1969. Graphite pencil, brush and ink, wash, and watercolor on graph paper, 22 × 21¾ in. (55.9 × 55.2 cm). Morgan Library and Museum, Gift of the Modern and Contemporary Collectors Committee, 2007.74.

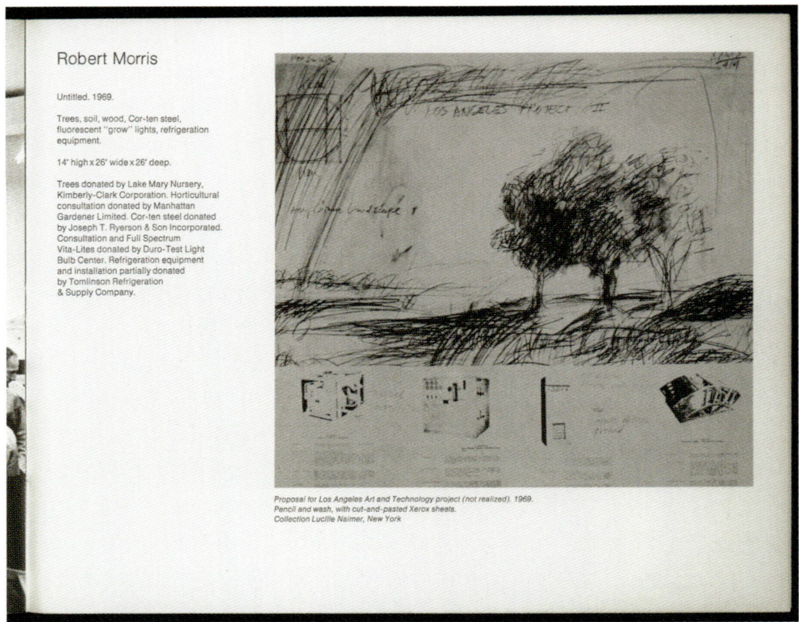

Fig. 91 Page from exhibition catalog *Spaces* at the Museum of Modern Art, December 1969.

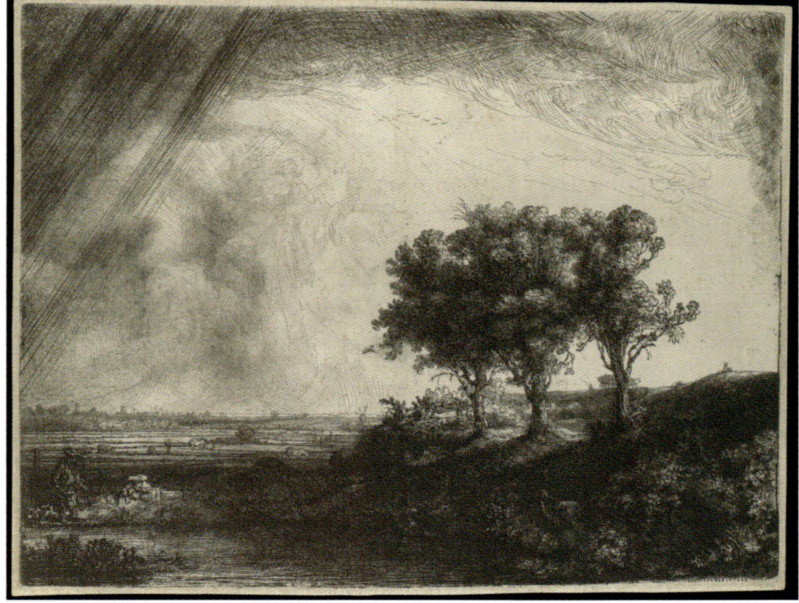

Fig. 92 Rembrandt van Rijn, *The Three Trees*, 1643. Etching, engraving, and drypoint, plate: 8⅜ × 10¹⁵⁄₁₆ in. (21.3 × 27.8 cm); sheet: 8⅜ × 11⅛ in. (21.3 × 28.3 cm); mount: 14¼ × 19¼ in. (36.2 × 48.9 cm). Metropolitan Museum of Art, H. O. Havemeyer Collection, Bequest of Mrs. H. O. Havemeyer, 1929, 29.107.31.

temperature.[66] In this sketch, floating cutout pictures of four enormous heating and cooling units unground the land on the middle and upper parts of the page, as do their typed descriptions. In the upper left corner, inchoate swirling lines connect the aboveground atmospheric conditions with the artificially generated air below.

The layering of trees and precipitation in the second sketch was also a spoof on Rembrandt van Rijn's print *The Three Trees* (1643), which the artist had likely seen while giving a talk at the Clark Art Institute in Massachusetts the previous year (fig. 92).[67] *The Three Trees* depicts a rainstorm near a clump of trees of roughly equal size, interspersed with human figures almost completely obscured by the dense etched lines, including a male artist sketching busily and thoughtfully at the top of a hill. This coupling of aeration and inspiration was no accident. In mixing his own present moment with the Dutch master's interest in etching weather and atmosphere, Morris presents us with drawing's highest goal. He dramatizes the artist's centuries-long struggle to represent land and atmosphere on a two-dimensional surface, and the difficulties inherent in bringing these things into being through the substrate of the lived body. Just as importantly, Morris's invocation of Rembrandt nods to the surging market for drawings in the later 1960s, when collectors and art historians alike fetishized drawing as a register of the artist's creative vision. Earlier that year, he had written that the rising interest in artists' drawings was a "hangover of the High Renaissance," wherein cross-hatchings could send critics and art historians into a diagnostic frenzy.[68] The citations in this proposal drawing thus emerge as both a reflection on the difficulty of representing changes in weather and a concession to art history as a discipline of material alchemy, bent on crystallizing state changes into clear narratives. History prefers object to matter, line to air, cross-hatchings to the disorder of rain.

Kinships between artists can also collapse linear histories, even subvert them. The scratch-out at the top-left quadrant of Morris's second plan drawing (see fig. 91) mirrors Rembrandt's patch of precipitation in the same space on the elder artist's sheet. Seen against Morris's scribble, Rembrandt's transversal lines loosen and appear less precious. The younger artist burlesques the mythologized scribble of the artist as a register of the modernist subject, while Rembrandt's sketching figure is at once something to which we might aspire, and a performance of Morris's ambivalent feelings about drawing itself.[69] "Marking goes on in a hysterical space," he had said, a space that "congealed into that threatening membrane" of the paper surface.[70] Almost all of his ongoing drawing series addressed this, from early exercises (explored in the Introduction) that made the paper surface into a Duchampian readymade to such later experiments as the *Blind Time* drawing series starting in 1973, in which he blindfolded himself and smeared graphite onto the paper using his hands. These series explored the congealment of gesture and idea onto paper's surface and harpooned the "rotting sack of Humanism" that he identified as his lifelong bête noire. At the same time, for Morris, drawing was an important gateway technique of the thinking artist—a technique that, despite his antipathy toward it, also generated a theoretical language for his own work, as well as a usable past.

Although it pulled Morris closer to the puzzles of simulating nature, *Portable Heater* was not realized. Tuchman viewed the drawings and tactfully called the project "ambitious."[71] Lear Siegler withdrew support for the project, citing the busy schedule of its director of engineers. No one else at Lear Siegler had "sufficient imagination" to continue with the work, it was claimed. The company's deference to artistic imagination exposed a broader problem within the Art and Technology program: many of the artists' proposals were so outsized in scale or visionary in scope that they bordered on the absurd. Andy Warhol's contribution called for a giant rain machine to spray a wall of mist in front of screen-printed paintings of daisies.[72]

Fortunately, new curatorial practices and emerging conceptual stances on drawing began to absorb the leftovers of projects both failed and successful. As new exhibitions animated the planning process in dynamic ways, Midtown and Lower Manhattan became dotted with galleries adapted from small postindustrial spaces, displaying plans and prototypes in hybridized office settings. These spaces gravitated toward the contemporary model of the project gallery, but their historical roots were also found in the liminal, often decaying spaces of older European avant-gardes. A notable example was John Gibson's Projects for Commissions gallery, whose exhibition *Ecologic Art* in 1969 included the rejected proposal drawings for Morris's *Portable Heater.* A review of this exhibition in the *East Village Other* emphasizes the simultaneously public and bureaucratic character of the space, calling it "less a gallery and more an office" and explicitly framing it as an environment. In this "office" (a word that reviewer Lil Picard cradles within quotation marks) one could find "collectors, nice friendly art-chicks, just groovy people rapping ART, drinking coffee from papercups and one can look at photos, diagrams, drawings—sometimes also at 'Samples' of art-projects hanging from the ceiling, or standing against a wall, or lying around on the windowsill-shelves. The place is informal." Picard compares the gallery to the Sturm Gallery in Berlin, which thrived between 1912 and 1925 and where Kurt Schwitters first showed. She characterizes Projects for Commissions as an exposition of the possibilities for avant-garde art "when Art wasn't Art-Industry yet," when "sculptures stood around on the windowsill, and nobody really even cared to look at them—and everybody could have walked out with a Schwitters and Herwardt Walden would not have missed it. . . . Things had been so casual, friendly and really hip."[73] The gallery is so casual that no one really notices the art nor affirms its aesthetic or monetary value. The plans and drawings in *Ecologic Art* do not just reflect on the expanded spatial and atmospheric possibilities inherent in the term *ecologic.* They themselves create a liminal space, a special ecology wrapped around an ethos of fleeting possibilities beyond Cold War bureaucratic systems of value, tied up with the possibility of their disappearance into thin air.

Against the backdrop of these debates and displays, the curator Marcia Tucker invited both Morris and Ferrer to participate in the exhibition *Anti-Illusion: Procedures/Materials* at the Whitney Museum in May 1969. After first planning to call the exhibition *Anti-Form,* after Robert Morris's essay, Tucker and cocurator James Monte settled on *Anti-Illusion,* a reference to the critic Clement Greenberg's assertion that contemporary painting should dispense with both illusion and representation.[74] The exhibition took up most of the galleries in the Whitney's newly opened building on Seventy-Fifth Street and Madison Avenue and scrutinized the recent trend of artists organizing their artwork spontaneously, both inside their studio spaces and out, using whatever materials were at hand. Although *Anti-Illusion* did not include drawings, its exhibition catalog featured documentary photographs of artists creating their in-gallery works, which yoked art making to process, behavior, and performance and helped to shift the locus of meaning from the finished work to its dynamic process of making, the traditional role of the sketch.

For *Anti-Illusion,* Morris and Ferrer each chose a different permutation of materiality, one invisible and one highly obstructive. For Morris's contribution, *Money,* he requested one hundred thousand dollars from the exhibition's budget, which he would invest in financial markets of his choosing. He would then split his earned profits with the museum, with the titular "procedures and materials" drawn from the invisible ebbs and flows of market investments. Ferrer, on the other hand, introduced two works that took the word *materials* more literally. For the first, he arranged for an ice-making company to drop off seven large blocks of ice on the Whitney Museum's concrete front walkway, which the critic Cindy Nemser apparently tripped over and complained about in her review.[75] In another untitled work he installed on the Whitney's fourth floor, he smeared a large passage of grease on the wall and then dumped bales of hay onto the greased wall. Some of the hay clung to the grease medium; some of it stuck to the top of the wall; some settled in a large pile in front of it. Ferrer wanted this entropic work to be as improvised as possible, despite having to disclose part of his plans so that the museum could prepare the wall with primer ahead of time. He aimed to "make a big, big mess" with the grease medium—he notes that all the other artists in the show prepared their process-based works inside their studios before the show's opening—to undermine the growing hegemony of practiced specialization in the art world.[76] The work's material also referenced the word *greaser,* an epithet used in the United States for Latinos at the time. The mess indexed an ambition to spontaneity that was decidedly modernist, as well as a layered and sticky racialized semantics.

Ferrer's biography, as a Puerto Rican artist participating in avant-garde discourses in 1960s New York, was enmeshed with his commitment to indeterminacy and mess in interesting ways. Born in Santurce, Puerto Rico, a cultured and densely populated part of the island, Ferrer traveled throughout his youth among New York, Los Angeles, and the elegant Santurce neighborhood of Miramar. He played jazz timbale drums as a music major at Syracuse University and later in East Harlem salsa clubs, while his stepbrother José Ferrer worked as an actor in Los Angeles and won an Oscar in 1950 for his starring role in *Cyrano de Bergerac.* After college Ferrer returned to Puerto Rico and studied at the university's main campus in Mayagüez with the Spanish surrealist Eugenio Fernández Granell. In 1953, when Ferrer was twenty-two years old, Granell took the younger artist to Europe, where he met Wifredo Lam, André Breton, Benjamin Péret, and other contributors to the surrealist movement. This left him with a deep interest in automatism, including automatic drawing and composition—another source of kinship with Morris, whose first artistic correspondents when he moved to New York City had been Marcel Duchamp and John Cage.[77]

As a postsurrealist diasporic artist with a devotion to music, word games, literature, and history, however, Ferrer was still little known enough in 1960s New York that downtown curators simply mentioned him as "a young artist from Puerto Rico."[78] Some organizations of which minimal artists were a part, including the Art Workers' Coalition, were beginning to foreground race and nation in activist discussions, debating the specific terms for inclusion: How many women artists should the group consist of? How many Black and Puerto Rican artists? One of the major schisms in early 1969 within the Art Workers' Coalition, in fact, concerned the degree to which an artist's ethnic or national identity should be made a legible category of analysis.[79] Meanwhile, calls for visibility among Spanish-speaking artists and citizens in New York were growing louder. The New York City Public Schools contracted with artist and educator Raphael Montañez Ortiz to produce educational materials for public school children highlighting Puerto Rican art and culture—a project that Ortiz turned into a proposal for the Museo del Barrio, a museum of Puerto Rican art in East Harlem.[80] Thus while Ferrer lived, worked, and exhibited near New York City's ground zero for Puerto Rican liberation, his career took off within an antiform milieu whose parochialism was only just beginning to abate.

When his work was unveiled at the opening event, Ferrer activated his cultural identity through his material's associations with otherness and filth. He stood in front of the hay on the fourth floor "dressed like a super-fly musician . . . on the scene in Latin America," instead of his usual daytime "proletarian attire" of jeans and dirty boots, which he called the "uniform" of the New York avant-garde. He shouted, in a high-pitched voice, "The greaser strikes!"[81] In this time and place, *greaser* and *grease* might have had multiple connotations for viewers: a lower-level employee in an automotive shop or shipyard; a slang term for a Mexican person, taken from insults against fighters in the Mexican-American War and expanding in the twentieth century to anyone of Latin American descent; or a youth subculture of working-class teenagers. Given that the greasy scrawl behind him resembled graffiti, it might also seem to give vandalism a lineage to the grease crayon that created lithographs, the popular, commercial, and sometimes radical medium of the nineteenth century. Whatever its thrust, Ferrer's act made the elite viewers at the opening immediately uncomfortable. "The reaction I perceived was that my work was excessive," he recalls.[82] His greaser call and flashy attire pervaded the atmosphere, too cacophonous for high culture. This rejection also makes visible the prescriptions and restrictions on what kind of artists could engage ecological themes in their work and in what ways. Anglo artists could traffic in trash and waste if they dressed as workers, but Latino artists could not spectacularize these same things through their own cultural lens.

     Prototypes of Empire

This exchange in the Whitney's galleries took place against a backdrop of strident public calls for Puerto Rican liberation both on the island and in the diaspora. The East Harlem neighborhood where Ferrer lived when he first arrived in New York became the site of numerous public struggles about the marginalized status of Puerto Rican immigrant communities. The Young Lords, an activist group formed in Chicago in 1968 to fight for self-determination for Puerto Rico and other colonized peoples, staged a "garbage offensive" in June 1969 to call attention to uncollected trash on the streets of East Harlem caused by inconsistent sanitation services to the neighborhood.[83] The offensive brought a new perspective on matter and accumulation and positioned the street as a locus of relations of power. An image of the offensive shot by Hiram Maristany, a twenty-one-year-old leader of the Young Lords, builds on the material politics of bodies that had begun in the violent summer of 1968 (fig. 93). A group of men and boys stands amid about a dozen overturned garbage cans, most of which had been left to get too full due to lack of consistent pickup from the New York City Sanitation Department, whose office was on Ninety-Ninth Street between First and Second Avenues.[84] Unlike the college-age protestors who made up the teeming masses in the streets of Paris, Berkeley, and Mexico City, these are local young men from the neighborhood, surveying the refuse in the streets with their sons. Maristany invoked a *backward politics* when he talked about the initiative, presenting it as a powerful harnessing of matter that could reverse Harlem citizens' position within New York urban social hierarchies: "You got to go backward to go forward."[85] The Young Lords marched to the sanitation office and demanded brooms, and Hiram's photographic series shows them sweeping the waves of dirt and trash into piles.

Several things are at work in these photos, but most notable is the particulate nature of the garbage, and the Young Lords' simultaneous exhaustion and determination as they confront its friability. Garbage scatters; its smaller

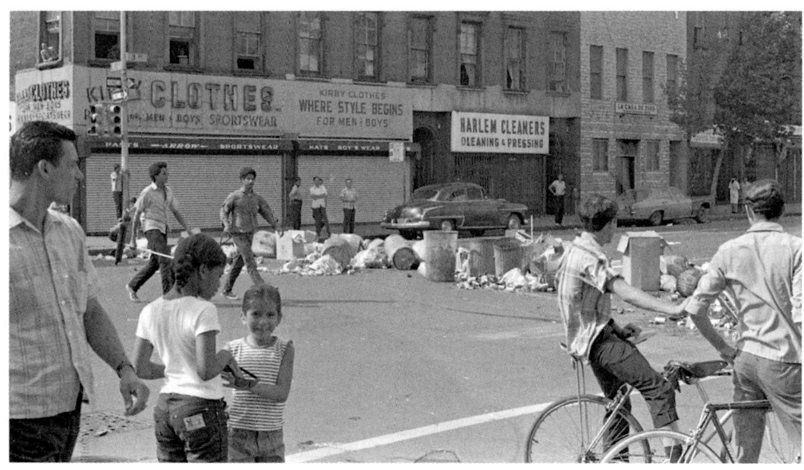

Fig. 93 Hiram Maristany, Young Lords at the Garbage Offensive, ca. July 1969.

particles erode the distinction between the discrete waste objects and their surroundings. Local media reports on the offensive were similarly indistinct. Some outlets reported that the Young Lords dumped garbage from overflowing cans into the streets and burned it "against a backdrop of decaying tenements, a low-income housing project and the Penn Central tracks that carry commuters to the suburbs," drawing attention to the ways that the neighborhood itself was abandoned material, left to accumulate and rot.[86] Young Lords member Jose Yglesias recalled, conversely, the force of the garbage's accumulation that then created the necessary discomfort to clean a long-neglected area of the city: "Suddenly in East Harlem last summer people began throwing garbage and wrecked furniture into the middle of the streets. . . . The police and sanitation workers would clear one intersection and find that two blocks away—east or west, downtown or up—another one was blocked with the kinds of debris that in middle-class sections of the city is not allowed to languish on the sidewalks. The Mayor's office got the message and a twenty-four-hour pickup of garbage was begun. For a while El Barrio . . . was cleaner than anyone remembered. With this 'garbage riot,' the Young Lords first made their presence felt in New York."[87] To mobilize discarded garbage was to reject the prescriptive and stereotyping languages of race and class, which often used garbage, dirt, and waste as its justification.

Ultimately, Morris proved to be an imperfect, and even problematic, cultural producer to probe Puerto Rico's geopolitics. While the performance generated rich failures and mistakes, the codes of empire did not emerge as particularly legible for the artist in the long term. "You have nothing to do with Puerto Rico," Morris insisted to Ferrer after the project concluded, affirming the downtown New York art world mandate for advanced creators to separate their theoretical commitments from cultural identity. For Morris, it seemed that Puerto Rico provided no worthwhile intellectual scaffolding for the younger artist's career. However, the two artists' respective work in 1968 and 1969 helped them conceptualize drawings as one of many different transport systems for matter, which had a direct effect on the burgeoning antiform and land art movements.[88] Castoffs of the earth itself—leaf litter, dirt, surface temperatures, gases—became increasingly popular materials for these artists, in both an extension of and a challenge to the biological metaphors of growth, organicism, and decay that had dominated modernist aesthetics.[89] Drawing on paper helped them negotiate capacious ways to animate these castoffs. Concerns with disorder were beginning to mix with urgent social questions of the moment: Did advanced societies have too much order? How much was too much? Natural materials helped to historicize the species hierarchies and Enlightenment-era taxonomies that had led to the military-industrial control of land and mass death in the postwar moment. To use Rosalind Krauss's terms, Morris's and Ferrer's separate and collaborative works contributed to an expanded field for sculpture, undermining the discrete art object and suspending it between two genres that sculpture had previously defined itself against: landscape and architecture.[90] If we return to Spinoza's idea, described in chapters 1 and 3, that only modal differences exist between materials in different states, then construction, preparatory, and performance ephemera were entangled with other throwaway castoffs, infusing space with impurities.

An implicit dream for these drawings is that they model the etymological possibilities of the word *propose;* they put something forward, ideally at a distance from practical concerns. In lying around casually, they summon into being the possibility that materials might be made to do new things. But Morris knew that this dream was at odds with drawing's relation to disciplinary powers and market economies, which instrumentalize designs and materials at the expense of the possible. Markets absorb ideas, recirculate them, and turn them into progress and money. For this reason, drawing for Morris was connected to development, but also to development's opposing poles of ruin, failure, and decay. Shortly after beginning undergraduate studies in art and engineering at the University of Missouri and the Kansas City Art Institute, Morris was drafted into the Korean War and dispatched with an air force battalion to build emergency airfields for military transport planes outside Seoul. The airfields, in fact, already existed in full on Morris's arrival; they had been constructed months earlier. Faced with no planned project to carry out, Morris's battalion invented a fictive one of their own that burlesqued the expansionist approach of the American military project. The team tunneled half a mile into a mountain, making drawings and engineering specifications to document the tunnel. After packing the dummy tunnel with dynamite, they erected a grandstand at a considerable distance from the mountain and invited engineering professionals from the region to witness its spectacular explosion. Drinks were served to the crowd at the behest of the military captains, and after a large group had gathered, Morris's team blew up the mountain. "So that was the event," Morris reported in an interview almost sixty years later. "I don't think I was ever so bored in my life as when I was in the Army."[91]

At no point does Morris give specifics about this mountain beyond the boring spectacle of its destruction. Sutured from his own memories, Morris's blasé account is less a map than a ghostly invocation. American military project plans were virtually authorless, containing no individual signatures; their dry and curling pages, if stacked together, would just vaguely spatialize the tens of thousands of builder-destroyers constituting the United States' presence in Southeast Asia. That Korea's eastern and southern Cenozoic-era mountains were one of the primary spaces that citizens buried their dead, a Confucianist and Shamanist practice, is not mentioned, nor is this practice noted in any English-language manuals for military development projects in the region.[92] Both in practice and in Morris's rueful account, the drawn plan enervates land, converting one form of currency into another. Its functions are purely performative: first to justify a lavish military development budget and then to fictionalize the mountain and transform it into inert material.[93]

For artists and designers deployed in overseas military projects during the Cold War, development was ineluctably linked with entropy and destruction. These projects wedded advanced research in academia to military-industrial tools. They ranged from land clearance, nuclear missile testing, and surveillance technology development to geoscoping wetlands, all infused with a sense of purpose and plenty. Their shaping effect on Vietnam-era artistic projects cannot be underestimated. Plan drawings propagated a liquid, flexible approach to currency and became a material matrix in which art or land or money or machines could all be endowed with similar transactive powers.[94] The drawings came to evoke the same inherent failures as all US-backed projects on majority-world land, rooted in what Georges Bataille called *the accursed share:* the irrecuperable waste components of any economy that arise as the result of capitalism's necessary excesses.[95] For Morris and his contemporaries, failed military development initiatives also dovetailed into other kinds of formless excess: pollution, decay, colonial modes of governance and control, which the artist was helpless to halt. "The artist wants to stop the massive hurricane of carnage, to separate the liberating revolution from the repressive war machine," wrote Robert Smithson in 1970. Smithson insisted that a truly clean revolution was impossible for politically minded artists and evoked Bataille's writings on the body's erogenous zones, using the sewer as a metaphor for personal and infrastructural progress. "As time goes by, pollution and other excreta are liable to turn the planet Earth into a more horrible pigpen."[96]

In sum, drawing positioned both the street and the natural world as *hysterical spaces,* especially when its material and market dynamics were accounted for. Works on paper not only framed terrain, landscape, and bodies as beyond human control but also reflected the failure of revolutionary projects of the 1960s writ large. By 1969, Morris had moved out of the apartment building he shared with Yvonne Rainer and stopped making objects for her dance performances. According to Morris, the Art Workers' Coalition was beginning to fracture and "people went in different directions."[97] Uninterested in incorporating questions of race and gender into the overall project of the group, Morris busied himself with the Art and Technology program at the Los Angeles County Museum of Art, his collaboration with Ferrer, and two or three site-specific outdoor projects that laid the groundwork for an emerging critical interest in the natural world. His works "[went] outside" and "[got] bigger" and, according to his own account, less engaged with performance traditions. He became more conscious of the ways human development could change landscape irrevocably.[98]

This set of drawings, the sculptural installation, the ensuing performance point to a complicated historical moment. The project arose in a space of exhaustion where numerous constructs were beginning to fracture and lose their efficacy: the possibility of fine art and protests effecting any real change against the war in Vietnam and the colonial occupation in French Indochina, the idea that a noncontinental American artist's work could be received with any real nuance or independently of the lens of exoticization, and performance as an exploratory medium. At the same time, awareness was rising of environmental damage as an extension of other forms of corporatized state violence and of the totalizing nature of state violence rendered *writ small* within Leo Castelli and other key critics' reception of anything remotely Puerto Rican. The utility of genre and method, long an object of critique for Morris, was beginning to die on the paper stage.

American artists at the end of the decade did not embrace sketches or so-called natural materials as a corrective to this state of affairs. Nor did drawings chart a common vision of US territorial occupations at home and abroad. To the contrary, this project dismantled the possibility of that common vision and centered violence as a material reality of lived experience within the dynamics of empire, rather than a distant abstraction. Morris and Ferrer's partnership, which they did not repeat, allowed drawing to contain, in a lasting and important sense, new possibilities for understanding constructions of nature and of violence. Each drawing's paper surface creates a horizon across which pervasive structural violence occurs in the context of numerous atmospheric phenomena, including tropical fantasies attached to Puerto Rico. But each one also undercuts its own value as a plan with a future. To borrow from Michel Foucault's construction of the document in political theory, each sketch asks for nothing but an "intrinsic description of" itself by modern historians.[99]

Most crucially, these drawings demonstrate the development of an idea while also committing to the constructedness of development. They use logic while denying its hegemony. What's more, they notate our lack of ability to assimilate the trauma of warfare and state violence writ large. Any sketch, any plan, always contains the possibility of its passing through the world unmade. Crucial to its status as a repository of visual memory is the carelessness that underpins it: a carelessness that is not without thought but creates an exhilarating wastefulness because thought-formation itself is so plentiful. Both Morris's and Ferrer's techniques showed that automatic responses are themselves remains—memories of rational orders, struggling to get out.[100] Morris, though invited to Puerto Rico as a "gran oportunidad" for its modern research university, organized with Ferrer an active lapse, a lapse trafficked by the speed of the drawn projection and the preposterousness and outrageousness inherent in speculation itself.

CHAPTER 5

Deep in the Surface

Charles White and the Vertices of History

She has a name and a face, but the rest of her body is nowhere to be found. The Anglicized biblical name Sarah sits above her head, stenciled in dark layers of sepia-colored oil wash in a post-no-bills font, while her gaze points upward (fig. 94).[1] The sum below her head announces to the viewer that this person—the entire body, head included—is worth $3,600. This oil wash drawing, *Wanted Poster Series #4,* which the artist Charles White created as one of a series of eighteen works between 1969 and 1974, mimics two of the most common representations of enslaved people in early American print culture: the wanted poster and the slave auction advertisement. In 1968, White's close friend Edmund W. Gordon gave him a pile of nineteenth-century newspapers, which included ample examples of both.[2] These papers provided the inspiration for the series, but the centered head and face in *Wanted Poster Series #4* are anachronistic on purpose. Originally, neither the auction posters nor the wanted posters featured personal images, instead relying on verbal descriptions of enslaved people's bodies and mannerisms.[3] The descriptions that were printed on the posters were calibrated to a predominantly (but not exclusively) white literate public, intended to mark people for sale or capture without them even knowing it. Further, the identification of enslaved people in the antebellum South was never based on empirical pictorial matching in the first place. Instead, enslavers relied on commercial and insurance records or rushed court hearings to confirm their captives' identities.[4] And so White's drawing, with its insistent affirmation of Sarah's personhood, demonstrates the miscarriages of reading, looking, and listening that the slave economy was designed to sustain.

Four typographic symbols of pointing hands direct the viewer's gaze insistently to this head, which sits inside an outlined rectangle like a modern portrait snapshot. These hands impart an urgency, creating a tie between the depicted head in the center and the live head that belongs to someone called Sarah.[5] Pointing hands have been used in print culture since the Middle Ages to channel the reader's attention to a particular part of a written text; by the nineteenth century they were incorporated into the visual language of advertising, used on wayfinding signs and event posters to direct readers to locations, to advertise performances, or to highlight sales.[6] These

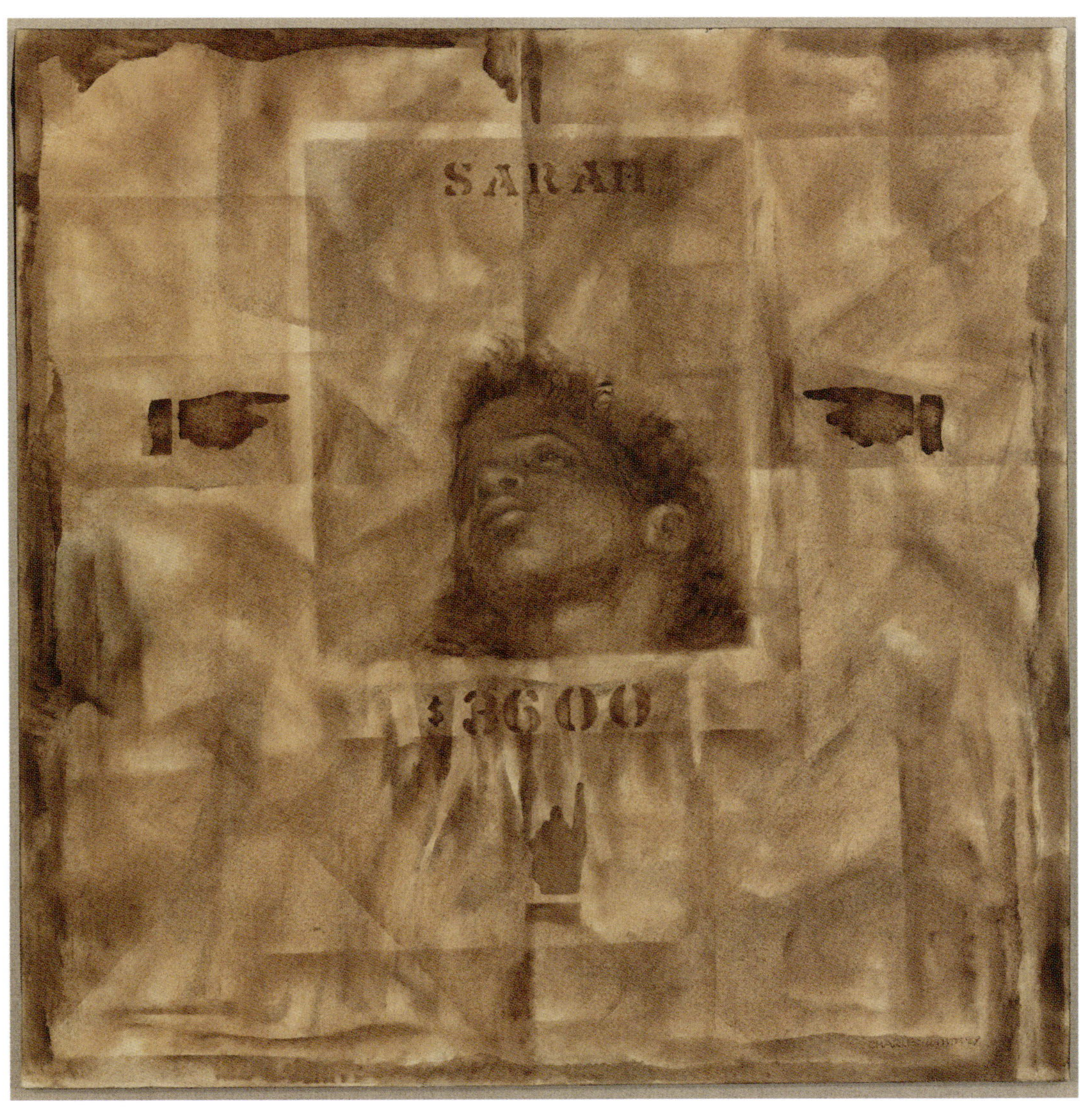

Fig. 94 Charles White, *Wanted Poster Series #4,* 1969. Oil on paper mounted on composition board, overall: 29⅜ × 29¼ in. (74.6 × 74.3 cm); image: 24 × 24 in. (61 × 61 cm). Whitney Museum of American Art, New York; purchase, with funds from The Hament Corporation, 70.41.

four hands also echo the cardinal directions on a map, which the page resembles with its crisscrossing of fold marks. The work's blend of typography and topography implicates space itself in the financialization of human bodies and implies a vast network of spectacles, forced passages, and returns. Is this a way to a lost body, a lost history, a lost image? The paper's folded and refolded surface hints that this person's state of fugitivity may be ongoing, reflecting Stefano Harney and Fred Moten's contention that "the slave is always already fugitive. The slave is constantly escaping being constantly undone."[7] Though the data on the paper surface are hazy, the hands press their point nevertheless; we know for whom to look.

In the fall of 1969, at the peak of his career as a graphic artist and educator, the fifty-year-old White created a series of eighteen drawings and lithographic prints that carried this theme. The first ten works used a challenging oil wash technique that had "no sustained precedent in his work up to that point."[8] This series is quite distinct from Robert Morris's distanced, colonized environments or Carolee Schneemann's inverted, shredded figures. Instead, White used oil wash to simulate the archival page, overlaying the present with the past to propose a new permutation of selfhood that resisted the United States' ongoing erasure of its racist history. The woman's face in *Wanted Poster Series #4,* depicted in the style of the realist artists Francisco Goya and Honoré Daumier that White so admired, is the face of an individual made *somebody* by dint of evidence.[9] But as her face mixes with the murky surface's folds and refolds, she becomes anybody and everybody, at once transparent and opaque.[10] "We're all fugitives," White quipped in 1969.[11]

Such a quip was in some ways autobiographical. Several of White's ancestors on his father's side had come to southern Missouri as enslaved people from Trinidad and Tobago, and five of his maternal ancestors in Mississippi, two uncles and three cousins, had been lynched.[12] His assertion also reflected a sober reality about US print culture: that it had long been a key instrument in upholding the legal grounds of slavery, with slave posters and auction advertisements naturalizing the body to the condition of flight. The remark gestured to the anxieties shared by African American citizens in the late 1960s, a moment marked by racially motivated assassinations, the intensification of protests into riots through police violence, and the surveillance and criminalization of Black radical leaders by the US government and local law enforcement. This chapter presses into these drawings' layers both materially and semantically to arrive at three main interventions that the *Wanted Poster* series made for the generation of the late 1960s. The first is the copresence of abuse and bodily integrity. Throughout the series, White juxtaposes expressive human figures with the forces that threaten those figures with annihilation: the printed matter of enslavement, as in *Wanted Poster Series #4,* or national symbols of racist violence. He folded these national symbols together with emotionally evocative, anatomically specific images to show the physical and biopolitical stakes of the printed word.

To put it another way using Gilles Deleuze's analysis of Spinoza, White detached the notion of *making* from any association with established ideas and instead sought to "free univocal Being from a state of indifference or neutrality" by placing the creative act and the act of erasure side by side.[13] Rather than contemplate these images diagnostically, we are compelled to look *with* White as his archive of lost, renegade, and escaped persons comes to presence. To divide the present from the past is another occasion where we, against Spinoza's recommendations, isolate the idea from the thing itself.

In melding human figures with national symbols and racist legal constructions, he demonstrated the fragility of each and made them both speak to what he called the "total environment" of Black lived experience.[14] He thus inserted himself into the semiotics-driven and systems-based art of the US neo-avant-garde despite his extended critical exclusion from that scene, as well as his exclusion from canonizing institutions such as the Los Angeles County Museum of Art. By 1969, that museum had yet to collect his work, despite his presence in other flagship American museums such as the Whitney Museum and the Museum of Modern Art in New York. The second intervention was the possibility for the diluted oil medium to contain and perform history. By adding liquid solvent to brown paint for the first ten drawings in this series, White made his resulting brown shades endlessly variable but semantically indistinct. Through a play of subtraction, accretion, and constructed depth in layers of thinned color, White's images could counter what Huey Copeland has called "the inability of figurative modalities of representation alone to address the structural logic of slavery and its ongoing effects."[15] The third was his endorsement of expanded modes of learning—something that, for White, was central to the project of Black liberation, both in the United States and around the globe.[16] White's art was inextricably bound together with education and self-determination, and it resisted the premise that knowledge could be centralized or unified. To actualize a liberated generation, an entirely new approach to knowledge must come into being.

The above three nodes are all manifestations of a central concern in White's art throughout his career, which is the interplay of accretion and removal, of erasure and building back up. Paper accrues even the most casual of notations with ease but is also generous with erasures and can expand or contract from its own flatness, as Richard Tuttle also learned. I have suggested in other chapters that artists and designers understood paper in the twentieth century as being in dialectical relation with creativity, sometimes generating it and sometimes obstructing it, but in White's work this dual power comes through in especially strong ways. Although White had seen paper as the media of liberation, he was also reflecting late in the decade on paper as the medium for official oppression, like colonial bureaucracies for Robert Morris and Rafael Ferrer, or capitalist excess for Carolee Schneemann. In building up to erase, and in erasing to make things more evident, White centered paper as part of the struggle against those powers—specifically, by expanding on his use of paper media in service of education and empowerment, so that people might see their own bodies as catalysts for sovereignty.

To connect these contributions, I follow a theoretical lineage in Black studies that imagines sensory phenomena as an antidote to language's divisive properties. White's own art and thought model this sensory unity. "My work takes shape around images and ideas that are centered within the vertex of a black life experience," White wrote in 1970, in the frontispiece for a folio of reproductions of the *Wanted Poster* series. "A nitty-gritty ghetto experience—resulting in contradictory emotions. Anguish—hope—love—despair—happiness—faith—lack of faith—dreams."[17] In mathematics, the vertex is the point at which multiple vectors meet; Spinoza uses the vertex to describe the properties of the intellect.[18] Such a metaphor would have appealed to someone as invested in graphic processes as White. The simulated folds and creases in the *Wanted Poster* series can also be interpreted as vertices, taking them beyond the realm of the motif and into that of method. And although White did not read Spinoza, the philosopher was visible in Black liberation discourses in the United States. Malcolm X called Spinoza "a black Spanish Jew" in his autobiography and declared that Spinoza's "pantheistic doctrine, something like the 'allness of God,' or 'God in everything,'" was one of the only recuperable postulates in the history of Western philosophy for Black thought.[19] White was not a pantheist, but he did consider sensory phenomena such as sounds, smells, and touch to be powerful tools for consolidating Black subjectivity. His concept of the total environment was a buffer against the loss of bodily agency wrought by physical and bureaucratic violence and centuries of disenfranchisement. It was a loss to which Sarah's visage in *Wanted Poster Series #4* testified and, also, in its layers of washed color, stood against.

White and others presented these new permutations of selfhood in a moment when full social and juridical oneness for people of color was proving almost impossible to achieve. National marches spurred the passage of the Civil Rights Act in 1964, which outlawed segregation in public places and mandated racial integration in schools and other public facilities, and the Voting Rights Act in 1965, which forbade discriminatory voting practices during elections. But as the photojournalist Leonard Freed noted, Black picketers were accused of "creating division" in an otherwise united country.[20] In the years immediately following the act's passage, many public spaces used signage, wayfinding signals, and impenetrable bureaucratic rituals to continue to prevent Black people from using them. In the South, "Whites Only" signs stayed up, or owners erected new ones announcing bars or restaurants as "private clubs" that refused Black people as members.[21] Some spaces closed altogether.[22] My analysis critiques language and signage while also maintaining awareness of language's discursive and physical effects. In this period, signs were not just a theoretical construct; they perpetrated violent bureaucratic fictions that organized and governed the body beyond the law.

Deep in the Surface

The late 1960s were marked by stark confrontations and troubling new realities for US Black liberation movements.[23] After Martin Luther King Jr.'s murder in Memphis, the civil rights community's faith in nonviolence as a means for generating meaningful political change had been shaken to its core.[24] Black separatism was gaining ground, eclipsing the messages of pan-African unity that predominated earlier in the decade.[25] Charles White's drawings that preceded the *Wanted Poster* series honored King in the wake of his death. The artist's general output expressed solidarity with activists who organized to help Black people maintain their dignity, like King, the Congress of Racial Equality, the Student Nonviolent Coordinating Committee (SNCC), and the Black Panthers.[26] But the FBI's program of covert and illegal investigations, COINTELPRO—the program that played a role in withdrawing Carolee Schneemann's *Illinois Central* from the Museum of Contemporary Art Chicago the previous year (see chapter 1)—was actively campaigning to undermine these activists' work. At that moment in Washington, DC, in fact, the Federal Bureau of Investigation released a series of posters urging viewers to look out for members of Black radical organizations including the Black Panther Party and the Nation of Islam. These groups' platforms included better education for children, solidarity with other African diasporas around the globe, and, in the case of the Black Panthers, armed resistance against police brutality, to name but a few. But the FBI lumped these groups into a single category of "possibly violent" extremists who were likely to "abandon [their] supposed obedience to white, liberal doctrines (non-violence)."[27] The groups were surveilled by police and accused of trumped-up or sometimes completely fabricated charges. The posters were part of a CIA-backed effort to determine whether Black radical activists were funded by foreign Communist governments, but also, according to one CIA operative, as an attempt to "neutralize" these thinkers and writers; "to try and get them in trouble with local authorities wherever they could."[28] The posters are a testament to the collaboration of domestic and national agencies to halt leftist activism in the United States, and show the degree to which activism was seen as tantamount to foreignness.

For Black citizens, the posters became a chilling genre of their own.[29] A prime example was the case of Leroy Eldridge Cleaver, who was taken to San Quentin State Prison in California after an armed conflict with the Oakland Police Department in April 1968, in which police officers killed Bobby Hutton, a seventeen-year-old unarmed Black Panther (fig. 95).[30] That October, Cleaver jumped bail and fled to Cuba. "There are a whole lot of people behind those walls who don't belong there," Cleaver remarked of his experience in prison—a charge that called attention to the carceral system's tendency to seize and absorb bodies indiscriminately.[31] Cleaver's poster is illustrated with mugshots from three separate occasions, three frontal and one in profile. The mugshot photographs, labeled for his arrests in 1966 and 1968, attempt to prove his criminality through their temporal progression: look at this moment when Cleaver's face was last captured by a police camera, then look at the time before that. This is serial photography at its most nefarious, designed to mortgage each nuance of Eldridge's head and face—from the thoughtful tilt of his head at the far left to his goatee at the right—to his future as a fugitive and, the federal government hoped, as a reincarcerated criminal. And although White had produced a seemingly nonviolent drawings program for the earlier part of that year, including his portfolio of reproduced drawings called "I Have a Dream," these themes would soon act as prompts in putting violence to work (fig. 96).

In fusing together visual archives of imprisonment, enslavement, and bodily commodification, White summons a long history of servitude to begin the task of rubbing it out.[32] The oil wash works in the *Wanted Poster* series used architectural tracing paper mounted on laminated construction chip board, which was widely available in hardware stores in White's neighborhood of Altadena, California.[33] He had moved there after having career success first in Chicago and later in New York City, where he himself had been a victim of several racially motivated beatings.[34] To make the works, the artist would dilute oil paint with a solvent, likely turpentine, and spread a layer of pigment onto the paper. Next, he would remove some of this layer

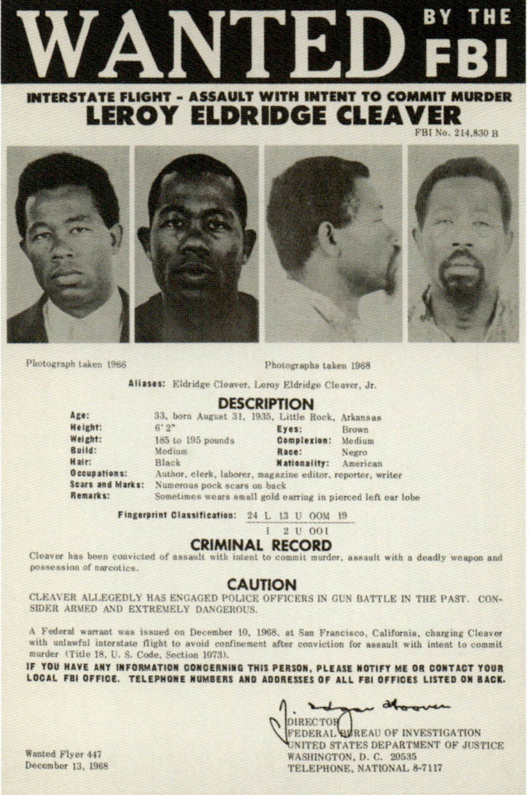

Fig. 95 Wanted by the FBI. Leroy Eldridge Cleaver. Interstate flight—assault with the intent to commit murder. United States, 1968.

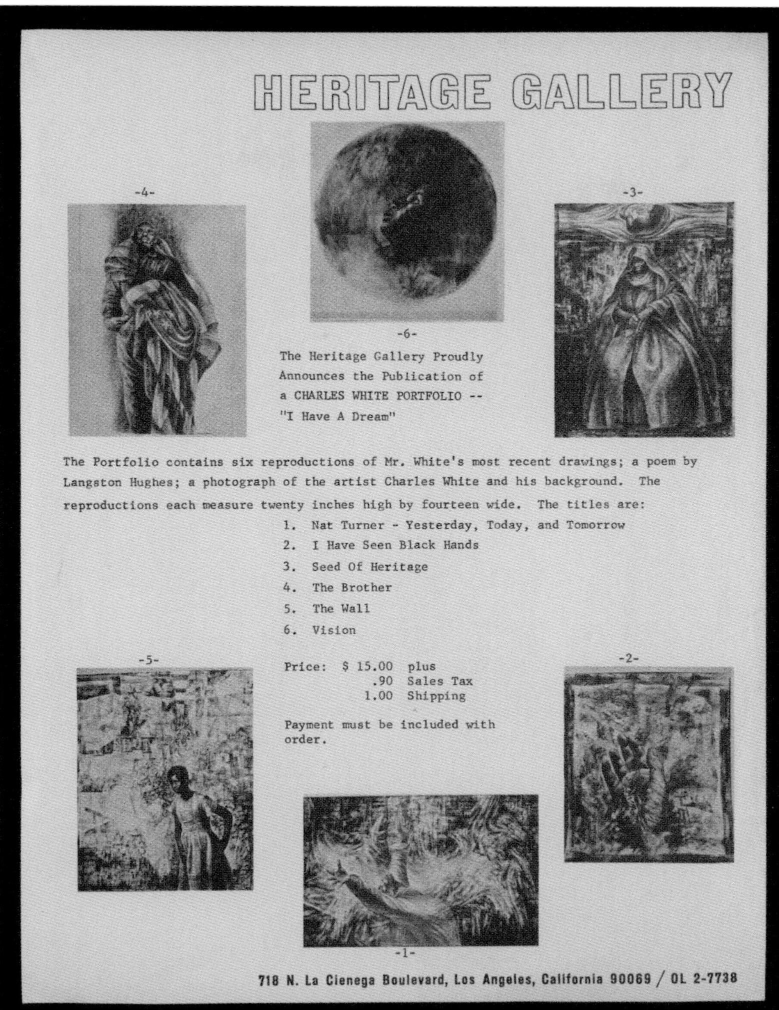

Fig. 96 Advertisement for "I Have a Dream," a portfolio of six reproductions by Charles White distributed by the Heritage Gallery, Los Angeles. Charles W. White Papers, Archives of American Art, Smithsonian Institution.

with solvent and then use "Q-tips, Kleenex, rags, balsa wood, brushes, and a whole slew of other things—all in one given work" to create the illusion of three dimensions by taking away, and then adding, successive layers of monochromatic diluted color.[35] With this highly tactile, subtractive method, White coaxed the image from layers of still-drying liquid, creating depth through successive acts of erasure and rebuilding.

To make these works, the artist conceded that he frequently "abuse[d] the surface [of his drawings] harshly" and "scrub[bed] into it with rags and a lot of tools."[36] Other scholars have remarked that such methods reveal his investment in material metaphors of violence.[37] But these methods are also congruent with White's broader interest in knowledge-formation and learning as intensive, even excruciating activities—the often-painful act of peeling things away from the surface to deepen the ground. The art historian Sarah Elizabeth Lewis has argued for "groundwork" as crucial for creating a metabolic relationship between one's medium and one's intellectual

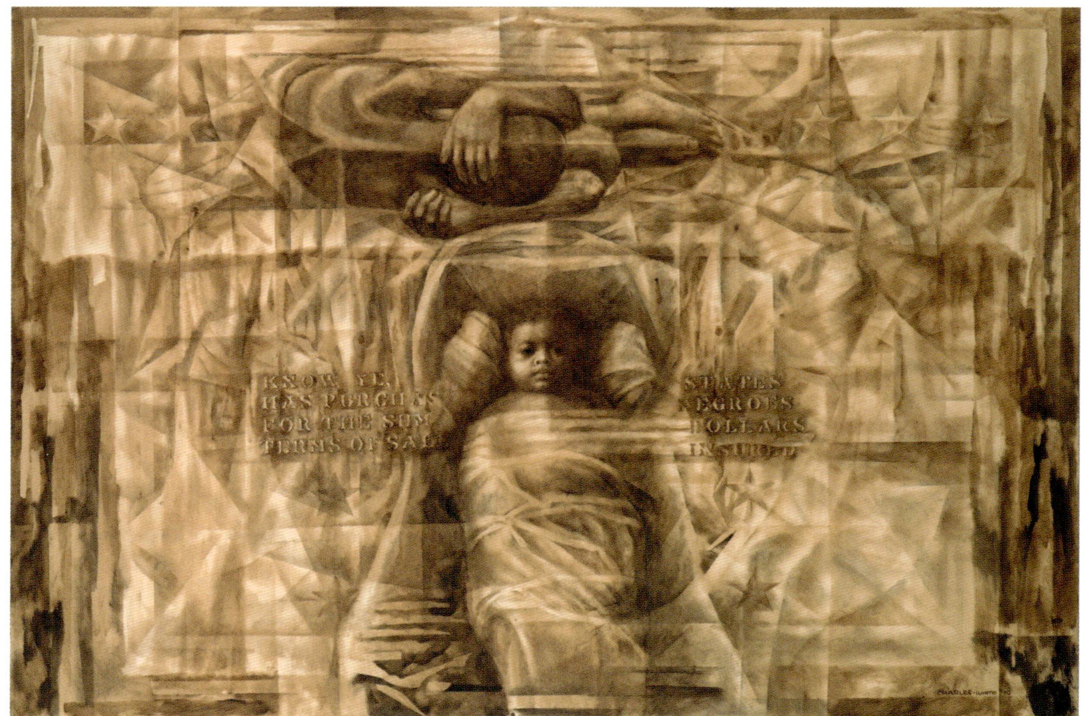

confrontation with history.[38] She identifies this dialogical relationship with the ground as central to the work of more contemporary Black American artists, such as Amy Sherald, Hank Willis Thomas, Kehinde Wiley, and Mark Bradford, but similar concepts also thrived among Black artists in the wake of King's assassination. Indeed, White's use of a popular botanical metaphor in a public lecture named the ground as an important locus of knowledge-formation. "You can't nourish anything until you establish the roots," he admonished a crowd gathered for "Black Artists: Art and Social Commentary," a panel of talks organized by the Black Arts Council at the Los Angeles County Museum of Art in 1969. "And even below that you go to the nitty gritty. Now, that's below the roots. Where the nitty gritty leaves off, that's where the roots begin." He similarly noted a change in the revolutionary attitudes of young artists in the late 1960s, one that was generative and ultimately positive: "Your brother's getting down to the nitty. And he's adding the gritty. Then he comes up through the roots. Then he grows a branch. He's gonna come, he's gonna blossom. . . . He's gonna unfold, and a bud is going to be revealed, and he's gonna blossom."[39] This refertilization suggests a counterstrategy for *whitewashing,* a blanket term for covering up a transgression that often appeared in discussions of racial erasure.[40]

Such generativity from the ground level required young artists to engage with their surroundings in active dialogue. "No matter how young you are you need to communicate with something, somebody," White said in a magazine interview the previous year. "You need to have some dialogue with your immediate family, with your peers as well as with your total

     Deep in the Surface

environment."[41] Like Tuttle's concept of the "complete electrical functioning of a human being" in this period, White's "total environment" encompassed many aspects of lived experience, both cherished and brutal: in this case, the supportive elements in a person's social circle and the historical forces that attempted to rob that person of selfhood.[42] This interlacing of rich community and imminent risk helps to explain the prominent presence of youths, babies, and children in the series. *Wanted Poster Series #10*, made in 1970, depicts two bodies, one a baby and the other a child (fig. 97). Both figures in the drawing link childhood to states of transit associated with bondage. In the top register, the youth's body is bent at the waist in a crouching position, invoking the cramped conditions for African captives in the holds of slave ships during the traumatic Middle Passage.[43] Below, a swaddled infant lies in a cradle that resembles the reed basket of the biblical Moses. Both figures are caught and bound, motionless, yet on the move. The texts on either side of them reference the terms that have caused them to be trafficked in this manner: "has purchased for the sum," "terms of sale," "negroes," "dollars," and "insurance." The boy sits on a starry fragment of the US flag, while the baby is layered next to and underneath the flanking text. They emerge, but only barely. In visualizing Black youth and babyhood, White presents possibilities for remembering a lost past, as well as for rebuilding the missing pieces of Black childhood more than a century later.

One of the largest drawings of the *Wanted Poster* series, *Wanted Poster Series #6* of 1969, shows two stacked but isolated figures: a woman pictured from head to torso, and a young boy seated in contemplation (fig. 98). These figures are the "darkest" in the image, having accrued the most wash, but also the most volumetric and defined. As in the other pictures, there is no clear relationship between the two persons other than their designation at the bottom of the image as "valuable"—a juxtaposition that once again recalls the severed natal ties that were commonplace when children were forcibly separated from their parents in the Atlantic slave trade. The work also collocates two flags in American history: the stars-and-bars flag of the Confederate States of America and the stars-and-stripes flag of the Republic. The center of the composition references article IV, section 2 of the US Constitution, which was ratified in 1787 and allows fugitives from justice in one state to be apprehended in any other state. This section includes the Fugitive Slave Clause, which mandates that "a person held to service or labor" in one state must be returned to their master in that same state if they escape bondage.[44] This law was never repealed, and White's citation of it mobilizes its continued threat to activists such as Eldridge Cleaver fleeing the FBI.

Symbols of nationhood were a rich field for investigation in the late 1960s. Many Black, so-called third world, and feminist artists such as Faith Ringgold, Clifford Joseph, and Kate Millett took up visual motifs of nationhood to highlight the United States' eagerness to protect its symbols in a way that did not extend to its citizens. At this moment, the American flag

Fig. 98 Charles White, *Wanted Poster Series #6*, 1969. Oil wash brushed and stenciled with masking out over traces of graphite, sheet: 59 × 27 × 2 in. (149.9 × 68.6 × 5.1 cm). Blanton Museum of Art, The University of Texas at Austin, Gift of Susan G. and Edmund W. Gordon to the units of Black Studies and the Blanton Museum of Art at The University of Texas at Austin, 2014.99.

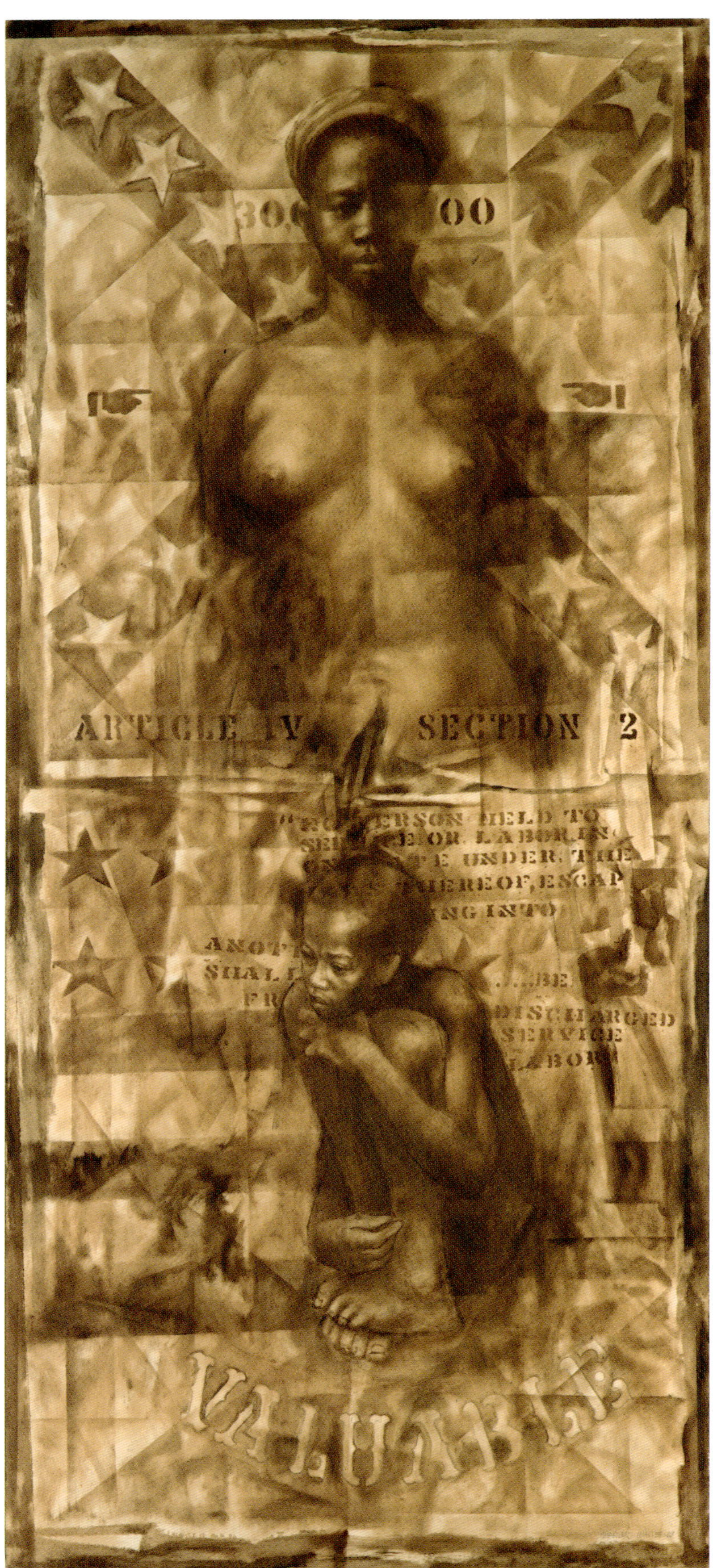

was accorded a sense of value and embodiment that outstripped that of US citizens of color. On July 5, 1968, Congress passed Public Law 90-381, otherwise known as the Flag Protection Act, which allowed for the fining and imprisonment of "whoever knowingly mutilates, defaces, physically defiles, burns, maintains on the floor or ground, or tramples upon any flag of the United States."[45] Stephen Radich, a New York gallery owner, was promptly fined for hosting an exhibition at his gallery of artwork that included creative revisions of the American flag. Amid fevered debates about the war's legitimacy and efficacy as a tool for capitalist nation-building, police officers in major urban areas such as New York and Los Angeles began sewing American flag patches on their uniforms and affixing US flag stickers on their patrol cars.[46] After completing *Wanted Poster Series #6* in 1969, White pointed out his purposeful conflation of national identity and white supremacist order: "The confederate flag in the back of the upper figure, a little bit of the union flag, bottom," he said, pointing to each. "Ain't no difference now baby."[47] Like the simulated folds that activate White's "vertex" of the Black experience, these symbols depart from the realm of the symbolic and become literally indelible.

Wanted Poster Series #6 is a reflection on *who* is wanted, *by whom*, and at what moments. As US Black viewers awaken to the fact that their ancestors had a price on their heads, they are right to wonder who else might be conflated with and exchanged for the legal tender of printed currency—currency that is also foldable.[48] Intimate family memories are only recoverable when we get "down to the nitty" of the glaring imposition of the national flag. White's ambit stands out in stark contrast to Clifford Joseph's painting *The Superman* (1966), which employs the same stacking of national symbols and an allied but quite different vision of bodily transparency (fig. 99). *The Superman* shows the phantom of US racialized violence in what Joseph hoped would be its twilight hour. It circulated nationally in 1971, when the Whitney Museum of American Art hosted a well-intentioned but critically calamitous exhibition *Contemporary Black Artists in America*. The Acts of Art Gallery, a Black-owned space at 15 Charles Street in New York's West Village, responded with an exhibition of work by Black artists called *Rebuttal to the Whitney Museum Exhibition* that included *The Superman*. Charles White saved a *New York Times* article on the two exhibitions, which featured a picture of *The Superman*.[49] However, the strong visual correlation between the two works suggests that he was aware of this work by the time he made *Wanted Poster Series #6*.

The Superman demonstrates the activist commitments that Joseph and White shared, but in contrast to White's robust bodies, the figure in Joseph's painting is skeletal and vulnerable. It is also doubly exposed. The Ku Klux Klan robe draped over his arm leaves him nude except for the symbol covering his genitals—a white cross with a drop of blood that symbolized the perceived genetic purity of whiteness—while the flesh covering his left ribcage over his heart has disappeared completely.[50] Like a parody of a

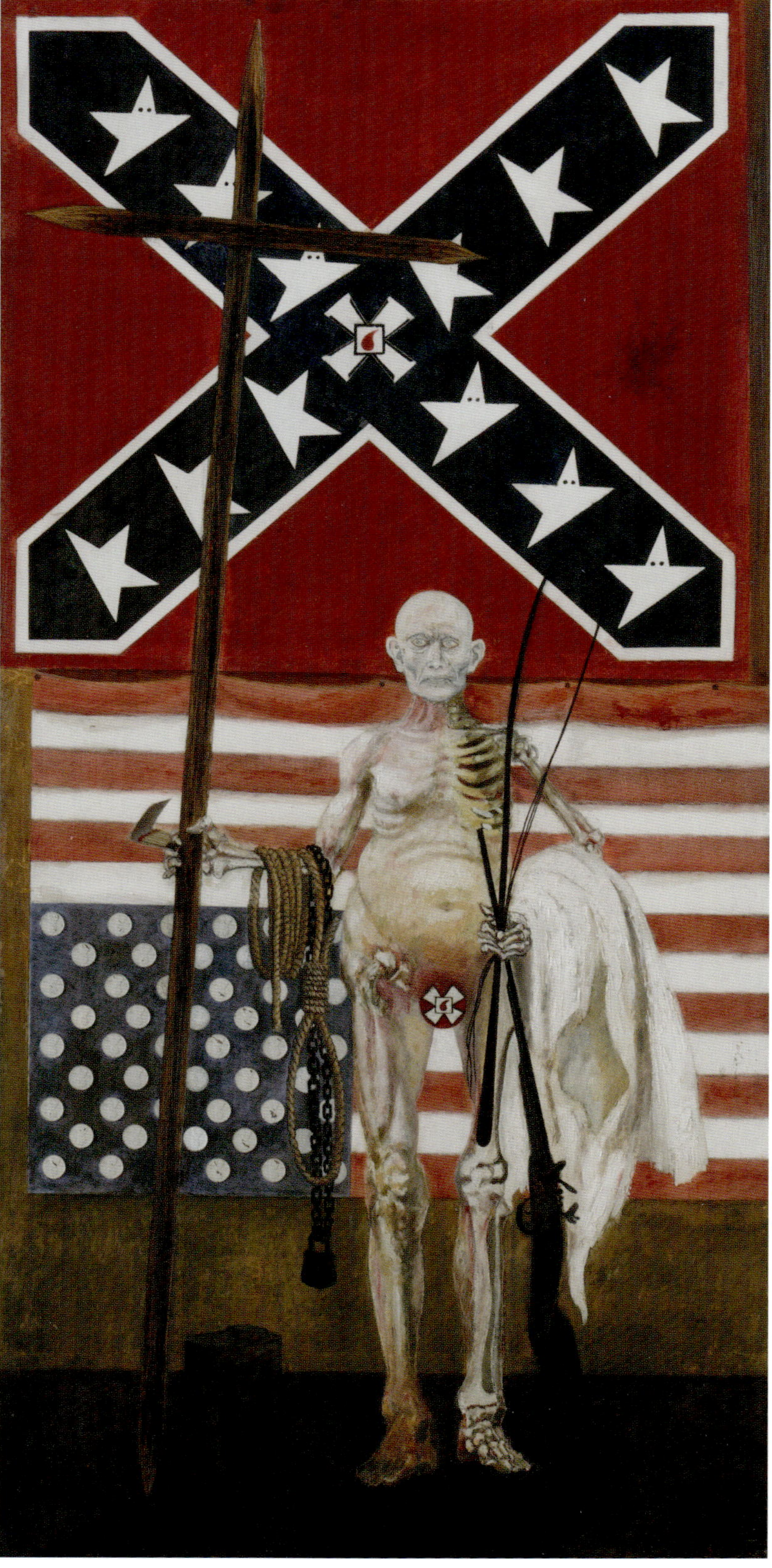

Fig. 99 Clifford W. Joseph, *The Superman,* 1966. Oil and mixed media (pennies) on board, 48 × 24 in. (121.9 × 61 cm).

Deep in the Surface

medical anatomical model, his muscles, oddly delicate and ill-used, are visible also. Here Joseph lays bare a stunning disjunction between that which white supremacists imagine themselves to be—armed with a whip, a gun, a rope, a Ku Klux Klan robe, a staked wooden cross, and a container of gasoline to burn the cross—and that which they reveal themselves to be: flabby flesh over bone. The only thing that sustains the figure's power are the coordinated national symbols behind him. Whereas Joseph neutralizes this power by taking the figure down to its structuring elements, White rebuilds the Black body's power and resilience by removing and adding progressive layers of the wash medium. *The Superman* is a symbol of various deaths, his own and others, but White's anonymous figures break free of the symbols that oppress and occlude them.

LIQUID HISTORIES

In the *Wanted Poster* series, the liquid medium also could function as a reservoir for historical memory. Kellie Jones has observed that Black American artists in the 1960s and 1970s were "obsessed with history," and this obsession often surfaced to demonstrate Black survival strategies as inherently regenerative.[51] As Langston Hughes asserted in his 1964 pro–civil rights play *Jerico-Jim Crow,* "Now they forced us to come—now America's got us, and we've got America, we're gonna be here a while."[52] White's surfaces in the *Wanted Poster* series play with this historical continuity by replicating the material sensations of kept memories: a paper page unfolded and refolded many times. The varied applications of diluted oil paint divide the sheet into squares or triangles that do not always correspond with paper's physics. In this way, the public notice announcing that someone is wanted by the police merges with the intimate, "keepable" materiality of a letter and of the archive in general. White would go on to use this technique in his *Love Letter* lithograph series in the early 1970s. His choice of color, which was restricted to browns in the first ten works in the series, foregrounds other tactile relations to history: the private liquid practice of the ink wash, which in umbers and burnt siennas were a common choice among Old Master painters since the early modern period, and the sepia-tinted photograph, which played a strong role in 1960s and 1970s picture-making. This brown wash was called brunaille when applied to painting practice and bistre in reference to subtractive ink wash, and it used a diluted base pigment of brown to develop a figure's texture, dimension, and depth.[53] A drawing attributed to Nicolaes Maes, a member of Rembrandt's school, provides a good illustration of the pigment's uses in early modern art (fig. 100). The medium creates shadows that also act as background, allowing a richer play of tonal variation.[54] The layers of oil wash thus resist the media of enslavement even as they replicate that media, providing a joyous corrective to servitude that routes through the infinite possibilities of monochrome.[55]

White's concept of the total environment emerged in part as a means for presenting human beings in relation to their surroundings, a commitment grounded in his own biography and personal experience. As early as the 1930s, fellow artists such as Todros Geller encouraged White to draw from his own life and neighborhood rather than making copies of established works of art.[56] This ignited a sustained interest in animating the specific relation between the human figure and its social context while at the same time maximizing the figure's emotional appeal to many different strata of viewers. His training at the School of the Art Institute of Chicago in the late 1930s and early 1940s included lessons in watercolors and diluted pigments, as well as familiarity with all kinds of solvents. He used watercolor washes in many colors to add visual interest and depth to his earliest figure sketches (figs. 101, 102). Each of these colored washes spotlights a human figure, giving them what Erica Moiah James has called a simultaneous "inscrutability" and "extended signification."[57] The washes in these sketchbook pages are an early instance of what Kerry James Marshall has called a "tendency toward pictorial action" in White's images of the human figure: abstract patterning that takes the figure outside time and space and places it into its own allover universe.[58] Their coronal patterns captured White's attention throughout his career and are a foundation for his *Wanted Poster* series wash technique. White's own commentary on the *Wanted Poster* series supports Marshall's observations; he said that each human figure depicted in the series is "both part of it and not part of it."[59] And although the British art critic Peter Clothier has argued that White's solitary figures derive their power from their "isolation from all semblance of social reference," these haloes of washed color, I suggest, allow them to

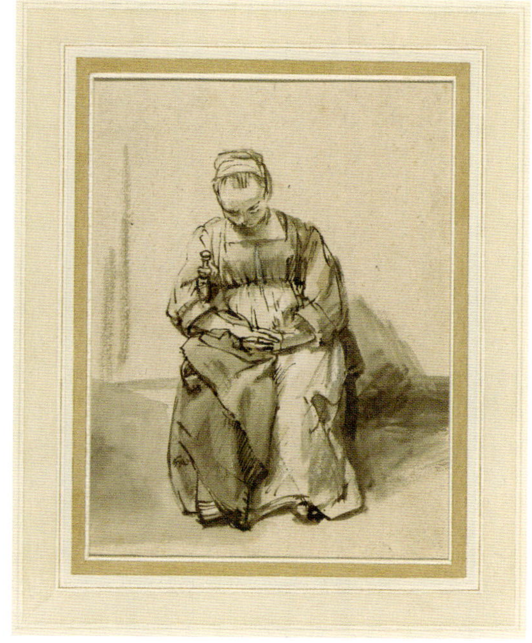

Fig. 100 Attributed to Nicolaes Maes (formerly attributed to Rembrandt Van Rijn), *Woman Asleep in a Chair*, ca. 1634–93. Pen and brown ink and wash, on paper; slight corrections in opaque white in the figure's bodice and skirt; framing line in brown ink, 7 13/16 × 6 1/16 in. (20 × 15.3 cm). Morgan Library and Museum, I, 199.

Deep in the Surface

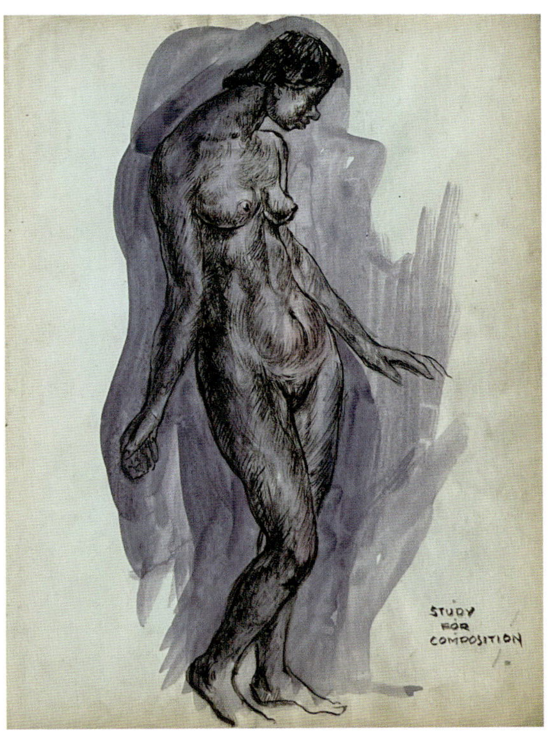

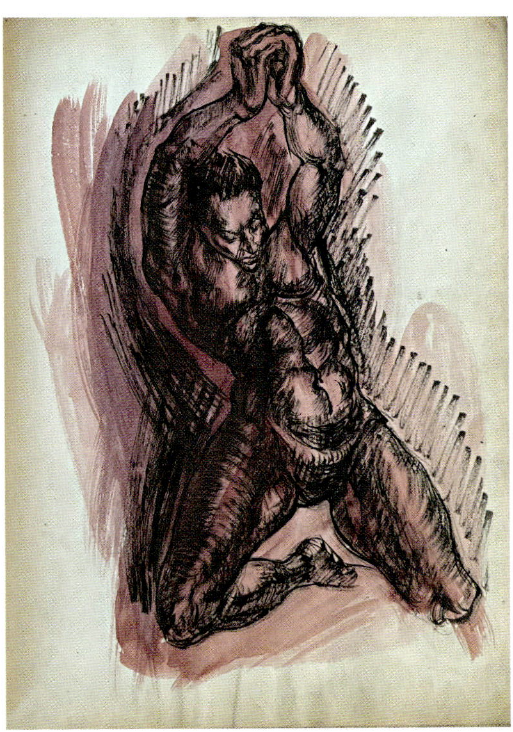

be mobilized in many different ways and in fact *add* social reference rather than subtract it.[60]

White's notes and sketches from the School of the Art Institute of Chicago also show the inspiration he took from West African sculpture and architecture. He sketched figurative sculptures in the Art Institute's collection, including those made by the Baoulé people from Ivory Coast, that were thought of as an enclosure for the soul of the deceased, a vehicle for the soul's continual dissemination in public (fig. 103).[61] For White, a person's body was situated alongside what his friend Ramon Price called "ancestral presences"—a network of past familial connections, close and distant, that could bear on one's experience in the present. As such, environment could constitute sound, smell, taste, and texture, as well as such social variables as historical memory and ancestral relations, archivally lost but recuperated through imagined narratives or prompts.[62] White had long been invested in illustrative graphic representations of African Americans and their histories, but by 1968, he was contemplating his own position as an ancestor, a progenitor of an art yet to come. He had accepted a position as professor of drawing and painting at the Otis Art Institute four years earlier, at a crucial moment when students nationwide were demanding that the imbalance (or more often the total absence) of Black faculty in higher education be corrected.[63] As his presence on the lecture circuit grew and his investments in pedagogy deepened, he used additive material processes to assemble his own long narrative of experiences and to make sense of his personal lineage.

Fig. 101 Charles White, untitled sketchbook page, ca. 1937–42. Charcoal, pastel, ink, graphite, pen and inks and watercolor on ivory wove paper, 10¼ × 8⅛ in. (26 × 20.5 cm). Art Institute of Chicago, 2006.259.

Fig. 102 Charles White, untitled sketchbook page, ca. 1937–42. Charcoal, pastel, ink, graphite, pen and inks and watercolor on ivory wove paper, 10¼ × 8⅛ in. (26 × 20.5 cm). Art Institute of Chicago, 2006.259.

This summoning of ancestry through material means, and the resulting emotional effects on the viewer, continued to attract many critical misconceptions. Kellie Jones has written that "the rise of pop, the enshrining of recognizable subject matter, finally permit[ted] the mainstream visibility of White's work on the West Coast in the early 1960s."[64] This is certainly the case, and his exhibitions in this decade were invariably "box-office smash[es] in the field of commercial exhibitions," to quote one *Artforum* critic in 1964.[65] Still, the artist recognized interpretive shortcomings in some of the critical commentary on his work. He asserted in his talk at the Los Angeles County Museum of Art in 1969, "I don't know whether what I do is art. I could care less whether it's labeled by any of the prominent critics in town 'art,' or whether they've missed the point of what I'm trying to say [entirely]." Writers for theoretically motivated fine art magazines including *Studio International* and *Artforum* praised White's work for its technical proficiency or its appeals to narrative or emotion or both. A review in *Artforum* in 1965 had backhandedly pronounced that White "gain[ed] a certain distinction" from being "able to calculate the effects of a wipe, or a bite, or a cut."[66] A review published the previous year wielded a baffling circular logic: "If occasionally too sentimental, it is not difficult to dismiss the flaw as inconsequential in respect for an artist whose sincerity bleeds all over the paper."[67] Though White's process was indeed technically advanced and his commitment to socially transformative pictures

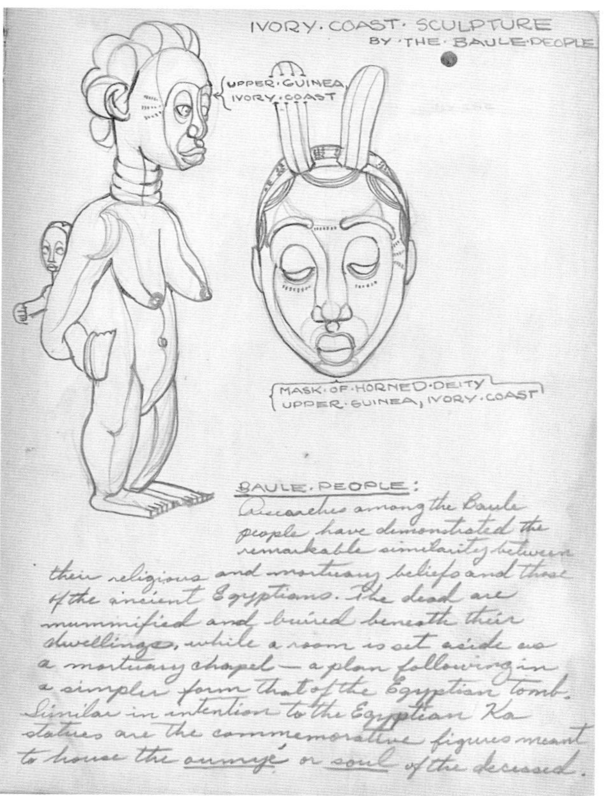

Fig. 103 Charles White, untitled sketchbook page, p. 58, ca. 1937–42. Charcoal, pastel, ink, graphite, pen and inks and watercolor on ivory wove paper, 10¼ × 8⅛ in. (26 × 20.5 cm). Art Institute of Chicago, 2006.259.

Deep in the Surface

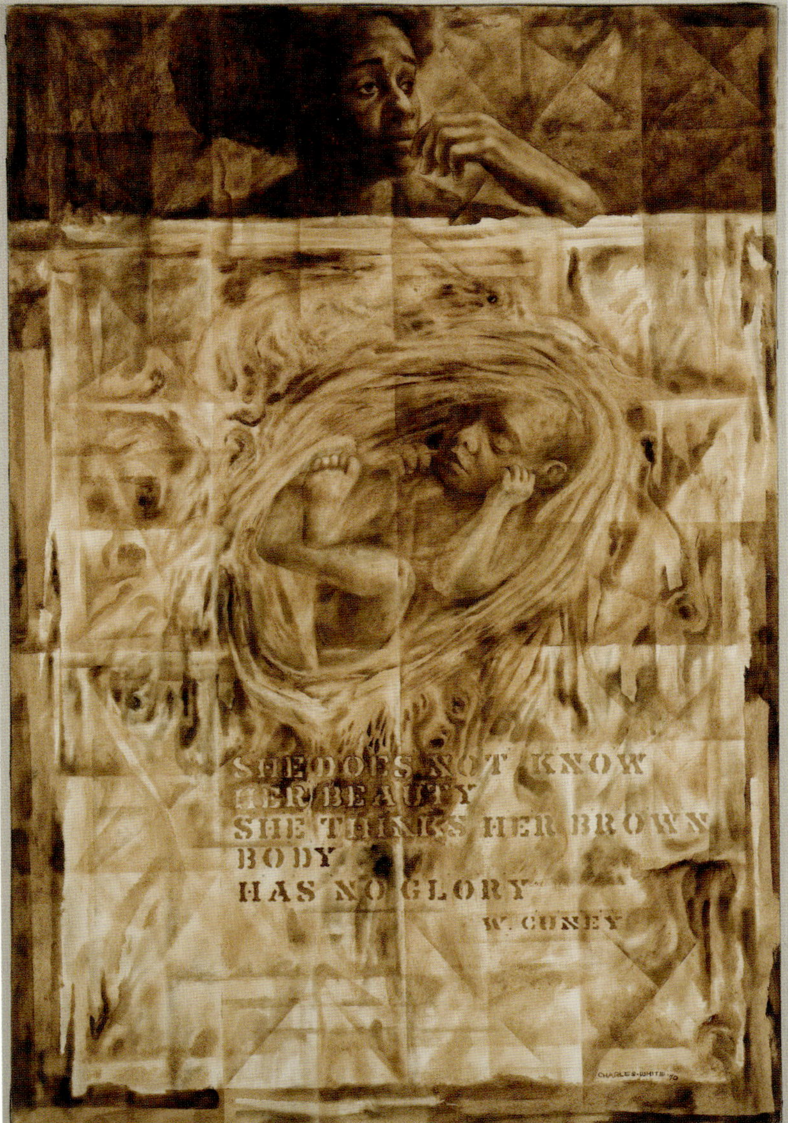

Fig. 104 Charles White, *She Does Not Know Her Beauty*, 1970. Oil wash on board, 40 × 28 in. (101.6 × 71.1 cm). Mott-Warsh Collection, Flint, MI, LN2018.1347.

in the realist style was unyielding, it is easy to see that these critics often missed the forest for the trees. For instance, the oil wash medium could accommodate the wide variations in pigmentation that White was skilled at articulating.[68] To achieve the range of browns in the first ten works of the *Wanted Poster* series, White used what conservators and scholars have identified as "a warm-brown paint," "a sepia tone," and "shades of burnt umber."[69] His drawing *She Does Not Know Her Beauty* of 1970 uses oil wash in its most explicit mode to date, to connect Black bodies past and present to a speculative African past (fig. 104). The work's title comes from William Waring Cuney's poem "No Images" (1924), which imagines new possibilities for reframing Black female beauty standards. "She does not know / her beauty," the poem begins, and suggests that this might change "If she / could dance / naked / under palm trees / and see her image in the river."[70] If

Cuney's title implies that "no images" yet exist to do this work, then White provides both an image and an answer in the woman's tilted head and wrinkled brow at the top of the composition and the baby in utero at its bottom. Diluting these tones made his passages of oil wash into an ideal corollary for the varying tones and undertones of African American skin, which the popular press was differentiating, celebrating, and even commodifying by the end of the decade.[71]

KNOWING A LOT: THE POWER OF EDUCATION

The material practices from the *Wanted* posters suggest that the discursive possibilities for addition and subtraction were just as important as their physical affordances. These practices were also connected to the material techniques of White's earlier ink works, many of which centered images of bodies as important teaching tools. His earliest drawings make lively use of things drawn and scratched out, with scratching and dry brushing (which spreads a wet medium across a dry surface) finding strong foothold. This wet technique squared with his techniques more broadly, which, unlike several other artists in this book, were operationalized to make imaged bodies more visible in more precise ways. Doing this with any unruly liquid medium—which could then be pushed and pulled by a dry implement— was another instance, for White, of an exciting point of contact between the possible and the practical. His earlier drawings are important to consider alongside this study, insofar as that they lay the foundation for a powerful conception of education: that learning, too, was a matter of constant difficult erasures and accruals and that real bodies were often caught between the limitless potential of knowledge and the harsh reality of its circumscription.

This connection to knowledge is once again made visible by tracing through White's remarks about atmosphere and environment. Although his interest in the environment was distant from contemporaneous scientific studies on ecology, these two discursive terrains did occasionally intersect. In the summer of 1969 when White began the *Wanted Poster* series, a biology professor at Southern Oregon College, Frank Lang, invited the artist to give a keynote talk at a conference entitled "Politics and Our Deteriorating Environment."[72] The conference was to include the folk singer Pete Seeger, as well as talks on population management, world hunger, and other problems of resource quantification and sustainability. Later that year, at the "Black Artists: Art and Social Commentary" panel in Los Angeles, White reflected on this invitation and expressed bafflement at his inclusion in the program. "It's a 3-day conference on pollution, conservation, urban affairs. . . . I don't know what the hell I'm doing there as an artist," he said—to the audience's uproarious laughter. But then he paused and reevaluated his own expertise. "I suppose I know a hell of a lot about urban affairs, having grown up in the ghetto of Chicago. Conservation: my folks were from

Mississippi, and they worked on farms, and they picked cotton and did all the things, so I know a little something about conservation. And culture . . . I know a whole lot about culture. I know a lot about culture. I know a lot about people."[73]

The knowledges that White juxtaposes here are obviously, even humorously, different: scholarly disciplines such as "urban affairs" and "conservation" are distant reflections of learned and lived behaviors that accompany urban life, or the agile adaptations that develop from having too little of this or that, or the habits designed to circumvent shortage. To experience such deprivations, and yet rise above nationalistic hate symbols so successfully, required a transversal relation to learning and education. If modernity in the American context was saturated with symbols that were historically weaponized to injure bodies of color and prevent Black thriving, then what was required, White wrote in a letter to playwright Lorraine Hansberry, must be nothing short of a "biting condemnation of ideas and images which dehumanize life."[74] As Amiri Baraka put it, this required "a thrilling language of ideas from the mouths of Black people . . . a thrill of meaning and music."[75] To take in information, synthesize knowledge, and process thought within a media landscape designed to affirm the status quo and uphold oppressive systems of power required new frameworks for knowing and methodologies for learning. White's close friend the educational theorist Edmund W. Gordon wrote extensively about this problem while collecting White's work and using his drawings as illustrations for his articles on educational topics. A former divinity school student, Gordon viewed psychology as a tool for assessing and improving basic human needs and correcting social inequities on a broad scale. While teaching and writing on psychology and educational theory at Yale University, Gordon became a key voice in theorizing "the achievement gap," having been one of the earliest specialists invited to assess the Head Start program after President Lyndon B. Johnson launched it in 1965.[76]

Gordon and White's relationship provides historical and theoretical context for White's visualizations of the struggle for educational independence in the postwar moment. Gordon's academic article "Relevance or Revolt" of 1969 was illustrated with three drawings by White and emphasized the need to reimagine the university education in the image of its broad and diverse surfeit of users. "Information mastery, management of knowledge, information analysis, cultural and intellectual competence are probably more important to all segments of our population now than ever before. It is the purposes to which knowledge and the pursuit of knowledge are committed that lack relevance to the central issues of our time," Gordon wrote.[77] Although White's experience teaching at art schools was quite different from Gordon's work in large universities, the artist's relationship to orthodox spaces of learning was also deeply critical. He had been a chronic truant in junior high and high school, alienated by the lack of content devoted to the cultural contributions of people of color.[78] He rejected the classroom in favor of the galleries at the Art Institute of Chicago and in favor of the library, where he spent entire days reading books of his own choosing.[79] In 1933, he joined the Negro Art Club, a group on the South Side of Chicago that raised money to send one of its members to classes at the School of the Art Institute each week. White's core principles extended from the premise that education was shared—the media of learning even acted as a coparent to the unsupervised White in his earliest childhood, when his mother dropped him off at the library while she ran errands—and knowledge could be indexed expansively and approached speculatively. White's concession to this basic epistemic need—a need that matched natural curiosity with a groundwork of researched, published information and family and community traditions—was foundational to his practice in the final two decades of his life, when his own work as an illustrator of Black historical education texts was reaching a twenty-year peak. Drawing was a portal to intellectual freedom; it allowed almost anyone to seize and reconstitute the tools that had been kept from them.

The civil rights communities of which White was a part saw media as generative of sensory social experience, as well as a product that inhered within it. In 1963, the Student Nonviolent Coordinating Committee (SNCC) laid out a platform for its Freedom Schools. Black students did not receive the same quality of education as white students across the southern states—a problem that rested with segregation but intersected with the project of modern learning as a whole. Students were "forced to live in an environment that is geared to quash intellectual curiosity, and different thinking," wrote SNCC leader and historian Charlie Cobb.[80] The Freedom Schools proposed an alternative curriculum, expandable into different

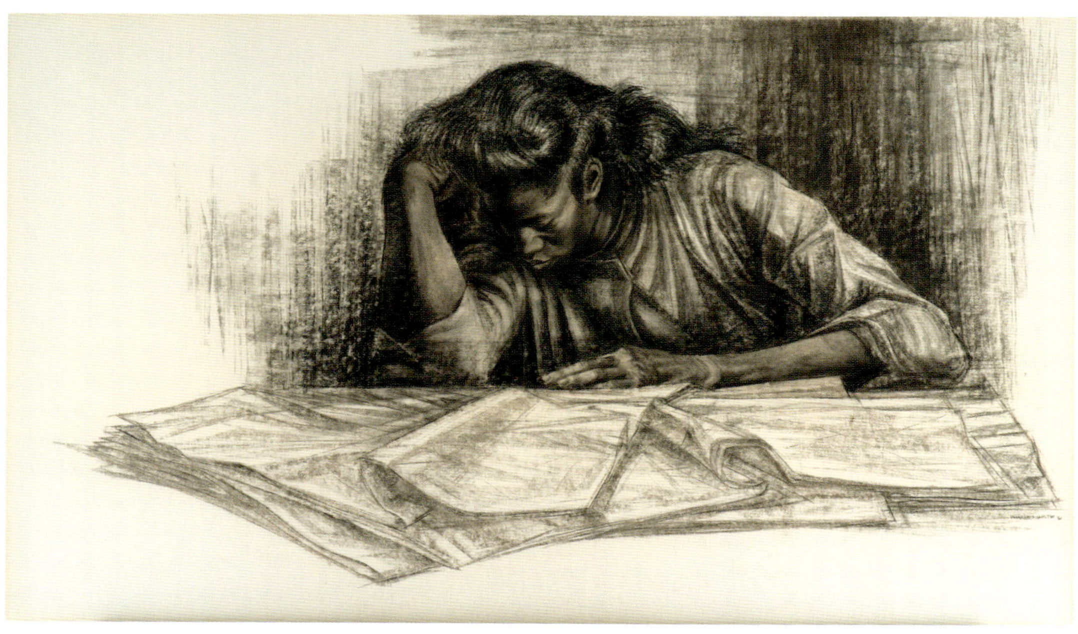

Fig. 105 Charles White, *Awaken from the Unknowing*, 1961. Compressed charcoal and brown and gray vine charcoal with scratching out, blending, and erasing on cold-pressed illustration board, sheet: 31 × 56 in. (78.7 × 142.2 cm). Gift of Susan G. and Edmund W. Gordon to the units of Black Studies and the Blanton Museum of Art at The University of Texas at Austin, 2014.83.

lengths and sizes, that included training in leadership skills, art, and music appreciation. Each branch of the school was encouraged to produce a student newspaper.

For the cover of the first Freedom School brochure, the SNCC reprinted a Charles White drawing titled *Awaken from the Unknowing* (fig. 105). The work shows a young girl bent over a stack of books and newspapers, poring over their contents. She is lost in thought, perhaps even exhausted from studying, with her face concealed from the light and by the cast shadow of her supporting hand. White leaves the drawing unfinished at its edges, allowing the white expanse of the paper beyond to amplify the young girl's solitude and independence. The textures of her hair and clothes, and the shaded vortex created by her bent arm and downturned face, are suffused with the same generative potential as the paper. We also see the same "abuse" of the surface that White would later reference in 1970, when he summarized his graphic practice for curator James E. Young. This is not a charcoal cloud produced by holding the tool held sideways, as with canonical modernist artists such as Georges Seurat. An added implement helped create the grooves on the paper's surface (White used art composition board for this work rather than commercial chipboard), which leaves behind a heated inversion of a needle scratching a record. Passages of charcoal pencil have been layered in and then scratched out again. The woman in the picture emerges in high-relief contrast, a fully formed mind rising from infinitude, as books and newspapers spread out into space. They spell out a system of possibilities that is limitless. There is more to come in this vision of the materials of learning as they extend from the human body that activates them through impulse. Rather than presenting printed knowledge as a given, White reminds us that language and erudition are confined to who can access them in real time and space. Education often came in a piecemeal state; for those excluded from orthodox spaces of knowledge or who escaped from such spaces because of intellectual incompatibilities diagnosed as deficiencies, it was an intricate, self-directed path. More images of children engaged in the act of contemplation—specifically, the face of his young neighbor, Elijah—soon became a companion motif (figs. 106, 107).

As Huey Copeland, Simone Browne, Teresa Carbone, and Darby English have amply demonstrated, the core tenets of art history—close looking and distanced empirical description—maintain strong ties to criminal investigation. The pictures in the *Wanted Poster* series mobilize drawing in service of the possibility that evidence is not merely the object of forensic examination but can also soak and leak into things; it can be unearthed, processed, supplemented, and reversed. Across the broader span of White's work, writing and drawing were fundamental entitlements, cementing the inherent freedoms of a private self with infinite possibilities to explore. Drawing and printed media were understood to act in dynamic mutuality with citizens as writers and makers, with the very act of citizenship connected intrinsically with the ability to respond to one's

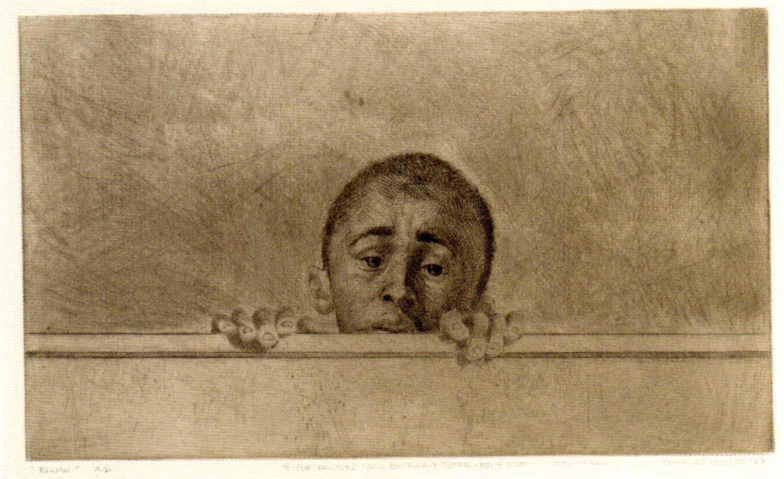

surroundings in kind. But drawing could also allow people to reconstitute their surroundings completely, confronting multiple histories, ancestral lineages, and violent national symbols. The oil wash works in the *Wanted Poster* series were attempts to uncover the difference between a human being's environment (and its role in affirming concepts of personhood) and ecology, between matter and symbol, between brutality and its irrepressible legal and juridical apparatus.[81] To exhume all these things was only the beginning.

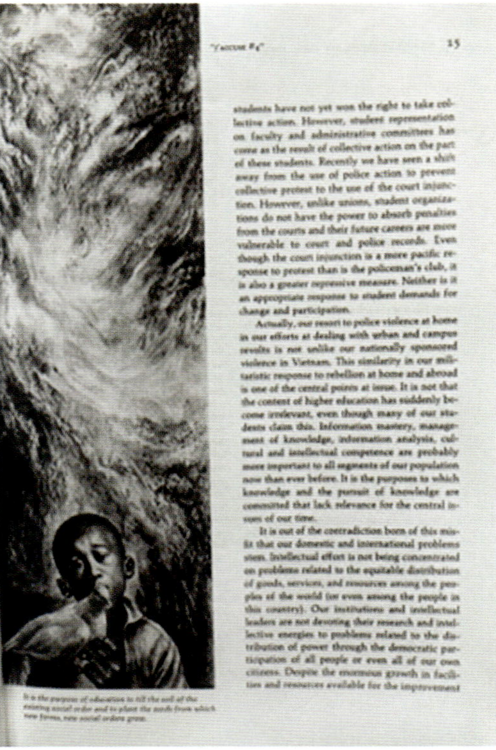

Fig. 107 Charles White, *J'Accuse #4*, featured in Edmund Gordon, "Relevance or Revolt," *Perspectives on Education* (Teachers College, Columbia University) 3, no. 1 (1969).

Deep in the Surface

Out of Paper and into the World

In the United States in the late twentieth century, debates on citizenship and visibility were inseparable from—and often occurred on top of—publicly available materials for learning, of which paper was irrefutably one. In this sense, artists in the postwar moment made works that summoned an implicit critique of the very thing you are holding in your hands or viewing on your screen right now: the work of historical writing. This book's narrative progression is itself an environment, bringing drawing's bounded, differently bodied, or streaming qualities to bear on a politics of the present. At the start of this story, artists were just beginning to test the drawing's constructive, representative functions. Together, we read and look alongside Robert Morris in New York as he mined the daily news and its attendant shocks and with Charles White in Los Angeles as he erased paper's surface and built it up again. As Carolee Schneemann's shreds of canceled bank checks cover the bodies of her performers in Chicago, we start to perceive the paper surface as a friable field too unstable to contain the human figure. In activating drawings as material assemblages, these artists explored pre-Spinozan thinkers such as Heraclitus or made legible inheritors of Spinoza including Alfred North Whitehead and Gilles Deleuze and Jane Bennett and Karen Barad. Still others, such as Sol LeWitt and Adrian Piper, engaged Spinoza in their drawing practice more directly, as modernism began its sunset period and the relation between ideas and empirical reality continued to come under critique.[1]

Throughout this story, we take part in their important ethical and political reflections through interrogating what kind of learning and experimenting constitutes knowledge and what kind does not. And in considering the paper page as a kind of streaming media material avant la lettre, it becomes clear that paper's mechanical standardization and mass availability made it an ideal site for reconciling the external world with the artist's lived body. To mark *any* surface in the postwar decades—decades that were themselves marked by the failures of colonialism, racial segregation, extractive capitalism, and nuclear armament—highlighted language's disjunctive relation to individual viewing and being.

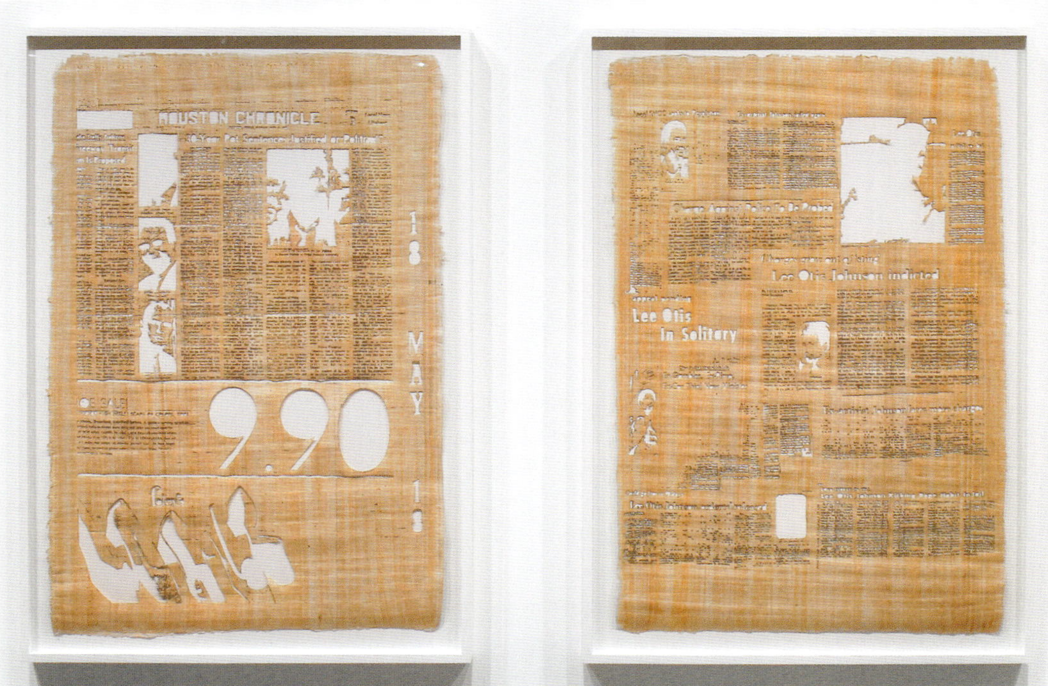

Fig. 108 Jamal Cyrus, *Eroding Witness, Season 3, Episode 20*, 2018. Diptych, laser-cut papyrus, each: 37 × 24½ in. (94 × 62.2 cm); framed: 40¼ × 28¾ in. (102.2 × 73 cm). Inman Gallery, Houston, TX.

The analog paper surface continues to be a dense starting point for artists and designers because of its links to viewing, touching, learning, and truth-construction. In the 1960s, it could bring users and observers *out of the world* or help them make worlds *out of paper:* this material was responsive, flexible, and semipermeable, like a human body or like thought itself, but one that also created distances between bodies through bureaucratic or juridical means. Originally an arena for the creation of categories in early modern art and ideas, paper became an engine for exploring "anarchic difference" and "acategorical thought," as Michel Foucault wrote in 1970.[2]

Thus, as we move from chapter 1, where Schneemann's drawings rotated from landscape to body, a methodology of extension derived from Spinoza's ethical writings encourages us to learn through unfolding and reaching outward. We learn that materials both proper and improper to paper could be shredded, wasted, and recycled, passed back through the environment, and then captured and reconstructed by voracious, image-hungry entertainment media. And this book's final pages, which you are reading in one iteration of many—and one whose final version will be replicated across different electronic text-reading platforms—conclude with Charles White's careful decisions about what kinds of violence to enact upon surfaces. What all this suggests is that even the most exhaustive accounts of drawing must reckon with the medium's complicated successes and failures at bringing new worlds into being at the end of the long 1960s. Turning away from explicitly utopian aims, these artists' projects leveraged the body as vulnerable, like paper, but also infinitely palimpsestic. Disappearing and being seen are two separate aims that works on paper accomplish.

     Epilogue

A contemporary example emerges in Jamal Cyrus's *Eroding Witness* series, which the Houston artist created in the second decade of the 2000s. During this moment, Cyrus began researching detailed archives of police violence against Black liberation movement leaders in the 1960s and 1970s. Using a laser etching machine, Cyrus burned a selection of news stories and FBI documents about the Black Power movement onto sheets of papyrus (fig. 108). For each work, the artist used the newspaper as its main design interface, invoking the journalist Alan Barth's 1943 assertion that the news is the "first draft of history."[3] For Cyrus, the paper material becomes a performative history-making space—a media space that freezes a narrative in a moment almost coextensive with the historical event.[4] Despite being titled like a television show, *Season 3, Episode 20* is a testimonial to what is missing, or, as the artist articulates it, to "the dissolution or the breakdown of historical memory . . . and particularly within the Black community of past political ideals and values."[5] The work's laser-cut image re-creates a *Houston Chronicle* story on the arrest of Black student activist Lee Otis Johnson by the Houston Police Department in the summer of 1969. Its visible headlines reek of the pretense of objective journalism: Lee Otis (the *Chronicle* omits his last name) has been indicted for passing a marijuana cigarette to an undercover police officer. Lee Otis is in solitary confinement. Is Lee Otis's thirty-year sentence justified, or is the Houston Police Department making a political example out of him? The laser-cut text has shredded the papyrus, so the information stamped into its fibers fades out rather than informs.

Like Morris's copying of the newspaper, Cyrus positions the news as a mechanism for narrating history that is prescriptive, yet brittle. The news stories appear on papyrus, a material made from the stem tissue of an Egyptian sedge grass and an African technology (fig. 109).[6] Unlike the flexible

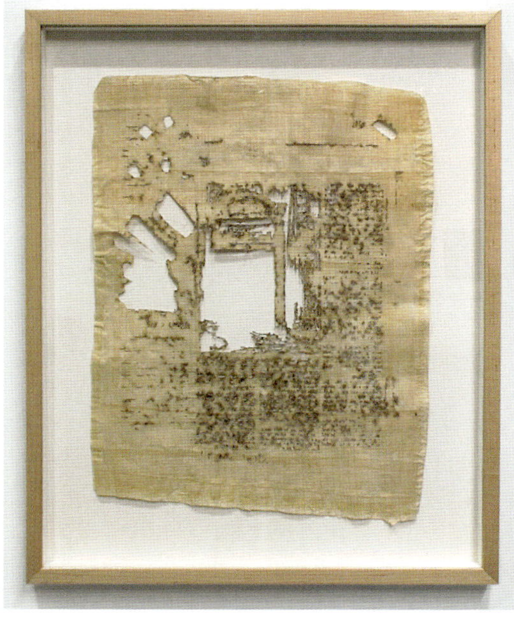

Fig. 109 Jamal Cyrus, *Eroding Witness* (*Episode #221*), 2011. Laser-cut papyrus, gouache, 17 × 14 in. (43.19 × 35.6 cm). Inman Gallery, Houston, TX.

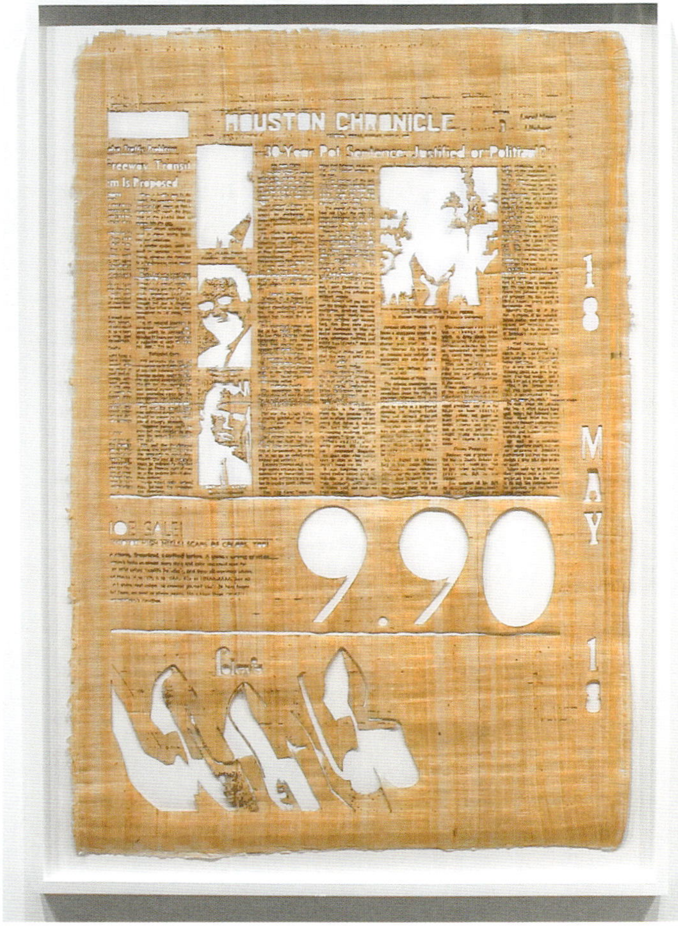

sheets of vellum or parchment made from animal skins that formed early modern codices and illuminated manuscripts, papyrus documents could not fold without cracking and required a large roll for long texts. And while these news stories perform the *possibility* that they might be fixed in time to create the first drafts of history, their structural inflexibility is the very thing that stops that transfer cold. Each page is suspended on hinges above a handmade paper backing; their manila color and gridded weave signal an entirely other time. The imprinted text on each sheet casts a shadow on the wall behind it, as an object or a body might (fig. 110). Johnson's story, which the *Houston Chronicle* narrates very differently than accounts in Houston's Black community circulars did, becomes an agent in the erosion of historical memory. The plant fibers perform the weight of media's erasure and history's decay.

Throughout this book, matter steps in to complicate "seeing" and "the shown" in important ways. From the late 1950s to the early 1970s, layered, combinatorial, and intuitive approaches to drawing set the stage for paper's shredding, recycling, recording, rapid prototyping, and cutting capabilities to come out, which in turn manifested a new, physicalized awareness of media's totalizing influence in contemporary art and the central role of

　　Epilogue

one's environment in every situation. How very tempting it is to understand this as a story of the body's disappearance, a swan song sung by enfleshed bodies in the twilight of humanism. But the human body didn't disappear as much as extend into its environment in select moments, and this is precisely the kind of juncture that holds meaning for our own contemporary existence. Our beings, our selves may be written or taken down; at the same time, we face the prospect of being thrown away or subjecting our remains to distortion and decay in a contemporary age when the durability of the device far exceeds that of the flesh. In the face of these threats, a consideration of materials and tools becomes more urgent. When tools are not made available for certain bodies to use, those bodies do not disappear; they simply invent new tools using the materials available to them. Linear articulations and tracings may never be truly detached from their support, particularly if those supports originate digitally.

Turning once again to Spinoza, the *extension* proves more and more relevant to parsing these postwar relations among makers, materials, and surroundings. In medieval and early modern philosophy, to be extended meant simply to have dimensions or to be spread out across time or space. Anything with substance was capable of extension, of being extended—power, passivity, inertia, interior space, leaking liquids, or drawn lines—and was distinct from thought insofar as thought was the agent that made substances divisible. In other words, Spinoza separated thought (or imagination) from extension in order to argue that "Measure, Time and Number are nothing other than modes of thinking, or rather, modes of imagining."[7] As Robert Morris, William Anastasi, and others in this book have argued, matter and space are infinite. To divide them is to *perform* thought, to imprint the body is to show division, and those divisions are the very things that we must analyze with great critical rigor.[8] It is vital, therefore, to survey paper's extensions as well as its record of thought, despite the conviction that the dominant narrative of industrial nations is that of a long march toward paperlessness. As the substrate, the filament, for knowledge and collective action, paper marks the problems and potentials of imagination, both in reaching for a better world and for closing down or delimiting certain parts of that world. By viewing the differences between real extensions and imagined divisions, new tensions come into focus—the tension within a material that clings close to the body and carries the rhetoric of private communication, for example. A bleached and flattened plane that dissolved into or pointed to whole environments, paper denatured ideas in the postwar period—and indeed, still does today.

Through this framework we can revisit the "conceptual turn" of the late 1960s and early 1970s, which includes such artists as Lawrence Weiner, Lothar Baumgarten, and On Kawara, and collectives including the New York Graphic Workshop. Much installation and site-specific work finds its genealogy in (and on) paper, as artists began to look differently at the industrial materials of downtown New York and harness design tropes from printed matter. As a result, the humanistic questions about mind and body previously associated with drawing became interrogations of power and territory. This is a sharp turn from earlier 1960s methods drawn from the live, collaborative ethos of Fluxus and Happenings, where drawn prototypes and event scores had a more private function and resisted institutional display and thus were more closely associated with the intimate or expressionist mode. Artists began using type on the exterior walls of buildings in the same few years that they installed paper documents in New York galleries. But in harnessing the atmospheric, omnipresent flows of modern information in ways that foretold the cloud-based streaming data universe of the twenty-first century, they also marked paper—and other disposable mass media picture interfaces—with a unique archival weight. That weight was different from the "ton of lead" that Lucy Lippard referred to when memorializing the era in 1973, but it imprinted on art history, nevertheless.

I have endeavored to show that paper never quite moved from being aesthetically marginalized or a critical curiosity in curatorial practices of the 1960s. Only when artists themselves made a firm case for exploring it as a public medium was it prioritized in the following years.[9] The medium naturalized very gradually for gallerists, aided by the popularization of international biennials and art fairs and their attendant shipping costs across global markets.[10] In art education, too, drawing had broken up into many different teaching tracks, and art schools and universities had begun to reduce their drawing programs; of the five artists featured here, three (Carolee Schneemann, William Anastasi, and Rafael Ferrer) had minimal exposure to drawing courses in their earliest training. Drawing's centrality instead lay in its divestment from the finished artwork and its discursive qualities that provoked speculative ideas. Drawings had a contentious relation to behaviors that were discussed according to the growing orthodoxies of social and behavioral theory. They could model relations between place and making that were less atomistic than gallery models promised at that moment. Consequently, the medium expanded and broke apart in the precise moment that it became a more legitimate collecting category in contemporary art, and also the moment when design became a firm part of discourses on ecology and capitalism—two ways to discuss human beings' place in the world and their instrumentalization within it.

As such, the work on paper sustained a multidirectional move toward a "post-medium condition," as Rosalind Krauss has called it. Such a condition "makes any simple, unitary identification of the work's physical support impossible."[11] This book's wide-ranging perspective on paper serves to complicate ideas about medium's lineage and instead prompt us all to contemplate the very ground of a practice, our tools and our spaces, to see what they do for us as we attempt to create conditions for something new to happen. As the long 1960s gave way to the denouements of the 1970s, paper continued to be a component of the artistic process. It continued to provide models for how to approach newer, disembodied multimedia streams that the popularization of film and tech tools permitted. While early sketches were still necessary in artistic practice, drawing's association with paper as its physical support waned. Full-color illustrated weekly circulars gave way to televised news and, eventually, streaming media. Sketch- and paper-based art pedagogies transposed themselves onto peer-to-peer ad hoc tech networks. According to Martha Rosler, artists' critiques shifted toward the media of communication that were "central to the hegemony of the newly ascendant middle classes" and that were more rarefied and expensive, such as televisions and computers.[12] The critiques of authorship spawned by structuralism in the wake of 1968 brought in a full, exuberant commitment to an "anti-drawing stance." Ultimately this freed drawings from their attachment to limiting terms including privacy, personal identity, and signature.[13]

There was also a flight at the end of the 1960s from the varying structures and systems that composed *environments* and instead toward *nature,* though few could agree on what that meant exactly. People—namely, white people with financial means—were encouraged to go back to the land; to look critically at cities, which resulted in rampant white flight and gentrification; and to dispense with the idea of personal authorship. New, communal spaces from Druid Heights to Kaliflower offered a return to the basic tools and skills for living, though most were still dependent on the Cartesian coordinates typical of designed spaces.[14] Earth Day was launched in 1970, and by 1971 the consensus among ecologists was that a true conservation movement could not rely on the fervor of a one-day celebration of natural resources.[15] The meeting in 1970 of the International Design Conference in Aspen, Colorado, was called "Environment by Design," though a group of French theorists issued a statement against the conference, cautioning against environmentalism as "a boy scout idealism, with a naive euphoria in a hygienic nature."[16] At the conference, the Container Corporation of America—the company that two years earlier had withdrawn Carolee Schneemann's contribution on waste and reuse from its sponsored exhibition, *Made with Paper*—selected a design by the twenty-three-year-old designer Gary Anderson as a recycling symbol that would mark commercial products with a commitment to environmental sensitivity, even as the biologist Thomas Edmondson was discussing before Congress his twenty years of research findings that indicted untreated raw sewage as the cause of nutrient imbalances in lakes and rivers.[17] Other activists in the ecological movement such as the biologist Barry Commoner called for human beings to reclaim "their place in the terrestrial ecosystem," that they had "broken out of the circle of life."[18] Environment increasingly came to signify not only the data and beings circulating within an architectural envelope or a structure but rather the outside of the rather complicated and frequently invoked term *civilization.* As Timothy Leary put it in 1967, "Urban living is spiritually suicidal. The cities of America are about to crumble as did Rome and Babylon. Go to the land. Go to the sea."[19] As the 1970s opened, artists' and designers' dreams of access and integration gave way to pursuits of imagined spaces that might be made real—some exclusive, some necessarily separatist, and all forged with revolutionary ardor.

As if in answer to this call, alternative exhibition spaces sprang up for art and design. The years 1969 through 1977 saw an unprecedented proliferation of spaces that sought to denature the canonizing museum as art's primary counting-house. In 1971, the curator Alanna Heiss founded the Institute for Art and Urban Resources in Queens, which converted abandoned or underutilized buildings throughout the New York metro area into artists' studios and cultural working spaces; the fruits of this labor included the Clocktower Gallery in the former New York Life Insurance Company building in Lower Manhattan and PS1 Contemporary Art Center in Queens. Artists Space, Creative Time, White Columns, and the Kitchen followed shortly thereafter. When Marcia Tucker was dismissed from the Whitney Museum of American Art due to controversy about her "pretentious and unprofessional" retrospective of Richard Tuttle's work—a retrospective in which some of the viewers scrawled notes in pencil next to Tuttle's wall drawings—she founded the New Museum of Contemporary Art inside the New School for Social Research on lower Fifth Avenue.[20] Printed Matter and the Drawing Center, which both opened in 1977, made drawings and ephemeral artworks central to the project of "exhibit[ing] art by living artists in their own neighborhood," as the Drawing Center's founding curator, Martha Beck, put it in announcing her departure from the Department of Drawings at the Museum of Modern Art as a critical assailment of Midtown Manhattan's changing demographics and cultural politics.[21] New institutional missions reflected ways that drawings and printed matter came to matter—as the tools of a thrumming contemporary moment and as market critique—and also harnessed New York's urban brickscape as a container and amplifier for emergent voices. If the decade of the 1960s was fueled by an envisioning of experimental possibilities, then Leary gave everyone permission to *go to* new surroundings, harmonizing with the new wave of alternative art spaces. Could we be getting somewhere?

But this escape was fractional, provisional, even exclusive. "The collectives in the 1970s were often predominantly white," Howardena Pindell says of this time. "If [white people] were not in charge, then business was not to be conducted."[22] Pindell's phrasing is poignant here: as a young MFA graduate of Yale University who was hired to work in the Arts Education department at MoMA in 1967, she entered the museum just before Martha Beck exited it. As a member of this highly feminized and less competitive department (despite her art degree from a top graduate program), she had a front-row seat to many varieties of art world business that might *be conducted,* to echo Pindell's use of the passive voice. She met Adrian Piper and Sol LeWitt in the burgeoning feminist and conceptual art scene of the early 1970s. In their work, these artists parodied bureaucratic forms including typed lists and placards, the purview of an acutely feminized sector of the art and cultural workforce.

Pindell would likely also have been aware of the several women's committees that staged a public demonstration in December 1970 just twenty-two blocks uptown from the building where she worked. The three groups—Women Artists in Revolution, Women Students and Artists for Black Artists' Liberation, and the Ad Hoc Women's Art Committee— printed a fake press release listing the Whitney Museum of American Art Annual Show's artist invitees at 50 percent women and 50 percent nonwhite artists.[23] They printed fake tickets, of which the Whitney agreed to honor the first hundred, screening all admission tickets for authenticity with an ultraviolet light. In exhibition spaces they left raw eggs and tampons individually printed with the 50/50 message.[24] When I think of Women Artists in Revolution's use of insistent little emblems—throwaway markers of their demands—I wonder where they ended up and whether anyone saved them. Let us not lose sight of paper's fragility and tendency to disintegrate, in the absence of curatorial intervention. What, then, does the history of paper tell us about the material givens of the archive and the conditions that make it possible for these makers' histories to be seen and discussed? As mentioned in chapter 1, how might paper allow us to think differently about the bodies kept separate from their surroundings through prescriptive designs or regulations? What models or lessons become legible when we follow the trail away from and out of drawing and toward surfacing, streaming, and reimaginings of separation?

In a departure from such media theorists as Marshall McLuhan who had focused on universal liberation from systems, many Black and feminist conceptual artists of the 1970s whose work aligned with burgeoning resistance movements stepped forward to answer this question. They made paper-based works that repeated the labor of the calculation, seizing its behavioral pathways including graph-making and data visualization, performing the significance of these operations for those most calculated and surveilled. Adrian Piper used paper's textured, tactile qualities to undermine the neutrality of the sketch, the legal document, and, eventually, the business card. Charles Gaines, who was acquainted with the New York gallery scene from his youth in Newark, New Jersey, and his time as an MFA student at the Rochester Institute of Technology, where he was the first Black student to gain an MFA, mapped photographs of trees and faces onto gridded graph paper. Pindell herself also made drawings and painting-sculptures that turned critical attention to the grid, a structure that has long appeared in modernist art as both an ordering device and an opening onto new possibilities. While drawing habituates us to streaming content, doing it on paper makes us aware of the politics of such a stream.

Most of us think that we can now live without paper, but we cannot. Numerous lessons from the first quarter of the twenty-first century confirm this: protest signs, whose materials have remained consistent for centuries, have become a barometer for how art institutions absorb and historicize other technologies of protest. The Smithsonian American Art Museum collected cardboard signs in the wake of George Floyd's murder by officers of the Minneapolis Police Department in the summer of 2020. That July, the Whitney

Museum of American Art began plans for an exhibition, *Collective Actions: Artist Interventions in a Time of Change,* that would put on display ephemeral objects artists had sold to raise money for Black Lives Matter and other organizations. (*Collective Actions* was eventually canceled after public pressure from the featured artists; the Whitney had acquired their work at discount prices designed to make them accessible for ordinary citizens to purchase.)[25] A new public discussion—indeed a new heyday—arose for objects that, to use Sampada Aranke's phrasing, were "designed to die."[26] Single-serving wrapped food items and Dixie cups returned with the global covid-19 pandemic of 2020 (and beyond), and vaccination cards had to be carried around in wallets. Archives and museum collections around the world closed their doors, halting research, as paper pages and books became vectors for disease.

It is clear that this medium now generates quite different extensions between bodies and their environments. Paper is biodegradable, but not as readily as we think it is. It is a distant adjunct to the digital tools of most professional training. Its surface makes a sound when touched, and so it is a candidate for the haunting sonics of autonomous sensory meridian response, or ASMR, videos. Sheets of analog paper, with their firm borders and boundaries, resist the automatic doubling of data scraping and other surveillance technologies tied to digital writing and image technologies. Paper sheets provide alternatives for drawing and writing in a time when the material conditions for information exchange increasingly mirror the tools that businesses use to manage productivity. If drawing and writing both map flows of energy, paper enacts limits.

Such a difference invites further thinking, not just about paper as a bounded space for information or ideas, but also about the things that paper has long failed to document, such as sounds, lost languages, or lost property. Professional practices in art history and visual studies that have concerned themselves with preservation are only just beginning to consider what has been, and what probably will remain, lost. In reviewing the many possibilities for what was in the 1960s called *environment,* we might consider in the twenty-first century how to withdraw from documentation as a central mechanism for history making and disclosure. Robert Morris told us that paper is a trap; Carolee Schneemann used shredded documents to reimagine capitalism's continual cycles of extraction and exploitation; William Anastasi offered a method for recording experiments that foreclosed on narratives of progress; Richard Tuttle showed that paper can create new spaces for being together, like a template that produces infinite copies; and Charles White revealed new ways of repairing violence. Following these ideas, we might attend to the absences yet to be perceived; the spaces in and around the "piece of" paper that appear in Jamal Cyrus's work as constitutive of representation itself. As new environments and bodies step forward to be counted, this methodology of the page mobilizes objects, surfaces, and tools as critically important, but not always forever, and not always fully whole.

Notes

INTRODUCTION

1. Seven years before Bernice Rose's landmark exhibition *Drawing Now* at the Museum of Modern Art in 1976, Peter Plagens attempted to unpack drawing's relationship to tradition and vanguardism by dividing contemporary drawing tendencies, from Frank Stella to Robert Rauschenberg to Claes Oldenburg, into the categories of surrealist and constructivist. "Good drawings today exist not only against a continuing realization of what drawing is, but they are products, more or less, of the modernist art in general," he insisted. What this indicates is that critical dialogues on drawing preoccupied themselves with concerns about training and talent. See Peter Plagens, "The Possibilities of Drawing," *Artforum* 8, no. 8 (1969): 31.

2. Morris, quoted in Thomas Krens, ed., *The Drawings of Robert Morris,* exh. cat. (Williamstown, MA: Williams College Museum of Art, 1982), n.p.

3. Rosalind Krauss has written that paper and canvas are both "structured by the lattice through which perspective will map the coordinates of external space," though those coordinates were held in place more firmly by the art canvas's commitments to the stretcher bar (and, by extension, the wall or other planar surface) until this convention receded at the end of the twentieth century. See Krauss, *The Optical Unconscious* (Cambridge, MA: MIT Press, 1993), 54.

4. Carolee Schneemann to Michael Kustow, December 19, 1967, in *Correspondence Course: An Epistolary History of Carolee Schneemann and Her Circle,* edited by Kristine Stiles (Durham, NC: Duke University Press), 119.

5. Diana Taylor, *The Archive and the Repertoire: Performing Cultural Memory in the Americas* (Durham, NC: Duke University Press, 2003), xx.

6. See especially James Nisbet, *Ecologies, Environments, and Energy Systems in the Art of the 1960s and 1970s* (Cambridge, MA: MIT Press, 2014), 4–11.

7. Laurence Schmidlin, "The Intermediality of Drawing: Toward a Theory of Reception?," *Kunstlicht* 32, no. 3 (2011): 30–37.

8. Buckminster Fuller coined this term in 1966 in his lecture "World Man," presented to the Princeton University School of Architecture at its inaugural Kassler Lecture, which Robert Morris and Carolee Schneemann would have known about. Reprinted in Daniel López-Pérez, ed., *R. Buckminster Fuller: World Man* (Princeton, NJ: Princeton University Press, 2013), 32–101.

9. Robert Morris, "Notes on the Phenomenology of Making," reprinted in *Continuous Project Altered Daily: The Writings of Robert Morris* (Cambridge, MA: MIT Press, 2013), 73.

10. Robert Morris, "Notes on Sculpture, Part 4: Beyond Objects," *Artforum* 7, no. 8 (1969): 54.

11. Charles White notes "total environment" in several places, including his "Soul and Art" lecture of 1969; White, "Soul of an Artist," *Soul Illustrated,* Winter 1968, 56. In 1961, he referred to "a human kind of oneness" that he felt in his early "environment" alongside other members of his creative community; see Charles White, "The Negro Artist Speaks," ca. 1961, unpublished typescript, Charles W. White Papers, box 4, folder 71, Archives of American Art, Smithsonian Institution (hereafter abbreviated as AAA). White's student David Hammons said in 1970, "I feel that my art relates to my total environment—my being a black, political, and social human being." Hammons, interview with Joseph E. Young, December 16, 1970, in *Three Graphic Artists: Charles White, David Hammons, Timothy Washington,* exh. cat. (Los Angeles: Los Angeles County Museum of Art, 1970), 7.

12. Oral history interview with Robert Morris, April 19–20, 2018, AAA.

13. Morris had had a wide range of experiences with loft living. He lived in the smallest section of his first studio on Bond Street to make room for the dance projects of his then-wife, the experimental choreographer Simone Forti, and their mutual friend, the choreographer Yvonne Rainer. For more on the relationship between minimalism and dance, see Burt Ramsay, "Minimalism, Theory, and the Dancing Body," in *Performative Traces: Judson Dance Theater* (Oxford: Taylor and Francis, 2006), 52–87; and Morris interview, AAA.

14. Oral history interview with Robert Morris, March 10, 1968, AAA.

15. Morris has repeatedly used the word "suspension" in relation to drawing, particularly in reference to the drawing's ability to "suspend" the indexical act of mark-making on its paper surface. See Jean-Pierre Criqui, "Rubbings, 1972," in *Robert Morris: The Mind/Body Problem,* exh. cat. (New York: Solomon R. Guggenheim Museum, 1994), 240.

16. Krens, *Drawings of Robert Morris.*

17. Morris has a particular affinity with nuclear technologies, stated most explicitly in his interview of 1990 with curator Phil Patton. Patton noted, "Of nothing else does [Morris] speak as passionately as the possibility of nuclear annihilation. His eyes light up hauntingly—'I am fascinated by all that power,' he says. 'It goes back to Xerxes, the raw power to create an empire. In the 20th century, the efficiency of it has increased exponentially. It's fascinating, the power that makes people do and build these things.'" Patton, "Robert Morris and the Fire Next Time," *ArtNews,* December 1983, 90.

18. The Associated Press photo appeared in such national newspapers as the *Washington Post* and *Seattle Post-Intelligencer* and in popular magazines including *Variety.* Myron Fortenberg, "Castro Bid for Talks Is Rejected," *Washington Post,* October 25, 1962; John Berry, "Disagreement in Ex-Comm," *Seattle Post-Intelligencer,* October 25, 1962.

19. Robert Morris, "Notes on Art and/as Land Reclamation," *October* 12 (Spring 1980): 92.

20. Eddie Chambers, http://www.eddiechambers.com/charles-white/otis-drawing-biennial/.

21. Toyin Ojih Odutola, Quoted in "How to See: Charles White," video produced by the Museum of Modern Art, New York, January 11, 2019, https://www.moma.org/magazine/articles/26.

22. *Station Wagon Living* (Dearborn, MI: Ford Motor Company, 1959).

23. Charles White, "Soul and Art," in *Black Artists: Art and Social Commentary*, panel at Los Angeles County Museum of Art, October 27, 1969. https://archive.org/details/clcmar_000039.

24. Erica Moiah James, "Charles White's *J'Accuse* and the Limits of Universal Blackness," *Archives of American Art Journal* 55, no. 2 (2016): 22.

25. White, "Soul of an Artist," 56.

26. Caroline Jones, *Machine in the Studio: Constructing the Postwar American Artist* (Chicago: University of Chicago Press, 1998), 1, 3.

27. In an interview in 1975, Elayne Varian connected the process-illuminating qualities of this project as squarely pedagogical: "[Finch College president] Dr. DeMarco liked the idea very much. It was an educational, uh, thing. And I am sort of educationally minded." Oral history interview with Elayne H. Varian, May 2, 1975, Archives of American Art, Smithsonian Institution.

28. Robert Morris, "Letters to John Cage," *October* 81 (Summer 1997): 75, 76.

29. Leo Steinberg, "Other Criteria," reprinted in *Other Criteria: Confrontations with Twentieth-Century Art* (New York: Oxford University Press, 1972), 84.

30. Jane Bennett, *Vibrant Matter: A Political Ecology of Things* (Durham, NC: Duke University Press, 2009), x.

31. Allan Kaprow, "The Shape of the Art Environment," *Artforum* 6, no. 10 (1968): 59.

32. See Deanna Petherbridge, *The Primacy of Drawing: Histories and Theories of Practice* (New Haven: Yale University Press, 2010); Kelly Chorpening and Rebecca Fortnum, eds., *A Companion to Contemporary Drawing* (Oxford: Wiley-Blackwell, 2020); Anna Lovatt, *Drawing Degree Zero: The Line from Minimal to Conceptual Art* (University Park: Pennsylvania State University Press, 2019); Laurence Schmidlin, *La Spatialisation du dessin dans l'art américain des années 1960 et 1970* (Paris: Les Presses du réel, 2019); and Cornelia H. Butler and Catherine de Zegher, *On Line: Drawing through the Twentieth Century*, exh. cat. (New York: Museum of Modern Art, 2010).

33. See Elise Archias, *The Concrete Body: Yvonne Rainer, Carolee Schneemann, Vito Acconci* (New Haven: Yale University Press, 2016); Jason Hoelscher, *Art as Information Ecology: Artworks, Artworlds, and Complex Systems Aesthetics* (Durham, NC: Duke University Press, 2021); and Nisbet, *Ecologies, Environments, and Energy Systems.*

34. Roland Barthes, "Cy Twombly: Works on Paper," in *The Responsibility of Forms: Critical Essays on Music, Art, and Representation*, translated by Richard Howard (New York: Hill and Wang, 1985), 160.

35. Barthes, "Cy Twombly," 174.

36. Roland Barthes, *Writing Degree Zero*, translated by A. Lavers and C. Smith (Boston: Beacon Press, 1970), 14.

37. Morris, "Letters to John Cage," 75.

38. Robert Morris, "Aligned with Nazca," in *Continuous Project Altered Daily*, 158.

39. Hoelscher, *Art as Information Ecology*, 78.

40. Spinoza, preface to *Ethics*, 102–3, quoted in Bennett, *Vibrant Matter*, x.

41. See John Berger, *Bento's Sketchbook* (New York: Verso, 2011).

42. Spinoza, quoted in Gilles Deleuze, *Expressionism in Philosophy: Spinoza*, translated by M. Joughin (New York: Zone Books, 2005), 87.

43. Bennett, *Vibrant Matter*, xi.

44. Louis Althusser, *Reading Capital: The Complete Edition*, translated by Ben Brewster and David Fernbach (1965; repr., London: Verso, 2015), 12, and on Marx, 233–34. First published as *Lire le capital* (Paris: François Maspero, 1965).

45. Martin Luther King Jr., *Strength to Love* (Philadelphia: Fortress Press, 1963), 13.

46. Deleuze, *Spinoza*, 4.

47. See Robert B. Genter, "Barnett Newman and the Anarchist Sublime," *Anarchist Studies* 25, no. 1 (2017): 11.

48. Heinrich Blücher, "Why and How We Study Philosophy," Blücher Archive, Bard College, 1952, https://www.bard.edu/bluecher/lectures.php.

49. *Sol LeWitt*, exh. cat. (The Hague: Gemeentemuseum, 1970), n.p.

50. Dia, "Dia Art Foundation to Present *A Friendship: Carl Andre's Works on Paper from the LeWitt Collection* at the Dan Flavin Art Institute," press release, February 7, 2014, https://www.diaart.org/about/press/dia-art-foundation-to-present-a-friendship-carl-andres-works-on-paper-from-the-lewitt-collection-at-the-dan-flavin-art-institute/type/text.

51. Gwen Allen, *Artists' Magazines: An Alternative Space for Art* (Cambridge, MA: MIT Press, 2011).

52. See JoAnn Yates, *Control through Communication: The Rise of System in American Management* (Baltimore: Johns Hopkins University Press, 1993); Craig Robertson, *The Filing Cabinet: A Vertical History of Information* (Minneapolis: University of Minnesota Press, 2021); and Lisa Gitelman, *Paper Knowledge: Toward a Media History of Documents* (Durham, NC: Duke University Press, 2014).

53. I am thinking specifically of Caitlin Haskell, ed., *Ray Johnson c/o*, exh. cat. (Chicago: Art Institute of Chicago, 2021).

54. Dick Higgins, "Introduction," in *Fantastic Architecture*, edited by Wolf Vostell and Dick Higgins (New York: Something Else Press, 1970), n.p.

55. No record exists as to why Schneemann's drawings were omitted from the project, but Schneemann has asserted generally that "no one" was interested in her drawings. Carolee Schneemann, interview with the author, New Paltz, NY, July 10, 2010.

56. Carolee Schneemann, "Parts of a Body House," in Vostell and Higgins, *Fantastic Architecture*, n.p.

57. Bruno Latour, "Drawing Things Together," in *The Map Reader: Theories of Mapping Practice and Cartographic Representation*, edited by Martin Dodge, Rob Kitchin, and Chris Perkins (Oxford: Wiley Blackwell, 2011), 66–67.

58. Schneemann, "Parts of a Body House," n.p.

59. Latour, "Drawing Things Together," 69.

60. Sarah Ahmed, *Living a Feminist Life* (Durham, NC: Duke University Press, 2017), 8.

61. Karen Barad, "Posthumanist Performativity: An Understanding of How Matter Comes to Matter," *Signs: Journal of Women in Culture and Society* 28, no. 3 (2003): 818.

62. See White, "Soul of an Artist," 56; and Schneenmann, quoted in Emma McCormick-Goodhart, "Carolee, She Was a Great Painter: Remembering Carolee Schneemann (1939–2019)," *Frieze*, March 15, 2019, https://www.frieze.com/article/carolee-she-was-great-painter-remembering-carolee-schneemann-1939–2019.

63. Steffani Jemison with Huey Copeland, "Drafts: Steffani Jemison on the Stroke, the Glyph, and the Mark," *Artforum* 57, no. 8 (2019): 150–51.

64. Donald Preziosi referred to the 1960s and 1970s as the beginning of such historiographic changes—changes that had significant impact on the study of paleolithic cave paintings. Preziosi, "Reckoning with the World," in *Rethinking Art History: Meditations on a Coy Science* (New Haven: Yale University Press, 1989), 126.

65. Herbert Marcuse, "On Science and Phenomenology," lecture presented February 13, 1964, at the Boston Colloquium for the Philosophy of Science and reprinted in *A Portrait of Twenty-Five Years: Boston Colloquium for the Philosophy of Science, 1960–1985*, edited by Robert S. Cohen and Marx X. Wartofsky (Dordrecht: D. Reidel, 1985), 19–30.

66. This history is oriented in relation to art in the 1960s in Robert M. Brain, "Representation on the Line: Graphic Recording Instruments and Scientific Modernism," in *From Energy to Information: Representation in Science and Technology, Art, and Literature*, edited by Linda Henderson and Bruce Clarke (Stanford, CA: Stanford University Press, 2002), 155–77; and David Lomas, "Becoming Machine: Surrealist Automatism and Some Contemporary Instances: Involuntary Drawing," *Tate Papers* no. 18 (Autumn 2012): https://www.tate.org.uk/research/tate-papers/18/becoming-machine-surrealist-automatism-and-some-contemporary-instances.

67. See, for instance, Charles Reich, *The Greening of America* (New York: Random House, 1970); Frances Moore Lappé, *Diet for a Small Planet* (London: Ballantine, 1971); and E. F. Schumacher, *Small Is Beautiful: A Study of Economics as If People Mattered* (London: Blond and Briggs, 1973).

68. For example, Antonin Artaud wrote, "To create art is to deprive a gesture of its reverberation in the organism, whereas this reverberation, if the gesture is made in the conditions and with the force required, incites the organism and, through it, the entire individuality, to take attitudes in harmony with the gesture." Artaud, *The Theatre and Its Double* (New York: Grove Press, 1958), 81. Although most artists of this generation were familiar with Artaud's work, Tuttle would have come into direct contact with Artaud's art and writing while collaborating with Galerie Hubert in Vienna for his artist's book *The Point from the Corner of the Room, 1973–74*. Artaud had been one of Galerie Hubert's first featured artists when it opened its space in 1971.

CHAPTER 1
WILD WASTE

1. Peter Holbrook, "The Chicago Saga of Carolee Schneemann," unpublished essay, n.d., Carolee Schneemann Papers, acc. no. 950001, series 3, box 5, folder 2, Getty Research Institute, Los Angeles (hereafter cited as Schneemann Papers).

2. By 1970, Schneemann's relationship to politics, and more specifically activist praxes, would grow more complicated as she continued to observe people's reactions to her filmic and live works. In a letter to James Tenney in early February of that year, she wrote about the importance of archival material to her projects, including the deployment of "tapes, transcripts, Chicago pig riot films," and physical training exercises to create political content that had an "organic impact," to reach the growing number of "stoned innocent heads" who believed that "if you get your head in the right place, it will come out all right." In another letter to Tenney ten days later, she wrote that "for myself and my friends there is no real interest in things political—it has all come to seem such an unreal farce," specifically the New Left political scene in New York City. "I know that I do not want to sacrifice my own time and energy to a historical process that has its own internal mass-dynamic and will probably turn out the same way with or without me. I want my life, a private (and yes! peaceful) life, becoming 'public' only when and where that will nourish the private." See Schneemann to James Tenney, February 3 and 12–13, 1970, both reprinted in *Correspondence Course: An Epistolary History of Carolee Schneemann and Her Circle*, edited by Kristine Stiles (Durham, NC: Duke University Press), 165, 171.

3. Photographs illustrating the preview performance were shot by a *Village Voice* photographer, who then distributed them to other publications. See Holbrook, "Chicago Saga of Carolee Schneemann."

4. Van Gordon Sauter, "Gooey 'Celebration' to Happen at Museum," *Chicago Daily News*, January 6, 1968.

5. Sauter's chief source of amusement seemed to be that Schneemann's homemade glue "didn't work" even as Schneemann "rolled about" within it. Sauter, "Gooey 'Celebration.'"

6. Carolee Schneemann, *More Than Meat Joy: Performance Works and Selected Writings*, 2nd ed. (Kingston, NY: McPherson, 1997), 165.

7. Carolee Schneemann to Michael Kustow, December 19, 1967, in Stiles, *Correspondence Course*, 119.

8. "Anything I perceive is active to my eye. The energy implicit in an area of paint (or cloth, paper, wood, glass…) is defined in terms of the time which it takes for the eye to journey through the implicit motion and direction of this area. The eye follows the building of forms… no matter what materials are used to establish these forms." Carolee Schneemann, "From the Notebooks, 1958–1963," in *Imaging Her Erotics: Essays, Interviews, Projects* (Cambridge, MA: MIT Press, 2003), 47.

9. Bruno Latour, "Spinoza Lecture I: Nature at the Cross-Roads: The Bifurcation of Nature and Its End," in *What Is the Style of Matters of Concern?* (Amsterdam: Van Gorcum, 2008), 17.

10. Sauter, "Gooey 'Celebration.'"

11. Jane Bennett, *Vibrant Matter: A Political Ecology of Things* (Durham, NC: Duke University Press, 2009), x.

12. According to Schneemann's performance diary: "American Container Corporation saw the Voice photos and doesn't want any of their paper used in my work; withdrawing their use of space!" Undated performance diary, Schneemann Papers, box 2, folder 2.

13. This is narrated in Schneemann, *More Than Meat Joy*, 169–70.

14. The Container Corporation of America's sponsorship of modernist art projects since the 1930s has attracted much

attention from scholars. See Susan Black, *The First Fifty Years: 1926–1976* (Chicago: Container Corporation of America, 1976); James Sloan Allen, *The Romance of Commerce and Culture: Capitalism, Modernism, and the Chicago-Aspen Crusade for Cultural Reform* (Chicago: University of Chicago Press, 1983); Neil Harris and Martina Roudabush Norelli, *Art, Design, and the Modern Corporation: The Collection of Container Corporation of America* (Washington, DC: Smithsonian Institution Press, 1985); Justus Nieland, "Container Culture: Film, Packaging, and the Design of Corporate Humanism at the CCA," *Post45*, February 12, 2021; and Alex J. Taylor, *Forms of Persuasion: Art and Corporate Image in the 1960s* (Berkeley: University of California Press, 2022).

15. Paul J. Smith, "Introduction," in *Made with Paper*, exh. cat. (Chicago: Museum of Contemporary Crafts, New York, and Museum of Contemporary Art Chicago, 1967), n.p.

16. Holbrook, "Chicago Saga of Carolee Schneemann."

17. Schneemann, *More Than Meat Joy*, 167.

18. Department of Information Services to Carolee Schneemann, 1968, Schneeman Papers, series 3, box 2, folder 3. Sylvie Laura Simmonds's dissertation on Schneemann's Kinetic Theatre in the 1960s foregrounds this work in the Cold War– and Vietnam-era investigations conducted by COINTELPRO, the CIA, and the FBI. See Simmonds, "A Countercultural Movement: Examining Carolee Schneemann's Kinetic Theatre between 1963 and 1970" (PhD diss., McGill University, 2013).

19. Holbrook, "Chicago Saga of Carolee Schneemann."

20. Carolee Schneemann, text for *Body Collage* (1967), 4:12 min., b&w, silent, 16mm film on video; performed and edited by Carolee Schneemann from 16mm b&w film footage by Gideon Bachmann; Electronic Arts Intermix.

21. Amelia Jones, *Body Art: Performing the Subject* (Minneapolis: University of Minnesota Press, 1998), 4.

22. Schneemann switched to store-bought adhesives relatively quickly in the performance. Though Sauter's review does not mention this iterative component, Schneemann recalls it herself, as recounted in Schneemann, *More Than Meat Joy*, 165.

23. Rosalind Krauss, "Flattening Space," *London Review of Books,* April 1, 2004, 30.

24. It is telling that she later locates the birth canal as a primary source of female creativity, a "source of interior knowledge … symbolized as the primary unit of spirit and flesh in Goddess worship." See Schneemann, "The Obscene Body/Politic," *Art Journal* 50, no. 4, *Censorship II* (1991): 33.

25. Spinoza's full statement on this matter clarifies his status as a precursor to science studies, vital materialist philosophy, and even feminism: "Extension is an attribute of God; i.e., God is an extended thing." See Spinoza, *Ethics*, in *Spinoza: Complete Works*, edited by Michael L. Morgan with translations by Samuel Shirley (Indianapolis: Hackett, 2002), 245.

26. Nina Wexelblatt and B. Jack Hanly, "Editors' Introduction: Uncertain Reserve," *Thresholds*, no. 49 (2021): 1.

27. Laura Mulvey, "Visual Pleasure and Narrative Cinema," in *Film Theory and Criticism: Introductory Readings*, edited by Leo Braudy, 5th ed. (Oxford: Oxford University Press, 1998), 804.

28. Several of Barbarella's costumes were commented on in the news media by late 1968. The film's costume designer, Jacques Fonteray, organized actor Jane Fonda's costumes in several scenes to consist of nothing but a sheaf of "natural" material that draped over Fonda's body. These textiles were frequently harmonized with her more conventional costumes so that they provided more mobile, labile iterations of female dress. In the original comic strip *Barbarella*, French writer and illustrator Jean-Claude Forest drew Barbarella shirtless or wearing midriff-baring outfits. See Linda Williams, "Make Love, Not War: Jane Fonda Comes Home," in *Sex Scene: Media and the Sexual Revolution*, edited by Eric Schaefer (Durham, NC: Duke University Press, 2014), 53–80.

29. As one journalist put it, London's fashion week in 1966 was dominated by a mixture of local and exotic materials, both recuperated from streams and taken from the natural world: "plastic hats, elastic jewelry … , and long-haired African monkey and American raccoon." Reuters, "Plastic Hats and Fun Furs Open London Showings," *New York Times*, January 18, 1966.

30. "Paper Profits," *Mademoiselle*, June 1967, 99–101.

31. See Herbert Marcuse, "On Science and Phenomenology," in *Boston Studies in the Philosophy of Science*, edited by Robert S. Cohen and Marx W. Wartofsky, vol. 2 (New York: Humanities Press, 1965), 279–90. In *An Essay on Liberation* (Boston: Beacon Press, 1969), Marcuse modifies his thesis somewhat: "Science and technology are the great vehicles of liberation, and … it is only their use and restriction in the repressive society which makes them into vehicles of domination" (15).

32. Marcuse, *Essay on Liberation*, 24.

33. Karen Barad, "Posthumanist Performativity: An Understanding of How Matter Comes to Matter," *Signs: Journal of Women in Culture and Society* 28, no. 3 (2003): 801.

34. While Laura Mulvey commended *Fuses* following its screening in London in 1968, she "was never able to write one word about it because it would somehow compromise or jeopardize the position that she wanted to structure and build." Interview with Kathy Constantinides, November 14, 1987, Schneemann Papers, box 73, folder 5.

35. "To use my body as an extension of my painting-constructions [in 1963] was to challenge and threaten the psychic territorial power lines by which women were admitted to the Art Stud Club." Schneemann, "Eye Body," December 1963, in *More Than Meat Joy*, 52. For a contextualization of Schneemann within feminist art and history, see Émilie Bouvard, "Carolee Schneemann: Feminism and History," in *Then and Now: Carolee Schneemann: Oeuvre d'histoires*, ed. Annabelle Ténèze, exh. cat. (Arles: Analogues, 2013), 67–92.

36. Antonin Artaud, when discussing his own drawings in 1946, described their crumbling and rotting materials as performative—a state of material decay called the *subjectile*. Jacques Derrida later affirmed paper as a simultaneously unruly and permeable surface, "a sort of skin with holes for pores." See Artaud, *Oeuvres complètes*, vol. 19 (Paris: Éditions Gallimard, 1984), 259; and Jacques Derrida and Mary Ann Caws, "Maddening the Subjectile," *Yale French Studies*, no. 84 (1994): 154–71, at 158.

37. See Richard Shiff, "Breath of Modernism (Metonymic Drift)," in *In Visible Touch: Modernism and Masculinity*, edited by Terry Smith (Chicago: University

of Chicago Press, 1997), 184–213; and Elise Archias, "Concretions: Carolee Schneemann," in *The Concrete Body: Yvonne Rainer, Carolee Schneemann, Vito Acconci* (New Haven: Yale University Press, 2016), chap. 2.

38. Both quotations are from the original performance program of *Illinois Central.* Only the second was incorporated into Schneemann's essay on the work in *More Than Meat Joy.* Schneemann Papers, box 5, folder 2.

39. John Massey, untitled essay, *Made with Paper,* exh. cat. (New York: Museum of Contemporary Crafts, Craftsman's Council of the U.S., and the Container Corporation of America, 1967), n.p.

40. Untitled exhibition text, *Made with Paper,* n.p.

41. William Pahlmann, a reviewer, re-marked, "I could not help wondering what would happen if [the paper works] got rained on." Pahlmann, "Paper Et Cet-era," *Chicago Tribune,* January 15, 1968.

42. Schneemann, quoted in Carolee Schneemann, Bonnie Marranca, and Claire MacDonald, "In the Beginning Is Drawing," *PAJ: A Journal of Performance and Art* 41, no. 2 (2019): 6.

43. Robert Vishny, "Fire Sales in Finance and Macroeconomics," *Journal of Economic Perspectives* 25, no. 1 (2011): 30.

44. It is worth noting that Schneemann listed this as a "kinetic theatre" piece in both the flyer advertising the work and a hand-collaged artist's resume she produced in 1970. This indicates her understanding of performance ephem-era as having the potential to reconstitute social space. Schneemann Papers, series 1, box 17, folder 10.

45. In this same year, she had traveled to Venice to see the Biennale, including Robert Rauschenberg's contribution. The Whitechapel exhibition had been noted for its general embrace of banal-ity, and critic Robert Melville connected the banality of Rauschenberg's subject matter with the inclusion of drawing as a "minor" medium. See Melville, "Mis-cellany: Fear of the Banal," *Architectural Review* (London), April 1964, 291–93; and "Carnival in Venice," *Newsweek,* July 6, 1964, 79.

46. Carolee Schneemann, interview with the author, Samuel Dorsky Museum of Art, New Paltz, NY, July 29, 2010.

47. Despite a special award at Cannes in 1968 and a commendation at the Yale Film Festival in 1972, as well as positive coverage in such media as *Variety* and the *San Francisco Express Times, Fuses*'s authentication in the critical record has happened relatively recently. As late as 1982, Schneemann's direct collabo-rators and contemporaries refused to acknowledge the film as important. Stan Brakhage, for instance, who had had a mutually nourishing creative relationship with Schneemann as she developed her early films, refused to speak about the film in public. See Schneemann to Stan Brakhage, June 21, 1982, in Stiles, *Corre-spondence Course,* 336.

48. *Fuses* and other performances were shut down with regularity late in the de-cade due to their featuring of full-frontal female and male nudity. These shut-downs included the Dialectics of Lib-eration Festival and reached their apex in the 1968 London Film Festival that used *Fuses* to test censorship laws in the United Kingdom. See Schneemann, "Interview with Kate Haug" and "Istory of a Girl Pornographer," in *Imaging Her Erotics,* 20–44, 138.

49. "Shifting Grounds: The Museum of Contemporary Art, Chicago," http://shifting-grounds.net/MCA/ontario-transitions.html.

50. Schneemann, *More Than Meat Joy,* 170.

51. Holbrook, "Chicago Saga."

52. Schneemann, *More Than Meat Joy,* 168.

53. Sauter, "Gooey 'Celebration.'"

54. Schneemann, *More Than Meat Joy,* 167.

55. Throughout this chapter I use "paper" to describe the material Schneemann employed in this performance series. By the time *Illinois Central* was developed, Schneemann's principal sources were large reams of mass-produced printer paper that were intended for use in office and commercial printing, along with castoff construction materials and studio waste gathered from the street surround-ing her loft. This type of paper lent these projects a specific panindustrial material-ity that harmonized with Schneemann's use of meats and fish from French and American butcher shops when she pro-duced *Meat Joy* the year before.

56. Schneemann, *More Than Meat Joy,* 171.

57. The legal precedent was the Supreme Court decision in *United States v. Roth,* which came down in June 1957 and held that erotic material had to be "utterly without redeeming social importance" to be banned from sale or withdrawn from public view. Local police took some latitude in determining the social value of artworks, which resulted in frequent shutdowns or rumors of shutdowns in art and performance spaces. United States v. Roth, 354 U.S. 476 (1957).

58. Branden W. Joseph, *Experimentations: John Cage in Music, Art, and Architecture* (New York: Bloomsbury Academic, 2016), 21.

59. Schneemann Papers, series 1, box 2, folder 2.2.

60. As the artist put it, "I was given a purple spangled dress and a knife and instructed to balance on a small shelf while stabbing the wall repeatedly for several nights." Carolee Schneemann, "Carolee Schneemann on Judson Dance Theater," *Artforum* 57, no. 1 (2018), https://www.artforum.com/print/201807/carolee-schneemann-76346.

61. Branden Joseph notes that Robert Rauschenberg explicitly rejected the notion of taking an object ready-made from the world in order to isolate it, in-sisting that his work acted as a dynamic supplement to the materials of modern life, a position that resisted traditional art history's logocentric logic of icono-graphic analysis. See Joseph, *Random Order: Robert Rauschenberg and the Neo-Avant-Garde* (Cambridge, MA: MIT Press, 2003), 7–9.

62. Allan Kaprow, "The Shape of the Art Environment," *Artforum* 6, no. 10 (1968): 32–33. Here Kaprow refers to Morris in particular, whose use of felt batting, Kaprow thought, allowed for "an observ-able theme and variation in the work" that arose "in the absence of strict hier-archies developed by the all-over tradi-tion of the last twenty years." Reprinted in Kaprow, *Essays on the Blurring of Art and Life* (Berkeley: University of California Press, 2003), 90, 92.

63. Liz Kotz, "Object, Action and Ephem-era," in *Concept Action Language: Pop-Art, Fluxus, Nouveau Realism, Arte Povera in the Mumok Collection,* texts by Liz Kotz, Susanne Neuburger et al., exh. cat. (Vienna: Mumok Collection, 2011), 40.

64. Allan Kaprow, "The Legacy of Jackson Pollock," *ArtNews,* October 1958, 55.

65. Schneemann, *More Than Meat Joy*, 119. *Village Voice* critic Jill Johnston identified the meats and fish as an example of "culture in its rudimentary state," "the beginning and the end of a thing," and "the matrix of unformulated activity whirling into shape and the phoenix which burns from rubbish and rises into the ashes." Johnston, "Meat Joy," *Village Voice*, November 26, 1964, 17.

66. An example is his *Rosalie/Red Cheek/ Temporary Letter/Stock (Cardboard)* from 1971. See "Robert Rauschenberg, Rosalie/Red Cheek/Temporary Letter/ Stock (Cardboard), 1971: Artwork Record," Rauschenberg Research Project, January 2014, San Francisco Museum of Modern Art, https://www.sfmoma .org/artwork/2013.149; quotation from Dorothy Gees Seckler, "The Artist Speaks: Robert Rauschenberg," *Art in America* 54, no. 3 (1966): 74.

67. Allen Kaprow, *Paintings, Environments, and Happenings* [ms, Old Bridge, NJ, 1960], quoted in William C. Seitz, *The Art of Assemblage*, exh. cat. (New York: Museum of Modern Art, 1961), 88, 152, note 89.

68. Kaprow quoted in Seitz, *Art of Assemblage*, 90, and similar comments in *New Forms—New Media*, exh. cat. (New York: Martha Jackson Gallery, October 1960).

69. Seitz, *Art of Assemblage*, 89.

70. In a letter to Alfred Barr, curator of the Museum of Modern Art, on April 24, 1950, Baldwin Smith, the chairman of the Department of Art and Archaeology at Princeton, expressed concerns about the scholarly rigor of Seitz's proposed dissertation on living artists and asked for Barr's help in developing criteria for what constituted an "objective analysis" of such artists. He requested Barr's expertise on, among other things, where to find scholarly sources. Alfred H. Barr, Jr., Papers, Museum of Modern Art, series 1.A, box 212, mf 2176:245. For a fuller record of their exchange of letters, see Garnett McCoy and Allen Rosenbaum, "A Continued Story: Alfred H. Barr, Jr., Princeton University, and William C. Seitz," *Archives of American Art Journal* 21, no. 3 (1981): 8–13.

71. Gilles Deleuze's secondary thesis at the Sorbonne in 1968, "Spinoza and the Problem of Expression," took this on directly. The book as published included a chapter titled "Spinoza versus Descartes." Gilles Deleuze, *Spinoza and the Problem of Expression* [reprinted PhD thesis] (Moscow: Institute of General Humanities Studies, 2014).

72. Carolee Schneemann, "From the Notebooks, 1962–1963," in *Imaging Her Erotics*, 47.

73. Carolee Schneemann, in Schneemann, Ann Daly, and Angela Rodgers, "Carolee Schneemann: A Life Drawing," *TDR: The Drama Review* 45, no. 2 (Summer 2001): 14.

74. Schneemann, quoted in Schneeman, Marranca, and MacDonald, "In the Beginning Is Drawing," 3.

75. Carolee Schneemann, interview with the author, New Paltz, NY, July 25, 2010.

76. Paul Klee, *Pedagogical Sketchbook*, translated by Sybil Moholy-Nagy (New York: Praeger, 1953), 16.

77. Dick Higgins, "Statement on Intermedia," August 3, 1966, reprinted in *Dé-coll/age (décollage) * 6*, ed. Wolf Vostell (Frankfurt: Typos Verlag; New York: Something Else Press, 1967).

78. Schneemann, quoted in Gene Youngblood, *Expanded Cinema* (New York: E. P. Dutton, 1970), 92.

79. Most notable of these industrial connections was the building at 80 Wooster Street that Schneemann's friend George Maciunas leased to start Fluxhouse Cooperative II. In 1967 the paper company that had occupied it for thirty-five years vacated it, and over the next two years it would host performances by Allen Kaprow, Yoko Ono, and Richard Foreman's Ontological-Hysteric Theater; it also housed Jonas Mekas's Film Makers Cinematheque (later, the Anthology Film Archives). Richard Kostelanetz, *Soho: The Rise and Fall of an Artists' Colony* (New York: Routledge, 2003), 45–46.

80. Carolee Schneemann, *Divisions and Rubble* (1967), published with performance notes in *Aspen* no. 6a: *The Performance Art Issue*, 1969, 1.

81. Schneemann, *Divisions and Rubble*, 6.

82. For more information on the Destruction in Art Symposium (DIAS) and the effects on both the US and Anglo-European avant-garde, see Kristine Stiles, "The Story of the Destruction in Art Symposium and the 'DIAS Effect,'" in *Gustav Metzger: History History*, exh. cat. (Berlin: Hatje Cantz, 2005), which is condensed from her doctoral dissertation on the DIAS.

83. Carolee Schneemann, "Divisions and Rubble at Judson 1967," *Aspen* no. 6a: *The Performance Art Issue*, 1969, 4.

84. Buckminster Fuller, *Operating Manual for Spaceship Earth* (1969), reprinted in *Buckminster Fuller: Anthology for the New Millennium*, ed. Thomas T. K. Zung (New York: St. Martin's Press, 2022), 137.

85. "Send me more Bucky Fuller texts," quoted in Stiles, *Correspondence Course*, 127.

86. Fuller named Charles Darwin and Thomas Malthus chief among these problematic frameworks, calling them "Great Pirates" who had hijacked Spaceship Earth. Fuller, *Operating Manual for Spaceship Earth*, 8th ed. (n.p.: Estate of R. Buckminster Fuller, 2008), 80.

87. Marshall McLuhan with Jerome Agel, "Printing, a Ditto Device," in *The Medium Is the Massage: An Inventory of Effects* (New York: Random House, 1967), 50–69.

88. Richard Schechner, "6 Axioms for Environmental Theatre," *Drama Review: TDR* 12, no. 3 (1968): 41–64, at 46.

89. Darko Suvin, "Reflections on Happenings," *Drama Review: TDR* 14, no. 3 (1970): 125–44, at 126.

90. Christopher Alexander, "A City Is Not a Tree," *Architectural Forum* 122, no. 1 (April 1965): 58–62. A second part of this essay was published in the May issue that year, that went even further to detach the tree as an abstract design versus a component of the natural world: "It must be emphasized, lest the orderly mind brink in horror from anything that is not clearly articulated and categorized in tree form, that the idea of overlap, ambiguity, multiplicity of aspect, and the semi-lattice, are not less orderly than the rigid tree, but more so. They represent a thicker, tougher, more subtle and more complex view of structure." Alexander, "A City Is Not a Tree," *Architectural Forum* 122, no. 2 (May 1965): 58.

91. Manfredo Tafuri, *Introduction to Theories and History of Architecture* (New York: Harper and Row, 1968), 157, translated from *Teorie e storia dell'architettura* (Rome: Laterza, 1968).

92. CASE was an early attempt to think about the total effects of an environment on human beings' growth and development, and it incorporated race as a specific category of analysis. But aside from intermittent proposals to improve public parks, there were few

mentions of the natural world, placing the city as a uniquely patterned environment. See Kenneth Frampton fonds, Conference of Architects for the Study of the Environment (CASE), Canadian Centre for Architecture, Montreal, Quebec.

93. Schneemann, interview with Alexandra Juhasz, December 1995, quoted in Juhasz, *Women of Vision: Histories in Feminist Film and Video* (Minneapolis: University of Minnesota Press, 2001), 69.

94. Schneemann, quoted in Schneemann, Marranca, and MacDonald, "In the Beginning Is Drawing," 4.

95. Heinrich Blücher, "V. Socrates" (1954), in *Two Lectures by Heinrich Blücher*, New School for Social Research, Lecture I: (In Two Parts), April 30, 1954, Lecture II: May 7, 1954, Lecture XII (S-II) 4-30-54 [Lecture 1, Part 1], 1. Blücher Archive, Bard College.

96. Translation adapted from Rosemary Mayer, Julia Ballerini, and Richard Milazzo, *Pontormo's Diary* (New York: Out of London Press, 1982), 59 (quotation also mentioned in Jessica Maratsos, "Pictorial Theology and the Paragone in Pontormo's Capponi Chapel," *Art History* 40, no. 5 [November 2017]: 939); Pontormo quoted in Paola Barocchi, comp., *Scritti d'arte del Cinquecento*, vol. 1 (Milan: R. Ricciardi, 1971): "Ma quello che io dissi troppo ardito ch'è la importanza si è superare la natura in volere dare spirito a una figura e farla parere viva e farla in piano" (506).

97. By the time Pontormo was included in the exhibition of fresco drawings and paintings at the Metropolitan Museum of Art in 1968, curator Henry Geldzahler would call the artist "an unquiet, restless experimentalist" with an "elusive style," paving the way for new critical affinities with mannerist art. Thomas Hoving et al., eds., *The Great Age of Fresco: Giotto to Pontormo: An Exhibition of Mural Paintings and Monumental Drawings*, exh. cat. (New York: Metropolitan Museum of Art, 1968), 212.

98. Janet Cox-Rearick, *The Drawings of Pontormo* (Cambridge, MA: Harvard University Press, 1964), 361.

99. The Morgan Library and Museum's object files contain photocopies from mannerist art historian Daniel B. Rowland's book *Mannerism: Style and Mood* (New Haven: Yale University Press, 1964). Rowland ruminates on what he identifies

as the figures' bonelessness: "No indication of the body underneath the skin … an assembly of surfaces" (17–18). Found in Morgan Library and Museum, Pontormo's *Standing Male Nude et al.*, 154.4, object file. And as early as 1958, Schneemann sensed this also. In a letter to her partner, James Tenney, she remarked on the "compelling head" featured in the elder artist's painting of a member of the Medici family in the Metropolitan Museum of Art. Carolee Schneemann to James Tenney, March 19, 1958, in Stiles, *Correspondence Course*, 24.

100. Kristine Stiles, "The Painter as Instrument of Real Time," in Schneemann, *Imaging Her Erotics*, 4.

101. Judith Butler, *Bodies That Matter: On the Discursive Limits of "Sex"* (New York: Routledge, 1993), 159.

102. Carolee Schneemann to Naomi Levinson, June 5, 1957, in Styles, *Correspondence Course*, 12.

103. *Plumb Line* referred to a tool that Schneemann's partner Tom Mulholm used frequently in his work as a carpenter. The film addressed Schneemann's reaction to "endless Vietnam atrocities and the dissolution of my long relationship with [James] Tenney," her partner of thirteen years. "The plumb line stands for a phallic measure, a phallic exploration and determination of space," she noted, but given her previous interest in the architecture of Venice and her specific mentions of Piazza San Marco's sixteenth-century clocktower, it can be assumed that Renaissance design principles were also close considerations. Quoted in M. M. Serra and Katherine Ramey, "Eye Body: The Cinematic Paintings of Carolee Schneemann," in *Women's Experimental Cinema: Critical Frameworks* (Durham, NC: Duke University Press, 2007), 116, 118.

104. Leon Battista Alberti, from Prologue and book 1 of *De re aedificatoria*, in *On the Art of Building in Ten Books*, translated by Joseph Rykwert with Neil Leach and Robert Tavernor (Cambridge, MA: MIT Press, 1988), 3, 5–6, 7.

105. Carolee Schneemann, "The Obscene Body/Politic," *Art Journal* 50, no. 4 (1991): 28.

106. Judith Rodenbeck has also identified sound as part of the "crystallographic" connective tissue of this work, rotating around Schneemann's proto-structuralist studies of the science

of language. I agree but find encoded within it a set of theories that highlight matter's potential to both penetrate and structure human interaction, so that the ropes and bodies not only "operate as drawing in space and as social prompt" but also establish drawing's potential to access resistance from nearly all material state. See Rodenbeck, "Schneemann's Crystal," in *Carolee Schneemann: Kinetic Painting*, edited by Sabine Breitweisser, exh. cat. (Salzburg: Museum der Moderne, 2015).

107. See, e.g., Jean Dubuffet's comment that "far from being filled with wonder at human reason, I find it one of the poorest and dullest things there is.… Trees, for example, trees amaze me and fill me with wonder. Man does not at all." Dubuffet, Valérie da Costa, and Fabrice Hergott, *Jean Dubuffet: Works, Writings, Interviews* (Barcelona: Polígrafa, 2006), 140.

108. In an interview with the art critic Barbara Rose in 1987, Rauschenberg remarked, "There's no such thing as 'better' material. It's just as unnatural for people to use oil paint as it is to use anything else." Rose, *An Interview with Robert Rauschenberg* (New York: Vintage Books, 1987), 58.

109. Butler, *Bodies That Matter*, 35–36.

110. Butler, *Bodies That Matter*, 36.

111. Schneemann conceded that the institutional disinterest in her drawings was a factor in her continuing to understand and speak of them as private. When asked about the nature of this institutional disinterest, she was agnostic about its implications, saying, "I don't know how to answer that." Schneemann, quoted in Schneeman, Marranca, and MacDonald, "In the Beginning Is Drawing," 109.

112. Bennett, *Vibrant Matter*, 62.

113. Carolee Schneemann, *More Than Meat Joy*, 167.

114. Schneemann, *More Than Meat Joy*, 169.

115. Schneemann, *More Than Meat Joy*, 171.

116. Schneemann, quoted in Robert Enright, "The Articulate Body: Carolee Schneemann in Conversation," *Bordercrossings*, no. 65 (February 1998): 21.

117. Carolee Schneemann to Daryl Chin, February 25, 1975, in Stiles, *Correspondence Course*, 238.

118. Rachel Carson, *Silent Spring*, 50th anniversary ed. (Boston: Mariner Books, 2002), 63.

119. Schneemann, Marranca, and MacDonald, "In the Beginning Is Drawing," 4.

120. "Well, the transformations are very demanding because to get the image in life, the life has to be changed radically. So that's why I was talking about the physical exercises that I had to invent to train people so that they could enter the realm of this sensory flow.… How you touch somebody, how you drag them, how you grab them, how you hold them. I realized I could never do this directly. I could never address the sensory constraints head-on. I had to evolve very subtle and odd exercises and so that's when I began to perform because I have to be able to do it, see what does this accomplish, how does it feel." Schneemann, quoted in Schneeman, Marranca, and MacDonald, "In the Beginning Is Drawing," 11.

121. William Pepper, "The Children of Vietnam," *Ramparts*, January 1967, n.p.

122. Daniel Berrigan, "History Is a Weapon: The Cantonsville 9 Statement," published in *The Cantonville Nine: An Act of Resistance*, pamphlet printed by the Cantonville Nine Defense League, n.p.

123. Adrienne Rich, "The Burning of Paper Instead of Children," in *The Will to Change: Poems, 1968–1970* (New York: W.W. Norton, 1971).

124. Schneemann, quoted in Youngblood, *Expanded Cinema*, 370.

125. Immanuel Kant, *Critique of Judgment*, translated by Werner S. Pluhar (Indianapolis: Hackett, 1987), 275.

CHAPTER 2
OFF THE RECORD

1. Gregory Battcock, "Four Artists Who Did Not Show in New York This Season," *Arts Magazine*, Summer 1968, 16–17.

2. For example, Donald Judd's argument that Dan Flavin's fluorescent light sculptures were "interior articulation but not interior structure; they made an interior exoskeleton"; Judd, "Aspects of Flavin's Work," in the exhibition catalog for Flavin's *Fluorescent Lights, Etc.*, National Gallery of Canada, Ottawa, October 1969, 27–30; the critic John Perrault also referred to Sol LeWitt's wall drawings at the Dwan Gallery as "everything and nothing" in a review. Perreault, "The Monet of Minimalism," *Village Voice*, October 1969, in Dwan Gallery Records, series 2, box 4, folder 2, Archives of American Art, Smithsonian Institution (hereafter abbreviated as AAA).

3. Gilles Deleuze, *The Fold: Liebnitz and the Baroque* (Minneapolis: University of Minnesota Press, 1993), 4.

4. Deleuze, *The Fold*, 4.

5. Spinoza, *Ethics*, II, *Postulates on the Body*, IV, in *Spinoza: Complete Works*, edited by Michael L. Morgan with translations by Samuel Shirley (Indianapolis: Hackett, 2002).

6. Alfred North Whitehead, *The Function of Reason* (Princeton, NJ: Princeton University Press, 1929), 26.

7. Anastasi recalls reading Maurice Merleau-Ponty by 1966, when he and Robert Morris shared a studio building. For a more detailed discussion of the spread of Merleau-Ponty's work within minimal and conceptual circles in the mid-1960s, see James Meyer, "Morris's 'Notes on Sculpture,'" in *Minimalism: Art and Polemics in the Sixties* (New Haven: Yale University Press, 2001), 153–66.

8. Such texts include, for instance, Erin Manning, *The Minor Gesture* (Durham, NC: Duke University Press, 2016); Erin Manning and Brian Massumi, *Thought in the Act: Passages in the Ecology of Experience* (Minneapolis: University of Minnesota Press, 2014); Ellen Tani, *Second Sight: The Paradox of Vision in Contemporary Art* (New York: Scala Arts, 2018); and Richard Shusterman, "Muscle Memory and the Somaesthetic Pathologies of Everyday Life," in *Thinking through the Body: Essays in Somaesthetics* (Cambridge: Cambridge University Press, 2012), 91–111. See also the earliest works of social performance theory, such as two publications by Erving Goffman, *The Presentation of Self in Everyday Life* (Edinburgh: University of Edinburgh, 1956), and *Relations in Public* (Piscataway, NJ: Transaction), 1971.

9. Anastasi, telephone conversation with the author, Macon, GA, December 27, 2018.

10. In interviews, Anastasi frequently concedes to his fascination with bureaucracy and infrastructure when he first began making work as a professional artist at the height of the Nuclear Age. "I found it so interesting that there was all this matter, all these buildings, that could be blown up in a blink of an eye. The sheer number of drivers, airplanes, and plane pilots that it would take to coordinate such destruction—we had it, right there, in America." Anastasi telephone conversation, December 27, 2018.

11. David Lomas expands on this in "Becoming Machine: Surrealist Automatism and Some Contemporary Instances: Involuntary Drawing," which grounds Anastasi's work in the modernist avant-garde fascination with recording devices. Lomas emphasizes passivity, positioning Anastasi's projects as natural inheritors of Marcel Duchamp's early experiments depicting human motion in his paintings. He proposes Duchamp's painting *Sad Young Man on a Train* (1911–12; Peggy Guggenheim Collection, Venice), for instance, as both Duchamp and Anastasi experimented with, as Lomas puts it, "the passivity of a body acted upon by mechanical forces." However, a couple of projects are also relevant when considering the emerging approaches to action and agency in downtown New York. Sol LeWitt's works *Run I–IV* (1962; LeWitt Collection [I, II and III] and Glenstone [IV]) and *Muybridge I* and *Muybridge II* (1964; LeWitt Collection) advance the proposition that physical action is always incommensurate with the technologies that seek to fix and record it. In positioning the camera as a machine that rigorously, invariably traces the human body without revealing many individual details about that body, LeWitt problematized the agency and primacy of the viewer. See Lomas, "Becoming Machine: Surrealist Automatism and Some Contemporary Instances: Involuntary Drawing," *Tate Papers* no. 18 (Autumn 2012), https://www.tate.org.uk/research/tate-papers/18/becoming-machine-surrealist-automatism-and-some-contemporary-instances; and James Meyer, "LeWitt at the Dwan Gallery," in *Minimalism: Art and Polemics in the Sixties* (New Haven: Yale University Press, 2001), 200–208.

12. Joshua Shannon, *The Recording Machine: Art and Fact during the Cold War* (New Haven: Yale University Press, 2017), 24.

13. Philip Guston had written a letter in 1964 recommending that Betty Parsons visit his studio after seeing Anastasi's plaster on tar paper works, which are no longer extant. Parsons's visit was

fruitful; she bought three works by the artist and gave him a solo show in 1964. William Anastasi, "Artist Statement," Foundation for Contemporary Arts, New York, 2009, https://www.foundationforcontemporaryarts.org/recipients/william-anastasi/. The drawings also facilitated his first connections with John Cage. Virginia Dwan sent the elder artist to Anastasi's apartment to pick up a drawing that would be offered in a Dwan Gallery benefit auction in late 1965, suggesting that he also looked at Anastasi's new sound sculptures. Anastasi, "Caged Chance," in *The Cage Dialogues: A Memoir* (Philadelphia: Slought Foundation, 2011), 1.

14. Anastasi had solo exhibitions in 1966 and 1967, and two group exhibitions in 1970. He was included in all four of Virginia Dwan's *Language* exhibitions from 1967 to 1970. A drawing by Anastasi was also part of the exhibition *Scale Models and Drawings* at the Dwan Gallery in 1967—the only work of Anastasi's that Dwan ever sold. See Dwan Gallery Records, series 2, boxes 2–3, AAA.

15. The entire quotations are worth reproducing here: "The fact is, I thought of the subway drawings as some kind of therapy when I first started making them. I didn't take them as seriously as I did my other drawings. I really thought drawing was drawing, and subway drawing was something else…. I now think it is part of what I do. In my other work I try to have the same kind of spontaneity that I see on the page when I do a subway drawing." "William Anastasi in Conversation with Rachel Nackman, March 12, New York," in *Notations: Contemporary Drawing as Idea and Process,* http://notations.aboutdrawing.org/william-anastasi/. He also stated, "My intention was to forget drawing, to forget art history, to forget art, to forget myself, if possible." Quoted in Toni Hildebrandt, *Entwurf und Entgrenzung: Kontradispositive der Zeichnung, 1955–1975* (Paderborn: Wilhelm Fink, 2017), 191.

16. Robert Morris, "Essay on Drawing," in *Pop Art Redefined,* edited by Suzi Gablik and John Russell (London: Thames and Hudson, 1969), 94–95. In this essay, the napkin was the chief bearer of this cliché and gave the art historian implicit permission to think like a psychoanalyst.

17. In an email, curator of drawings Esther Adler confirmed the presence of cotton fibers in the Modern's napkins dating from the early 2000s. "A history of our orders from The Modern in the early 2000s confirms that the restaurant switched from cotton-blend napkins to double reinforced crepe (DNC) disposable napkins around the time that Anastasi made this work." Adler, email to author, January 29, 2020.

18. "Anastasi in Conversation with Nackman."

19. See Jacqueline Lichtenstein, "The Artist-Painter and the Philosopher-Sculptor," in *The Blind Spot: An Essay on the Relations between Painting and Sculpture in the Modern Age,* translated by Chris Miller (Los Angeles: Getty Research Institute, 2008), 55–89.

20. Linda Dalrymple Henderson, *Duchamp in Context: Science and Technology in the* Large Glass *and Related Works* (Princeton, NJ: Princeton University Press, 1998), 59.

21. Anastasi, interview with Anne Barclay Morgan, *Art Papers,* November/December 1995, 25.

22. Ian Burn, "The 'Sixties: Crisis and Aftermath," *Art and Text* 1, no. 1 (1981): 52.

23. Walter Benjamin, "The Task of the Translator," in *Walter Benjamin: Selected Writings,* vol. 1: *1913–1926,* edited by Marcus Bullock and Michael W. Jennings (Cambridge, MA: Harvard University Press, 1996), 254.

24. "Anastasi in Conversation with Nackman."

25. Margaret MacNamidhe, "Histories of Skill and De-Skilling in Art Schools," course lecture, Week 1, various dates, School of the Art Institute, Chicago, ca. 2021.

26. William Anastasi, interview with the author, New York, February 16, 2013.

27. Anastasi interview, February 16, 2013.

28. According to Anastasi, this neighborhood, then just beginning to be called Alphabet City, was "the cheapest [he] could find." Anastasi, in "William Anastasi and Thomas McEvilley: A Conversation," in *William Anastasi: A Selection of Works from 1960 to 1989,* edited by Charles F. Stuckey (New York: Scott Hanson Gallery, 1989), 7.

29. Anastasi frequently mentions his own aspirations to be an artist alongside quoting his mother's admiration for the profession. "It wasn't until 1960 before I began to whisper to myself, nervously, 'Maybe you are, after all, an artist.'" Anastasi, "Artist Statement," Foundation for Contemporary Arts, New York, 2009.

30. Quoted in Richard Milazzo, "Living at Bludgeon's Height: Libido, Religion, and the Living History of Conceptual Art," in *William Anastasi,* exh. cat. (Modena: Emilio Mazzoli Galleria d'Arte Contemporanea), 8.

31. See Anastasi, in "William Anastasi and Thomas McEvilley," 15; and Anastasi, interviews with the author, New York, February 16, 2013, and June 15 and August 17, 2016.

32. Aristotle informed Alberti's position on line and drawing, which was that new forms could only be created if the form preexists in the mind of the creator. According to Alberti, the act of building was divided into two parts: *disegno,* which concerned itself with form, and construction, which concerned itself with matter. Leon Battista Alberti, *De re aedificatoria,* reprinted in *On the Art of Building in Ten Books,* translated by Joseph Rykwert with Neil Leach and Robert Tavernor (Cambridge, MA: MIT Press, 1988), 11–19.

33. The original source for this quotation comes from Anastasi's studies of Duchamp rather than from extant interviews with the artist. Anastasi was aware of Duchamp's editorial project begun in 1917, *The Blind Man,* which began as a defense for his ready-made sculpture, and for which he wrote a defense of *Fountain,* stating, "Whether Mr. Mutt with his own hands made the fountain or not has no importance. He CHOSE it. He took an ordinary article of life, placed it so that its useful significance disappeared under the new title and point of view—created a new thought for that object." The scholarly consensus is that Duchamp viewed choice, particularly when exercised independently of aesthetic criteria, as a kind of intuitive, "blind" practice. Of *The Blind Man* magazine, Ann Collins Goodyear writes, "The title both raised the question of just who might be considered 'blind,' as well as the privileged perception of a 'second sight' that renders apparent truths obfuscated by the distractions of the physical world." *The Blind Man* no. 2 (1917): 5; Goodyear, "'Emerging Modernisms' and 'The Blind Man,'" June 24, 2019, Bowdoin College Museum of Art, https://www.bowdoin.edu/art-museum/news/2019/emerging-modernisms-and-the-blind-man.html.

34. Dr. Violet Staub de Laszlo, Jackson Pollock's therapist, confirmed this in a letter that released Pollock from Selective Service due to his mental illness. Staub de Laszlo to the Examining Medical Officer of the Selective Service System, May 3, 1941, Jackson Pollock and Lee Krasner Papers, circa 1914–84, AAA.

35. Letter to the editor, *Artforum* 6, no. 5 (1968), https://www.artforum.com /print/196801/letters-71513.

36. Heraclitus, a pre-Socratic philosopher, was likely attractive to artists in this community because his work is known only through quotations and translations by other philosophers, which meant that his ideas were flexible and anecdotally constituted. See Heraclitus, *Fragments: A Text and Translation,* translated by T. M. Robinson (Toronto: University of Toronto Press, 1987).

37. Robert Smithson, "A Sedimentation of the Mind: Earth Proposals," *Artforum* 7, no. 1 (1968): 83.

38. Smithson, "Sedimentation of the Mind," 83.

39. Ann Reynolds and others have noted Smithson's abiding preoccupation with various "elsewhere[s]," from the salt flats of Rozel Point, Utah, to the shores of the Yucatán Peninsula. Reynolds points out a commonality between these two contemporaries that might otherwise go unnoticed: that in referencing anything that is absent—either through its linear deposits, as Anastasi had, or by assembling matter from a distant place into a pile—that "elsewhere" is a marker of an absent place as well as an absent premise, impossible to access except in the present. See Reynolds, *Robert Smithson: Learning from New Jersey and Elsewhere* (Cambridge, MA: MIT Press, 2003), 182, note 127, in which she makes use of Alain Robbe-Grillet's statement, "For of course an elsewhere is no more possible than a formerly."

40. Schneemann disliked this aspect of John Cage's (and, we presume, by extension Anastasi's) practice, calling it "fro-ZEN." See Burt Ramsay, *Judson Dance Theater: Performative Traces* (New York: Routledge, 2006), 166.

41. Quoted in *William Anastasi: A Retrospective, 1960–1995,* exh. cat. (Philadelphia: Galleries at Moore, Moore College of Art and Design, 1995), 25.

42. See Jean-Michel Rabaté and Aaron Levy, "Preface: Interpretation Becomes Art," in *William Anastasi's Pataphysical Society: Jarry, Joyce, Duchamp, and Cage* (Philadelphia: Slought Foundation, 2005), ix.

43. Yvonne Rainer, "A Quasi Survey of Some 'Minimalist' Tendencies in the Quantitatively Minimal Dance Activity amidst the Plethora, or an Analysis of Trio A," written in 1966 and first published in Gregory Battcock, ed., *Minimal Art: A Critical Anthology* (New York: E. P. Dutton, 1968), 270.

44. Robert Morris, "Notes on Sculpture, Part 3," *Artforum* 5, no. 6 (1967): 128.

45. Bernard Green, "Gooey 'Celebration' to Happen at the Museum," *Chicago Sun-Times,* January 11, 1968.

46. Anastasi, quoted in Stuckey, *William Anastasi,* 7; Anastasi interview, February 16, 2013.

47. See Richard Shiff, "Donald Judd: Fast Thinking," in *Donald Judd: Late Work,* exh. cat. (New York: Pace Wildenstein, 2000), 4–23.

48. John Cage, "Lecture on Nothing," *Incontri Musicali* no. 3 (August 1959): 19, reprinted in Cage, *Silence: Lectures and Writings* (Middletown, CT: Wesleyan University Press, 1961), 110.

49. James Meyer points out that Robert Morris's strongest contribution to art criticism—"Notes on Sculpture," one and two, which he published in 1966—began as a parody of the formalist criticism of Clement Greenberg and Michael Fried. Anastasi's approach took a resolutely amateurish approach to art history and technical knowledge generally, in contradistinction to Morris's appropriations. See Meyer, *Minimalism: Art and Polemics in the Sixties* (New Haven: Yale University Press, 2001), 155. This stupidity was connected—implicitly and explicitly— with a desire to decouple art from standardized, narrative knowledge formations. Anastasi remarked in an interview in 2001, "A delegation from the NEA once asked Cage whom they felt they should support. He suggested they support an artist who didn't have a clue where his next idea would come from. They were shocked, but I totally agree. I feel like Duchamp who was never entirely convinced that what he was doing actually constituted art." In Lars Movin, "Only Ideas Can Be Art," in *Information* (Copenhagen), January 9, 2001.

50. Jacques Rancière, *The Ignorant Schoolmaster: Five Lessons in Intellectual Emancipation,* translated by Kristin Ross (Stanford, CA: Stanford University Press, 1991), 15.

51. Of the hundred pages of notes that he produced for the *Large Glass,* Duchamp published three sets of them in his lifetime: the *Box of 1914,* which contained photographs of sixteen pages of notes mounted on board; the *Green Box* of 1934, which contained ninety-four total documents, including lithographs of eighty-three notes and drawings; and *A l'Infinitif (The White Box),* trans. Marcel Duchamp and Cleve Gray (New York: Cordier and Ekstrom, 1966), which contained seventy-nine facsimile notes in seven black paper folders. The contents of all three volumes were reproduced in *The Salt Seller: The Writings of Marcel Duchamp (Marchand du sel),* edited by Michel Sanouillet and Elmer Peterson (New York: Oxford University Press, 1973). The publication of his notes and plans, and by extension their translation into English, was integral to critical framings of his work.

52. Duchamp, "The Green Box," in Sanouillet and Peterson, *Salt Seller,* 49.

53. Marcel Duchamp, interview with James Johnson Sweeney, in Sanouillet and Peterson, *Salt Seller,* 133. Anastasi first admired and encountered Duchamp's work at the Philadelphia Museum of Art in 1958, right after Louise and Walter Arensberg had brought their artworks there after diverting their enormous textile fortune into nightly artists' salons and the study of cryptography. Anastasi mentions this first encounter with Duchamp's works in Richard Milazzo, *William Anastasi: Paintings, Small Works, Drawings,* exh. cat. (Modena: Galleria Emilio Mazzoli, 2009), 119. The rest of this information, including Walter Arensberg's two books, *The Cryptography of Dante* and *The Cryptography of Shakespeare,* comes from "Arensberg Archives: Historical Note," Arensberg Archives, Philadelphia Museum of Art.

54. Quoted in Sanouillet and Peterson, *Salt Seller,* 49.

55. Jacques Rancière, *The Intervals of Cinema,* translated by John Howe (London: Verso, 2014), 7–8.

56. Claes Oldenburg, "Extractions from the Studio Notes," *Artforum* 4, no. 5 (1966): 32.

57. Anastasi has on occasion connected his own work to surrealism. He

collaborated on a book that attached him to Alfred Jarry, Marcel Duchamp, James Joyce, and John Cage, and his essay for that book pointed out the many connections among Duchamp, Jarry, and the surrealists. He has also mentioned automatic drawing in numerous interviews, conceding that the inspiration for his unsighted or automatic works in the early 1960s came through discourse on automatism and abstract expressionism. See Anastasi, "Jarry in Duchamp," in Rabaté and Levy, *William Anastasi's Pataphysical Society*, 33–34; Milazzo, "Living at Bludgeon's Height," in *William Anastasi*, 41; and Anastasi interviews, February 16, 2013, and November 11, 2015.

58. The question of exactly what constituted professionalism and how much professional dedication was needed to advance one's practice is complicated. Robert Morris has repeatedly uncoupled professional success as an artist from wage labor in this period. "You didn't have to work full-time to pay your rent, like you do today," he said to an interviewer. "You had time to visit your friends, sit around and talk, or just think about things. You had leisure, to be lazy or to think about things. To write things down." But Dorothea Rockburne makes plain a more raw and energetic commitment to professional success, stating that "everyone [in the downtown scene] was so busy kicking ass that we didn't have time to hole up together and get cozy in winter." What is most notable here is both artists' Marxist notation of thought and knowledge-production, as distinct from waged work and physical comfort. Anastasi's position is clear, however: he credits his active dating life as the thing that distracted him from advancing his work at Dwan and other galleries. Oral history interview with Robert Morris, April 19–20, 2018, AAA; Dorothea Rockburne, interview with the author, New York, March 1, 2015; and Anastasi interview, February 16, 2013.

59. See, e.g., Julia Bryan-Wilson, *Art Workers: Radical Practice in the Vietnam War Era* (Berkeley: University of California Press, 2009); Francis Frascina, *Art, Politics and Dissent: Aspects of the Art Left in Sixties America* (Manchester: Manchester University Press, 1999); and Julie Ault, ed., *Alternative Art, New York, 1965–1985* (Minneapolis: University of Minnesota Press, 2002).

60. Bryan-Wilson, *Art Workers*, 15.

61. Roy Ascott, "The Construction of Change," *Cambridge Opinion 37, Modern Art in Britain* (January 1964): 37, quoted in Lucy Lippard, *Six Years: The Dematerialization of the Art Object from 1966 to 1972* (Berkeley: University of California Press, 1997), 2.

62. Harold Rosenberg, "The American Action Painters," *Art News*, 51, no. 8 (1952): 48. A more current history of the commodification of artistic actions can be found in Christa Noel Robbins, *Artist as Author: Action and Intent in Late-Modernist American Painting* (Chicago: University of Chicago Press, 2021), 89–113.

63. Gregory Battcock, "Wall Paintings and the Wall," *Arts Magazine*, December 1970–January 1971, 24.

64. The stenographic translation process went beyond the purely linguistic. The *Gregg Shorthand* anniversary edition, the most popular instruction manual between 1929 and McGraw Hill's newer textbooks in the postwar period, refers to stereographic symbols as "brief forms" rather than the previous convention of "wordsigns," indicating a shift from viewing text and words as the basis of communication, to forms as illustrative of spoken sounds. See John Robert Gregg, *Gregg Shorthand: A Light-Line Phonography for the Million*, anniversary edition (New York: Gregg, 1929), iii.

65. Quoted in "William Anastasi Discusses This Drawing," multimedia accompaniment to "Robert Brennan on William Anastasi," in *Art=Text=Art: Private Languages/Public Systems: Drawings, Prints and Artists Books from the Sally and Wynn Kramarsky Collection*, exh. cat. (Buffalo: Anderson Gallery, University at Buffalo, State University of New York, 2013).

66. E. Goossen, "Carl Andre," *New York Herald Tribune*, April 9, 1966.

67. Lucy Lippard, "New York Letter," *Art International*, September 1965, 58–59.

68. Maurice Merleau-Ponty, *The Phenomenology of Perception* [1945] (New York: Routledge Classics, 2002), 149–50.

69. Between 1945 and 1965, essays and compendia abounded analyzing the "habits" of social classes in the United States. In addition to the cultural historian Russell Lyne's famous "Highbrow, Middlebrow, Lowbrow" (*Harper's*, 1948), see Alfred Kinsey, *Sexual Behavior in the Human Male* (Philadelphia: W. B. Saunders, 1948); and Leo Bogart, *The Age of Television: A Study of Viewing Habits and the Impact of Television on American Life* (New York: Frederick Ungar, 1956). On habit and artistic practice, see also Henry Geldzahler, "An Interview with Helen Frankenthaler, *Artforum* 4, no. 2 (1965): 36–38. Frankenthaler stated in 1965 that "'gesture' must appear out of necessity rather than habit."

70. See Anastasi, "William Anastasi and Thomas McEvilley," in Stuckey, *William Anastasi*, 15; and Anastasi interview, February 16, 2013.

71. Catherine Malabou, "The Relation between Habit and the Fold," lecture at the European Graduate School, Division of Philosophy, Art and Critical Thought, Saas-Fee, Switzerland, August 12, 2017, https://www.youtube.com/watch?v=EglV1eVTrpU.

72. Malabou, "Relation between Habit and the Fold."

73. Quoted in *William Anastasi: A Retrospective*, 19.

74. Janet M. Hooks, "Women's Occupations through Seven Decades," *United States Department of Labor, Women's Bureau Bulletin* no. 218 (1947): 75.

75. Friedrich Kittler, *Gramophone, Film, Typewriter*, translated by Geoffrey Winthrop-Young and Michael Wetz (Stanford, CA: Stanford University Press, 1999), 183.

76. In Duchamp's manuscript notes, exhibited at MoMA in 1966, he wrote about his own experiments with mechanical actions as having the potential to produce a new alphabet of visual forms, an "ideal stenography" that could serve as "a language of phenomena themselves." In fact, Duchamp rested the entire visual vocabulary of *The Bride Stripped Bare by Her Bachelors* on the possibility that the bride and other figures could be interchanged with text. See David Joselit, *Infinite Regress* (Cambridge, MA: MIT Press), 55; Marcel Duchamp, *À l'Infinitif (La Boîte Blanche) [In the Infinitive (The White Box)]*, 1912–20, published 1966, Museum of Modern Art, New York. Linda Henderson expands on stenography in her book *Duchamp in Context*, 106; Charles A. Cramer examines Duchamp's references to stenography and translation in "Duchamp from Syntax to Bride: Sa Langue dans Sa Joue," *Word and Image* 13, no. 3 (1997): 279–303.

77. Mina Loy, "O Marcel—Otherwise I Have Also Been to Louise's," *Blind Man* 2 (May 1917): 14.

78. Walt Whitman, preface to the 1855 edition of *Leaves of Grass*, as quoted in Susan Sontag, *On Photography* (New York: Farrar, Straus and Giroux, 1977), 23. Originally printed as "Freak Show," *New York Review of Books*, November 15, 1973, 13–19.

79. Sontag, *On Photography*, 22.

80. Jacques Derrida, "Otobiographies: The Teaching of Nietzsche and the Politics of the Proper Name," in *The Ear of the Other: Otobiography, Transference, Translation: Texts and Discussions with Jacques Derrida*, translated by Christie McDonald (Lincoln: University of Nebraska Press, 1988), 37.

81. Nietzsche, quoted in Derrida, *Ear of the Other*, 36.

82. Manning, *Minor Gesture*, 52.

83. Alex Potts, "The Interrogation of Medium in the Art of the 1960s," *Art History*, April 2004, 291.

84. Laura Hoptman, *Drawing Now: Eight Propositions*, exh. cat. (New York: Museum of Modern Art, 2002), 11.

85. Jacques Derrida, *Of Grammatology*, translated by Gayatri Chakravorty Spivak (Baltimore: Johns Hopkins University Press, 1998), 17.

86. Jacques Derrida, "Scribble: Writing-Power," in *The Derrida Reader: Writing Performances*, edited by Julian Wolfreys (Lincoln: University of Nebraska Press, 1998), 58.

87. Gordon Brown, "Light: Object and Image," *Arts Magazine* (Summer 1963): 64.

88. This behavioral approach to teaching Gregg shorthand, known as the Direct Method, gained ground in the 1930s, when a series of broad revisions to standard stenographic curricula would take effect in the United States. For more on this history, see Lindsey Jancay, "Shorthand and the Stenographic Image" (MA thesis, School of the Art Institute of Chicago, 2018).

89. Rancière, *Intervals of Cinema*, 7.

90. Long-playing records were not the norm in the 1940s; to promote them, stores selling televisions would frequently include a free LP player. The *Philadelphia Inquirer*, for instance, had several LP giveaways in the 1940s. Anastasi credits this as the root of his record collecting and affinity for high-quality stereo equipment, but this wasn't unique; Willem de Kooning also enjoyed fine stereos, and it was not unusual for a big sale to warrant the purchase of a new system. Anastasi, interview with the author, New York, June 4, 2014; see also Mark Stevens and Annalyn Swan, "The $700 Music Machine," in *de Kooning: An American Master* (New York: Alfred A. Knopf, 2006), 81–92.

91. Max Weintraub and Dove Bradshaw, eds., *William Anastasi: Sound Works, 1963–2013*, exh. cat. (New York: Bertha and Karl Leubsdorf Art Gallery, Hunter College, 2013).

92. Allan Solomon and Ugo Mulas, *New York: The New Art Scene* (New York: Holt, Rinehart and Winston, 1967), 29.

93. Skira published sixty-eight of these books between 1950 and 1969, as opposed to half as many in any other twenty-year period.

94. Frank Getlein, "Art Books: High Tide," *Nation*, December 1, 1958, 21.

95. Robert Richman, "Everyman's Museum," *Nation*, December 21, 1953, 20–21.

96. In the exhibition's catalog, William C. Seitz named Duchamp, along with Guillaume Apollinaire and André Breton, "accumulators of avant-garde ideas," so this display that emphasized quantity of materials was not accidental. Seitz, *The Art of Assemblage*, exh. cat. (New York: Museum of Modern Art, 1961), 14.

97. Grace Glueck, "A Mixed Bag, Lively and Tempting: Waddell's Houses Show of CORE Unit 300 Artists Offer View of Current Scene," *New York Times*, April 29, 1967.

98. William Anastasi, interview with the author, New York, November 1, 2013.

99. Milazzi, *William Anastasi*, 8. Anastasi, quoted by Yvette Lee, assistant curator for special projects, Whitney Museum of American Art, April 12, 2001.

100. As Marcel Duchamp reflected in an interview, "You have to approach something with an indifference, as if you had no aesthetic emotion. The choice of readymades is always based on visual indifference and, at the same time, on the total absence of good or bad taste." Quoted in Pierre Cabanne, *Dialogues with Marcel Duchamp*, translated by Ron Padgett (New York: Viking, 1971), 48.

101. Anastasi, *Cage Dialogues*, 2.

102. Clement Greenberg, "The Crisis of the Easel Picture," *Partisan Review* 15, no. 4 (1948): 481–84.

103. Anastasi, *Cage Dialogues*, 1.

104. "First at the Dwan," *Women's Wear Daily*, February 1, 1966, 39.

105. These mutual interests culminated in Anastasi's book-essay that established a completely speculative line of knowledge and influence through Duchamp, Jarry, and Joyce (through *Ulysses* and *Finnegans Wake*). See Levy and Rabaté, *William Anastasi's Pataphysical Society*, 47; Anastasi, *Cage Dialogues*, 37.

106. Lisa Gitelman, *Paper Knowledge: Toward a Media History of Documents* (Durham, NC: Duke University Press, 2014).

107. Murray Schumach, "Subways and Buses Roar Back to Life: Transit System Quickly Resumes," *New York Times*, January 14, 1966.

108. Trisha Brown remarked in 2010, "Mayor John Lindsay wanted to redevelop and raze the whole area of SoHo, but the project didn't go ahead. We were quite visible and viable in those days." In "All Work, All Play: In Conversation with Laurie Anderson, Trisha Brown, Jane Crawford, RoseLee Goldberg, Alanna Heiss and Lydia Yee," in *Laurie Anderson, Trisha Brown, Gordon Matta-Clark: Pioneers of the Downtown Scene, New York 1970s*, edited by Lydia Yee (New York: Prestel, 2011), 70.

109. John P. Callahan, "New Look Dawns at Grand Central: Bleak Shuttle Area Cheered by Tiles in City's Colors," *New York Times*, December 11, 1966.

110. "Down the Subway Tracks," *New York Times*, May 23, 1970.

111. Ralph Ellison, *The Invisible Man* (New York: Random House, 1952), 78.

112. Anastasi, *Cage Dialogues*, 65. Confirmed in an interview with the author, New York, September 8, 2017.

113. Clarence Taylor, *Fight the Power: African Americans and the Long History of Police Brutality in New York City* (New York: NYU Press, 2019).

114. William Anastasi, interview with the author, New York, February 15, 2015.

115. Anastasi frequently refers to the following quotation: "Repetition is an indestructible garment that fits closely and tenderly, neither binds nor sags.

Hope is a lovely maiden who slips away between one's fingers; recollection is a beautiful old woman with whom one is never satisfied at the moment; repetition is a beloved wife of whom one never wearies, for one only becomes weary of what is new. One never grows weary of the old, and when one has that, one is happy." See Søren Kierkegaard, *Repetition: A Venture in Experimental Psychology*, in *Kierkegaard: Fear and Trembling / Repetition*, translated by Howard V. Hong and Edna H. Hong (Princeton, NJ: Princeton University Press, 1983), 132. There are also many provocative emerging theories on the aestheticization of information. See, for instance, the documents and essays from workshops conducted at Harvard University in 2014 and its subsequent colloquium of 2015, "Beautiful Data," which discussed not only the aesthetic potential of data but also how institutions such as museums might appropriately exhibit data. (I remain ambivalent about the pure aesthetic potential of data itself, but this colloquium makes Anastasi's work an interesting precursor for dealing with this problem.) See "Beautiful Data," Metalab, http://beautifuldata.metalab.harvard.edu/.

116. Sol LeWitt, "Sentences on Conceptual Art," first published in *0 to 9* (New York), 1969, and *Art-Language* (England), May 1969, reprinted in *Sol LeWitt*, edited by Alicia Legg, exh. cat. (New York: Museum of Modern Art, 1978), 168.

117. Erin Manning and Brian Massumi's use of the word *affordance* aligns with Anastasi's prioritizing of his own body position in relation to the apertures and closures of urban space: "The particular angle is that of your body getting ahead. The opening is how the field appears as an affordance for your getting-ahead." Manning and Massumi, *Thought in the Act*, 9–10.

118. William Anastasi as told to Dove Bradshaw, email to author, September 5, 2017.

119. Henri Focillon articulates the moral weight of dominant handedness beautifully: "The hands are not a pair of passively identical twins. Nor are they to be distinguished like younger and older children, or like two girls with unequal talents, one trained in all skills, the other a serf dulled by the monotony of hard work…. The left hand can be made to perform all the duties of the right." Focillon, "In Praise of Hands," in *The Life of Forms in Art*, translated by George Kubler (Princeton, NJ: Princeton University Press, 1992), 161.

120. Duran Kimball, *Business Shorthand* (Sydney, Australia: Wentworth, 1900), 9–10.

121. Salvador Dalí, "The Object as Revealed in Surrealist Experiment" (1932), reprinted in *The Collected Writings of Salvador Dalí*, edited by Haim Finkelstein (Cambridge: Cambridge University Press, 1998), 236.

122. Numerous writings on surrealism in the 1960s mention wonder and reverie or emphasize the benefits of intuitive, uncalculated ways of being. See, for instance, Annette Michelson, who in 1966 quoted André Breton: "diametrical, steadfast, and categorical opposition to any attempt at a definition of formal beauty in terms of a deliberate effort of perfection incumbent upon man"; or Lucy Lippard, in an introduction to her edited volume on surrealists from 1971; or Roger Cardinal and Robert Stuart Short's assertion that surrealist techniques help to "recuperate man's lost powers." See Michelson, "Breton's Aesthetics: The Peripeties of Metaphor," *Artforum* 5, no. 1 (1966): 73; Lippard, ed., *Surrealists on Art* (Englewood Cliffs, NJ: Prentice Hall, 1974), 11–25; and Cardinal and Stuart Short, *Surrealism: Permanent Revelation* (London: Studio Vista/Dutton, 1970), 9.

123. Cardinal and Short, *Surrealism*, 60.

124. The Clocktower Gallery programs in the 1970s were devoted to creative merging of art and urban space, including the politicized use of office spaces. As part of the Institute for Art and Urban Resources, it converted abandoned and underused buildings in New York to art studios and exhibition spaces. Along with PS1 Contemporary Art Center, the Clocktower Gallery became permanent facilities of the institute in 1972. It is possible that Alanna Heiss found the clerical component of Anastasi's work attractive and arranged for him to be accorded the budget for three different speakers for the three nights of the performance. See Julie Ault, *Alternative Art, New York, 1965–1985: A Cultural Politics Book for the Social Text Collective* (Minneapolis: University of Minnesota Press, 2002), 33, 270; also confirmed in William Anastasi, telephone conversation with the author, Macon, GA, December 26, 2018.

CHAPTER 3
CUTTING INTO THINGS

1. Oral history interview with Richard Tuttle, November 14–17, 2016, Archives of American Art, Smithsonian Institution (hereafter abbreviated as AAA).

2. Gordon B. Washburn, untitled essay, in *Richard Tuttle: Constructed Paintings*, exh. cat. (New York: Betty Parsons Gallery, 1965).

3. Gallery activities included a specific invitation for children, with such children's activities as being asked to "sign" a drawing pad for the show. See Leo Lehrman, "Grab Bag," *Vogue Children's Fashions*, Spring/Summer 1964. Other activities are noted in Betty Parsons Gallery Papers, box 19, folders 3 and 4, AAA.

4. Robert Pincus-Witten was comparing Richard Tuttle's boxes to Lucas Samaras's small painted celluloid cubes, which averaged about four to six inches in height and were displayed in Samaras's earliest exhibitions as a group in a Plexiglass case. Pincus-Witten, "Richard Tuttle," *Artforum* 8, no. 6 (1970): 64.

5. Marcia Tucker, *Richard Tuttle*, exh. cat. (New York: Whitney Museum of American Art, 1975), 20.

6. Richard Tuttle, "For 'ABC Art,'" unpublished artist's statement printed in Barbara Rose, "ABC Art," *Art in America* 53, no. 5 (1966): 60.

7. So popular was the box form, in fact, that Brian O'Doherty organized *The Box Show* in January 1965, in which Tuttle's boxes were included. This reference to his own "white boxes" were a concession to the box as a formal and stylistic trope, but one that was not without humor. "Byron Gallery Press Release" for "The Box Show" by Brian O'Doherty, February 2, 1965, Byron Gallery Records, 1959–1991, box 12, folder 2, AAA.

8. Jeffrey Weiss, *Robert Morris: Object Sculpture, 1960–1965* (New Haven: Yale University Press, 2014), 49; Veronica Roberts, *Converging Lines: Eva Hesse and Sol LeWitt*, exh. cat. (Austin, TX: Blanton Museum of Art, 2014), 21.

9. Brian O'Doherty, essay manuscript, Byron Gallery Records, box 12, folder 1, AAA. I was alerted to this essay in Laura Lake Smith's illuminating dissertation, "Imagining the In-Between: The Serial Art of Richard Tuttle" (PhD diss., University of Georgia, 2017), 38, note 50.

10. Mel Bochner insisted that Eva Hesse's "cubes with the hairy interiors were sexual puns on the word *box.*" Bochner, quoted in *Eva Hesse,* edited by Mignon Nixon (Cambridge, MA: MIT Press, 2002), 42. For a thorough inventory of these early box exhibitions, see Veronica Roberts, "Opening LeWitt's Early Boxes," in *Converging Lines,* 37–55.

11. Benedict Spinoza, *Improvement of the Understanding: Ethics and Correspondence of Benedict de Spinoza* (Baltimore: Johns Hopkins University Press, 1999), 79, 81.

12. Richard Tuttle, "How to Duplicate Your Cloth Piece a Thousand Times—," in *Other Ideas,* exh. cat. (Detroit, MI: Detroit Institute of Arts, 1969), n.p.

13. Interestingly, chance and systems theory—two methods that also distanced art making from the artist's private creative faculties—was an emerging priority for neo-Dada and conceptual artists and accomplished this same goal. Mel Bochner's quotation of Arnold Schoenberg in his essay "The Serial Attitude" of 1967 is illustrative here: "My desire was for a conscious control over the new means and forms that arise in every artist's mind." This agnostic approach to control was a common variable but still left art's matter and form in the hands (so to speak) of the artist seeking to make visible a particular system—in other words, conceptual art maintained the same bifurcation between form and matter, the same distance between thought and the "object" of thought's expression, as did abstract expressionism. Bochner, "The Serial Attitude," *Artforum* 6, no. 4 (1967): 29.

14. Karen Barad, "Diffracting Diffraction: Cutting Together-Apart," *Parallax* 20, no. 3 (2014): 179.

15. Christine Knauer, "Race and/in War," in *At War: The Military and American Culture in the Twentieth Century and Beyond,* edited by David Kieran and Edwin A. Martini (New Brunswick, NJ: Rutgers University Press, 2018), 168–94, at 184.

16. Dave Hickey, "Fire on the Water," in *Lynda Benglis,* edited by Franck Gautherot, Caroline Hancock, and Seung-Duk Kim, exh. cat. (Eindhoven: Stedelijk Van Abbemuseum, 2009), 149.

17. This impasse was highly visible in critics' anxious responses to artworks late in the decade that had to do with documentation—works that were often discussed in terms of the possible and the impossible. In his review of Tuttle's fabric pieces and Douglas Huebler's drawings at the Eugenia Butler Gallery in September 1969, Thomas H. Garver wrote, "Eugenia Butler's Gallery becomes increasingly 'conceptual' or 'impossible' as her exhibitions progress. One has the feeling that the work of all her artists might easily be packed in a retentive mind and removed in toto without altering the gallery in the slightest." The sense here is that these object-documents revealed things that may have taken place in some other place or time—and that this was the thing Garver found most vexing. Garver, "Richard Diebenkorn, Richard Tuttle, Douglas Huebler," *Artforum* 8, no. 1 (1969): 67.

18. Eve Meltzer, *Systems We Have Loved: Conceptual Art, Affect, and the Antihumanist Turn* (Chicago: University of Chicago Press, 2013); Johanna Gosse and Timothy Stott, ed., *Nervous Systems: Art, Systems, and Politics since the 1960s* (Durham, NC: Duke University Press, 2022); Mette Gieskes, "The Politics of System in the Art of Carl Andre, Donald Judd, and Robert Morris" (PhD diss., University of Texas at Austin, 2006).

19. Richard Tuttle, "150 Words on My Work," *Art International,* May 15, 1968, 48.

20. Pincus-Witten, "Richard Tuttle," 64.

21. Samuel Wagstaff, "Looking at Modern Art: Trinity College Reading Program," n.d., Samuel L. Wagstaff Papers, box 3, folder 23, AAA.

22. Florence Berkman, "Pop Art on Exhibition: Free, Far Out," *Hartford (CT) Times,* January 11, 1964.

23. Cornelia H. Butler, "Framed Drawings," in *The Art of Richard Tuttle,* edited by Madeleine Grynsztejn, exh. cat. (San Francisco: San Francisco Museum of Modern Art, 2005), 59.

24. Caroline Jones cites the studio as a space that affirmed and circumscribed the hermetic, private nature of the artist's body: "The public role played by the private studio in postwar American art was both paradoxical and crucial to the development of an international modern art in New York. The Manhattan studio was a public figure for all that was private, a visible yet inaccessible source for all that was meaningful in the abstract art object…. Even when the ends of one's fingertips seemed distant, alienated from the core of meaning (the self), then the world beyond the studio was impossibly remote." Jones, *Machine in the Studio: Constructing the Postwar American Artist* (Chicago: University of Chicago Press), 20.

25. Harold Rosenberg, "The American Action Painters," *Art News* 51, no. 8 (1952): 22–23, 48–50, at 49 (emphasis added).

26. Jasper Johns, Notes from sketchbook A, p. 42, ca. 1963–64, transcribed in Kirk Varnedoe and Christel Hollevoet, *Jasper Johns: Writings, Sketchbook Notes, Interviews* (New York: Museum of Modern Art / Harry N. Abrams, 2002), 54.

27. Rosenberg, "American Action Painters," 22.

28. Benedict Spinoza, *The Ethics,* reprinted in *Improvement of the Understanding: Ethics and Correspondence of Benedict de Spinoza,* translated by R. H. M. Elwes (New York: Wiley, 1901), 77.

29. Anne Wagner, "Review: The Art of Richard Tuttle, San Francisco Museum of Modern Art," *Artforum* 44, no. 2 (2005): https://www.artforum.com/print/reviews/200508/richard-tuttle-9508.

30. Karen Barad, *Meeting the Universe Halfway: Quantum Physics and the Entanglement of Matter and Meaning* (Durham, NC: Duke University Press, 2007), 175.

31. Tuttle, quoted in Robert Pincus-Witten, "The Art of Richard Tuttle," in *Postminimalism* (New York: Out of London Press, 1977), 67.

32. Charles Reich, *The Greening of America* (New York: Random House, 1970), 14.

33. Reich, *Greening of America,* 11.

34. Reich, *Greening of America,* 12.

35. The full quotation is: "We but mirror the world. All the tendencies present in the outer world are to be found in the world of our body. If we could change ourselves, the tendencies in the world would also change. As a man changes his own nature, so does the attitude of the world change towards him…. We need not wait to see what others do." Gandhi, *The Collected Works of Mahatma Gandhi,* vol. 12 (Publications Division, Ministry of Information and Broadcasting, Government of India, 1964), 158.

36. Whitehead caught the attention of Louis Finkelstein, a lecturer at the Yale School of Art when Tuttle was there. Finkelstein's lecture on the philosopher in 1973 introduced his work as a "forebear of numerous curiosities that I'd say were very current." Finkelstein, Lecture on the

Philosophy of Alfred North Whitehead, March 23, 1973, Louis Finkelstein Papers, box 10, folder 7, AAA.

37. Phyllis Braff, "Recalling a Notable Logician-Philosopher Connecting with the Art World," *Brooklyn Rail,* November 2016, https://brooklynrail.org/2016/11/criticspage/recalling-a-notable-logician-philosopher-connecting-with-the-art-world.

38. Alfred North Whitehead, *The Concept of Nature* (Cambridge: Cambridge University Press, 1920), 172.

39. Alfred North Whitehead, *The Function of Reason* (Boston: Beacon Press, 1929), 58. Whitehead displays serious myopia regarding which cultures have developed what he calls "abstract schemes of morphology," which were important for introducing "Speculation" into "Reason." For instance, Whitehead felt that Greek mathematics were superior to the "comparative stagnation of Asiatic civilizations," a position that Tuttle did not share. See Whitehead, *Function of Reason,* 57–58.

40. Whitehead, *Function of Reason,* 31–32.

41. Whitehead, *Function of Reason,* 65.

42. See Ann Gibson, "Lesbian Identity and the Politics of Representation in Betty Parsons's Gallery," in Whitney Davis, ed., *Gay and Lesbian Studies in Art History* (New York: The Haworth Press, 1994), 245–70.

43. Agnes Martin, quoted in Anne M. G. Wagner, *A House Divided: American Art since 1955* (Los Angeles: University of California Press, 2012), 205, note 8.

44. The implied colonialist mindset of this idea reveals itself more explicitly when Rose quotes the critic John Ashbery: "Ashbery has asked if art can be excellent if anybody can do it. He concludes that "what matters is the artist's will to discover, rather than the manual skills he may share with hundreds of other artists. Anybody could have discovered America, but only Columbus did."

45. Tuttle, "Paper Is Place," unpublished exhibition catalog essay for the exhibition *Radikal auf Papier,* Aargauer Kunsthaus, Aarau, Switzerland, January 7, 1990.

46. Richard Tuttle to Samuel Wagstaff, May 3, 1964, Samuel L. Wagstaff Papers, box 2, folder 28, AAA.

47. Chris Martin, "In Conversation: Richard Tuttle," *Brooklyn Rail,* December 2004–January 2005, https://brooklynrail.org/2005/01/art/richard-tuttle.

48. *Department of Defense Appropriations for 1969; Hearings before the Subcommittee of the Committee on Appropriations, House of Representatives, Ninetieth Congress, Second Session* (Washington, DC: US Government Printing Office, 1968), 424.

49. *Department of Defense Appropriations for 1963: Hearings before the Subcommittee of the Committee on Appropriations, House of Representatives, Eighty-Seventh Congress, Second Session, Parts 5–6* (Washington, DC: US Government Printing Office, 1962), 31–32.

50. Garcia was expelled on the grounds of "failure to adapt," which includes an entry-level performance discharge justification of "not suited to the military lifestyle." The only other possibilities for expulsion at that time were a Section 8 diagnosis, which Tuttle managed to attain, or a court-martial for a more serious offense. Blair Jackson, *Garcia: An American Life* (New York: Penguin Books, 2000), 26.

51. *Department of Defense Appropriations for 1962: Hearings before the Subcommittee of the Committee on Appropriations, House of Representatives, Eighty-Seventh Congress, First Session* (Washington, DC: US Government Printing Office, 1962), 467.

52. Tuttle to Wagstaff, May 3, 1964, Samuel L. Wagstaff Papers, box 2, folder 28, AAA.

53. Tuttle to Wagstaff, January 29, 1964, Samuel L. Wagstaff Papers, box 2, folder 28, AAA.

54. Suzanne Hudson, Hixson-Lied lecture, University of Nebraska, Lincoln, October 16, 2019.

55. Hudson, Hixson-Lied lecture.

56. Hudson has connected Bob Ross's traumatic experience with military service to his interest in staging the learning of art as a social good. "Art for Therapy's Sake: Suzanne Hudson Looks at the Legacy of TV's Bob Ross," UC Santa Barbara, interview with Suzanne Hudson, https://www.hfa.ucsb.edu/news-entries/2018/2/11/art-for-therapys-sake-suzanne-hudson-looks-at-the-legacy-of-tvs-bob-ross.

57. Pincus-Witten, "Art of Richard Tuttle," 69.

58. The critic Mary Josephson mentioned this in her review of Tuttle's exhibition at the Betty Parsons Gallery in 1972. Josephson, "Richard Tuttle at Betty Parsons," *Art in America* 60, no. 3 (1972): 33. The curator Marcia Tucker was even more explicit when she wrote in the catalog essay for Tuttle's 1975 retrospective exhibition, "Dyed and wrinkled, they are stored crumpled in a canvas bag and installed with small nails, therefore negating their potential objecthood." Marcia Tucker, ed., *Richard Tuttle,* exh. cat. (New York: Whitney Museum of American Art, 1975), 6.

59. Martin Heidegger, *What Is a Thing?,* translated by W. B. Barton Jr. and Vera Deutsch (Chicago: Henry Regnery, 1967), 18.

60. Richard Tuttle, "Is Line / Fulmination?," lecture presented at "Minding the Time: New Perspectives on Old Master Drawings," symposium at the Morgan Library and Museum, May 9, 2017.

61. Gordon Washburn, essay for *Richard Tuttle,* exh. cat. (New York: Betty Parsons Gallery, 1965), n.p.; Stuart Preston, *New York Times,* May 1, 1969; Lucy Lippard, "New York Letter," *Art International* 9, no. 9 (1965): 39.

62. Emily Wasserman, "Richard Tuttle," *Artforum* 6, no. 7 (1968): 56–57; Wasserman, "Alan Shields, Paula Cooper Gallery, 529 W 21st Street," *Artforum* 7, no. 9 (1969): 64.

63. Richard Tuttle, "Dear Mr. Herbig," in *Bilder, Objekte, Filme, Konzepte,* exh. cat. (Munich: Städtische Galerie im Lenbachhaus, 1973), 160.

64. Pamela Lee, "Some Kinds of Duration: The Temporality of Drawing as Process Art," in Cornelia Butler, *Afterimage: Drawing through Process,* exh. cat. (Los Angeles: Museum of Contemporary Art, 1999), 43.

65. Richard Tuttle, "How to Duplicate Your Cloth Piece a Thousand Times—," in *Other Ideas,* exh. cat. (Detroit, MI: Detroit Institute of Arts, 1969), n.p.

66. I borrow the phrase "aesthetic target" from Richard Shiff, who has written about the deep and varied interests among artists in the 1960s in the confluence of perception and awareness. See Shiff, "An Imitation, Not a Copy: Richard Shiff on Bridget Riley," *Art Newspaper,* September 14, 2017, https://www.theartnewspaper.com/2017/09/14/an-imitation-not-a-copy-richard-shiff-on-what-bridget-riley-learned-from-georges-seurat.

67. Rudolf Arnheim, *Art and Visual Perception: A Psychology of the Creative Eye*, 2nd ed. (Berkeley: University of California Press, 1974), 11.

68. Arnheim, *Art and Visual Perception*, 16–17.

69. Maurice Merleau-Ponty, *The Phenomenology of Perception*, translated by Colin Smith (London: Routledge, 2002), 46–47.

70. Tuttle, "Dear Mr. Herbig," 160.

71. Barad, "Diffracting Diffraction," 175.

72. Merleau-Ponty, *Phenomenology of Perception*, 118–22.

73. Rosalind Krauss, "Sense and Sensibility: Reflections on Illusionism in Post-'60s Sculpture," *Artforum* 12, no. 3 (1973): 43–53, at 46.

74. Krauss, "Sense and Sensibility," 122.

75. Tuttle interview, AAA.

76. Richard Tuttle, phone conversation with the author, April 28, 2017.

77. Tuttle, "Is Line / Fulmination?"

78. Richard Tuttle, untitled commentary for a survey on artists' opinions regarding documenta 5, in Bruce Kurtz, "Documenta 5: A Critical Preview," *Arts Magazine* 46, no. 8 (1972): 39

79. These methods are imbricated with one another. Richard Tuttle mentions "Vogel's use of attribution, [which] he learned at the institute," and applied to his methods for collecting contemporary artists. Tuttle, email to the author, April 28, 2017.

80. See, e.g., Smith, "Imaging the In-Between"; Tuttle affirmed the complexities of his interest in repetition and serial drawing in Osman Can Yerebakan, "Dissimilarity in Unity: Richard Tuttle Interviewed," *BOMB*, December 9, 2019, https://bombmagazine.org/articles /dissimilarity-in-unity-richard-tuttle -interviewed/.

81. One may allude from the numerous writings on Western drawing that, since drawing has been so closely linked with personality and biography, to draw a finished work after the fact would be akin to returning to the self after it had unfolded or formed in the moment. Carmen Bambach has discussed this connection among drawing, process, and personality extensively, including in her essay "Il Divin' Disegnatore," in *Michelangelo: Divine Draftsman and Designer* (New York: Metropolitan Museum of Art, 2017), 15–30.

82. Jock Truman, Tuttle's dealer at the Betty Parsons Gallery, gave the work to the Museum of Modern Art in 1974 in anticipation of Bernice Rose's exhibition on contemporary drawing there the following year. It is clear that Tuttle's interest in making drawings was in part facilitated by pragmatism. Truman sought to expand the market for Tuttle's works while also encouraging collecting institutions such as MoMA to make a less risky investment than a large work might have been. This makes sense in the wake of depressed art prices at the beginning of the 1970s, an inversion of the soaring prices of the previous decade. For more information on Truman's promotion of Tuttle's work, see John T. Paoletti, *From Minimal to Conceptual Art: Works from the Dorothy and Herbert Vogel Collection*, exh. cat. (Washington, DC: National Gallery of Art, 1994), 120.

83. Pincus-Witten, "Art of Richard Tuttle," 67.

84. Barad, "Diffracting Diffraction," 176.

85. This is discussed in "Precision: Richard Tuttle with Jennifer Gross," in *Seeing Intimacy: Richard Tuttle on Paper*, exh. cat. (New York: Craig F. Starr Gallery, 2010), n.p.

86. *Richard Tuttle: Das 11. Papierachteck und Wandmalieren / The 11th Paper Octagonal and Paintings for the Wall*, exh. cat. (Munich: Kunstraum München, 1973), insert.

87. See Katie Anania, "Drawing, Intimacy and Privacy in American Studio Art Practice, 1963–1979" (PhD diss., University of Texas at Austin, 2016).

88. Tuttle, untitled commentary, 39. Judith Butler, *Gender Trouble*, 3rd ed. (New York: Taylor and Francis, 2002), 174.

89. Richard Tuttle, *40 Tage: Zeichnungen* (Bonn: Galerie Erhard Klein; Vienna: Galerie Hubert Winter, 1989), n.p. Richard Tuttle, *A Fair Sampling: Collected Writings, 1966–2019*, edited by Dieter Schwarz (Cologne: Walther König, 2020), 180.

90. Dorothy Vogel to Ruth E. Fine, "Interview with Herb and Dorothy Vogel," in Paoletti, *From Minimal to Conceptual Art*, 70.

91. Dorothy Vogel, interview with the author, New York, February 17, 2015. See also Tuttle's essay in *Richard Tuttle*, exh. cat. (Amsterdam: Stedelijk Museum, 1979), 14.

92. See, e.g., Alfred Schmela, letters to Fänn Schniewind and Willy Schniewind, 1960–70, Galerie Schmela records, acc. no. 2007.M.17, box 13, folder 18, Getty Research Institute, Los Angeles.

93. Lynda Benglis, telephone interview with the author, April 28, 2017.

94. Benglis interview.

95. Flora Miller Biddle and Fiona Donovan, *The Whitney Women and the Museum They Made: A Family Memoir* (New York: Simon and Schuster, 2017), 59.

96. Biddle and Donovan, *Whitney Women*, 61.

97. Jacques Derrida, *The Politics of Friendship*, translated by George Collins (New York: Verso Books, 2005), 17, 29.

98. A note on a bill of sale for the *1st Paper Octagonal* includes a note that the work could be "removed with water before scraping." Bill of sale to Giuseppe Rebecchini for *1st Paper Octagonal*, November 22, 1978, Betty Parsons Gallery Papers, box 25, folder 20, AAA.

99. Vogel interview. See also Tuttle's essay in *Richard Tuttle*, exh. cat. (Amsterdam: Stedelijk Museum, 1979), 14.

100. Douglas Crimp, "Reviews and Previews," *Art News* 72, no. 6 (1973): 99.

101. Richard Tuttle, untitled essay in *Using Walls (Indoors)*, exh. cat. (New York: Jewish Museum, 1970), n.p.

102. As Dorothy Vogel said, "The octagon aged so beautifully; it changed color slowly over years and years until it became yellowed, like a letter." Vogel to Ruth E. Fine, "Interview with Herb and Dorothy Vogel," 89.

103. Pincus-Witten, "Art of Richard Tuttle," 67. In an indirect affirmation of this stance on waste, Tuttle said that his family, particularly his grandmother, was "against conspicuous consumption." Tuttle interview, AAA.

104. *American Thrift* (Chevrolet Division, General Motors Corporation, 1962), film, https://archive.org/details/0836 _American_Thrift_19_31_29_00.

105. Vogel interview.

106. Karl Marx, *Capital: A Critique of Political Economy*, vol. 1, translated by Samuel Moore and Edward Aveling (New York: Modem Library, 1906), 209.

107. Benglis interview.

108. Tucker, *Richard Tuttle*, 82.

109. Harald Szeemann, ed., *Live in Your Head: When Attitudes Become Form:*

Works—Concepts—Processes—Situations—Information, exh. cat. (Bern: Kunsthalle Bern, 1969), n.p. Phillip Morris would purchase the Miller Brewing Company the following year, solidifying the company's advancement into the world of lifestyle brands in that decade.

110. See, for instance, R. A. Tamol, "Experimental Low Delivery Cigarettes—Project False," Philip Morris test records, May 5, 1966, Bates No. 1000702644, http://legacy.library.ucsf.edu/tid/naw44e00.

111. Szeemann, *Live in Your Head,* n.p.

112. Scott Burton, "Notes on the New," in Szeemann, *Live in Your Head,* n.p.

113. "What Is a Museum? A Dialogue between Allan Kaprow and Robert Smithson," reprinted in *Robert Smithson: Collected Writings,* edited by Jack Flam (Berkeley: University of California Press, 1996), 44.

114. Donald Judd, "Complaints Part II," *Arts Magazine* 47, no. 5 (1973): 30.

115. Richard Tuttle to Samuel Wagstaff, October 22, 1970, Samuel Wagstaff, Jr., Records, series 1, box 2, Detroit Museum of Arts.

116. "The Drawing and Print Club," *Bulletin of the Detroit Institute of Arts* 46, no. 3 (1967): 66.

117. The practices for displaying Family Dog and other rock posters in the late 1960s and early 1970s ram the gamut from small commercial expo displays to fine art museums. Wagstaff, for instance, justified the collection and display of rock music posters by gesturing to the "hordes of student-aesthetes" who might be attracted to rock poster exhibitions. Samuel Wagstaff, Jr., Records. An overview of rock poster markets and other display practices appears in Ryan Moore, "Break on Through: The Counterculture and the Climax of American Modernism," in *Countercultures and Popular Music,* edited by Sheila Whiteley and Jedediah Sklower (New York: Taylor and Francis, 2014), 29–44.

118. Jacques Derrida states that "the radical disruption of any context" is "the protocol of any code." Derrida, "Signature Event Context," in *Margins of Philosophy,* translated by Alan Bass (Chicago: University of Chicago Press, 1982), 1, 8.

119. Reich, *Greening of America,* 20.

120. Richard Tuttle, "Interview: Drawing and Exhibitions," published on PBS.org, September 2005, and reprinted on Art21.org, November 2011, https://art21.org/read/richard-tuttle-drawing-and-exhibitions/.

121. Dylan Kerr, "Richard Tuttle on Why He Finds Solace in the Spirituality of Art—Not Religion," interview with the artist, *Artspace,* April 27, 2016, https://www.artspace.com/magazine/interviews_features/qa/richard-tuttle-interview-53738.

CHAPTER 4
PROTOTYPES OF EMPIRE

Epigraphs: Hannah Arendt, *The Human Condition* (Garden City, NY: Doubleday Anchor Books, 1959), 250; Morse Peckham, *Man's Rage for Chaos: Biology, Behavior and the Arts* (New York: Chilton Books, 1966), xi.

1. Manuel Maldonado-Denis, *Puerto Rico: Una interpretación histórico-social* (Mexico City: Siglo Ventiuno Editores, 1980), 174.

2. Victor Hernández Cruz, "Loíza Althea," in *Mainland: Poems* (New York: Random House, 1973), 19.

3. Rafael Hernández Colón, who worked to publicize Puerto Rico's plebiscite vote for independence in 1967, recalls choosing the coconut (*Cocos nucifera*) palm as an icon to represent the statehood option when designing the ballot for the referendum. The coconut, which was to indicate statehood to voters who would not read, formed the party logo of the pro-statehood New Progressive Party. See Rafael Hernández Colón, *Vientos de Cambio: Memorias de Rafael Hernández Colón* (Ramallo Bros, 2004), 119.

4. Rafael Ferrer, quoted in Mario García Torres, "An Interview with Rafael Ferrer," in *9 at Leo Castelli* (San Juan, PR: Instituto de Cultura Puertorriqueña, 2009), 12.

5. The university's art gallery, El Museo de Bellas Artes Colegial, had been inaugurated in 1960 and was intended to expand the scope of Puerto Rico's cultural offerings beyond the urban center of San Juan, "a tono con las necesidades del pueblo colegial" [in tune with the needs of a college town]. José Enrique Arrarás, the university's chancellor, supported the dean, Stuart Ramos, in his ambition to expand the cultural offerings of the university; between 1960 and 1975, Roy Lichtenstein, Robert Morris, Frank Stella, Lucio Fontana, Leo Castelli, and José Luís Cuevas would visit. Fidel Torres, "Nuestro museo," *Campus* 2, no. 12 (1960): 4; Amanda Carmona Bosch, "Mayagüez, 1966–1971: Edad de oro de las artes plásticas en Puerto Rico," *Mayagüez Sabe a Mango,* n.d.

6. Throughout the project, Morris and Ferrer engage the spatial politics of the university. On one hand, the campus was a premiere metropolitan university, second only to the University of Puerto Rico—Río Piedras in San Juan. On the other, the campus was devoted primarily to agricultural and mechanical training until the late 1950s, when one of the agricultural buildings was annexed to create the fine arts department and the university art museum. See Zorali De Feria and Sandra Aponte, "MUSA y la colección permanente del Recinto Universitario de Mayagüez," *Visión Doble: Revista de Crítica e Historia del Arte,* April 14, 2019, 4.

7. James Nisbet, *Ecologies, Environments, and Energy Systems in Art of the 1960s and 70s* (Cambridge, MA: MIT Press, 2014), 139.

8. Two of the drawings are mentioned in Terrie Sultan's exhibition catalog for the Corcoran Gallery of Art, *Inability to Endure or Deny the World: Representation and Text in the Work of Robert Morris,* exh. cat. (Washington, DC: Corcoran Gallery of Art, 1990). Sultan notes that "these drawings serve as plans that outline the physical activity Morris wished to realize in his art projects, and in many cases they were the only surviving records of what were envisioned as temporary situations" (15). Five of them were included in *Robert Morris: El dibujo como pensamiento / The Drawing as Thought,* exh. cat. (Valencia, Spain: IVAM Centre Julio González, 2011).

9. Joshua Kind and Michael Flanagan, "Rafael Ferrer: An interview," in *Rafael Ferrer,* exh. cat. (New York: Nancy Hoffman Gallery, 1987), 8.

10. The Brazilian artist Regina Silveira, who also taught at Mayagüez during this time, notes that, through Arrarás, "the campus developed an interchange with notable artists such as Italian Germano Celant…, Robert Morris, … Barbara Rose, and others. Dean Arrarás himself was a collector of contemporary art and personal friend of influential people from the New York art scene like Leo Castelli and Roy Liechtenstein. This highly creative, closed environment very different

from that of the island went on for about four years." Cynthia Garcia, "Labyrinth of Life: A Conversation with Regina Silveira," Newcity Brazil, October 19, 2018, https://www.newcitybrazil.com/2018/10/09/labyrinth-of-life-a-conversation-with-regina-silveira/.

11. Quoted in Francoise Ferrer, email to the author, November 19, 2022.

12. Sol LeWitt, "Paragraphs on Conceptual Art," *Artforum* 5, no. 10 (1967): 80.

13. Carl Andre, quoted in *Sol LeWitt: 100 Views*, edited by Susan Cross and Denise Markovich, exh. cat. (Boston: MASS MoCA, 2009), 91.

14. Barbara Rose, "Claes Oldenburg's Soft Machines," *Artforum* 5, no. 10 (1967): 33.

15. The project also registered the artists' mounting frustrations with *form* that came to characterize the antiform and land art movements, showing its problematic connections with the more instrumentalizing and market-friendly term *style*. Style could be historicized, hierarchized, applied to systems of value, and used to mythologize the artist's sovereign, bounded power. The site-specific projects that emerged in the late 1960s were interesting to Morris and Ferrer because they seemed to escape the market implications of artistic style. But as Morris wrote in 1979, "Site-specific works can hardly be described as commodity production items. They seem to assume the role of a service function rather than that of object production. Yet the majority of those artists showing a sustained interest in site-specific work—in either realized or proposed projects—conform to the 'established style variation' mode characteristic of commodity object production." The only workable solution, Morris speculated, was to understand site-specific and land art as a form of land reclamation, to be undertaken as a civic or community conservation effort. From Morris, "Earthworks: Land Reclamation as Sculpture," lecture delivered July 31, 1979, revised as "Notes on Art and/as Land Reclamation," reprinted in *Continuous Project Altered Daily: The Writings of Robert Morris* (Cambridge, MA: MIT Press, 1993), 224.

16. Joan Kee, *Models of Integrity: Art and Law in Post-Sixties America* (Berkeley: University of California Press, 2019), 67.

17. Sol LeWitt remarked in 1969, "Some people's [artist] work only exists in the documentation…. the wall things of mine are a good example because once a show is over, they're destroyed. The only thing that remains is a photograph of the wall, a drawing of the drawing, and maybe a verbal description of how to draw it. By the thing itself is gone…. That's why I want to be able to use this kind of method that Seth was working on, because that's the only way these things would be available in his catalogues." Sol LeWitt and Patricia Norvell, "Sol LeWitt: June 12, 1969," in *Recording Conceptual Art: Early Interviews with Barry, Huebler, Kaltenbach, LeWitt, Morris, Oppenheim, Siegelaub, Smithson, and Weiner,* edited by Alexander Alberro and Patricia Norvell (Berkeley: University of California Press, 2001), 122.

18. The Menil Collection, the Detroit Institute of Arts, and the Walker Art Center all had thriving collectors' clubs that used prints as an organ for social interactions between middle-class members. The Walker, with the support of its collectors' club, produced the first US run of the print series *Continuous Monument* by the Italian radical architecture collective Superstudio. At the Detroit Institute of Arts, curator Samuel Wagstaff cultivated this group with mixers and entry-level print purchases, and Jermayne MacAgy pursued a similar strategy as she developed the Contemporary Arts Association in Houston a decade earlier. Wagstaff's involvement with the collectors' club is mentioned in chapter 3 of this book.

19. I refer here to Patricia Johanson's 150 sketches for a domestic garden, which she submitted to *House and Garden* at their request in March 1969, but then the magazine refused to publish them. They have since been cataloged at the Dumbarton Oaks Research Library and in Xin Wu, *Patricia Johanson's House and Garden Commission: Re-Construction of Modernity* (Washington, DC: Dumbarton Oaks Research Library and Collection, 2008).

20. This is a common note about Morris's work: that his critiques of systems extended to the very systems of labor and value that made artistic "work" seem special, removed from, or independent from the larger pathways of capitalism. But Morris's written instructions, and their value as a "remainder" of the art process, have so far received scant attention. For earlier remarks on Morris and labor, see Julia Bryan-Wilson, "Hard Hats and Art Strikes: Robert Morris in 1970," *Art Bulletin* 89, no. 2 (2007): 344; and Andrew Chesher, "Desublimating the Gestalt: Towards an Archaeology of Robert Morris's Anti Form," *Zeitschrift für Ästhetik und Allgemeine Kunstwissenschaft (ZÄK)* 19 (2021): 22.

21. Ferrer mentions this in his "Autobiography" in *Deseo: An Adventure* (Cincinnati: Contemporary Arts Center, 1973), 48–55, at 54.

22. *Revista de Arte* was part and parcel of the new campus expansions and increased support for the arts and humanities there. See untitled editor's introduction, *Revista de Arte,* folder 9, Archivo de la *Revista de Arte* (Mayagüez), Museo de Reina Sofia.

23. "La falta de formalismo y de ideas preconcebidas con que los dos enfocaron la que iba a ser exposición hizo que la idea de ésta evolucionase normal y lógicamente hacia la interesantisima serie de actuaciones septembrinas." Ángel Crespo, "Los eventos Morris en el campus de Mayagüez," *Revista de Arte* no. 3 (1969): 12.

24. David Rodriguez Graciani, a member of the student resistance, gives a thorough account of the demonstrations in his ¿Rebelion o Protest? *La Lucha Estudiantil en Puerto Rico* (Rio Piedras, PR: Ediciones Puerto, 1972).

25. Such a mobilization is congruent with earlier performance scores by George Brecht and others, who declared (with recourse to John Cage, whom Morris also admired), "Events are an extension of music." George Brecht, "An Interview with George Brecht by Irmeline Lebeer" (1973), in *An Introduction to George Brecht's "Book of the Tumbler,"* Henry Martin (Milan: Multipla Edizioni, 1978), 84.

26. Morris mentioned Gestalt psychology numerous times in his early writings, as did Carolee Schneemann. His "Notes on Sculpture" essays, published in *Artforum* between February 1966 and June 1967, make several references to gestalt theory, which Morris had encountered while an undergraduate at Reed College and later through the writings of Maurice Merleau-Ponty. See Morris, "Notes on Sculpture," *Artforum* 4, no. 6 (1966): 42–44, reprinted in Gregory Battcock, ed., *Minimal Art: A Critical Anthology* (New York: E. P. Dutton, 1968).

27. Peckham, *Man's Rage for Chaos,* 321–22.

28. This is how Morris also reckoned with what he considered the binary problematic of language. Mixed with his references to Peckham are references to de Saussure's categorizations of analog and digital linguistic modes. See Robert Morris, "Some Notes on the Phenomenology of Making," *Artforum* 8, no. 8 (1970), reprinted in *Continuous Project Altered Daily*, 81.

29. It is worth noting that Latour prioritizes theorists of technology and curators from the 1960s and 1970s in his discussions of drawing. Samuel Y. Edgerton's studies from the 1970s of Renaissance scientific drawing figure especially heavily here.

30. Eugene S. Ferguson quoting Samuel Y. Edgerton, quoted in Bruno Latour, "Visualisation and Cognition: Drawing Things Together," in *Knowledge and Society: Studies in the Sociology of Culture Past and Present*, edited by Elizabeth Long and Henrika Kuklick, vol. 6 (Greenwich, CT: Jai Press, 1986), 8.

31. Morris, interview with Rosalind Krauss, undated, Morris Archives, Gardiner, NY. Published as "Robert Morris: Autour du problème corps/esprit/ Around the Mind/Body Problem," *art press*, July–August 1994, 24–32.

32. In a text for *Artforum* on Nazca drawings in Peru, Morris diagnosed the minimalist sculptures of the 1960s as weighed down by schematic thinking, far too reliant on the gridded "plan view" of preparatory drawings: "The insistence on the rational placement of units in minimal art as linear or grid extensions was borrowed from painting's ordering. Minimal art's diagrammatic aspect was derived from plans generated by drawings on flat pages." Morris, "Aligned with Nazca," *Artforum* 14, no. 2 (1975): 29.

33. The literature scholar Morse Peckham, who himself came from the British Army Air Corps, insisted that communication was by its very nature imperfect and consisted of behaviors that had been mutually and habitually reinforced between speakers. It is no surprise that Morris cites Peckham in his arguments against diagrammatic thinking. Peckham, *Man's Rage for Chaos*, 49.

34. Morris, "Aligned with Nazca," 29. Although Morris asserted this in relation to Nazca drawings, we can also consider it a holdover from his and Donald Judd's initial reactions to Michael Fried's essay

"Art and Objecthood," in which he diagnosed minimalism as overly theatrical. See Michael Fried, "Art and Objecthood," *Artforum* 5, no. 10 (1967): 12–23; and Judd, "Complaints: Part I," *Studio International*, April 1969, 182.

35. Peckham refers to this, with recourse to Alfred North Whitehead, as "misplaced concreteness"—the way a structure is hypostatized from a limited set of observations. Peckham, *Man's Rage for Chaos*, 27.

36. Julia Bryan-Wilson's accounts of Vietnam-era artists including Morris who identified themselves as workers amply demonstrates this. See Bryan-Wilson, "Robert Morris's Art Strike," in *Art Workers: Radical Practice in the Vietnam War Era* (Berkeley: University of California Press, 2011), 83–126.

37. Clement Greenberg, "On the Role of Nature in Modernist Painting," originally published as "The Role of Nature in Modernist Painting," *Partisan Review*, January 1949, and edited and republished in Greenberg, *Art and Culture: Critical Essays* (Boston: Beacon Press, 1961), 173.

38. Félix Rodríguez, Che Guevara's executioner, was a Cuban exile turned CIA Special Activities operative who advised Bolivian troops during the manhunt leading up to Guevara's death. For more on the American art community's reception of Guevara's death, including the circulation of his postmortem photographs, see Michael Casey, *Che's Afterlife: The Legacy of an Image* (New York: Vintage, 2009), 183. See also Bjorn Kumm, "The Death of Che Guevara," *New Republic*, November 11, 1967.

39. See, e.g., "10 Dead as Violence Continues in Major U.S. Cities; Troops Sent to Washington, Chicago, Detroit," *Toledo (OH) Blade*, April 5, 1968; and Walter McCall, "12th Street Erupts: Ghettoes React to King's Death," *Windsor (ON) Star*, April 5, 1968.

40. Martin Arnold, "Puerto Rico Is Concerned about Image," *New York Times*, March 14, 1971.

41. Morris later expressed doubt, in fact, that it is possible to make art or have ideas at all in such a climate. "In a century of profound violence and failed political programs," he wrote, "it seems there is a comparable 'postideological' despondency. Currently, in the face of an empty present and a cancelled future, a

political and intellectual quietism is set at idle beneath the materialistic roar." Morris, "Three Folds in the Fabric and Four Autobiographical Asides as Allegories (or Interruptions)," *Art in America* 77, no. 11 (1989): 149.

42. Morris linked the "political unrest and disbelief in U.S. political actions" in the 1960s with the breakdown of abstract expressionism, for instance. Morris, "American Quartet," *Art in America* 69, no. 10 (1981): 99.

43. Bruno Latour, "Atmosphère, Atmosphère," in *Olafur Eliasson: The Weather Project*, exh. cat. (London: Tate Modern, 2003), 31. In this essay, he credits the philosopher Peter Sloterdijk with using air and meteorology to locate "other ways of escaping the narrow constraints of modernism."

44. In this way, it was not unlike Marcel Duchamp's mocking of vision in his work *Étant donnés: 1° la chute d'eau, 2° le gaz d'éclairage…* (Given: 1. The Waterfall, 2. The Illuminating Gas…; 1946–66), which went on view at the Philadelphia Museum of Art following Duchamp's death in 1968. Morris would have known of this work. One of his lithographs from 1970 of war memorials included one, *Trench with Chlorine Gas*, that referred to a broad spectrum of chemical weapons used since World War I.

45. These projects are well documented. Ernesto B. Vigil, *The Crusade for Justice: Chicano Militancy and the Government's War on Dissent* (Madison: University of Wisconsin Press, 1999), chaps. 3–7.

46. Lucy Lippard, "Escape Attempts," in *Six Years: The Dematerialization of the Art Object from 1966 to 1972* (Berkeley: University of California Press, 1997), x.

47. Rafael Ferrer, statement in "The Artist and Politics: A Symposium," *Artforum* 9, no. 1 (1970): 35–39, at 36.

48. In "Notes on Land Art as Reclamation," Morris opined on art's relation to commodity markets, suggesting that many kinds of art could serve a "public relations function": "Exhibition in any art gallery… participates in the commodity structure. None of the historical monumental works known today would have been made if the artists had refused to work… because of either questionable sponsorship or disagreement with the ends to which the art was used. It is an illusion that artists have ever had anything to say about the functions of

their works." Morris, "Notes on Art and/as Land Reclamation," *October* 12 (Spring 1980): 87–102, 98.

49. José Trías Monge, *Puerto Rico: The Trials of the Oldest Colony in the World* (New Haven: Yale University Press, 1999), 166.

50. Robert William Anderson, *Party Politics in Puerto Rico* (Stanford, CA: Stanford University Press, 1965), 14.

51. This was the first of several essays in which he would mention drawing as an embattled part of the artistic process.

52. Robert Morris, "Anti Form," reprinted in *Continuous Project Altered Daily*, 41.

53. Morris, "Anti Form," 43. Sam Wagstaff said that his show *Black, White and Grey* had been organized around "big [minimal] pieces" and that all works were "pretty difficult art … these pictures don't meet you half way." Samuel Wagstaff to Robert Morris, cited in Meyer, *Minimalism: Art and Polemics in the Sixties* (New Haven: Yale University Press, 2001); Florence Berkman, "Pop Art Exhibition Free, Far Out," *Hartford (CT) Times*, January 11, 1964.

54. Morris, "Anti Form," 44.

55. Pamela Lee, "Some Kinds of Duration: The Temporality of Drawing as Process Art," in Cornelia Butler, *Afterimage: Drawing as Process*, exh. cat. (Los Angeles: Museum of Contemporary Art, Los Angeles, 1999), 89.

56. Spinoza's work represents one of the earliest challenges to Descartes's mind-body dualism, though Spinoza also used many of Descartes's ideas as foundational to his own. In US academic philosophy in the postwar period, materialist theories by T. T. Place, Herbert Feigl, J. J. C. Smart, and others also undermined or deemphasized the Cartesian model. The artist Adrian Piper discusses this intellectual history in several of her autobiographical writings, as well as in "An Open Letter to Donald Kuspit," reprinted in Piper, *Out of Order, Out of Sight: Selected Writings in Art Criticism, 1967–1992*, vol. 2 (Cambridge, MA: MIT Press, 1996), 107–26.

57. "Each one of those needles makes a little different kind of mark. The paper is very special. There are many lines. There are eight lines I believe from eight parts of the brain. For me it's interesting to look at." Paul Cummings, Oral history interview with Robert Morris, March 10,

1968, Archives of American Art, Smithsonian Institution (hereafter abbreviated as AAA).

58. Morris interview, 46.

59. Robert Morris, "The Present Tense of Space," reprinted in *Continuous Project Altered Daily*, 199.

60. Suzaan Boettger, *Earthworks: Art and the Landscape of the Sixties* (Berkeley: University of California Press, 2003), 6.

61. Morris to Lear Siegler, Inc., June 1969, quoted in Gail R. Scott, "Robert Morris," in *A Report on the Art and Technology Program of the Los Angeles County Museum of Art, 1967–1971*, edited by Maurice Tuchman (Los Angeles: Los Angeles County Museum of Art, 1971), 239.

62. Morris to Lear Siegler, Inc., March 3, 1969, quoted in Scott, "Robert Morris," 239.

63. Morris, proposal to Art and Technology Program, September 16, 1969, quoted in Scott, "Robert Morris," 240.

64. Matthias Koddenberg places proposal drawings for large-scale site-specific artworks into the context of postwar design in Koddenberg, *Christo and Jeanne-Claude: In/Out Studio* (Dortmund: Kettler, 2021).

65. The percentage of American households that included some form of air conditioning increased three- to fivefold in all regions of the United States between 1960 and 1970. See Jeff Biddle, "Explaining the Spread of Residential Air Conditioning, 1955–1980," *Explorations in Economic History* 45, no. 4 (2008): 402–23; and Gail Cooper, *Air-Conditioning America: Engineers and the Controlled Environment, 1900–1960* (Baltimore: Johns Hopkins University Press, 1998).

66. Morris had already explored implanting objects under the earth's surface in *Continuous Project Altered Daily*, which included holes and buried material that shifted each day. But exactly how Lear Siegler was to dig the holes for this project is not mentioned.

67. Morris may have seen this work at a Wildenstein gallery exhibition to benefit the Committee to Rescue Italian Art in the wake of the flood in 1966 in Florence, Italy. See Committee to Rescue Italian Art (CRIA), *The Italian Heritage*, exh. cat. (New York: Wildenstein, 1967).

68. Robert Morris, "On Drawing," in *Pop Art Redefined*, edited by Suzi Gablik and John Russell (London, 1969), 94–95.

69. See Amelia Jones, "The 'Pollockian Performative' and the Revision of the Modernist Subject," in *Body Art: Performing the Subject* (Minneapolis: University of Minnesota Press, 1998), 53–102.

70. Morris interview.

71. Maurice Tuchman wrote, "We were usually reluctant to follow through on proposals which seemed too completely designed, or thought out in advance, so that the corporation's role would simply be a question of executing a previously conceived plan, rather than collaborating actively in both the conception and execution of an idea." Tuchman, *Report on the Art and Technology Program*, 19.

72. Jane Livingston, "Andy Warhol," in Tuchman, *Report on the Art and Technology Program*, 331–37.

73. Lil Picard, "Art," *East Village Other*, March 7, 1969, 10.

74. Rafael Ferrer, "'Nothing … Is What It Is,'" lecture presented at the 141st Annual Meeting of the Association for Public Art, Philadelphia Museum of Art, May 13, 2013, https://www.youtube.com/watch?v=s_OdyEWkzMg.

75. The original proposed exhibition title was *Anti-Form*, after Morris's essay of April 1968 in *Artforum*, but the other artists objected, citing concerns about being positioned as Morris's followers. Marcia Tucker, *A Short Life of Trouble: Forty Years in the New York Art World* (Berkeley: University of California Press, 2008), 81–82.

76. Cindy Nemser, "The Art of Frustration," *Art Education* 24, no. 2 (1971): 12.

77. A detailed record of this correspondence is published in Robert Morris, "Letters to John Cage," *October* 81 (Summer 1997): 70–79.

78. Tucker, *Short Life of Trouble*, 82.

79. In Morris's discussions of the AWC, he maintains that his interest in the group weakened when race and gender began to enter the coalition's discussions. "I maybe went to a few meetings, but I wasn't part of it. They were a group of artists, and they had different agendas: race, women, and so on. So it went—it didn't have much unity [and] it kind of fractured [after that]." New research indicates that the AWC successfully expanded its platform to include New Left priorities such as racism and sexism; the end of Morris's participation did not mark the close of the group as a

whole. Rafael Ferrer, notably, continued to attend AWC meetings. Oral history interview with Robert Morris, April 19–20, 2018, AAA; Artworkers Coalition, "Documents 1," 1969, Primary Information, 2008, http://web.archive.org/web /20150303203637/http://primary information.org/files/FDoc.pdf.

80. Lauren Rosati, *Alternative Histories: New York Art Spaces, 1960 to 2010* (Cambridge, MA: MIT Press 2012), 116.

81. Mario García Torres, "An Interview with Rafael Ferrer," in García Torres, *9 at Leo Castelli,* 11.

82. "In Conversation: Lynne Warren with Rafael Ferrer," *MCA Magazine,* Summer 2015, 29.

83. Johanna Fernández has noted the importance of documentary photography to the Young Lords' activist program, especially the photographs of Hiram Maristany, the group's unofficial photographer. While Maristany's images of the "garbage offensive" were not published until late summer 1969, Ferrer, who had lived in East Harlem, would certainly have been aware of these protests in his former neighborhood. See Fernández, *Young Lords: A Radical History* (Chapel Hill: University of North Carolina Press, 2019), 91–114.

84. "Mapping Resistance: The Young Lords in El Barrio," https:// www.mappingresistance.com /copy-of-3rd-avenue-and-111th-st.

85. Daniel José Older, "Garbage Fires for Freedom: When Puerto Rican Activists Took Over New York's Streets," *New York Times,* October 11, 2019.

86. Joseph P. Fried, "East Harlem Youths Explain Garbage-Dumping Demonstration," *New York Times,* August 19, 1969.

87. Jose Yglesias, "Right On with the Young Lords," *New York Times,* June 7, 1970.

88. This is visible as early as 1969 in the Earth Art Symposium at Cornell University, when artists like Robert Smithson, Hans Haacke, and other speakers identified drawing as a means of making tracks or being "immersed in a site that you're scanning" (Smithson). Haacke and others also noted their propensity to engage disciplinary tools such as printouts, aerial scans, and gridded maps. Transcript of Earth Art Symposium, Cornell University, 1969, 1, 11, 23, Robert Smithson and Nancy Holt Papers, box 2, folder 48, AAA.

89. This applied most acutely to modernist standards for sculptural form. Smithson noted this when he wrote in 1966, "Although anatomy is rarely taught in our art schools, the metaphors of anatomical and biological science linger in the minds of some of our most important abstract artists." Robert Smithson, "Quasi-Infinities and the Waning of Space," *Arts Magazine* 2 (November 1966): 29.

90. Rosalind Krauss, "Sculpture in the Expanded Field," *October* 8 (Spring 1979): 30–44, at 38.

91. Morris interview, 2018, AAA.

92. Jessie Kindig discusses the destruction of mountain ranges in "Korea in War for Peace: Race, Empire and the Korean War" (PhD diss., University of Washington, 2014).

93. Morris, for instance, made an "infantry archive" in 1970 that focused on dead soldiers, but the body of the mountain acts here in a really different way. See Christophe Cherix, "An Experience Bank: The Drawings of Robert Morris," in *Robert Morris,* exh. cat. (New Paltz, NY: Samuel Dorsky Museum, 2001), 6.

94. For more on art as currency, see David Joselit, "Art Flow," *Guernica,* December 3, 2012.

95. Georges Bataille, *The Accursed Share: An Essay on General Economy,* vol. 1 (Brooklyn, NY: Zone Books, 1997). See also Pamela Lee's footnoting of Bataille in *Object to Be Destroyed: Gordon Matta-Clark* (Cambridge, MA: MIT Press, 2001), 237.

96. Robert Smithson, contribution to "The Artist and Politics: A Symposium," *Artforum* 9, no. 1 (1970): 39.

97. Morris interview, 2018.

98. Morris interview, 2018.

99. Michel Foucault, *The Archaeology of Knowledge* (New York: Pantheon Books, 1972), 7.

100. Morris wrote that "what ties a lot of work together is its sharing of the 'automated' step in the making process, which has been enlisted as a powerful ally in the recovery of means or time and in increasing the coherence of the making phase itself." Morris, "Some Notes on the Phenomenology of Making," *Artforum* 8, no. 8 (1970), reprinted in *Continuous Project Altered Daily,* 91.

CHAPTER 5
DEEP IN THE SURFACE

1. This font is also historically dissimilar from the ones commonly used in enslaved "wanted" posters and advertising auctions of enslaved people. It was, however, a popular font for both official and public graffiti signage, which photographer Darryl Cowherd immortalized in his photographs of St. Louis after nationwide riots in Black neighborhoods in 1966 and 1967. See Janet Dees, ed., *A Site of Struggle: American Art against Anti-Black Violence* (Princeton, NJ: Princeton University Press, 2022), 19–29.

2. Ilene Susan Fort, "Charles White's Art and Activism in Southern California," in *Charles White: A Retrospective,* edited by Sarah Kelly Oehler and Esther Adler, exh. cat. (New York: Museum of Modern Art, 2018), 132.

3. Kellie Jones notes that most of the distinguishing features mentioned in these posters were scars from abuse. See Kellie Jones, *South of Pico: African American Artists in Los Angeles in the 1960s and 1970s* (Durham, NC: Duke University Press, 2017), 46.

4. See Gordon S. Barker, *Fugitive Slaves and the Unfinished American Revolution: Eight Cases, 1848–1856* (Jefferson, NC: McFarland, 2013); R. J. M. Blackett, *The Captive's Quest for Freedom: Fugitive Slaves, the 1850 Fugitive Slave Law, and the Politics of Slavery* (New York: Cambridge University Press, 2018); R. J. M. Blackett, *Making Freedom: The Underground Railroad and the Politics of Slavery* (Chapel Hill: University of North Carolina Press, 2013); Stanley W. Campbell, *The Slave Catchers: Enforcement of the Fugitive Slave Law, 1850–1860* (Chapel Hill: University of North Carolina Press, 1970). Campbell's volume was the first historical monograph in English to assert that, contrary to previous consensus among midcentury historians, federal officials and ordinary citizens in the northern states had collaborated in a dense network of the capture of slaves and their return to enslaved conditions.

5. Pointing hands have a long history in modern art and linguistic theory as references to the indexical trace—that is, they impart a sense of direct contact with a physical referent. In her essay "Notes on the Index: Seventies Art in America," Rosalind Krauss misidentifies

the manicule in Marcel Duchamp's *Tu m'* as "a realistically painted hand," identifying nevertheless the work that this hand does: "establishing the connection between the linguistic signifier 'this,' and its referent." Krauss, "Notes on the Index: Seventies Art in America," *October* 3 (Spring 1977): 70–71.

6. Voytek Bialkowski, Christine DeLuca, and Kalina Lafreniere, "Manicules," in *Architectures of the Book,* University of Saskatchewan Humanities and Fine Arts Digital Research Centre, updated February 5, 2022, https://drc.usask.ca/projects /archbook/manicules.php#footnote12. The literary and textual history scholar William H. Sherman notes that the manicule existed without a name for centuries: "Everyone knows what the symbol is and does when they see it, but almost nobody knows what to call it. There is no single word, in fact, that will conjure it up for everyone—and I would even suggest that it may be the most pervasive feature in the history of textual culture that does not have a standard name." Sherman, "Toward a History of the Manicule," unpublished paper, December 2004, revised March 2005, http:// www.livesandletters.ac.uk/papers/FOR _2005_04_001.pdf.

7. Stefano Harney and Fred Moten, *All Incomplete* (Brooklyn, NY: Autonomedia, 2021), 85.

8. Mark Pascale, "'Graphic Interpreter of the Black People': Charles White as Draftsman and Printmaker," Oehler and Adler, *Charles White: A Retrospective,* 40.

9. See, for instance, Bridget R. Cooks's exhibition *The Black Index,* which shows how Black artists have used "self-representation as an antidote to colonialist images" (New York: Hunter College Art Galleries, 2021), 9.

10. In Charles White's essay "Humanist Art," he mentions Rembrandt van Rijn, Francisco Goya, Honoré Daumier, and Käthe Kollwitz as his most admired predecessors. See White, "Humanist Art," *Masses and Mainstream* 7, no. 5 (1954): 61.

11. Charles White, "Soul and Art," in "Black Artists: Art and Social Commentary," panel at Los Angeles County Museum of Art, October 27, 1969.

12. Oral history interview with Charles W. White, March 9, 1965, Archives of American Art, Smithsonian Institution (hereafter abbreviated as AAA).

13. Gilles Deleuze, *Expressionism in Philosophy: Spinoza* (Brooklyn, NY: Zone Books, 1990), 333.

14. White distilled his understanding of "total environment" across various talks and interviews in the 1960s, which I list on page 207, note 11 of this book. But his broad references to the Black political experience intersected with conversations on ecology at US universities when White was invited to give a keynote address at the Politics and Our Deteriorating Environment Symposium at Southern Oregon College in early November 1969. This symposium's themes resonated with art-ecology events like the Earth Art Symposium at Cornell University, held that February. Pamphlets for the Oregon symposium quoted White's claim that art was "one of the most tangible means of … relating to society with a oneness of thinking and feeling." See Charles W. White papers, Box 6, folder 33, and Box 13, Folder 11, AAA.

15. Huey Copeland, *Bound to Appear: Race, Slavery, and the Site of Multicultural Blackness in America* (Chicago: University of Chicago Press), 11.

16. White associated learning with a range of modalities, including sound and physical sensations. This expansive approach to learning and knowing was nourished through his involvement in projects like *Songs Belafonte Sings* (1962), a book by the singer Harry Belafonte for which White created the illustrations. *Songs Belafonte Sings* anthologized the sung musical forms of the Black Atlantic diaspora. Belafonte, *Songs Belafonte Sings* (New York: Duell, Sloan and Pearce, 1962).

17. Charles White, untitled text in *Wanted Poster Series* folio (Los Angeles: Heritage Gallery, 1970).

18. The vertex appears once in Spinoza's *Treatise on the Emendation of the Intellect,* as a tool for determining the source of ideas formed in the mind. He says that since the mind is capable of visualizing, for instance, "a cone cut in an oblique plane so that the angle of inclination is greater than the angle at the vertex of the cone," this power of comparative logic allows human beings to think critically about where their ideas come from. Baruch Spinoza, *Treatise on the Emendation of the Intellect,* in *Spinoza: Complete Works,* translated by Samuel Shirley (Indianapolis: Hackett, 2002), 29.

19. Malcolm X and Alex Haley, *Autobiography of Malcolm X* (New York: Random House, 1964), 193.

20. Quoted in Leonard Freed, *Black in White America* (New York: Grossman, 1968), 75.

21. Freed, *Black in White America,* 32–33, 132–35.

22. Consider, for instance, the now-infamous letter of 1961 from Troy H. Middleton, resident of Louisiana State University, to Harry Ransom, president of the University of Texas at Austin, which stated that "our Negro students have made no attempt to attend social functions, participate in athletic contests, go in the swimming pool, etc. If they did, we would, for example, discontinue the operation of the swimming pool." Troy H. Middleton to Harry Ransom, October 27, 1961, LSU University Archives, Hill Memorial Library.

23. Robert Morris and Charles White never corresponded, but White would have no doubt associated Morris with the "obscurity and anti-humanism" that the elder artist had diagnosed in American art by the late 1950s. White, "Humanist Art," *Masses and Mainstream* 7, no. 5 (1954): 61.

24. White, "Soul of an Artist," 56.

25. Erica Moiah James's article "Charles White's *J'Accuse* and the Limits of Universal Blackness" beautifully documents White's evolving positions with respect to pan-Africanism. See James, "Charles White's *J'Accuse* and the Limits of Universal Blackness," *Archives of American Art Journal* 55, no. 2 (2016): 4–25.

26. White described himself in 1968 as having been "a loose knit kind of militant" rather than "rebellious the way young people are today" but also acknowledged the potential for violent uprisings to result in rebirth. In his talk in 1969, he said, "It's a very interesting thing … that it took a Watts to make people conscious of the fact that the brother was out here painting, and was acting, and had all these great talents going for him.… Maybe we'll take another incident to build a museum to house the brothers' work." White, "Soul of an Artist," 56; and White, "Soul and Art."

27. "COINTELPRO: The FBI's Covert Action Programs against American Citizens," in *Supplementary Detailed Staff Reports on*

Intelligence Activities and the Rights of Americans, book 3, Ninth Congress, Second Session, April 24, 1976, 6, note 3.

28. Seymour M. Hirsh, "C.I.A. Reportedly Recruited Blacks for Surveillance of Panther Party," *New York Times*, March 17, 1978.

29. See Simone Browne, *Dark Matters: On the Surveillance of Blackness* (Durham, NC: Duke University Press, 2015).

30. Henry Louis Gates Jr., "Interview with Eldridge Cleaver," *Frontline*, PBS, Spring 1997.

31. "Address Given by Eldridge Cleaver at a Rally Given a Few Days before He Was Scheduled to Return to Jail," *Ramparts*, December 14–28, 1968, 8.

32. I am grateful to Katherine Lennard for a productive discussion of these operations.

33. Mark Pascale, School of the Art Institute of Chicago, to Holly Borham, Blanton Museum of Art, email, July 15, 2015.

34. Leon Edel, "Hoodlums Slug Four in Race Incidents in Greenwich Village," *PM* April 14, 1947, in Charles W. White Papers, box 10, folder 34, AAA.

35. Charles White, interview with Joseph E. Young, December 16, 1970, in *Three Graphic Artists*, 5.

36. White interview, December 16, 1970.

37. Veronica Roberts and Kellie Jones both illuminate this series through the framework of visual signifiers of violence; it is a fertile starting point for considering White's increasing difficulty in this period processing his own anger and disappointment.

38. Sarah Elizabeth Lewis has proposed the notion of "groundwork aesthetics"— contemporary art that "wrestle[s] with the discourse on looking at images of racial violence but also challenge[s] how we define the very environment of the artist and the form that resistance can take." To do this, she shows how contemporary African American artists play with the depiction and performance of "the ground" to highlight "bodies denied [an] upright position of self-sovereignty and agency." Lewis, "Groundwork: Race and Aesthetics in the Era of Stand Your Ground Law," *Art Journal* 79, no. 4 (2020): 97, 112.

39. White, "Soul and Art."

40. See Aruna D'Souza, *Whitewalling: Art, Race, and Protest in Three Acts* (New York: Badlands Unlimited, 2018), 19–29.

41. White, "Soul of an Artist," 54.

42. Lewis, "Groundwork," 97, 112.

43. White would certainly have been conversant with the Middle Passage as a trope in Black liberation discourses of the 1960s. White's friend Lorraine Hansberry's play *A Raisin in the Sun* (1959) references the Middle Passage, and it is a central theme in her unfinished, posthumously published play *Les Blancs*.

44. Kermit Hall, *The Oxford Companion to the Supreme Court of the United States* (Oxford: Oxford University Press, 2005), 925.

45. Summary, "82 Stat. 291—An Act to prohibit desecration of the flag and for other purposes," in Ninetieth Congress, Second Session, 1968, https://www .govinfo.gov/app/details/STATUTE-82 /STATUTE-82-Pg291-2/summary.

46. John R. Vile, *The American Flag: An Encyclopedia of the Stars and Stripes in U.S. History, Culture, and Law* (Santa Barbara, CA: ABC/CLIO), 125.

47. White, "Soul and Art."

48. White noted in his talk, "All these names and prices I got off reproductions of original posters. 30 dollars, price. They used to hold dollar raffles. Dollar raffle, win a human being." White, "Soul and Art."

49. A copy of John Canaday's review of this exhibition, "Black Artists on View in 2 Exhibitions," *New York Times*, April 7, 1971, is found in the Charles W. White Papers, box 12, folder 40, AAA.

50. This is known as the Mystic Insignia of a Klansman (MIOAK) and dates to the first decades of the twentieth century. Michael R. Ronczkowski, *Terrorism and Organized Hate Crime: Intelligence Gathering, Analysis and Investigations*, 3rd ed. (New York: Taylor and Francis, 2011), 281.

51. Jones, *South of Pico*, 137.

52. Langston Hughes, *Jerico-Jim Crow*, 1964, directed by Alvin Ailey and William Hairston; music arranged and directed by Hugh Porter. A flyer advertising a CORE-sponsored performance of this work at the Sanctuary at 143 West Thirteenth Street in New York City, a Jewish temple that had been converted from a Presbyterian church sanctuary in 1949, and illustrated with WHITE DRAWING TITLE, is found in the Charles W. White Papers, box 2, folder 47, AAA.

53. This insignia is recorded in a hearing in 1966 of the House Committee on Un-American Activities, Eighty-Ninth Congress, Second Session, July 20, 21, 22, 1966, 2171, 2175.

54. White, "Soul and Art."

55. Jaleh Mansoor's commentary on monochrome springs to mind here, as "a kind of transit station negotiating … fraught political vectors," including "the refusal of a national culture." Insofar as nineteenth-century slave media constitute a national culture for the broader Atlantic world, it is interesting to consider the materiality of paint and photography in relation to White's view of nation, especially given his sympathies with newly liberated African republics earlier in the decade. Mansoor, *Marshall Plan Modernism: Italian Postwar Abstraction and the Beginnings of Autonomia* (Durham, NC: Duke University Press, 2016), 22.

56. Pascale, "'Graphic Interpreter of the Black People,'" 40.

57. James, "Charles White's J'Accuse," 22.

58. Kerry James Marshall, untitled lecture at *Charles White: Beyond Images of Dignity*, Museum of Modern Art, New York, November 7, 2018, https://www.moma .org/calendar/events/4716.

59. White, "Soul and Art."

60. Peter Clothier, "Charles White: A Critical Perspective," in *Images of Dignity: A Retrospective of the Work of Charles White*, exh. cat. (New York: Studio Museum, Harlem, 1982), 25.

61. Charles White, untitled sketchbook pages, p. 58, c. 1937–1942, Art Institute of Chicago.

62. Quoted in Clothier, "Charles White: A Critical Perspective," 25.

63. Fort, "Charles White's Art and Activism in Southern California," 128.

64. Jones, *South of Pico*, 36.

65. Curt Opliger, "Review: Charles White, Heritage Gallery, Los Angeles," *Artforum* 2, no. 10 (1964): 19.

66. William Wilson, "Review: Charles White and Ernest Lacy, Heritage Gallery, Los Angeles," *Artforum* 4, no. 3 (1965): 15.

67. Opliger, "Review," 19.

68. See Belafonte, *Songs Belafonte Sings*.

69. Pascale, "'Graphic Interpreter of the Black People,'" 45; Jones, *South of Pico*, 46; Esther Adler, *Charles White: Black*

Pope (New York: Museum of Modern Art, 2017), 42.

70. William Waring Cuney, "No Images," in *Storefront Church* (London: Paul Breman, 1973).

71. Susannah Walker documents this trajectory in "'Black Is Beautiful': Redefining Beauty in the 1960s and 70s," in *Style and Status: Selling Beauty to African American Women, 1920–1975* (Lexington: University Press of Kentucky, 2007); and Walker, "Black Is Profitable: The Commodification of the Afro, 1960–1975," *Enterprise and Society* 1, no. 3 (2000): 536–64.

72. Lang likely knew of White's work because of the artist's participation in Oregon Southern College's Fine Arts Festival in 1966, three years earlier. Charles W. White Papers, box 6, folder 33, AAA.

73. White, "Soul and Art."

74. Charles White and Frances Barrett White to Lorraine Hansberry, no date, Charles W. White Papers, box 3, folder 22, AAA.

75. Amiri Baraka, "Sweet Lorraine," in *The LeRoi Jones/Amiri Baraka Reader*, edited by William J. Harris, 2nd ed. (New York: Thunder's Mouth, 2000), 525, 527.

76. See Edmund W. Gordon and Doxey A. Wilkerson, "Compensatory Education for the Disadvantaged, Programs and Practices—Preschool through College," *Journal of Human Resources* 4 (1969): 114–16. This was Gordon's first publication that gave a statistical analysis of supplementary education in general, focusing on early Head Start programs. Gordon later offered the following qualitative reflection on Head Start specifically: "As a political and social endeavor, it has turned out to be one of the most successful and effective of the federal government's experiments. When one looks at it in terms of its potential for what it could be, I'm more inclined to call it a failure because we are a long way from what we'd hoped for. It has become identified as a child development project and we had thought of it as a family and community development project." M. Price, "The Man Who Gave Head Start a Start," *Monitor on Psychology* 42, no. 10 (2011): 86.

77. Edmund W. Gordon, "Relevance or Revolt," *Perspectives on Education* (Teachers College, Columbia University), 3, no. 1 (1969): 15.

78. White, "Soul of an Artist," 54.

79. White, "Soul of an Artist," 54.

80. Charlie Cobb, "Prospectus for Summer Freedom School Program in Mississippi," 1964, Harry J. Bowie Papers, 1964–1967, Wisconsin Historical Society, Archives Main Stacks, mss 31, box 1, folder 4.

81. See Copeland, *Bound to Appear*, 19; Browne, *Dark Matters*, 1–30; Teresa Carbone, "Exhibit A: Evidence and the Art Object," in *Witness: Art and Civil Rights in the Sixties*, edited by Teresa Carbone and Kellie Jones (New York: Monacelli, 2014); and Darby English, *To Describe a Life: Notes on the Intersection of Art and Race Terror* (New Haven: Yale University Press, 2019), v–vi.

EPILOGUE

1. Adrian Piper has written that Spinoza was important to her early development as a philosopher, which then had strong bearing on her artistic practice. See her discussion of Spinoza's thinking in Piper, "Philosophy en Route to Reality: A Bumpy Ride," *Journal of World Philosophies* 4 (Winter 2019): 106–18.

2. Michel Foucault, "Theatrum Philosophicum" (review of Jacques Deleuze's *The Logic of Sense* and *Difference and Repetition*), *Critique* 282 (1970): 885–908, reprinted in *Aesthetics, Method and Epistemology: The Essential Works of Foucault*, edited by J. D. Faubion, vol. 2 (New York: New Press, 1998), 358.

3. Alan Barth, review of *The Autobiography of a Curmudgeon* by Harold L. Ickes, *New Republic* 108 (1943): 677.

4. Alysia Nicole Harris discusses the ways that this series makes meaningful differences reveal themselves, even within this very moment of coextensivity. She references Steven Matijico's essay on the *Eroding Witness* series, which points out that "the ghosts of words like 'police fired first' and 'who helped police set up Carl Hampton' reveal how mournfully Black newspapers decried Hampton's murder as an instance of police terror, while the Houston Post relegates it to a footnote, refusing to announce it on the front page." Harris, "In the Soil, in the Sound: Houston's Jamal Cyrus Gets to the Root of Southern Black Aesthetics," November 17, 2022, *Scalawag*, https://scalawagmagazine.org/2022/11/jamal-cyrus-black-aesthetic/.

5. "Artist Interview: Jamal Cyrus," Blaffer Art Museum, Houston, TX, August 3, 2021.

6. Papyrus is an Egyptian technology that is often accused of historical whitewashing, reframed as a white Western innovation rather than one whose botanical origins lie in many parts of the African continent. See Charles C. Okigbo, ed., *Development and Communication in Africa* (Lanham, MD: Rowman and Littlefield, 2003), 180; Molefi Kete Asante, "Afrocentricity: The Theory of Social Change," in *Multiversity India* (self-pub., 2003); Gloria Emeagwali, "African Indigenous Knowledge Systems and the Legacy of Africa," in *Indigenous Knowledge Systems and Development in Africa*, edited by Samuel Ojo Oloruntoba, Adeshina Afolayan, and Olajumoke Yakob-Haliso (New York: Palgrave Macmillan, 2020), 37–55.

7. Baruch Spinoza to Louis Meyer, April 20, 1663, reprinted in *Spinoza: The Letters*, translated by Samuel Shirley (Indianapolis: Hackett, 1995), 105.

8. Robert Morris noted in 1978, "Anytime the object has become specific, singular, dense, articulated and self-contained, it has already succeeded in removing itself from space." He later revised his argument to place the experience of any object as inevitably falling into the trap of continuous semiotic relations, even when the object was completely co-present with the observer and with the space surrounding it. Morris's assertion is in line with Spinoza's, that the notion of "the infinite" is so confounding precisely because it exceeds perceptual faculties and thought. See Morris, "The Present Tense of Space," reprinted in *Continuous Project Altered Daily: The Writings of Robert Morris* (Cambridge, MA: MIT Press, 2013); and Morris, "American Quartet," *Art in America* 69, no. 10 (1981): 256.

9. See Anna Lovatt, *Drawing Degree Zero: The Line from Minimal to Conceptual Art* (University Park: Pennsylvania State University Press, 2019).

10. When Alfred Barr compiled his book *Painting and Sculpture in the Museum of Modern Art, 1929–1967*, no distinct category existed for drawings. Even such artists as Claes Oldenburg and Ed Ruscha, for whom the exhibition of drawings or working objects became frontal to their oeuvres, merited entries only for painting and sculpture. To denote MoMA's accessions of drawing, Barr simply wrote,

"Also, drawings and a print," or "Also, a film on the artist in the Study Collection," in the entry for the cataloged finished works. See Barr, ed., *Painting and Sculpture at the Museum of Modern Art, 1929–1967* (New York: Museum of Modern Art, 1977), 540, 541. Barr's frequent mention of the "Study Collection" compels us to think further about the evolving position of works on paper as a category. The study collection was composed of works that were relevant to scholarly research but were not exhibitable as works of art. It was clear that by 1967, drawings were not classified as works of art, but most of them did not go into the Study Collection either. Indeed, many of the drawings I analyze here actively resist such classifications.

11. Rosalind Krauss, "Two Moments from the Post-Medium Condition," *October* 116 (Spring 2006): 56.

12. Martha Rosler, "Video: Shedding the Utopian Moment," in *Decoys and Disruptions: Selected Writings, 1975–2001* (Cambridge, MA: MIT Press, 2004), 59.

13. Douglas Crimp, "New York Letter," *Art International* 4, no. 17 (1973): 57.

14. These were among the few communes that the *New York Times* noted by name in a story surveying the "over two hundred" such collectives nationwide. A substantial portion of the story was devoted to the design and living arrangements for the collectives, with Albert Solnit, the chief of advance planning for Marin County, commenting on commune design. Bill Kovach, "Communes Spread as the Young Reject Old Values," *New York Times*, December 17, 1970.

15. "Earth Week '71 Is a Muted Affair: '70 Fervor Is Replaced by Dedication Leaders Say," *New York Times*, April 18, 1971.

16. "Statement by the French Group: The Environmental Witch Hunt," in *The Aspen Papers: Twenty Years of Design Theory from the International Design Conference in Aspen*, edited by Reyner Banham (New York: Praeger, 1974), 208.

17. W. T. Edmondson, G. C. Anderson, and Donald R. Peterson, "Artificial Eutrophication of Lake Washington," *Limnology and Oceanography* 1 (1956): 47–53.

18. Barry Commoner, "Population and 'Affluence,'" in *The Closing Circle: Nature, Man, and Technology* (New York: Alfred A. Knopf, 1971), 212.

19. Timothy Leary, *Start Your Own Religion* (Millbrook, NY: Kriya Press for Sri Ram Ashrama, League for Spiritual Discovery, 1967), 9.

20. David Bourdon, "Playing Hide and Seek at the Whitney," *Village Voice*, September 29, 1975. Marcia Tucker also recalls that visitors to the Whitney tried to pull Tuttle's wire pieces from the wall—a set of interventions that underscores my position that the works foregrounded a "casual" environment whose performance residue conflicted with the behavioral expectations for Madison Avenue museumgoers. Tucker, *A Short Life of Trouble: Forty Years in the New York Art World* (Berkeley: University of California Press, 2008), 113.

21. "The Drawing Center: A History," n.d., pamphlet published under institutional imprint, n.p., Drawing Center archives, New York.

22. Howardena Pindell, "On Making a Video—Free, White and 21," in *The Heart of the Question: The Writings and Paintings of Howardena Pindell* (New York: Midmarch Arts Press, 1997), 68.

23. Grace Glueck, "Women Artists Demonstrate at Whitney," *New York Times*, December 12, 1970.

24. This prompted Harold Rosenberg to comment glibly on the feminists' "arithmetical position on art," as reported in Glueck, "Women Artists Demonstrate at Whitney."

25. See Julia Jacobs and Zachary Small, "Whitney Cancels Show That Included Works Bought at Fund-Raisers," *New York Times*, August 25, 2020.

26. Sampada Aranke, untitled talk at "Serious Play: Radical Publications and Their Histories," panel at the School of Art, Art History and Design, University of Nebraska–Lincoln, March 29, 2021.

Index

Duchamp, Marcel, works by: *The Blind Man*, 215n33; *Boîte-en-Valise*, 93, 109; *The Bride Stripped Bare by Her Bachelors*, 217n76; *Large Glass*, 216n51; *Tu m'*, 228n5; *The White Box (A l'Infinitif)* (collection of notes), 82, *82*, 216n51, 217n76
Dunham, Katherine, 10
Dwan, Virginia, 23, 95, 97
Dwan Gallery, 23; Anastasi in *Language* exhibitions (1967–70), 215n14; Anastasi's solo exhibitions, 21, 73, 215n14; benefit auction, Anastasi participating in, 97, 215n13; *Scale Models and Drawings* (1967), 98, 215n14; *William Anastasi: Sound Works* (1965), 97, *97*, 215n13

Earth Day, 203
EAT (Experiments with Art and Technology), 48, 152
ecological sensibility: Bennett on, 14; *Ecological Art* exhibition (1969), 166; ecology as scientific discipline, 2; Morris and making within a larger ecosystem, 7; Schneemann's feminist ecological framework, 26, 27, 35, 40, 45–49, 67; Spinoza's materialist philosophy and, 12–14; state power's effects on, 151; Tuttle's dynamic ecosystem, 134; White on difference between environment and ecology, 196. *See also* environment
Edmondson, Thomas, 203
electrical functioning of human being, 135, 183
empathy, 47–48, 55
empire and colonialism, 3, 113, 145, 150, 153, 160, 172, 177
English, Darby, 195
Enlightenment philosophers, 14, 49, 75, 98
entanglements: Anastasi and, 71–74, 76–77, 86–87, 91, 93; drawings as, 12, 27; Latour and, 147; Morris and, 14; paper between artist's body and notions of space, 2, 80, 104, 111; Puerto Rico's reality enmeshed with cultural myths of the tropics, 157; Schneemann and, 26, 27, 34, 35, 40, 59, 61
environment: Anastasi and Cage on use of environmental sounds, 98; architects using natural patterns as inspiration, 50; artists' consciousness of environmental damage, 173; Carson's *Silent Spring*'s effect on artists, 61; condemnation of urban living, 203; Earth Day, 203; Fuller and, 49; Illinois's use of industrial agriculture, *24*, *28*, 59, 64; Kaprow and out-of-door space, 49–50; media environment of McLuhan, 49; Morris and, 162–65; paper in semantics of, 1, 12; return to the land, 203; Schneemann

on destruction of, 29, 49, 60, 64–67, 210n18; small-scale interactions and, 21, 116–17; Whitehead and, 117–18; White uncovering difference between environment and ecology, 196. *See also* ecological sensibility; recycling
existentialism, 92
expansion/extension: body as extension of painting and drawing, 34, 198, 201, 210n24; environment's extension by drawing, 37–38, 198; medieval and early modern meaning of, 201; paper's scale expanding to match the task, 160; Spinoza's concept of expansion, 112, 116, 198, 201; Tuttle's expansion of space, 113, 133, 144
Expo '67 (Montreal), 49

Family Dog (rock promotion collective), 141, 223n117; *James Gurley (Tribal Stomp #2)*, *141*; *Redskin*, *142*
Fantastic Architecture (1967 cover), 16–17, *17*
FBI, 22, 179, 183, 199, 210n18
femininity, 18, 58
feminism: anti-Cartesian theories of embodiment and, 72; control masking potentiality, 19; cultural vacillations of vision in treatment of female bodies, 55–56; drawings and, 2; early 1970s burgeoning feminist art scene, 183, 204–5; landscape genre deconstructed by feminist artists, 50; matter as medium for reimagining who and what counts, 19–20; Mulvey on woman's image in symbolism, 33, 34; philosophy's history of dividing material qualities by gender, 58; poststructuralist feminist ecological approach, 20, 67; Schneemann's feminist ecological framework, 26, 27, 35, 40, 45–49, 67; Schneemann's interest in feminist art history, 32, 39; Spinoza on extension as divine attribute and, 210n25
Ferguson, Eugene S., 155
Ferré, Luis A., 157
Ferrer, Rafael, 22, 145, 150–58; antiform and land art movements, 170; antiform artworks by, 150, 168, 224n15; art milieu of, 23; background of, 167–68, 202; materials for, 152; Morris's association with, 145–60, 170, 172–73, 177; performance plans probing US colonial interventions in Puerto Rico, 3; as Puerto Rican artist in Anglo-dominated artistic and political milieu, 158, 167–68; Puerto Rican preparatory visit with Morris, 148, 150; sculpture's expansion and, 170–71; in Whitney's *Anti-Illusion* exhibition (1969), 166–67, 168. *See also* *Frarmrroreerofibseaterlr*

Festival of Free Expression (Paris), 39, 44
Finch College, 10, 208n27
Flag Protection Act (1968), 185
Flavin, Dan, 109, 214n2
Floyd, George, 205
Fluxus, 20, 23, 72, 78, 79, 202
Focillon, Henri, 219n119
folded paper, 3, 7, 21, 68–70, 74, 78, 176, 178, 187
Fonteray, Jacques, 210n28
Foreman, Richard, 212n79
Forest, Jean-Claude, 210n28
Fortnum, Rebecca, 12
Foucault, Michel, 173, 198
Frampton, Kenneth, 50
Frarmrroreerofibseaterlr (Morris), 22, 145–60, 172–73; anger and resentment toward proposals of, 158; capitalist state's failings revealed through, 158, 167; connecting visionary projects and public gaze, 151; dependence on plan drawings, 156; failure as possibility for, 151–56, 173; *Field Fold*, 154, *154*; lack of formalism and preconceived ideas, 153; landscape's ties to social control and state violence, 149; as material memory banks, 147, 173; mirroring paper's role as medium of order and bureaucracy, 147; Morris and Ferrer collaborating in, 22, 145–56, *155*, 158–60, 170, 177; Morris ill-suited for creating art for, 148, 170, 225n41; origins of title, 145; paper ballots in referendum on Puerto Rican statehood, 158; planning documents highlighting mode of instability, 152; prototype drawings for, 145, 148–50, 158–59, 173, 223n8; Puerto Rican preparatory visit of Morris and Ferrer, 148, 150; *Rock Work*, 159, *159*; *Skywriter*, 148, *149*, 152, 159; snare drummer in, 153; spatial politics of university and, 223n6; structural violence and, 157, 173; supply list for, 151, 152–53, *152*; *3rd Bulldozer Event*, 145–47, *146*; *U.S. Flag Burial*, 148, *149*
Freed, Leonard, 178
Fried, Michael, 216n49, 225n34
Frost, Robert, 55
fugitives, 176, 183
Fugitive Slave Clause, 183
Fuller, Buckminster, 17, 207n8; *Operating Manual for Spaceship Earth*, 48–49, 212n86

Gag Law (1948), 146
Gaines, Charles, 205
Gandhi, Mahatma, 117, 220n35
garbage. *See* debris and trash
Garcia, Jerry, 119, 221n50
Geller, Todros, 188

Illustration Credits